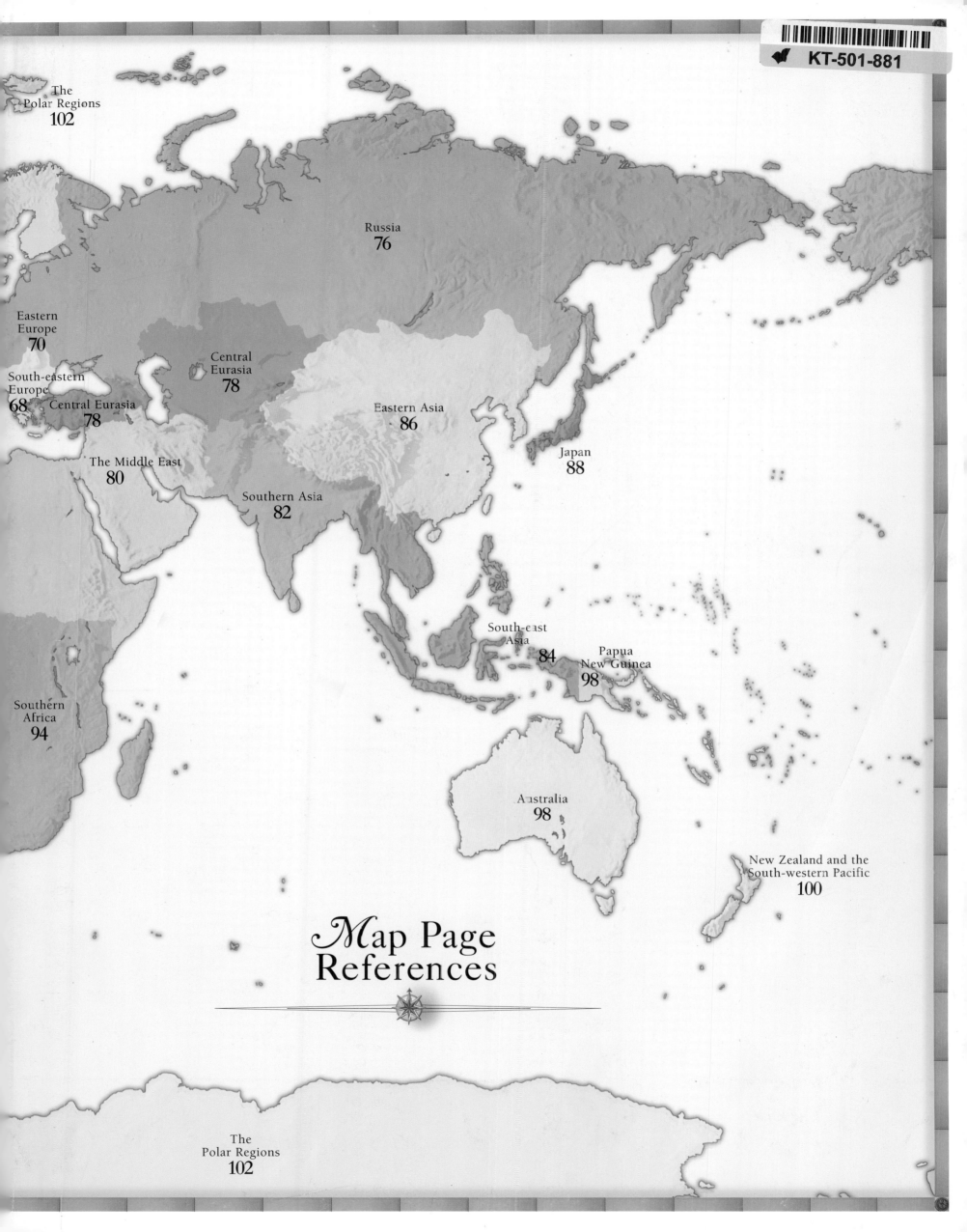

The Polar Regions 102

Eastern Europe 70

South-eastern Europe 68

Central Eurasia 78

Russia 76

Central Eurasia 78

The Middle East 80

Eastern Asia 86

Japan 88

Southern Asia 82

South-east Asia 84

Papua New Guinea 98

Southern Africa 94

Australia 98

New Zealand and the South-western Pacific 100

The Polar Regions 102

Map Page
References

THE READER'S DIGEST
Children's Atlas
of the World

The Reader's Digest
Children's Atlas of the World

A Reader's Digest® Children's Book,
published 1998 by Victoria House Publishing Ltd,
King's Court, Parsonage Lane, Bath BA1 1ER,
a subsidiary of The Reader's Digest Association, Inc.

Conceived and produced by Weldon Owen Pty Limited
43 Victoria Street, McMahons Point, NSW, 2060, Australia
A member of the Weldon Owen Group of Companies
Sydney • San Francisco

READER'S DIGEST CHILDREN'S BOOKS
General Manager: Vivian Antonangeli
Creative Consultant: Michael J. Morris
Group Publisher: Rosanna Hansen
Senior Editor: Cathy Jones
Editor: Louise Pritchard
Assistant Editor: Sarah Williams
UK Consultant: Deborah Hall

WELDON OWEN PTY LTD
Chairman: John Owen
Publisher: Sheena Coupe

Design Concept: John Bull
Managing Editor: Ariana Klepac
Art Director: Sue Burk

Project Editor: Scott Forbes
Consulting Editor: Colin Sale
Editorial Assistant: Anne Ferrier
Text: Scott Forbes

Senior Designer: Hilda Mendham
Designer, Thematic Spreads: Lena Lowe
Pre-press Co-ordinator: Jocelyne Best
Computer Production: Laura Sassin, Amanda Woodward
Computer Graphics: Stuart McVicar
Jacket Design: John Bull

Senior Picture Researcher: Anne Ferrier
Picture Researcher: Peter Barker
Archives: Rita Joseph

Illustrators: Susanna Addario,
Andrew Beckett/illustration, André Boos,
Anne Bowman, Greg Bridges, Danny Burke,
Martin Camm, Fiammetta Dogi, Simone End,
Giuliano Fornari, Chris Forsey,
John Francis/Bernard Thornton Artists, U.K.,
Jon Gittoes, Ray Grinaway, Terry Hadler/Bernard Thornton
Artists, U.K., Tim Hayward/Bernard Thornton Artists, U.K.,
David Kirshner, Frank Knight, Mike Lamble,
James McKinnon, Peter Mennim, Nicola Oram,
Tony Pyrzakowski, Oliver Rennert, Barbara Rodanska,
Claudia Saraceni, Michael Saunders, Peter Schouten,
Stephen Seymour/Bernard Thornton Artists, U.K.,
Marco Sparaciari, Sharif Tarabay/illustration,
Steve Trevaskis, Thomas Trojer, Genevieve Wallace,
Trevor Weekes, Rod Westblade, Ann Winterbotham

Maps: Digital Wisdom Publishing Ltd
Flags: Flag Society of Australia

Production Manager: Caroline Webber
Production Assistant: Kylie Lawson
Vice President International Sales: Stuart Laurence

British Library Cataloguing in Publication Data
A catalogue record for this book is available from
the British Library.

Colour Reproduction by Colourscan Co Pte Ltd
Printed by Toppan Printing Co, (H.K.) Ltd
Printed in China

A WELDON OWEN PRODUCTION

THE READER'S DIGEST
Children's Atlas
of the World

Consulting Editor: Colin Sale

A Reader's Digest Children's Book

CONTENTS

How to Use This Atlas 6

Maps and Mapmaking 8

How to Read a Map 10

Planet Earth 12

An Ever-Changing Planet 14

Weather and Climate 16

The Living World 18

Our Natural Resources 20

The Human Family 22

A Shrinking World 24

Planet in Peril 26

The Physical World 28

Countries of the World 30

NORTH AMERICA 32

Western Canada and Alaska 34

Eastern Canada 36

North-eastern United States 38

Southern United States 40

Central United States 42

Western United States 44

Mexico, Central America and
the Caribbean 46

SOUTH AMERICA 48

Northern South America 50

Southern South America 52

EUROPE 54

The United Kingdom and the Republic of Ireland 56

Spain and Portugal 58

France 60

The Low Countries 62

Western Central Europe 64

Italy 66

South-eastern Europe 68

Eastern Europe 70

Northern Europe 72

ASIA 74

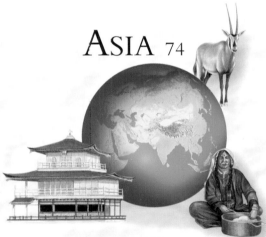

Russia 76

Central Eurasia 78

The Middle East 80

Southern Asia 82

South-east Asia 84

Eastern Asia 86

Japan 88

AFRICA 90

Northern Africa 92

Southern Africa 94

AUSTRALIA AND OCEANIA 96

Australia and Papua New Guinea 98

New Zealand and the South-western Pacific 100

The Polar Regions 102

World Fact File 104

Glossary 120

Index and Gazetteer 122

Acknowledgments 128

How to Use This Atlas

THE READER'S DIGEST CHILDREN'S ATLAS OF THE WORLD takes you on a fascinating tour of our extraordinary world. Before you start, read the sections called Maps and Mapmaking and How to Read a Map. There you will find out about different kinds of maps and how they are made, and learn how to read and use maps. The remaining introductory pages are a guide to our planet, Earth. They show you where it is located in the Solar System, what it is made of, how its landscapes have been shaped and how weather, wildlife and peoples vary around the world. The atlas maps are divided into seven parts – one for each of the continents of North America, South America, Europe, Asia, Africa, and Australia and Oceania, and one for the polar regions. Each part begins with a continent map that includes country lists and shows the most important features of the landscape. The continent map is followed by a series of illustrated maps which are packed with facts, pictures and activities. The sample maps and notes on these two pages explain the features on both types of map. At the back of the atlas you will find the World Fact File. This provides useful information on all of the world's countries and major territories. Finally, there is a glossary of terms used in this book, as well as a gazetteer – a geographical index that helps you to find places on the maps.

Continent Facts Includes the size of the continent, its population and the names of its countries.

ILLUSTRATED MAP

Country list A list of the countries or states on the map, their populations and capital cities.

France

FRANCE, THE LARGEST COUNTRY in western Europe, has a varied climate and landscape. In the north, the weather is mild and wet, and much of the land is flat. As you travel south, the climate becomes warmer and the land more mountainous. Three-quarters of the population live in towns and cities, but most of the country is farmland, and France is Europe's leading farming country. The northern plains are covered in fields of wheat and sugar beet, and in central and southern France vineyards dot the hillsides – more wine is produced in France than in any other country except Italy. The area around Paris, the capital, is the most densely populated region. It is home to one-fifth of the country's population and most of its industries. Several great rivers, including the Seine and the Loire, cross France's northern and western plains. These waterways were once the country's main transport routes, and their banks are lined with historic villages and magnificent castles known as châteaux. In the south, the mountains of the Pyrenees and the Alps separate France from Spain and Italy. Among their snow-capped peaks lie popular ski resorts, and national parks that are home to eagles, marmots and goat-like antelopes called chamois. Along the Mediterranean coast there are many busy beach resorts. Near the Italian border lies Monaco, the second-smallest country in the world. Monaco is famous for its casinos and its annual Grand Prix motor race.

FRANCE
POPULATION: 58,109,000 • CAPITAL: Paris
MONACO
POPULATION: 31,500 • CAPITAL: MONACO

Amazing Fact This box contains fascinating facts about the area on the map.

◆ AMAZING FACT ◆

France is now connected to Great Britain by an undersea rail link known as the Channel Tunnel. The tunnel took seven years to build and includes two rail tracks. Trains take 35 minutes to pass through the tunnel. People can travel from London to Paris in about three hours.

Physical map Shows the main features of the landscape.

CONTINENT MAP

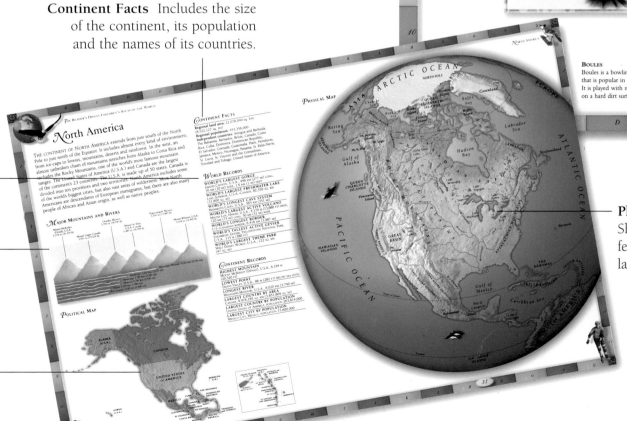

North America

THE CONTINENT OF NORTH AMERICA extends from just south of the North Pole to just north of the Equator. It includes almost every kind of environment, from ice caps to forests, mountains, deserts and rainforest. In the west, an almost unbroken chain of mountains stretches from Alaska to in Costa Rica and includes the Rocky Mountains, one of the world's most famous mountain ranges. The United States of America (U.S.A.) and Canada are the largest of the continent's 23 countries. The U.S.A. is made up of 50 states. Canada is divided into ten provinces and two territories. North America includes some of the world's biggest cities, but also vast areas of wilderness, but there are also many people of African and Asian origin, as well as native peoples.

Records A list of the tallest, longest and largest features of the continent.

Size comparison Shows how the continent's most important mountains and rivers would compare if you could see them side-by-side.

Political map Shows all the countries within the continent.

Coloured border
Each part of the atlas has a different coloured border.

Map reader's grid The letters and numbers on the border help you find places on the map. See page 10 to find out how to use the grid.

Projects By trying these activities and experiments, you can learn more about a topic or a part of the world.

KEY TO MAP SYMBOLS

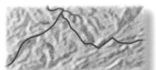

country border

regional (state) border

disputed border

MARTINIQUE
(FRANCE)

territory, and country to which it belongs

●Baltimore
◉ANNAPOLIS
★WASHINGTON, D.C.

✪ national capital
◉ regional capital
● city or town

Arno

river

Lake Ontario

lake

▲Ben Nevis
1,343 m (4,406 ft)

major mountain

Ⓔ African elephants

Ⓔ endangered animal

The France Map

ENGLAND

France See World Fact File page 107

Dunkerque
Calais
Boulogne • Nuclear energy • Lille
BELGIUM
LUXEMBOURG
Mussels
Potatoes
Dieppe • Sugar beet • Amiens
Channel Tunnel
Cherbourg • Le Havre • Rouen • GERMANY
Mont-St Michel
Bayeux Tapestry • Reims • Metz • Nuclear energy
Car manufacturing • Nancy • Strasbourg
PARIS • Iron ore • Iron and steel • Wine
Versailles • Fashion
Camembert cheese • Champagne • Seine • Troyes
Rennes • Chartres Cathedral • Eiffel Tower • Folk costume
Motor car racing Le Mans • Tour de France
Dairy cattle • Gaul fort
St-Nazaire • Tours • Dijon • Chapel of Notre Dame du Haut
Nantes • Mustard • Mountain climbing
FRANCE • Besançon
Château de Chambord • Bourges • Dairy cattle • SWITZERLAND
T.G.V. high-speed train • Doubs
La Rochelle • Beef cattle • Sheep • Seal • Marmot
Textiles • Mont Blanc 4,807 m (15,771 ft)
Tungsten • Farmer with goats • Coal • Lyon
Tourism • Chamois
Limoges china • St-Étienne • French bread • Grenoble • Skiing
Château de la Brède • Wine
Oysters • MASSIF CENTRALE • ITALY
Bordeaux • Lascaux cave paintings • Nuclear energy
Wine • Hunting for truffles • Avignon • Harvesting lavender • Perfume • Casino, Monte Carlo
French bread • Aircraft manufacturing • Cannes Film Festival • Nice • Mackerel
Biarritz • Natural gas • Toulouse • Montpellier • MONACO • Cannes
Boules • Walled town of Carcassonne • Pont du Gard • Marseille • Tourism • Water-skiing
PYRENEES • Sailing • Flamingo
SPAIN • ANDORRA • Solar furnace • Perpignan
structure in the Tower was erected exhibition of 1889 by André-Gustave Eiffel.
Mediterranean Sea
Osprey • Corsica • Tourism
Ajaccio • Statue of Napoleon

TOUR DE FRANCE
France's most famous sporting event, this cycle race around the entire country covers about 4,000 kilometres (2,500 mi).

SCALE
MILES
0 25 50 75 100
KILOMETRES
0 50 100 150

N
W E
S

PROJECT: Cave Painting

The cave paintings at Lascaux were created about 15,000 years ago. Here's how you can create your own painting that will look thousands of years old.

❶ Stuff a strong paper bag with crumpled newspaper and then staple the bag closed.

❷ Mix some glue and sand and use this to paint the whole bag. When it dries it will look like a rock.

❸ Collect three or four different coloured soils. Sift out the lumps and then mix each colour with glue to make earth paints. (Add water if the paints are too thick.) Now you are ready to paint. You can paint animals living in your area, as did the artists who created the Lascaux cave paintings.

LOOK AGAIN

• Which cathedral lies south-west of Paris?
• Name a horned animal found in the Pyrenees.
• What kind of food is produced in Dijon?
• Which small country is located east of Nice?

Look Again
To answer these questions, you'll need to look closely at the information on the map.

Locator globe
This globe shows where the area on the map is located.

LOCATION

Illustrations These show the people, places, wildlife and activities in the area on the map.

Feature illustrations These illustrations provide extra information about some of the map illustrations.

Scale The scale bar helps you to calculate distances on the map. To find out how to do this, see page 10.

Compass The compass helps you find north. To find out how to use the compass, see page 10.

KEY TO MAP COLOURS

Desert and semi-desert

Forest and grassland

Tundra

Ice-cap

Maps and Mapmaking

A MAP IS A PICTURE that represents an area of land on the Earth's surface. Any area, no matter how large or small, can be drawn as a map. Some maps show a small area such as a town; others show the whole world. Maps usually show areas that are much larger than the page they are printed on, so features are drawn much smaller than they really are. This is called drawing to scale. The bigger the area of a map, the smaller the features have to be drawn. Maps that show a small area and a large amount of detail are called large-scale maps. Maps that show a large area and a small amount of detail are called small-scale maps. On most maps, features are represented by lines, colours and symbols. For example, on a map of a town, black outlines may indicate streets, and coloured shapes may show buildings. On a map of a country, towns may appear as simple black dots, and rivers as blue lines. A book of maps – like the one you are reading now – is called an atlas. An atlas usually contains maps of the whole world as well as maps of countries and continents.

MAPPING THE WORLD

Each of these maps shows the location of Riverford School, but each is drawn to a different scale.

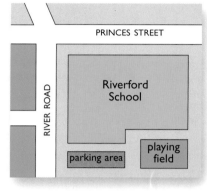

In this map of Riverford School, lines, coloured shapes and labels are used to show the school, nearby streets and other features. Maps of small areas like this are often called street maps.

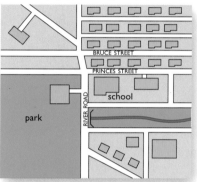

This is a map of Riverford town. Because the area of the map is larger, less detail can be shown. You can now see that the school is near houses, a park and a river, but you can no longer see the school parking area or playing field.

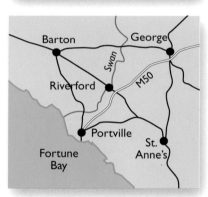

This map shows the region around Riverford. The town is now represented by a simple black dot, so you can no longer see the school or the streets. But you can see that Riverford is near water, and that it is linked to other towns by major and minor roads.

◆ AMAZING FACT ◆

In Greek mythology, Atlas was a man who led a rebellion against the gods. As a punishment for this act, he was made to support the world on his shoulders. When the first books of maps were published in the 16th century, many had an illustration of Atlas carrying a globe on their covers. As a result, a book of maps soon became known as an atlas.

◆ PROJECT: *Mapping Your Neighbourhood* ◆

You can draw a map of your neighbourhood. To do this you will have to think about where places are, how far apart they are, and what shape they are. You may need to go for a walk and make a list of the things you want to show on your map.

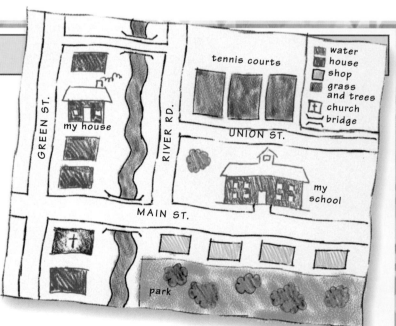

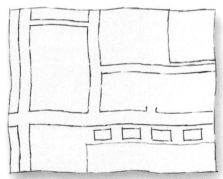

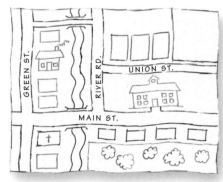

❶ Once you have decided what you are going to include, draw in the streets.

❷ Then add shapes to represent features such as buildings, parks and rivers. Label the streets.

❸ Now colour in your map. Use one colour for houses, one for streets, and so on. Draw a key to show what the colours represent. Finally, add labels for important places such as your home and school.

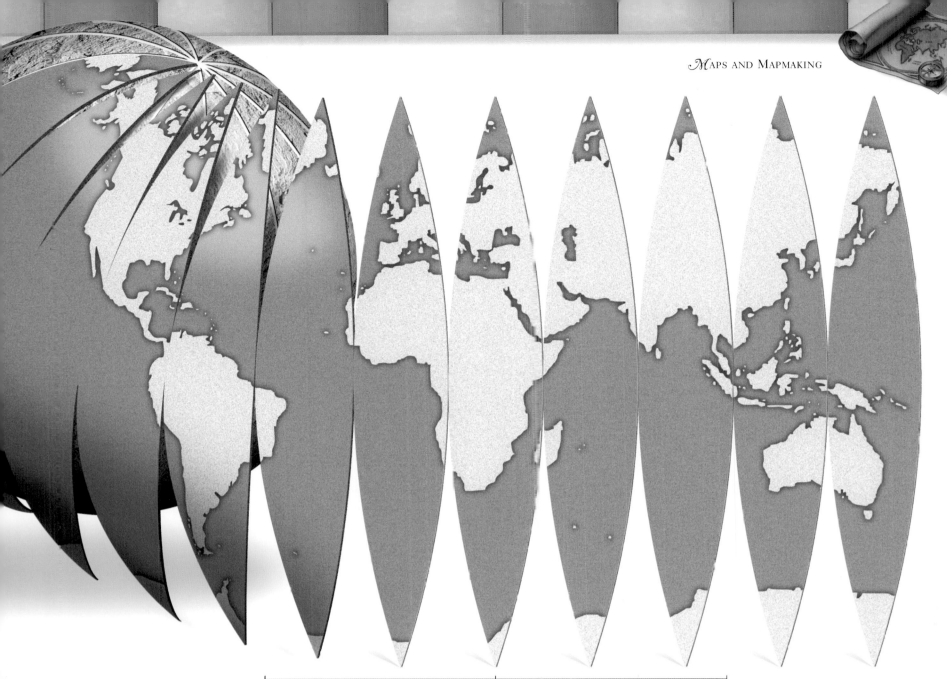

MAKING MAPS

People who make maps are known as mapmakers or cartographers. Before aeroplanes and spacecraft were invented, mapmakers used information supplied by travellers and explorers to make maps. Nowadays, most maps are based on surveys and on photographs taken by satellites positioned in space, high above the Earth. Mapmakers face one major problem: the Earth is round, but most maps have to be flat. A globe is the most accurate kind of map because it is the same shape as the Earth. But if you tried to create a flat map by simply peeling off the surface of a globe, you would have to divide the peel into pieces, or segments. You can test this for yourself by carefully peeling an orange in one piece and trying to flatten out the skin. You will find that it is impossible to make the peel lie flat without breaking it. In order to create a flat map, mapmakers have to stretch and squash the segments of the globe. The different ways in which they do this are known as projections. There are many types of projections, and each creates a slightly different map.

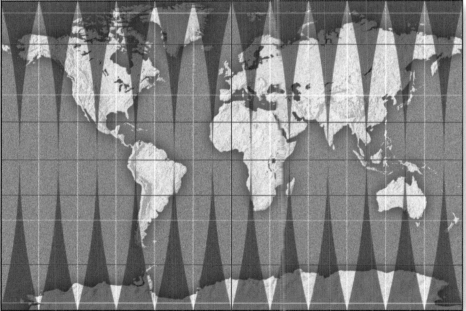

Arctic
Circle
(66.5°N)

Tropic of
Cancer
(23.5°N)

Equator
(0°)

Tropic of
Capricorn
(23.5°S)

Antarctic
Circle
(66.5°S)

180°   Greenwich Meridian (0°)   180°

A FLAT EARTH

As shown above, the surface of the globe can be divided into segments. To create a flat, rectangular map like the one on the left, mapmakers must fill in the gaps between the segments. To help them do this and plot locations, mapmakers use lines of latitude (horizontal lines) and longitude (vertical lines).

LINES AROUND THE WORLD

Mapmakers use a grid system to plot locations on the globe. Lines of longitude are drawn between the North Pole and the South Pole and are measured in degrees east or west of the Greenwich Meridian (0°). Lines of latitude are drawn in a west-east direction and measured in degrees north or south of the Equator (0°). The Equator divides the world into the northern and southern hemispheres. The Greenwich Meridian and the 180° line separate the eastern and western hemispheres.

How to Read a Map

MAPS ARE PACKED WITH INFORMATION. Some maps show you where countries are, what size and shape they are, and where they are in relation to other countries. Maps can also tell you about a region's climate, landscape, vegetation, towns and cities, and transport routes. Once you have learnt how to read maps, you can use an atlas to find out many things about countries all around the world.

FINDING PLACES

Most maps and atlases use a gazetteer and a grid system to help you find places. You look for the place name in the gazetteer – an index of place names, which usually appears at the back of the atlas – and then use the grid reference to find the location on the relevant map. Normally, a map grid consists of a series of letters along the top and bottom of the page and a series of numbers down the sides. Take a look at the map of Australia on the right. The grid reference for the city of Melbourne is H8. To find Melbourne, look at the letters on the top or bottom border and find H. Then find 8 on the left- or right-hand border. Imagine a line running down the page between the two Hs and another running across the page between the two 8s. (You can use a ruler to help you line up the numbers.) You will find Melbourne near where these lines would meet.

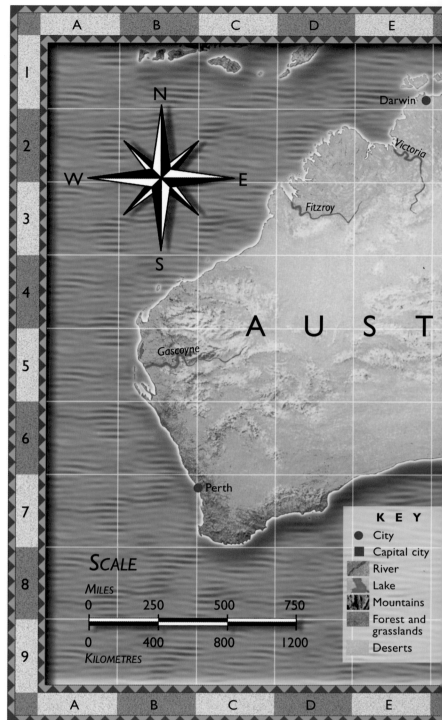

USING THE MAP GRID
In the gazetteer of this book, each place name is followed by a grid reference. The grid reference for the city of Nashville, Tennessee, in the United States is 41 L4. To locate Nashville, turn to page 41 and find L and 4 on the grid. Trace a line down from L and another across from 4. Nashville is near the intersection of the two lines.

DESCRIBING DIRECTION
A map usually has a compass symbol, which indicates the direction of north (N) on the map. Sometimes, as on the map above, it also shows the directions of south (S), east (E) and west (W). You can use the points of a compass to describe where places are. For example, on the map above you can say that Sydney is east (E) of Adelaide and that Brisbane is north (N) of Sydney. Brisbane is both north and east of Adelaide, so we can use a combination of compass points and say that Brisbane is north-east (NE) of Adelaide. But Brisbane is further to the east of Adelaide than it is to the north of it. So, if we want to be even more accurate, we can describe Brisbane as being east-north-east (ENE) of Adelaide. The compass above left shows all the combinations of compass points that you can use to describe direction.

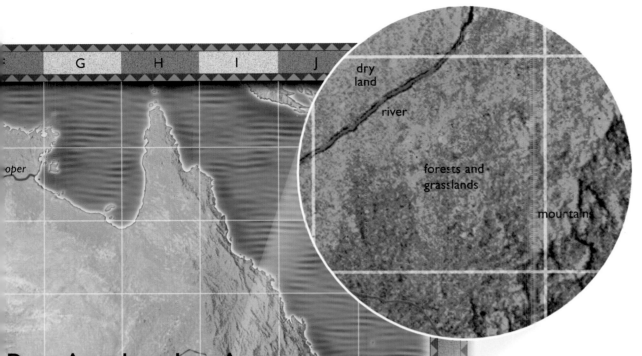

dry
land

river

forests and
grasslands

mountains

G H I J

oper

RALIA

Lake
Eyre

Cooper Creek

Darling

Lachlan

Murray

Adelaide

Brisbane

Sydney

CANBERRA

Melbourne

Hobart

G H I J K

5

6

7

8

9

COLOUR KEYS

On this map of Australia, dark shading indicates mountains. Green represents forests and grasslands, and orange shows desert and other dry land. Areas of water such as oceans, lakes and rivers are all coloured blue.

THE LIE OF THE LAND

The colours of a map may tell you something about a region's landscape, vegetation and climate. Often, shading is used to show mountain ranges, and colours are used to represent different kinds of vegetation. Green normally represents forests or grasslands, while yellow or orange indicates an area of dry land such as desert. On many maps, a special symbol, such as a square or star, is used to indicate a capital city. Most maps and atlases have a key that explains these features. In this atlas, you will find the key on page 7.

MEASURING DISTANCE

Most maps have a scale. This shows how distance on the map compares with real distance. Many scales appear as a bar that is divided into sections, as do the ones used in this book. In the scale shown on the map above, each section on the top part of the bar is equal to 250 miles, and each section on the bottom of the bar represents 400 kilometres. The project on this page shows you how to use this type of scale to measure distances on a map. Scales can also be written like this:

1:1,000,000

This shows that the map has been reduced 1,000,000 times. Distances on the ground are therefore 1,000,000 times greater than they are on the map. Thus 1 centimetre on the map is equal to 1,000,000 cm, or 10 km, and 1 in on the map is equal to 1,000,000 in, or 15¾ mi. Other scales are written like this:

1 cm = 10 km

This shows that 1 centimetre on the map corresponds to 10 kilometres in real distance.

◆ PROJECT: *Using a Scale* ◆

To measure the distance between Perth and Sydney on the map at left, follow these steps:

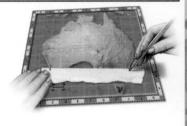

❶ Place the straight edge of a piece of paper on the map so that it lines up the dots of the two cities. Mark their positions on the paper.

❷ Place the paper next to the scale so that one of the dots lines up with zero. The scale is shorter than the distance, so mark the paper where the scale ends and note the distance it represents.

Place the mark back at zero and repeat these steps as often as necessary. Add the figures to calculate the distance between the cities.

You can also use the scale to measure distances along curved lines.

❶ Place a piece of string on the map along the Darling River, bending it to match the course of the river.

❷ Grasp the string at each end of the river, then straighten it out and measure it against the scale. You can then calculate the length of the river.

N

Planet Earth

WE LIVE ON A SMALL PLANET in a tiny part of a vast universe. Our part of the universe is called the Solar System. There are nine planets in the Solar System, and they move around, or orbit, a star that we call the Sun. Enormous groups of stars are known as galaxies. Our galaxy is called the Milky Way and it is made up of at least one billion stars. There are many millions of galaxies in the universe and each one is surrounded by a vast, empty space. The Solar System formed about 5,000 million years ago from a swirling cloud of dust and gases. The hot, central part of the cloud became the Sun, while further out, rocks and gases combined to form the planets. Other rock fragments became asteroids, or minor planets.

◆ AMAZING FACTS ◆

- Our galaxy looks like this. The faint, glowing arms of this galaxy are clouds of stars. Each of these stars is like our Sun and may have its own system of planets.

- It would take a jet aircraft travelling at 800 kilometres per hour (500 mph) six years to reach Venus and about 1,600 years to reach Pluto.

ROUND AND ROUND

As each planet orbits the Sun, it also spins, or rotates, on its axis – an imaginary line through its centre. Earth rotates once every 24 hours, and takes one year to orbit the Sun. Planets near the Sun orbit more quickly than those further away. Asteroids also orbit the Sun. Most are located between Mars and Jupiter, in an area known as the asteroid belt. The planets and asteroids are all held in their orbits by gravity, a powerful force that pulls them towards the Sun. Without this force, they would fly off into space.

THE PLANETS IN PERSPECTIVE

The illustration below shows the relative distances between the planets, as well as how long each planet takes to orbit the Sun (a year for that planet) and how long it takes to spin on its axis (a day for that planet).

Sun

Mercury Year: 88 Earth days. Day: 59 Earth days.

Venus Year: 225 Earth days. Day: 243 Earth days.

Earth Year: 365.25 days. Day: 24 hours.

Mars Year: 1.9 Earth years. Day: 24.6 hours.

Asteroid Belt

Jupiter Year: 11.9 Earth years. Day: 9.8 hours.

Saturn Year: 29.5 Earth years. Day: 10.2 hours.

Uranus Year: 84 Earth years. Day: 17.9 hours.

✦ PROJECT: *Space Mobile* ✦

You can make your own mobile of the Solar System to hang up in your bedroom or in your classroom at school.

❶ First, collect some paper, coloured pens, string or cotton thread, scissors and a coat-hanger.

❷ Draw the Sun and each of the planets and colour them. Make sure you copy the colours and relative sizes of the planets as shown in the illustrations on these pages.

❸ Carefully cut out each planet using a pair of scissors.

❹ Make a small hole in the top of each planet with the point of a pen or pencil and thread a length of string through the hole.

❺ Tie the Sun and the planets to the bottom of the coat-hanger. Place the Sun in the middle and arrange the planets on either side of it in the order shown in the illustration on these pages. Don't forget that some planets are closer together than others.

❻ When all the planets are in place, the mobile is ready to hang.

WORLD IN MOTION

As Earth turns on its axis, we move in and out of the Sun's light. Day begins as we move into the light. As we turn away from the Sun, night falls. Because Earth is tilted at an angle, the amount of sunlight reaching different parts of the world varies throughout the year. When part of Earth is tilted towards the Sun, it is summer there. When it is tilted away from the Sun, it is winter.

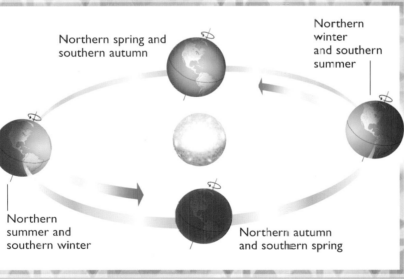

Northern spring and southern autumn

Northern winter and southern summer

Northern summer and southern winter

Northern autumn and southern spring

FIT FOR LIFE

Some planets are surrounded by a layer of gases called an atmosphere. As far as we know, Earth is the only planet in the Solar System with an atmosphere that contains sufficient water and oxygen for life to flourish. Our atmosphere is so thin that if the planet were the size of an apple, the atmosphere would be only as thick as the peel.

Neptune Year: 165 Earth years. Day: 19.2 hours.

Pluto Year: 248 Earth years. Day: 6.4 Earth days.

*A*n Ever-Changing Planet

THE EARTH IS SHAPED like a large ball. Inside are several layers made of different materials. As the Earth formed, heavy minerals such as iron and nickel sank to the centre, while lighter materials rose to the middle and upper levels. At first, the upper levels consisted entirely of hot, liquid rock, but as the Earth cooled, the outside solidified to form a thin, hard crust. This crust broke into several pieces, known as lithospheric plates. These plates float on the liquid, molten rock – or magma – underneath and are constantly moving, although you cannot feel the movement. Energy from the Earth's core creates powerful convection currents that force the plates together and apart. This happens extremely slowly, but over millions of years these movements shape and shift the surface of the Earth, causing earthquakes and volcanic eruptions and forming mountains and islands.

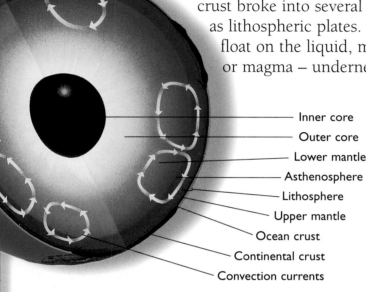

- Inner core
- Outer core
- Lower mantle
- Asthenosphere
- Lithosphere
- Upper mantle
- Ocean crust
- Continental crust
- Convection currents

INSIDE EARTH

Our planet's solid iron inner core is surrounded by an outer core of liquid iron and nickel. Above this is a layer of solid rock called the lower mantle and a wide band of quite soft rock known as the asthenosphere. The Earth's outer layer is called the lithosphere. It consists of the solid rock of the upper mantle, and the crust. Crust under the land (continental crust) is usually thicker than crust under the sea (ocean crust). In the Earth's core, temperatures reach more than 3,000°C (5,400°F). This heat creates strong convection currents that push the crust in different directions.

◆ *P*ROJECTS: *Folding the Crust* ◆

❶ Cut a paper plate in half. These halves represent two of the Earth's lithospheric plates.

❷ Using sticky tape, attach a sheet of paper to the plate halves. The paper represents the Earth's crust.

❸ If you slide one half of the plate under the other, the paper buckles. Similarly, when two of the Earth's plates collide, their crusts fold, forming mountains.

❶ Take a sheet of paper, fold it in half and continue to fold it.

❷ After six folds, it becomes difficult to fold the paper any further. In the same way, the thicker the Earth's crust, the greater the force required to fold it.

Spreading plates

Hot-spot volcanoes

Coastal collisions

Coastal Collisions
When thin, dense ocean crust meets thick continental crust, the thin crust slides under the thicker crust. Magma rises to the surface and forms a line of volcanoes. This process formed Mount St. Helens in the U.S.A.

Hot-Spot Volcanoes
Weaknesses in the middle of plates, known as hot spots, allow magma from the asthenosphere to burst through the crust and form volcanoes. The Hawaiian Islands were created by hot-spot volcanoes.

Spreading Plates
Circulating magma may force plates apart. Where the plates separate, magma rises through the gap, then cools and hardens to form a ridge. Normally this happens under the sea, but it happens on land in Iceland.

WORLD IN MOTION
Convection currents cause the Earth's plates to collide, separate and slide past each other. The effects of these movements are shown in the illustration above and in the photographs on the right.

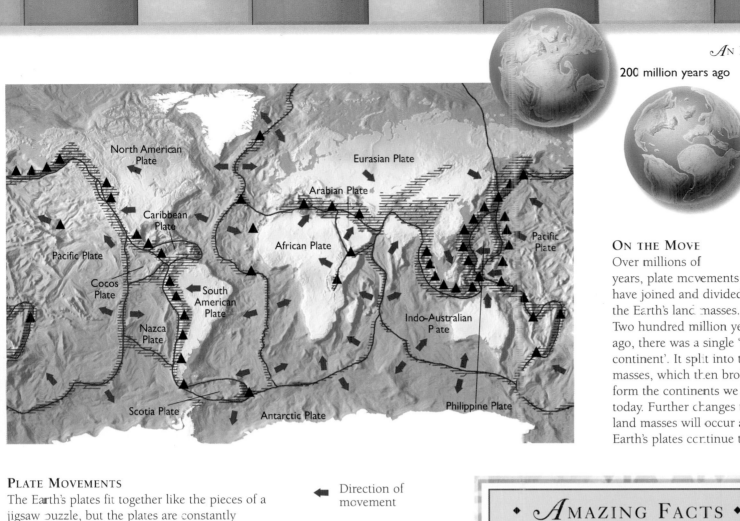

200 million years ago

90 million years ago

Present

60 million years from now

ON THE MOVE

Over millions of years, plate movements have joined and divided the Earth's land masses. Two hundred million years ago, there was a single 'super continent'. It split into two land masses, which then broke up to form the continents we know today. Further changes to these land masses will occur as the Earth's plates continue to drift.

PLATE MOVEMENTS

The Earth's plates fit together like the pieces of a jigsaw puzzle, but the plates are constantly moving. This map shows the direction in which each plate moves. Most volcanoes and earthquakes occur where plates meet. This means that countries in the centre of plates, such as Australia, have few earthquakes and volcanoes, whereas countries at the edges of plates, such as Japan, have many.

← Direction of movement

▲ Volcanoes

⬡ Earthquake zones

◆ AMAZING FACTS ◆

- When the island volcano of Krakatoa in Indonesia erupted on August 27, 1883, the explosion was heard up to 4,800 kilometres (3,000 mi) away!
- More than 500,000 earthquakes occur every year. Fortunately, most of these are too weak to cause any damage.

Sliding plates

Folding crust

Undersea collisions

Sliding Plates
A fault line forms where two plates slide past each other. The friction between the plates creates earthquakes. These occur regularly along the San Andreas fault in California, U.S.A., as part of the coastline slides northward.

Folding Crust
When two plates with crusts of similar thickness collide, the edge of one plate slides under the other, and the crusts buckle and fold to form mountains. This process created the massive Himalayas mountain range in Asia.

Undersea Collisions
When two plates with ocean crust collide, one may sink beneath the other, forming a deep trench. In places, magma bursts through the crust to form volcanic islands. The islands of Japan formed in this way.

◆ LOOK AGAIN ◆

- What is the Earth's inner core made of?
- What kind of volcanoes formed the Hawaiian Islands?
- Where are earthquakes most likely to occur?

Weather and Climate

OUR WEATHER MAY CHANGE from day to day, but we usually experience the same kind of weather from year to year. The pattern of weather that occurs in a region over a long period is known as the climate. The climate of an area depends on three main factors: how far north or south of the Equator it is (its latitude), how high it is (its altitude), and how close it is to the sea. As a result of the Earth's orbit and its round shape, sunlight warms areas near the Equator more than areas near the poles. Tropical regions are therefore hot all year round, and the poles are always cold. Areas between the tropics and the poles are temperate. This means that they have warm summers and cool winters. Mountains are colder than lowland areas because as you climb higher the atmosphere becomes thinner and retains less heat. In coastal regions, sea breezes and ocean currents also affect the climate. Usually they prevent the weather from becoming too hot or too cold. Where winds blow inland from the sea, they are usually moist and bring high rainfall.

WIND PATTERNS

Because hot air rises and cold air sinks, the Sun's uneven heating of the Earth's surface causes air to circulate as shown in the large diagram below. These patterns of air circulation are deflected by the planet's rotation, and form the major wind systems shown on the globe below right. These winds carry warm or cold, moist or dry air, and are an important influence on the Earth's climates.

Air Circulation

Air flows poleward from the south-west

Air flows toward the Equator from the north-east

Cold easterly winds blow from the poles.

Warm and cold air meet, creating a belt of stormy, wet weather.

Upper air cools and sinks, creating dry conditions.

Warm, moist air rises at the Equator, clouds form and rain falls.

60°N

30°N

Equator

WORLD CLIMATES

The world can be divided into eight major climate zones, which are shown on this map and described on these pages. Ocean currents influence many of these climates. For example, north-western Europe has a mild climate as a result of the warm waters of the Gulf Stream.

warm currents   cool currents

Cold Temperate
These regions have long, bitterly cold and snowy winters. Their summers are usually mild and damp.

Mountain
Mountains are normally colder, wetter and windier than neighbouring regions that lie nearer sea level.

Polar
The polar regions are extremely cold for most of the year. Although snow falls regularly, the poles are relatively dry.

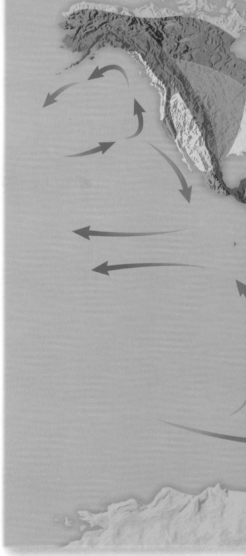

Wind Systems

Polar easterlies

Westerlies

Trade winds

Westerlies

Polar easterlies

Wet Temperate
Wet temperate regions have four distinct seasons, with cool, wet winters and warm, wet summers.

Dry Temperate
Rainfall is relatively low in these regions. Most areas have mild, wet winters and hot, dry summers.

Desert and Semi-desert
These are dry, barren areas with very low rainfall. They are usually hot by day, but may be cold, or even frosty, at night.

Subtropical
In summer, these regions are hot and wet like tropical areas. In winter, they are dry and mild like deserts.

Tropical
The tropics are hot and wet. In some areas, it rains all year round. In others, most of the rain falls in summer.

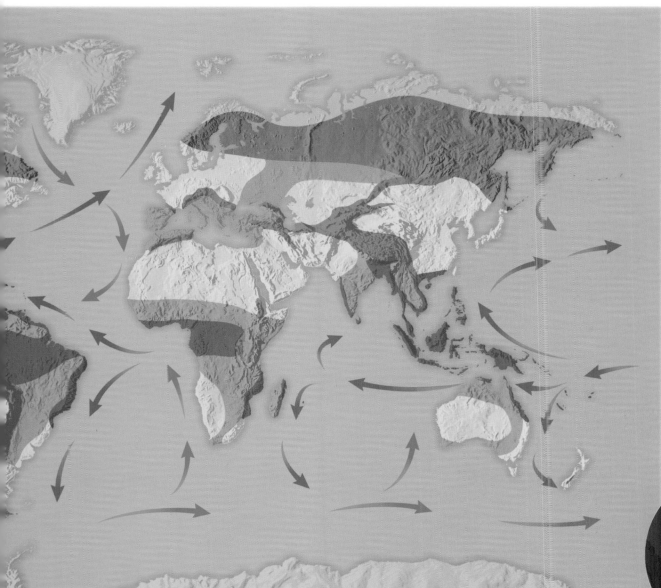

◆ AMAZING FACT ◆

Thunderstorms are most common in tropical areas, but occur all over the world. At least 20,000 storms occur each day, and at any one time about 2,000 may be taking place. Lightning from these storms strikes the ground as frequently as 100 times every second.

ENERGY FROM THE SUN
Because the Earth is shaped like a ball, the Sun strikes it more directly near the Equator than at the poles. This is why tropical areas are hot and the polar regions are cold.

◆ PROJECT: *Why the Poles Are Colder Than the Equator* ◆

❶ In a dark room, shine a torch a few centimetres above, and at right angles to, a flat surface such as a tabletop. Observe the shape and brightness of the patch of light.

❷ Tilt the torch and note how the light changes. When the light strikes the surface from directly overhead, the patch of light is small and intense. When the light strikes the table at an angle, the patch is larger and weaker.

In a similar way, sunlight is most intense at the Equator, where it strikes the ground from directly overhead. At the poles, the light strikes the Earth at an angle and is spread across a wider area, making it much weaker.

The Living World

ALMOST EVERY PART OF OUR PLANET is inhabited by an amazing variety of living things. So far, scientists have named about two million kinds, or species, of plants and animals, but there may be between 10 and 100 million species on Earth! All living things inhabit the biosphere, which is made up of the land, oceans and atmosphere. Within the biosphere, there are many kinds of environment. Over millions of years, plants and animals have gradually altered their bodies and behaviour to suit particular environments. This process is known as adaptation. Together, an environment and its inhabitants are known as an ecosystem. The living things in an ecosystem depend on each other for food and other resources. For example, vegetation provides food for plant-eating animals (herbivores) which may in turn be eaten by meat-eating animals (carnivores). These close relationships mean that damage to one part of an ecosystem is likely to affect every other part of it.

GLOBAL ECOSYSTEMS

Each of the Earth's environments has its own community of plants and animals. This illustration shows how ecosystems change between the tropical rainforests (far left) and the polar ice-caps (far right).

Oceans

The oceans contain a huge variety of species that have adapted to life under water. Marine plants include many kinds of seaweed. Animals include sea mammals such as seals and whales, coral, and thousands of fish species.

Tropical Rainforests

The hot, humid weather of the tropics creates dense forests that are home to more species than any other environment. Monkeys and birds live high in the trees, while jaguars and other mammals prowl the forest floor.

Subtropical Savannahs

With rain falling only in summer, subtropical areas have few trees. The African savannah grasslands support herds of herbivores such as zebras, which are hunted by lions and other carnivores. Vultures and other scavengers eat the leftovers.

Deserts and Semi-deserts

Desert species have adapted to drought. Some plants, such as cacti, store water in their stems. Others have long roots that reach water far underground. In hot deserts, many animals come out only at night, when it is cooler.

WORLD ENVIRONMENTS

Because the weather determines the types of plants that grow, the Earth's environments are closely related to its climate zones.

- Tropical rainforests
- Subtropical savannahs
- Deserts and semi-deserts
- Temperate grasslands and shrub woodlands
- Temperate forests
- Coniferous forests
- Mountains
- Polar ice-caps and tundra

◆ AMAZING FACT ◆

The world's largest flower, the rafflesia, is found in the rainforests of South-east Asia. It can measure up to one metre (3 ft) in diameter. It gives off a smell like rotting flesh which attracts insects.

Mountains

The higher the land, the less vegetation there is and the colder and windier it gets. Thick fur coats keep many mountain animals warm. Some species, such as mountain goats, have special hooves that help them climb rocky slopes.

Polar Ice-caps and Tundra

The ice-caps are bitterly cold and offer little shelter. Some animals have fur and a thick layer of fat to keep them warm. Tundra is treeless land that surrounds the Arctic ice-cap. Its low shrubs feed hares, lemmings and other herbivores.

Temperate Grasslands and Shrub Woodlands

Moderate rainfall creates grasslands and shrub woodlands. Grasslands attract herbivores such as bison and are ideal hunting grounds for birds of prey. There is little shelter, so some animals live in burrows.

Temperate Forests

Trees grow well in wet temperate regions. In areas with cold winters, most of the trees are deciduous, which means that they shed their leaves in autumn. Some animals migrate in winter; others survive on food stored during summer.

Coniferous Forests

Cold temperate regions are covered by forests of evergreen trees called conifers. Shaped so that snow slides off them, these trees are well adapted to the cold winters. Many animals have thick fur, and some hibernate during winter.

◆ LOOK AGAIN ◆

- Name a plant-eating animal that lives on the African savannah.
- Which plants store water in their stems?
- How have animals adapted to mountain environments?

Our Natural Resources

THE EARTH PROVIDES US with everything that we need to live. Its atmosphere, rivers and lakes supply fresh water which, with sunshine and soil, enables plants to grow. In turn, plants produce vital supplies of oxygen and provide us and other animals with food. Animals supply humans with meat, wool and dairy products. Plants also provide timber, fuel and textiles such as cotton. All these resources – water, plants, crops, animals – are renewable. This means that if we manage them carefully they will never run out. Other resources are non-renewable. They do not regrow or replenish themselves and will eventually be used up. They include minerals, precious stones and fossil fuels. Minerals – such as clay, chalk and many metals – and precious stones – such as diamonds and emeralds – have a wide range of uses, particularly in industry. Coal, oil and gas supply most of the energy we need for lighting and heating our homes and for fuelling our cars. They are known as fossil fuels because they are the remains of animals and plants buried deep underground millions of years ago. Some of these non-renewable resources may run out within the next 50 years. Because of this, and because burning fossil fuels creates pollution, scientists are trying to find ways of using renewable resources (Sun, wind and sea) to supply some energy.

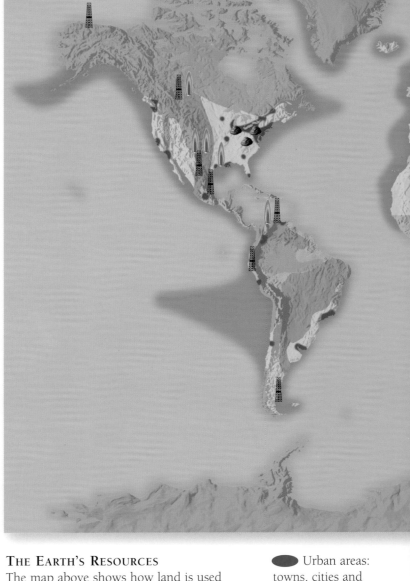

ENERGY SUPPLIES

The illustration below shows our principal sources of energy. As the chart on the right indicates, coal, oil and gas still supply most of our fuel. But alternative energy supplies such as wind and solar power are being developed in many parts of the world. As reserves of fossil fuels run out, these sources will become increasingly important.

Energy Use

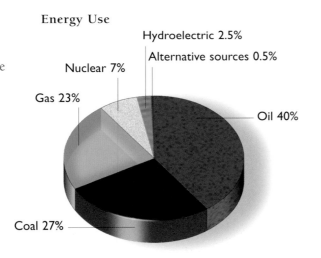

- Hydroelectric 2.5%
- Alternative sources 0.5%
- Nuclear 7%
- Gas 23%
- Oil 40%
- Coal 27%

THE EARTH'S RESOURCES

The map above shows how land is used in different parts of the world, and where major fuel reserves are located.

- Major gas field
- Major coal field
- Major oil field

- Urban areas: towns, cities and industries
- Areas with large farms where people grow crops and raise animals for sale

Oil
Oil and gas are found together in certain rocks in the Earth's crust. They are extracted by drilling from sea or land rigs.

Coal
Coal is more plentiful than other fossil fuels. It can be collected by digging at the surface or by mining deep underground.

Uranium
Uranium is an element known to be a radioactive metal. It is used as a fuel in nuclear power stations to produce electricity.

Geothermal Power
In some parts of the world, ground water is heated by hot volcanic rocks, creating steam that is used to generate power.

THE WATER CYCLE

A process known as the water cycle provides us with a regular supply of fresh water. Water in oceans, lakes and rivers is constantly evaporating into the air, where it exists as water vapour. The warmer the air, the more water vapour it can hold. When air cools, its ability to hold water decreases, and some of the water vapour turns, or condenses, into tiny water droplets or ice crystals. These droplets or crystals form clouds. If the droplets or crystals combine and become heavy enough, they fall as rain or snow. Water that falls on land drains into rivers, lakes and underground channels. It then flows into the sea, replenishing the oceans and completing the water cycle.

◆ PROJECT: *Create a Water Cycle* ◆

This simple experiment will show you how the water cycle works.

❶ Cool a long, metal spoon or ladle by placing it in a freezer for a few minutes. Choose a spoon with a wooden handle.

❷ Ask an adult to help you boil some water in a kettle or saucepan.

❸ As the water boils, the warm air above the water rises. As it starts to cool, it condenses and forms clouds of steam.

❹ Hold the cold spoon over the steam, being careful not to burn yourself. The cooling effect of the cold metal causes the water vapour to condense more quickly and form droplets of water on the underside of the spoon.

❺ The droplets grow in size until they become heavy enough to fall, just like rain. Some of the droplets may fall back into the kettle or saucepan, replenishing the water supply.

Areas with small farms where people grow crops and raise animals mainly for their own use

Grassland areas used for grazing large numbers of animals

Deserts, dry grasslands and tundra used for grazing small numbers of animals

Forested areas with some farming, hunting and mining

Areas that are too cold or dry for farming, but include some mining and hunting

Major fishing grounds

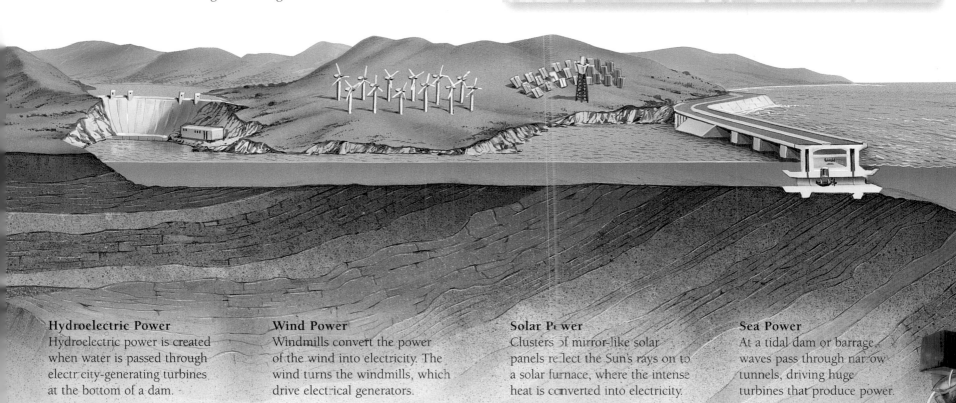

Hydroelectric Power
Hydroelectric power is created when water is passed through electricity-generating turbines at the bottom of a dam.

Wind Power
Windmills convert the power of the wind into electricity. The wind turns the windmills, which drive electrical generators.

Solar Power
Clusters of mirror-like solar panels reflect the Sun's rays on to a solar furnace, where the intense heat is converted into electricity.

Sea Power
At a tidal dam or barrage, waves pass through narrow tunnels, driving huge turbines that produce power.

The Human Family

OUR PLANET IS HOME to about 5.8 billion people. This population is not spread evenly over the Earth's land masses. Instead, people are concentrated where resources are plentiful, or can be easily obtained by trade. Therefore, few people live in deserts or polar regions, but many live in fertile areas, close to energy sources, and near rivers and coasts. The world's population is now growing more quickly than ever before. In the time it takes you to read this sentence, more than 20 babies will have been born. Since 1950 the number of people on the Earth has more than doubled. This growth is the result of a longer life expectancy due to improved medical services, and a high birth rate in some parts of the world. The most rapid population growth occurs in developing countries – poorer countries with little industry or technology. It is difficult for these countries to feed and take care of their growing populations, so many of them are urging their people to have fewer children.

NATIONAL POPULATIONS

This diagram shows the 10 countries with the world's largest populations. China has by far the biggest population – in fact, one in every five people in the world lives in China!

WHERE PEOPLE LIVE

The dots on this map show the world's most densely populated areas.

Developed countries
Developing countries

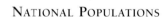

China	India	U.S.A.	Indonesia	Brazil	Russia	Pakistan	Bangladesh	Japan	Nigeria
1.2 billion	937 million	264 million	204 million	161 million	150 million	132 million	128 million	126 million	101 million

CROWDED COUNTRIES

Some countries are densely populated – a large population lives in a small area. Others are sparsely populated – a small population occupies a large area.

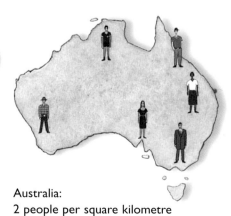

The Netherlands: 400 people per square kilometre (1,000 per sq. mi)

Australia: 2 people per square kilometre (6 per sq. mi)

GROWING CITIES

As countries develop, people move to cities to look for work in factories and businesses. This comparison of the populations of Paris, France, and Jakarta, Indonesia, shows these cities in developing countries are now growing more rapidly than those in developed countries.

Paris Jakarta

1970 8.5 million 3.9 million **1990** 9.3 million 9.3 million **2010** 9.6 million 19.2 million

◆ AMAZING FACTS ◆

- Every second, three babies are born.
- If the world's population were spread out evenly over its land masses, each person would occupy an area larger than four football pitches.

- Standing side by side, everyone in the world could fit on to the island of Jamaica.

POPULATION GROWTH

Every four days, one million children are born. If the world's population continues to grow at this rate, it will have reached 10 billion by the year 2100. The populations of developing countries are expanding rapidly while those of developed countries are growing slowly or decreasing.

- Developing countries
- Developed countries

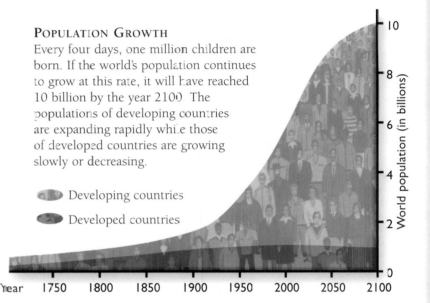

RICH AND POOR

Countries with large industries and high levels of technology are described as developed countries. People in these parts of the world are generally wealthy and have many possessions. In countries with little industry and technology, people are poorer and have few possessions. These countries are described as developing countries. Although they are home to far fewer people, developed countries are much richer and use a much larger proportion of the world's resources than developing countries. This map divides the countries into developed and developing countries.

Developed countries:
make up 20% of the world's population
own 80% of the world's wealth
use 70% of the world's energy

Developing countries:
make up 80% of the world's population
own 20% of the world's wealth
use 30% of the world's energy

◆ PROJECT: Languages ◆

More than 3,000 languages are spoken around the world, but more than one-third of the world's population speaks one of the following six languages. So you can learn to say hello to more than two billion people!

hello
English
(350 million speakers)

你好
ni hao
Chinese
(1 billion speakers)

مرحبا
mar-ha-ban
Arabic
(150 million speakers)

¡hola!
o-la
Spanish
(250 million speakers)

नमस्ते
na-ma-stay
Hindi
(200 million speakers)

привет!
pree-vyet
Russian
(150 million speakers)

A Shrinking World

In 1850, the journey between London and New York took about three weeks. Now the same distance can be travelled in just over three hours. This dramatic difference has altered our view of the world. Countries now seem closer together than ever before – the world seems to be shrinking! Faster means of transportation, along with recently developed technologies, have greatly increased international trade and communication. Aeroplanes can carry goods to the other side of the world within a day. Fresh foods, such as meat, fruit and vegetables, which would previously have spoiled before they reached their destinations, can now be transported over long distances in refrigerated container ships. Modern telecommunications – telephone, fax and electronic mail services – allow businesses to deal directly with customers anywhere in the world. Telecommunications also enable us to increase our understanding of other places and peoples. We can watch television programmes about other countries, speak to people on the other side of the world by telephone, and make friends on computer networks such as the Internet.

 1860: Clipper ship, 3 weeks

 1910: *Mauretania* steamship, 5 days

1939: Boeing 314 Clipper seaplane, 24 hours

Today: Concorde supersonic jet, 3½ hours

Transatlantic Transportation

In the mid-19th century, a clipper ship was the fastest means of transportation between New York and London. The exact length of the journey depended on the weather, but the trip usually took about three weeks. By 1910, the steamship *Mauretania* had cut the Atlantic crossing to five days. In 1939, the Boeing 314 Clipper seaplane provided the first passenger aircraft service across the Atlantic, with a flight time of about 24 hours. Today, the Concorde supersonic jet can complete the same trip in three and a half hours.

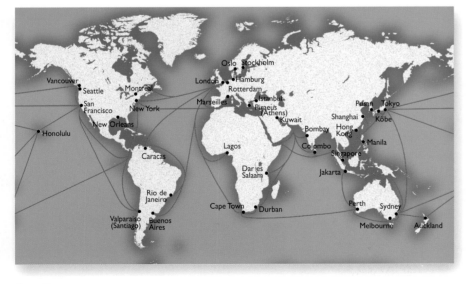

Sea Routes

Today, few people travel by sea, but goods of all kinds are transported by container ships and tankers. This map shows the world's most important shipping routes and busiest ports. Rotterdam in the Netherlands handles more cargo than any other seaport.

Air Routes

Flying is now the most popular form of international travel. This map shows the busiest international air routes and airports. Heathrow in London handles more international flights than any other airport, but Chicago's O'Hare Airport is the world's busiest, with more than 2,000 planes landing and taking off each day.

INTERNATIONAL TRADE

The countries of the world exchange a wide variety of goods. Countries that have more raw materials and produce more food and goods than they need export some of those materials to countries that have few resources. Other countries export little because they need all their own resources. In the diagram below, the arrows indicate the direction of trade in three categories of goods: food, raw materials (including minerals, fuels and timber), and manufactured goods (goods that are made in factories, such as cars and electrical equipment). The illustrations show the most important products in each region.

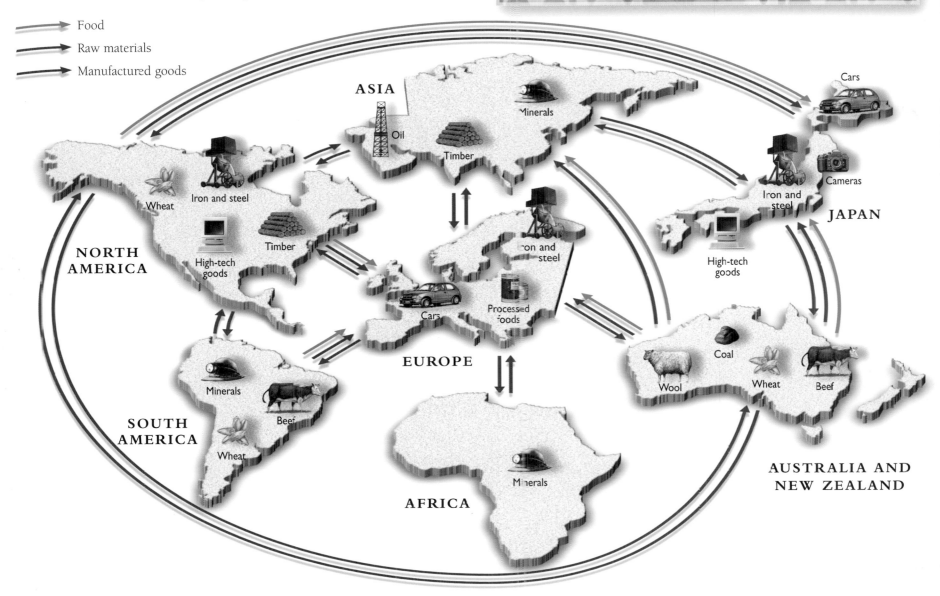

- → Food
- → Raw materials
- → Manufactured goods

ASIA
Oil
Timber
Minerals

NORTH AMERICA
Wheat
Iron and steel
High-tech goods
Timber

SOUTH AMERICA
Minerals
Beef
Wheat

EUROPE
Iron and steel
Cars
Processed foods

AFRICA
Minerals

JAPAN
Cars
Cameras
Iron and steel
High-tech goods

AUSTRALIA AND NEW ZEALAND
Wool
Coal
Wheat
Beef

◆ *L*OOK AGAIN ◆

- If it is midday in England, what is the time in eastern Australia?
- Which is New Zealand's busiest port?
- What kinds of manufactured goods does Japan export?

TIME ZONES

The world is divided into 24 time zones, and time is measured in hours ahead of or behind the time in Greenwich, England. The time is the same throughout each zone and is usually one hour ahead of or behind the neighbouring time zones. The International Date Line marks where one day ends, and another begins.

-12 -11 -10 -9 -8 -7 -6 -5 -4 -3 -2 -1 0 +1 +2 +3 +4 +5 +6 +7 +8 +9 +10 +11 +12

NORTH AMERICA   Greenwich   EUROPE   ASIA
International Date Line
AFRICA
SOUTH AMERICA
AUSTRALIA
International Date Line

12am 1am 2am 3am 4am 5am 6am 7am 8am 9am 10am 11am 12pm 1pm 2pm 3pm 4pm 5pm 6pm 7pm 8pm 9pm 10pm 11pm 12am

A VIRTUAL WORLD

Computers are changing the ways in which we work, relax and communicate. You can now send electronic mail (e-mail) and other digital information from one computer to another almost anywhere in the world. You can also read magazines, hear music and even shop using information networks such as the Internet. Some networks allow you to speak directly to other people and even see them on your computer screen. This is called video conferencing. In the future, more and more people are likely to use computers for shopping, entertainment and business.

Planet in Peril

THE FUTURE OF OUR PLANET is at risk, now more than ever before. In the last 200 years, rapid population growth and the development of industry and technology have magnified the effect of our activities on the environment. Supplies of fossil fuels and other non-renewable resources are running out. We are over-using the soil, forests and fishing grounds, and no longer giving these renewable resources a chance to recover. Waste from our homes and industries is poisoning water supplies, and gases from our cars and factories are polluting the air we breathe. Increasing air pollution may even be changing the climate. Scientists all over the world are trying to find ways to preserve resources and limit the damage we are doing to the Earth. Through simple activities such as recycling, using our cars less and buying environmentally friendly products, we can all play a part in protecting the Earth and preserving its resources for future generations.

• *A*MAZING FACTS •

- A hectare (2.47 acres) of Brazilian rainforest is destroyed every 20 seconds.
- Every day, more than 50 species become extinct. This is mainly the result of human activities such as forestry and hunting.

A GLOBAL CRISIS

This map shows that environmental problems affect almost every part of the Earth. The most serious problems are described and illustrated on these pages.

- Existing deserts
- Areas at risk of becoming deserts
- Existing rainforest
- Cleared rainforest
- Cities with severe air pollution
- Areas affected by acid rain
- Polluted waterways
- Heavy oil slicks created by shipping
- Light oil slicks created by shipping
- Major nuclear accidents
- Major oil tanker disasters
- Major oil rig explosions

Holding Back the Desert

In dry parts of the world, overgrazing and clearing the land of its natural vegetation can turn fertile areas into desert. To keep deserts from spreading further, we need to manage better the land we farm and replant trees and shrubs.

Saving the Forests

Vast areas of natural forest are being cleared to supply timber, fuel and paper, and to make way for towns and farms. You can help protect the world's forests and reduce the need for more wood by recycling paper. Replanting trees also helps.

Reducing Air Pollution

Cars and factories fill the air with grime and poisonous gases. Industries and car manufacturers are trying to reduce such pollution. You can also help by walking, cycling or using public transport instead of travelling by car.

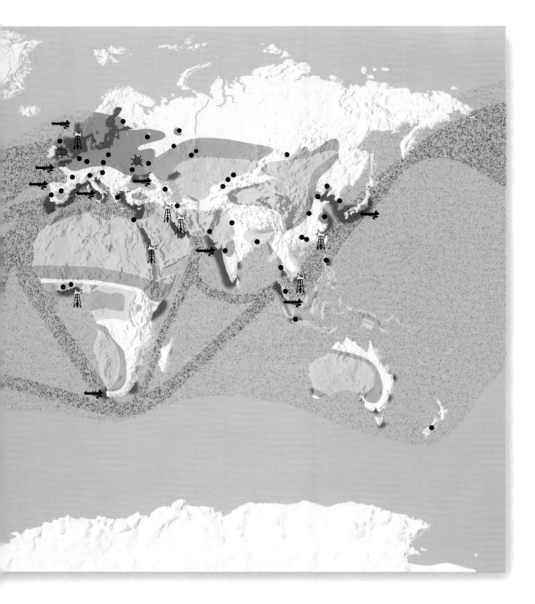

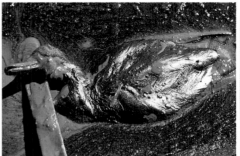

Oil Spills
Oil and other pollutants spilled by ships are a threat to wildlife. In 1989, oil spilt by the tanker *Exxon Valdez* off the coast of Alaska, in the United States, killed thousands of animals, including 350,000 seabirds.

Nuclear Accidents
Nuclear accidents occur rarely but can be devastating. In 1986, an accident at the Chernobyl nuclear power plant in the Ukraine released a cloud of radioactive gas across Europe, poisoning land, crops and people.

Oil Well Explosions
Accidents on oil and gas rigs can cause major environmental problems. During the Gulf War in Kuwait in 1992, hundreds of oil wells were set on fire, causing serious water and air pollution throughout the region.

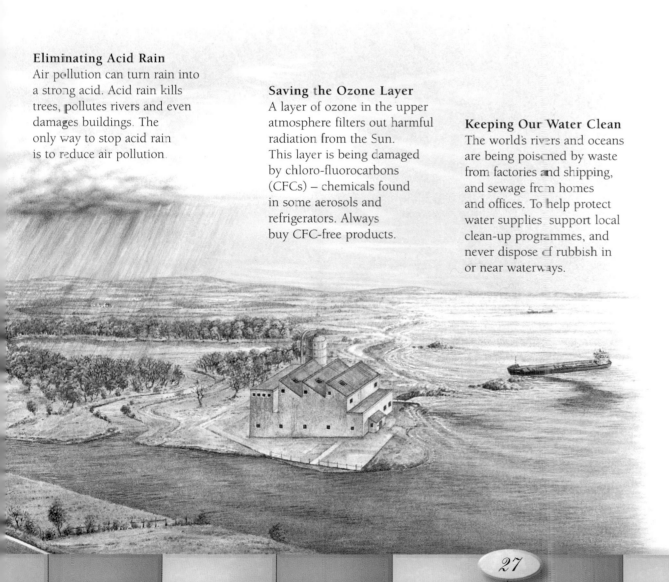

Eliminating Acid Rain
Air pollution can turn rain into a strong acid. Acid rain kills trees, pollutes rivers and even damages buildings. The only way to stop acid rain is to reduce air pollution.

Saving the Ozone Layer
A layer of ozone in the upper atmosphere filters out harmful radiation from the Sun. This layer is being damaged by chloro-fluorocarbons (CFCs) – chemicals found in some aerosols and refrigerators. Always buy CFC-free products.

Keeping Our Water Clean
The world's rivers and oceans are being poisoned by waste from factories and shipping, and sewage from homes and offices. To help protect water supplies, support local clean-up programmes, and never dispose of rubbish in or near waterways.

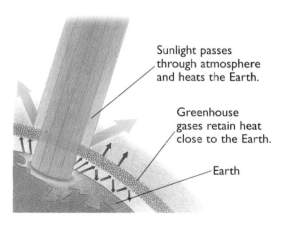

Sunlight passes through atmosphere and heats the Earth.

Greenhouse gases retain heat close to the Earth.

Earth

GLOBAL WARMING
Gases in the atmosphere, known as greenhouse gases, keep the Earth warm by trapping some of the energy that comes from the Sun. But the burning of fossil fuels is raising the levels of these gases, causing the planet to warm up too much. If this continues, some fertile land may turn into desert, and ice-caps may melt, causing flooding in lowland areas. Most countries are trying to reduce greenhouse gas emissions.

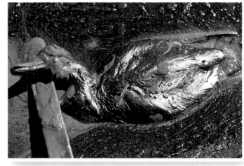

• LOOK AGAIN •
- How can we prevent acid rain?
- Which gases keep the Earth warm?
- How can you help protect the ozone layer?

The Physical World

WE CALL OUR PLANET EARTH, but more than two-thirds of its surface is covered by salt water. Large areas of salt water are called oceans, and smaller areas are known as seas. There are four oceans – the Pacific, Atlantic, Indian and Arctic – and many seas. The Pacific Ocean alone is larger than all of Earth's land masses combined. Land covers only 29 per cent of our planet's surface. Its shape and the kind of soil and vegetation that cover it vary enormously from place to place. Throughout the world there are hills, mountains and areas of flat land called plains. Trees and other plants cover many parts of the Earth, but some places have almost no vegetation. Deserts – very dry areas with sparse vegetation – cover about one-fifth of the world's land. The polar regions and many mountain tops are covered in ice and snow. The seas, too, have their mountains and valleys. Deep trenches are found in most oceans, and mountains on many islands are actually the tops of undersea mountains. For instance, Mauna Kea, on the island of Hawaii in the Pacific Ocean, is 10,205 metres (33,480 ft) high, measured from the sea floor to its highest point. That's far taller than Mount Everest, the highest mountain on land.

PHYSICAL FACTS

Circumference of Earth around the Equator: 40,067 km (24,902 mi)
Area of sea: 362,033,000 sq. km (139,782,000 sq. mi)
Area of land above sea level: 148,021,000 sq. km (57,151,000 sq. mi)
Largest ocean: Pacific Ocean, 166,241,700 sq. km (64,186,300 sq. mi)
Largest land mass: Eurasia (Europe and Asia), 53,698,000 sq. km (20,733,000 sq. mi)
Deepest ocean trench: Mariana Trench, Pacific Ocean, 10,911 m (35,797 ft)
Largest island: Greenland, 2,175,000 sq. km (840,000 sq. mi)

◆ AMAZING FACT ◆

Almost all of the water on Earth – 97.3 per cent – is salt water. Less than 3 per cent is fresh water, and two-thirds of this is locked up in ice-caps and glaciers. That leaves less than 1 per cent in rivers, lakes and underground channels.

ARCTIC OCEAN

Spitsbergen
SVALBARD
FRANZ JOSEF LAND
SEVERNAYA ZEMLYA
Greenland
Sea
NOVAYA ZEMLYA
Barents Sea
Kara
Sea
Laptev Sea
NEW SIBERIAN
ISLANDS
East
Siberian
Sea
Chukchi
Sea
Jan Mayen
Island
Iceland
Norwegian
Sea
SCANDINAVIA
Dvina
Yenisey
CENTRAL
SIBERIAN
PLATEAU
Lena
Bering Strait
FAEROE
ISLANDS
North
Sea
Volga
URAL MOUNTAINS
WESTERN
SIBERIAN
PLAIN
Ob
Yenisey
Angara
Lena
Amur
Bering Sea
ALEUTIAN ISLANDS
Ireland
BRITISH
ISLES
EUROPEAN PLAIN
Dnieper
EUROPE
Ob
Irtysh
SIBERIA
Lake
Baikal
ALEUTIAN TRENCH
CHANNEL
ISLANDS
CARPATHIAN
MTS.
Danube
KIRGIZ
STEPPE
ASIA
ALPS
Black Sea
Caspian Sea
Aral
Sea
Lake
Balkhash
GOBI
DESERT
KURIL ISLANDS
KURIL TRENCH
AZORES
Mediterranean Sea
ATLAS MTS.
Euphrates
ZAGROS MTS.
HINDU KUSH
TIAN SHAN
KUNLUN MTS.
PLATEAU
OF TIBET
Huang (Yellow)
Sea of Japan
Hokkaidō
Honshū
NORTH-WEST
PACIFIC
BASIN
PACIFIC
MADEIRA
Tigris
Nile
Red Sea
ARABIAN
PENINSULA
HIMALAYAS
Jiang (Yangtze)
East China
Sea
MIDWAY
ISLANDS
CANARY
ISLANDS
SAHARA DESERT
NUBIAN
DESERT
Arabian
Sea
DECCAN
Ganges
Bay of
Bengal
Mekong
Taiwan
South
China
Sea
Luzon
PHILIPPINE
BASIN
MARIANA
ISLANDS
Wake
Island
MARIANA TRENCH
MID-PACIFIC MOUNTAINS
OCEAN
CAPE VERDE
ISLANDS
SAHEL
AFRICA
LACCADIVE
ISLANDS
ANDAMAN
ISLANDS
NICOBAR
ISLANDS
Sri
Lanka
PHILIPPINE TRENCH
PHILIPPINE ISLANDS
Philippine
Sea
Palau
Guam
MICRONESIA
MARSHALL ISLANDS
CENTRAL
PACIFIC
BASIN
Johnston
Atoll
Niger
Gulf of
Guinea
Uele
Ubangi
Congo
Kasai
CONGO
BASIN
GREAT RIFT VALLEY
Lake
Victoria
MALDIVES
CAROLINE ISLANDS
Nauru
MELANESIA
OCEANIA
GILBERT
ISLANDS
Ascension
SEYCHELLES
MID-INDIAN
BASIN
NINETY-EAST RIDGE
Sumatra
Borneo
New
Guinea
SOLOMON ISLANDS
Tuvalu
Tokelau
MARTIN VAZ
ISLANDS
St. Helena
Zambezi
COMOROS ISLANDS
Mayotte
Madagascar
Mauritius
Réunion
MID-INDIAN RIDGE
INDIAN
OCEAN
Christmas
Island
JAVA TRENCH
Java
COCOS (KEELING)
ISLANDS
WHARTON
BASIN
Coral
Sea
Vanuatu
New
Caledonia
FIJI
ISLANDS
Niue
SAMOA
ISLANDS
Tonga
MID-ATLANTIC RIDGE
KALAHARI
DESERT
NAMIB DESERT
Orange
GREAT SANDY
DESERT
SIMPSON
DESERT
GREAT DIVIDING RANGE
Norfolk
Island
KERMADEC
ISLANDS
KERMADEC TRENCH
TONGA TRENCH
WALVIS RIDGE
Tristan da Cunha
Gough Island
CAPE OF
GOOD HOPE
AUSTRALIA
GREAT VICTORIAN
DESERT
Lake
Eyre
Darling
Murray
NEW
ZEALAND
North
Island
CHATHAM
ISLANDS
Amsterdam
Island
SOUTH-WEST INDIAN RIDGE
SOUTH-EAST INDIAN RIDGE
Great Australian
Bight
Tasmania
Tasman
Sea
South
Island
St. Paul
Island
CROZET
ISLANDS
KERGUÉLEN
ISLANDS
Macquarie
Island
AUCKLAND
ISLANDS
SOUTH
SANDWICH
ISLANDS
PRINCE EDWARD
ISLANDS
Bouvet Island
HEARD AND McDONALD
ISLANDS
ATLANTIC-INDIAN
BASIN
SOUTH INDIAN
BASIN

ANTARCTICA

Ross
Sea

Countries of the World

APART FROM ANTARCTICA, which has no permanent population, all the land on Earth is divided into countries. There are almost 200 countries in the world, and each country has its own government and its own laws. The world's smallest country, the Vatican City, measures about one-half of a square kilometre (0.17 sq. mi). That's about the size of 100 football fields. The largest country in the world, Russia, is 39 million times bigger! The lines that separate countries are called borders. On this world map, the countries are shown in different colours so that you can see the borders clearly. Borders may be straight or curved. Some are formed by rivers or mountain ranges; others cross lakes or seas. The sizes of countries and the shapes of their borders often change. Sometimes a large country divides into smaller countries because groups of people want to form separate countries. Neighbouring countries often disagree about where a border ought to be. Such disputes have led to wars in many parts of the world. In this atlas, disputed borders are shown by a dotted line. Many countries govern areas of land in other parts of the world. These are called territories. On a map, the name of the governing country usually appears in brackets after the name of the territory.

POLITICAL FACTS

Number of countries: around 200
Largest countries:
Russia, 17,075,383 sq. km (6,592,812 sq. mi)
Canada, 9,976,185 sq. km (3,851,809 sq. mi)
China, 9,583,000 sq. km (3,700,000 sq. mi)
Smallest country: Vatican City, 0.44 sq. km
(0.17 sq. mi)
Longest border: U.S.-Canada, 6,416 km
(3,987 mi)

• LOOK AGAIN •

The following shapes represent countries shown on the world map on the right. Can you find and name them?

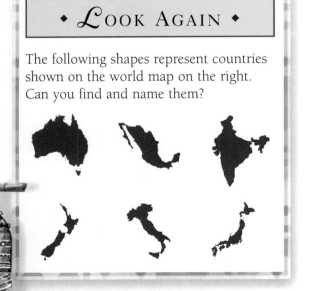

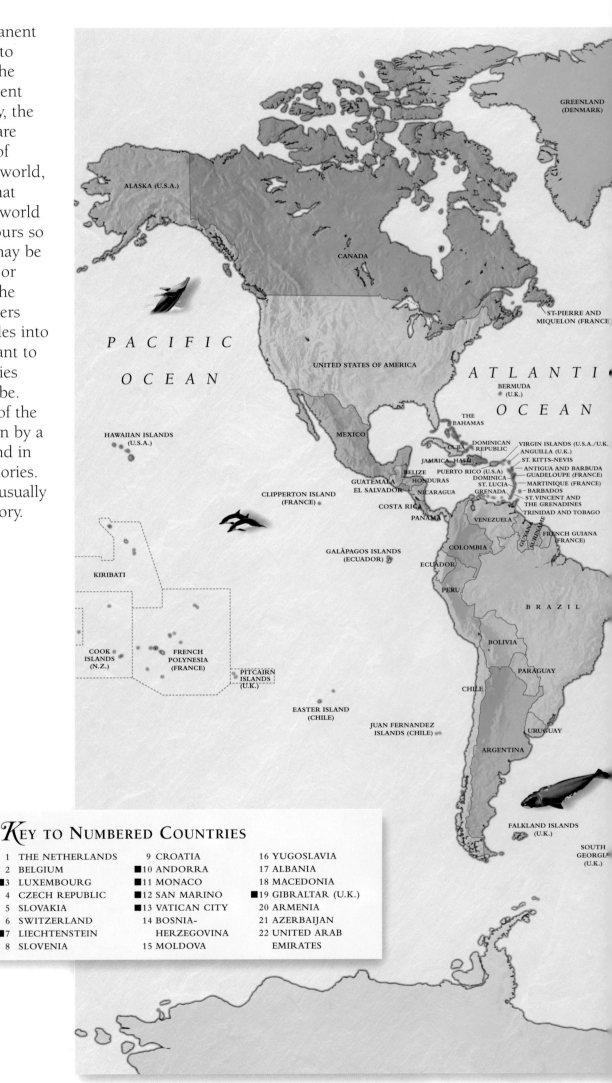

KEY TO NUMBERED COUNTRIES

1 THE NETHERLANDS	9 CROATIA	16 YUGOSLAVIA
2 BELGIUM	10 ANDORRA	17 ALBANIA
3 LUXEMBOURG	11 MONACO	18 MACEDONIA
4 CZECH REPUBLIC	12 SAN MARINO	19 GIBRALTAR (U.K.)
5 SLOVAKIA	13 VATICAN CITY	20 ARMENIA
6 SWITZERLAND	14 BOSNIA-	21 AZERBAIJAN
7 LIECHTENSTEIN	HERZEGOVINA	22 UNITED ARAB
8 SLOVENIA	15 MOLDOVA	EMIRATES

J   K   L   M   N   O   P   Q

2

3

4

5

6

7

8

9

10

11

ARCTIC OCEAN

SVALBARD
(NORWAY)

JAN MAYEN ISLAND
(NORWAY)

ICELAND

FAEROE ISLANDS
(DENMARK)

SWEDEN   FINLAND

NORWAY

ESTONIA

DENMARK   LATVIA
LITHUANIA

UNITED   RUSSIA
KINGDOM

IRELAND   POLAND   BELARUS

GERMANY

FRANCE   AUSTRIA   HUNGARY   UKRAINE

ROMANIA

ITALY   BULGARIA

GREECE   TURKEY

MALTA   CYPRUS   SYRIA

TUNISIA   LEBANON   IRAQ   IRAN   AFGHANISTAN

MOROCCO   ISRAEL   JORDAN   KUWAIT

CANARY ISLANDS   BAHRAIN
(SPAIN)   QATAR   PAKISTAN

WESTERN   ALGERIA   LIBYA   EGYPT   SAUDI
SAHARA   ARABIA   OMAN

MAURITANIA   MALI   NIGER   CHAD   SUDAN   ERITREA
                                                                                YEMEN

SENEGAL   BURKINA   NIGERIA   DJIBOUTI
GAMBIA   FASO   CENTRAL   ETHIOPIA
GUINEA-BISSAU   GUINEA   AFRICAN
S. LEONE   CAMEROON   REPUBLIC   SOMALIA
LIBERIA
CÔTE D'IVOIRE   EQUATORIAL   KENYA
(IVORY COAST)   GUINEA   GABON   DEMOCRATIC   UGANDA
SÃO TOMÉ   CONGO   REPUBLIC OF   RWANDA
AND PRÍNCIPE   THE CONGO   BURUNDI
                              (ZAIRE)   TANZANIA

ASCENSION
(U.K.)

ANGOLA   ZAMBIA   MALAWI

ST. HELENA AND DEPENDENCIES
(U.K.)   NAMIBIA   ZIMBABWE   MOZAMBIQUE
MARTIN VAZ ISLANDS   BOTSWANA   MADAGASCAR
(BRAZIL)   SWAZILAND
                              LESOTHO
                              SOUTH
                              AFRICA

TRISTAN DA CUNHA
(U.K.)

GOUGH ISLAND
(U.K.)

PRINCE EDWARD ISLANDS   CROZET ISLANDS
(SOUTH AFRICA)   (FRANCE)

KERGUÉLEN ISLANDS
(FRANCE)

SOUTH
SANDWICH ISLANDS   BOUVET ISLAND   HEARD AND McDONALD ISLANDS
(U.K.)   (NORWAY)   (AUSTRALIA)

RUSSIA

KAZAKSTAN

UZBEKISTAN   KYRGYZSTAN
TURKMENISTAN   TAJIKISTAN
GEORGIA

MONGOLIA

CHINA   NORTH
KOREA
SOUTH KOREA

JAPAN

NEPAL   BHUTAN

INDIA   BANGLADESH   MACAO
                    MYANMAR   (PORTUGAL)   TAIWAN
                    (BURMA)   LAOS
LACCADIVE   ANDAMAN   THAILAND   VIETNAM   PHILIPPINES
ISLANDS   ISLANDS
(INDIA)   (INDIA)   CAMBODIA
NICOBAR
ISLANDS   BRUNEI
SRI   (INDIA)   MALAYSIA
LANKA
MALDIVES   SINGAPORE   INDONESIA

PACIFIC
OCEAN

MIDWAY ISLANDS
(U.S.A.)

NORTHERN   WAKE ISLAND
MARIANA   (U.S.A.)
ISLANDS
(U.S.A.)   MARSHALL
ISLANDS   JOHNSTON
GUAM (U.S.A.)   ATOLL (U.S.A.)

PALAU   FEDERATED STATES
OF MICRONESIA

NAURU   KIRIBATI

PAPUA
NEW   SOLOMON
GUINEA   ISLANDS   TUVALU   TOKELAU
(N.Z.)
WALLIS AND   WESTERN
VANUATU   FUTUNA   SAMOA
(FRANCE)   AMERICAN
NEW   FIJI   SAMOA
CALEDONIA   (U.S.A.)
(FRANCE)   TONGA   NIUE
(N.Z.)

NORFOLK ISLAND
(AUSTRALIA)   KERMADEC ISLAND
(N.Z.)

BRITISH INDIAN
OCEAN TERRITORY (U.K.)

CHRISTMAS ISLAND
(AUSTRALIA)

COCOS (KEELING) ISLANDS
(AUSTRALIA)

SEYCHELLES

COMOROS
MAYOTTE
(FRANCE)

MAURITIUS
RÉUNION (FRANCE)

INDIAN

OCEAN

AMSTERDAM ISLAND
(FRANCE)

ST. PAUL ISLAND
(FRANCE)

AUSTRALIA

NEW
ZEALAND   CHATHAM ISLANDS
(N.Z.)

AUCKLAND ISLANDS
(N.Z.)

MACQUARIE ISLAND   CAMPBELL ISLAND
(AUSTRALIA)   (N.Z.)

PACIFIC

OCEAN

ATLANTIC

OCEAN

AZORES
(PORTUGAL)
PORTUGAL   SPAIN

MADEIRA
(PORTUGAL)

CAPE
VERDE
ISLANDS

ANTARCTICA

J   K   L   M   N   O   P   Q

North America

THE CONTINENT OF NORTH AMERICA extends from just south of the North Pole to just north of the Equator. It includes almost every kind of environment, from ice-caps to forests, mountains, deserts and rainforest. In the west, an almost unbroken chain of mountains stretches from Alaska to Costa Rica and includes the Rocky Mountains, one of the world's most famous mountain ranges. The United States of America (U.S.A.) and Canada are the largest of the continent's 23 countries. The U.S.A. is made up of 50 states. Canada is divided into ten provinces and two territories. North America includes some of the world's biggest cities, but also vast areas of wilderness. Most North Americans are descendants of European immigrants, but there are also many people of African and Asian origin, as well as native peoples.

Major Mountains and Rivers

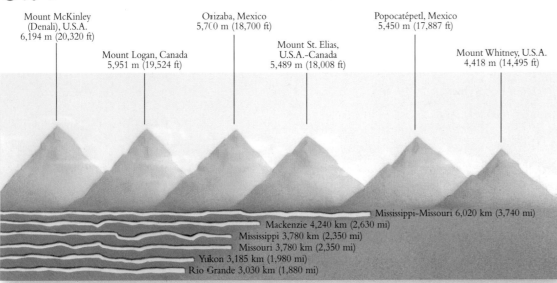

Mount McKinley (Denali), U.S.A. 6,194 m (20,320 ft)

Mount Logan, Canada 5,951 m (19,524 ft)

Orizaba, Mexico 5,700 m (18,700 ft)

Mount St. Elias, U.S.A.-Canada 5,489 m (18,008 ft)

Popocatépetl, Mexico 5,450 m (17,887 ft)

Mount Whitney, U.S.A. 4,418 m (14,495 ft)

Mississippi-Missouri 6,020 km (3,740 mi)
Mackenzie 4,240 km (2,630 mi)
Mississippi 3,780 km (2,350 mi)
Missouri 3,780 km (2,350 mi)
Yukon 3,185 km (1,980 mi)
Rio Grande 3,030 km (1,880 mi)

Political Map

ALASKA (U.S.A.)

CANADA

UNITED STATES of AMERICA

HAWAII (U.S.A.)

MEXICO

CUBA

BERMUDA (U.K.)

THE BAHAMAS

DOMINICAN REPUBLIC

JAMAICA

BELIZE
HONDURAS
HAITI

GUATEMALA

NICARAGUA

EL SALVADOR

COSTA RICA

PANAMA

TRINIDAD and TOBAGO

SOUTH AMERICA

ANGUILLA (U.K.)
VIRGIN ISLANDS (U.S.A./U.K.)
ANTIGUA and BARBUDA
ST. KITTS–NEVIS
GUADELOUPE (FRANCE)
PUERTO RICO (U.S.A.)
DOMINICA
MARTINIQUE (FRANCE)
ST. LUCIA
ST. VINCENT and THE GRENADINES
BARBADOS
GRENADA

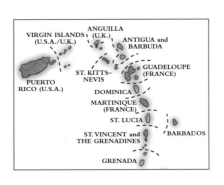

Continent Facts

Regional land area: 22,078,049 sq. km (8,522,127 sq. mi)
Regional population: 453,356,000
Independent countries: Antigua and Barbuda, The Bahamas, Barbados, Belize, Canada, Costa Rica, Cuba, Dominica, Dominican Republic, El Salvador, Grenada, Guatemala, Haiti, Honduras, Jamaica, Mexico, Nicaragua, Panama, St. Kitts–Nevis, St. Lucia, St. Vincent and the Grenadines, Trinidad and Tobago, United States of America

World Records

WORLD'S LARGEST GORGE
GRAND CANYON, U.S.A., 446 KM (277 MI) LONG, 16 KM (10 MI) WIDE, 1.6 KM (1 MI) DEEP

WORLD'S LARGEST FRESHWATER LAKE
LAKE SUPERIOR, U.S.A.-CANADA, 82,350 SQ. KM (31,800 SQ. MI)

WORLD'S LONGEST CAVE SYSTEM
MAMMOTH CAVES, U.S.A., 565 KM (351 MI)

WORLD'S LARGEST ACTIVE VOLCANO
MAUNA LOA, U.S.A., 4,170 M (13,680 FT) HIGH, 120 KM (75 MI) LONG, 50 KM (31 MI) WIDE

WORLD'S LONGEST BORDER
U.S.-CANADIAN BORDER, 6,416 KM (3,987 MI)

WORLD'S TALLEST ACTIVE GEYSER
STEAMBOAT GEYSER, YELLOWSTONE NATIONAL PARK, U.S.A., 115 M (380 FT)

WORLD'S LARGEST THEME PARK
WALT DISNEY WORLD, U.S.A., 122 SQ. KM (47 SQ. MI)

Continent Records

HIGHEST MOUNTAIN
MOUNT MCKINLEY (DENALI), U.S.A., 6,194 M (20,320 FT)

LOWEST POINT
DEATH VALLEY, U.S.A., 86 M (282 FT) BELOW SEA LEVEL

LONGEST RIVER
MISSISSIPPI-MISSOURI, U.S.A., 6,020 KM (3,740 MI)

LARGEST COUNTRY BY AREA
CANADA, 9,976,185 SQ. KM (3,851,809 SQ. MI)

LARGEST COUNTRY BY POPULATION
UNITED STATES OF AMERICA, population 263,814,000

LARGEST CITY BY POPULATION
MEXICO CITY, MEXICO, population 15,600,000

ASIA

PHYSICAL MAP

ARCTIC OCEAN

× NORTH POLE

Chukchi
Sea

Ellesmere
Island

Beaufort
Sea

Banks
Island

QUEEN
ELIZABETH
ISLANDS

Greenland

Baffin
Bay

EUROPE

Bering
Sea

BROOKS RANGE

Yukon

Mackenzie

Victoria
Island

Baffin
Island

ALEUTIAN ISLANDS

Mt. McKinley
(Denali)

Mt. Logan

Mt. St. Elias

Great
Bear
Lake

Arctic Circle

Labrador
Sea

Gulf of
Alaska

Great Slave
Lake

C
A
N
A
D
I
A
N

Hudson
Bay

LABRADOR

QUEEN
CHARLOTTE
ISLANDS

COAST MTS.

ROCKY
MOUNTAINS

G
R
E
A
T

S
H
I
E
L
D

Newfoundland

ATLANTIC OCEAN

Vancouver
Island

Lake
Winnipeg

PACIFIC OCEAN

COAST RANGES

Missouri

P
L
A
I
N
S

Lake
Nipigon

Lake
Superior

Lake
Huron

St. Lawrence

HAWAIIAN
ISLANDS

GREAT
BASIN

Great
Salt
Lake

Mississippi

Missouri

Lake
Michigan

Lake
Ontario

Lake
Erie

Mt.
Whitney

Colorado

Ohio

APPALACHIAN MOUNTAINS

Bermuda

SIERRA NEVADA

SIERRA MADRE OCCIDENTAL

SIERRA MADRE ORIENTAL

Rio Grande

Mississippi

Gulf of California

Tropic of Cancer

THE
BAHAMAS

LESSER ANTILLES

GREATER ANTILLES

Gulf of
Mexico

Bay of
Campeche

Caribbean Sea

Popocatépetl

Orizaba

SOUTH AMERICA

Lake
Nicaragua

Equator

GALÁPAGOS
ISLANDS

10

11

Western Canada and Alaska

CANADA, THE WORLD'S SECOND-LARGEST country, covers more than half of North America. Northern Canada is a vast, chilly wilderness where bears fish icy rivers for salmon and wolves hunt caribou across snow-covered plains. Few people live in this cold environment: the North-west Territories occupy one-third of Canada, but the province's population of 65,800 could be contained in a large sports stadium. Eighty per cent of Canada's residents live within 300 kilometres (185 mi) of the southern border, where the climate is milder and the land is more fertile. The prairie grassland that covers parts of Alberta, Manitoba and Saskatchewan is one of the world's most

productive farming regions. These provinces also supply most of Canada's oil and gas. West of the towering Rocky Mountains is the Pacific coastline, a maze of islands and narrow waterways. In the Gulf of Alaska, glaciers creep down the mountains toward the shore, while seals and whales swim in the bays. Alaska is not part of Canada. It is the biggest state in the U.S.A. but it is separated from the rest of the country by Canada. More than half of Alaska's lands are wildlife refuges, and the state contains some of North America's largest oil fields.

ALASKA (U.S.A.)
POPULATION: 603,600 ✹ CAPITAL: JUNEAU

ALBERTA
POPULATION: 2,747,000 ✹ CAPITAL: EDMONTON

BRITISH COLUMBIA
POPULATION: 3,766,000 ✹ CAPITAL: VICTORIA

MANITOBA
POPULATION: 1,137,500 ✹ CAPITAL: WINNIPEG

NORTHWEST TERRITORIES
POPULATION: 65,800 ✹ CAPITAL: YELLOWKNIFE

SASKATCHEWAN
POPULATION: 1,015,600 ✹ CAPITAL: REGINA

YUKON TERRITORY
POPULATION: 30,100 ✹ CAPITAL: WHITEHORSE

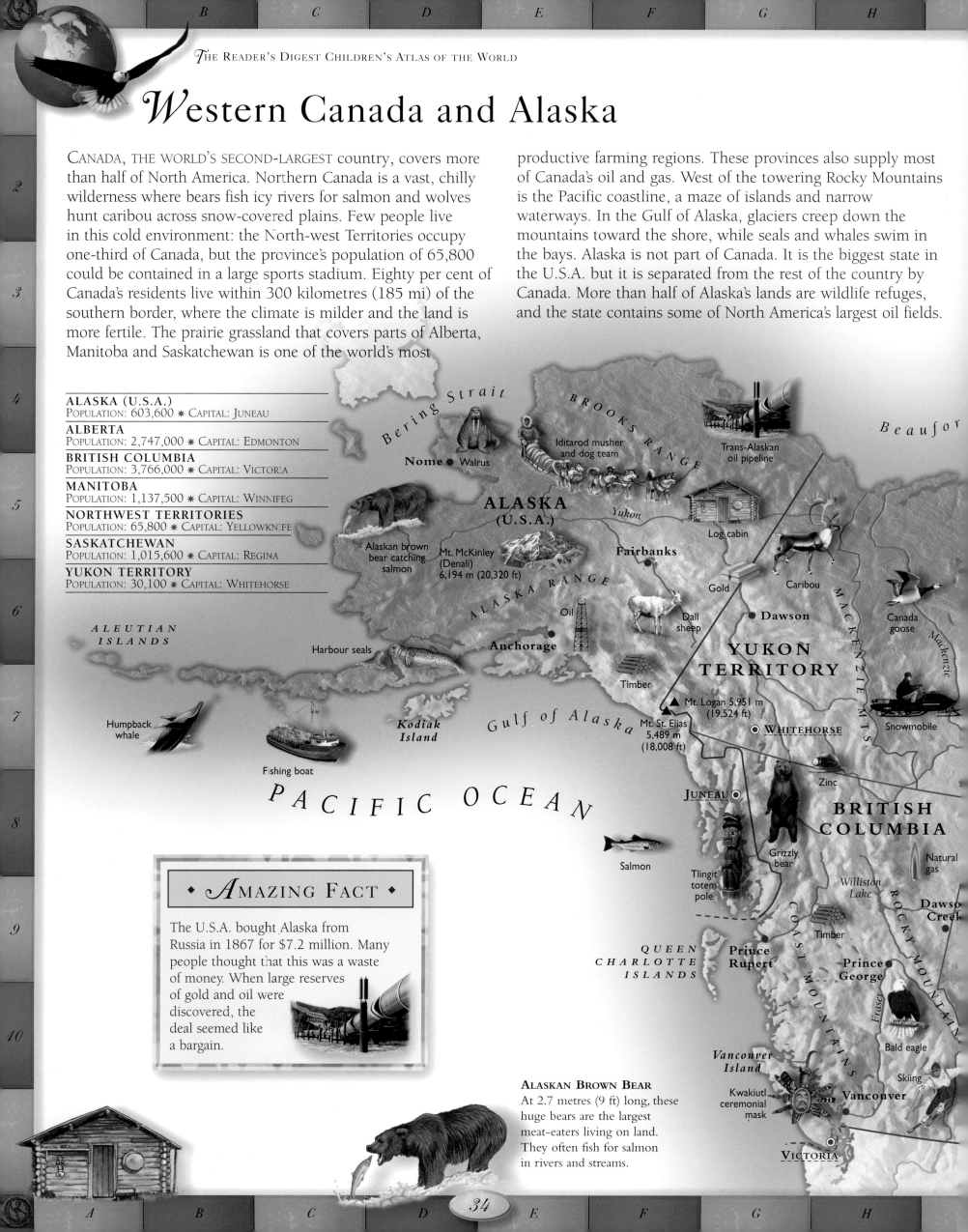

Bering Strait

BROOKS RANGE

Beaufor

Nome ● Walrus

Iditarod musher and dog team

Trans-Alaskan oil pipeline

ALASKA (U.S.A.)

Yukon

Log cabin

Alaskan brown bear catching salmon

Mt. McKinley (Denali) 6,194 m (20,320 ft)

Fairbanks

Caribou

ALASKA RANGE

Gold

Canada goose

ALEUTIAN ISLANDS

Oil

Dall sheep

Dawson

YUKON TERRITORY

Mackenzie

Anchorage

Harbour seals

Timber

Mt. Logan 5,951 m (19,524 ft)

MACKENZIE MTS.

Humpback whale

Kodiak Island

Gulf of Alaska

Mt. St. Elias 5,489 m (18,008 ft)

WHITEHORSE

Snowmobile

Fishing boat

PACIFIC OCEAN

Salmon

JUNEAU

Zinc

BRITISH COLUMBIA

Grizzly bear

Natural gas

♦ AMAZING FACT ♦

The U.S.A. bought Alaska from Russia in 1867 for $7.2 million. Many people thought that this was a waste of money. When large reserves of gold and oil were discovered, the deal seemed like a bargain.

Tlingit totem pole

Williston Lake

Dawso Creek

QUEEN CHARLOTTE ISLANDS

Prince Rupert

Prince George

ROCKY MOUNTAIN

COAST MOUNTAINS

Timber

Fraser

Bald eagle

Vancouver Island

Skiing

Kwakiutl ceremonial mask

Vancouver

ALASKAN BROWN BEAR
At 2.7 metres (9 ft) long, these huge bears are the largest meat-eaters living on land. They often fish for salmon in rivers and streams.

VICTORIA

ARCTIC OCEAN

Narwhal

Ellesmere Island

Musk ox

QUEEN ELIZABETH ISLANDS

Polar bears

PARRY ISLANDS

Arctic fox

◆ PROJECT: *Inuit Finger Masks* ◆

In ceremonies and rituals, the Inuit use tiny finger masks to represent their spirit ancestors. The masks are often carved from wood or stone, but you can make some out of cardboard.

❶ Cut out a circle about 10 centimetres (4 in) in diameter. Cut two small holes at the bottom of the circle large enough for your fingers to poke through.

❷ Draw a face in the centre of the circle and colour it. Cut a fringe in the cardboard, or glue feathers or beads around the face.

❸ To perform with the mask, move your hand slowly from side to side to the beat of a drum.

Somerset Island

Prince of Wales Island

Baffin Bay

GREENLAND

Davis Strait

Baffin Island

Inuit building igloo

Banks Island

Snow goose

Arctic hare

Victoria Island

Traditional church

Innuit fishing through ice

Kittiwake

Harp seals

Sea

Great Bear Lake

Silver

Wolf

Igloo-shaped houses

Southampton Island

Hudson Strait

LOCATION

QUÉBEC

NORTHWEST TERRITORIES

YELLOWKNIFE

Seaplane

Gold

Grey jay

Moose

Hudson Bay

Ⓔ Beluga whale

Great Slave Lake

CANADA

Slave

Peace

Zinc and lead

Lake Athabasca

Uranium

Reindeer Lake

Beaver

Nelson

Nickel and copper

Churchill

Churchill

N

E

W

S

ALBERTA

Edmonton dinosaur fossils

arley

Mountie

MANITOBA

ONTARIO

SCALE

MILES

0   100   200   300

Oil

Natural gas

Wheat

Saskatchewan

Saskatoon

EDMONTON

SASKATCHEWAN

Gold

Lake Winnipeg

0   100   200   300   400   500

KILOMETRES

• Calgary

REGINA

Grain stores

WINNIPEG

ROYAL CANADIAN MOUNTED POLICE (MOUNTIES)
Canada's national police force was founded in 1873 to prevent disputes between native tribes and European traders.

Calgary Stampede

Legislative Building

Eastern Canada

ABOUT 60 PER CENT OF THE POPULATION of Canada live along the shores of the St. Lawrence River and the Great Lakes, an area that occupies only 2 per cent of the country's land area. From the early 17th century onwards, European immigrants settled here because the land was fertile and the waterways provided transportation routes. Today, the region is home to many of Canada's biggest cities, including the two largest, Toronto and Montréal. Canada has two main languages – English and French. The majority of French speakers live in the province of Québec, which was once a French territory. The forests, lakes and rivers that cover most of Québec and Ontario provide a wealth of resources. Québec's forestry industry produces about 12 per cent of the world's pulp and paper. Hydroelectric power stations create so much electricity that Québec and Ontario can export energy. The climate of eastern Canada ranges from temperate in the south to arctic in the north. For nine months of the year, Hudson Bay is frozen, allowing polar bears to prowl the pack-ice in search of food. Off Newfoundland's north shore float huge icebergs measuring up to 45 metres (150 ft) high. Further south, enormous tides surge in and out of the bays. In the Bay of Fundy, the sea can rise 15 metres (50 ft) at high tide – high enough to cover a four-storey building!

NEW BRUNSWICK
POPULATION: 760,100 ✳ CAPITAL: FREDERICTON

NEWFOUNDLAND
POPULATION: 575,400 ✳ CAPITAL: ST. JOHN'S

NOVA SCOTIA
POPULATION: 937,800 ✳ CAPITAL: HALIFAX

ONTARIO
POPULATION: 11,100,000 ✳ CAPITAL: TORONTO

PRINCE EDWARD ISLAND
POPULATION: 136,100 ✳ CAPITAL: CHARLOTTETOWN

QUÉBEC
POPULATION: 7,334,000 ✳ CAPITAL: QUÉBEC

✦ LOOK AGAIN ✦

● Which city is Canada's national capital?

● Which endangered sea mammal swims off the east coast of Newfoundland?

● What kind of mineral is mined in Newfoundland?

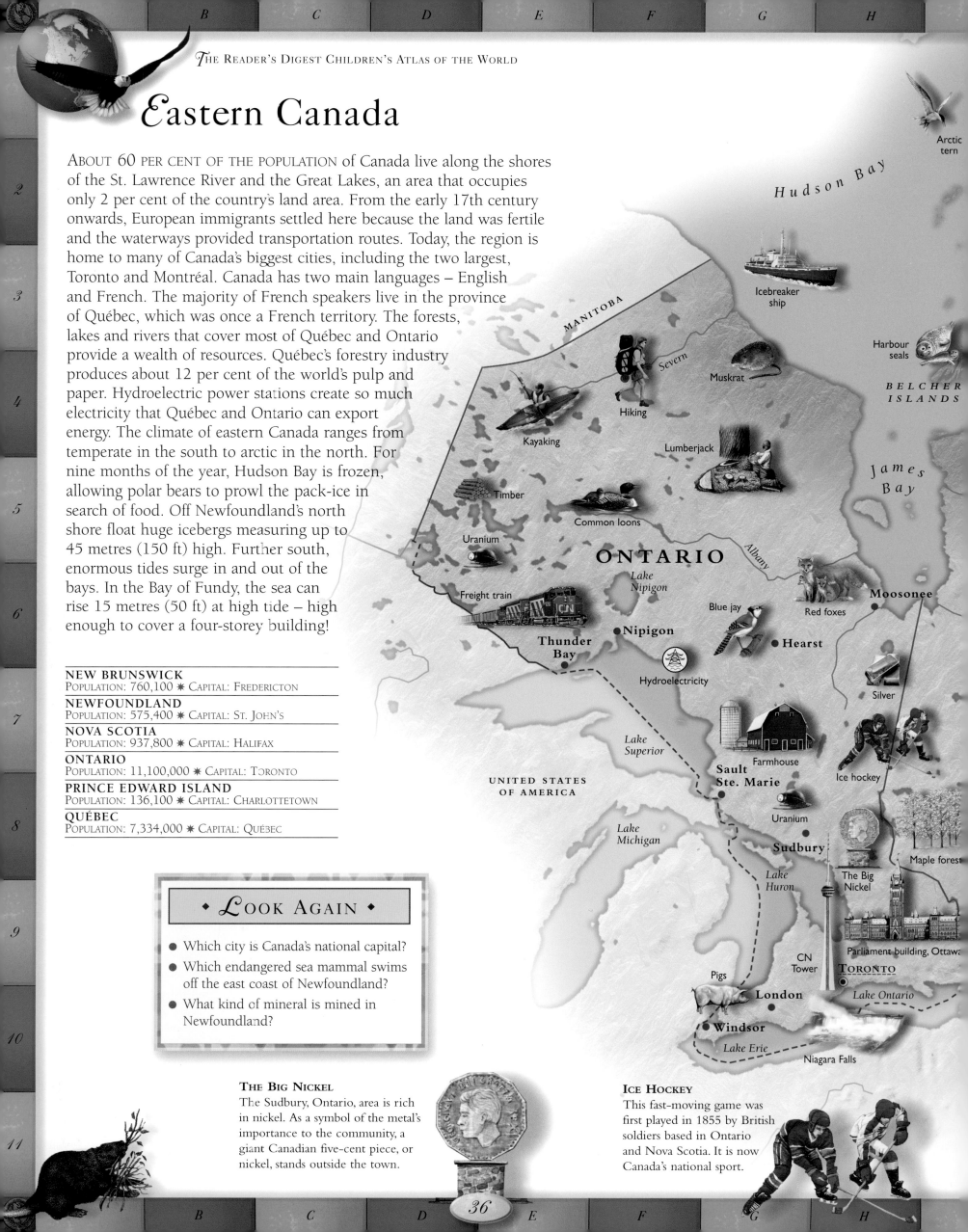

Arctic tern

Hudson Bay

MANITOBA

Icebreaker ship

Harbour seals

BELCHER ISLANDS

Severn

Muskrat

Hiking

Kayaking

Lumberjack

James Bay

Timber

Common loons

Uranium

ONTARIO

Albany

Lake Nipigon

Blue jay

Red foxes

Moosonee

Freight train

Nipigon

Hearst

Thunder Bay

Hydroelectricity

Silver

Lake Superior

UNITED STATES OF AMERICA

Farmhouse

Ice hockey

Sault Ste. Marie

Lake Michigan

Uranium

Sudbury

Maple forest

Lake Huron

The Big Nickel

Pigs

CN Tower

Parliament building, Ottawa

London

Lake Ontario

Windsor

Lake Erie

Niagara Falls

TORONTO

THE BIG NICKEL
The Sudbury, Ontario, area is rich in nickel. As a symbol of the metal's importance to the community, a giant Canadian five-cent piece, or nickel, stands outside the town.

ICE HOCKEY
This fast-moving game was first played in 1855 by British soldiers based in Ontario and Nova Scotia. It is now Canada's national sport.

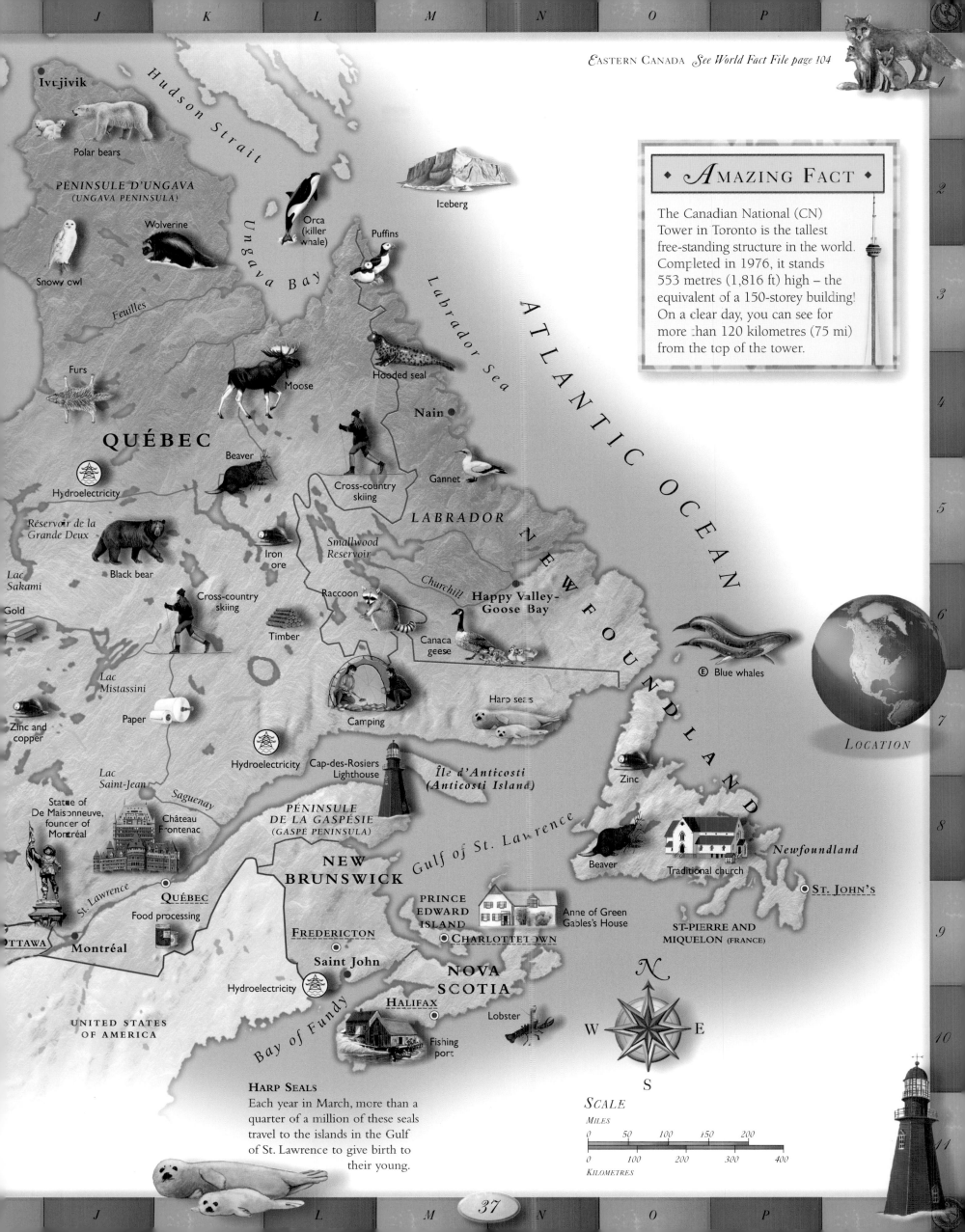

Ivujivik

Hudson Strait

Polar bears

PÉNINSULE D'UNGAVA
(UNGAVA PENINSULA)

Wolverine

Snowy owl

Ungava Bay

Orca
(killer
whale)

Puffins

Iceberg

Feuilles

Furs

Moose

Labrador Sea

Hooded seal

Nain

ATLANTIC OCEAN

QUÉBEC

Beaver

Hydroelectricity

Cross-country
skiing

Gannet

LABRADOR

Réservoir de la
Grande Deux

Smallwood
Reservoir

Lac
Sakami

Black bear

Iron
ore

Churchill

**Happy Valley-
Goose Bay**

NEWFOUNDLAND

Gold

Cross-country
skiing

Raccoon

Zinc and
copper

Lac
Mistassini

Paper

Timber

Canada
geese

Blue whales

Camping

Harp seals

Hydroelectricity

Lac
Saint-Jean

Cap-des-Rosiers
Lighthouse

Île d'Anticosti
(Anticosti Island)

Zinc

Saguenay

Statue of
De Maisonneuve,
founder of
Montréal

Château
Frontenac

PÉNINSULE
DE LA GASPÉSIE
(GASPÉ PENINSULA)

Gulf of St. Lawrence

Beaver

Traditional church

Newfoundland

St. Lawrence

**NEW
BRUNSWICK**

QUÉBEC

Food processing

OTTAWA

Montréal

FREDERICTON

Saint John

Hydroelectricity

**PRINCE
EDWARD
ISLAND**

CHARLOTTETOWN

Anne of Green
Gables's House

**ST-PIERRE AND
MIQUELON (FRANCE)**

ST. JOHN'S

**NOVA
SCOTIA**

HALIFAX

Lobster

UNITED STATES
OF AMERICA

Bay of Fundy

Fishing
port

LOCATION

HARP SEALS
Each year in March, more than a
quarter of a million of these seals
travel to the islands in the Gulf
of St. Lawrence to give birth to
their young.

N W E S

SCALE

MILES

0   50   100   150   200

0   100   200   300   400

KILOMETRES

North-eastern United States

THE NORTH-EAST U.S.A. is home to 65 million people – more than one-quarter of the population of the U.S.A. From Boston in the north to Washington, D.C. in the south, a line of great cities stretches for over 640 kilometres (400 mi) along the Atlantic shore. Including its suburbs, New York City is home to more than 16 million people. It is the largest city in the U.S.A. and the third largest in the world. New York is one of the world's leading centres of trade, industry and culture. The heart of the city is the island of Manhattan, where giant skyscrapers, including some of the world's tallest, tower over long, straight streets packed with people and traffic.

The Appalachian Mountains separate the cities of the coast from the Great Lakes and the plains of the interior. They stretch for more than 2,600 kilometres (600 mi) from northern Alabama, in the southern U.S.A., to northern Maine. In the south, these mountains are rich in minerals – Kentucky produces more coal than any other state. Farms occupy many Appalachian valleys, but large areas of the mountains are covered by deciduous forests, where black bears forage for blueberries and otters swim in the streams. In autumn, these forests provide spectacular displays of colour, as their leaves change from green to brilliant shades of orange, red and gold.

CONNECTICUT
POPULATION: 3,275,000 ✳ CAPITAL: HARTFORD

DELAWARE
POPULATION: 717,200 ✳ CAPITAL: DOVER

DISTRICT OF COLUMBIA
POPULATION: 554,200 ✳ CAPITAL: WASHINGTON, D.C.

KENTUCKY
POPULATION: 3,860,000 ✳ CAPITAL: FRANKFORT

MAINE
POPULATION: 1,241,000 ✳ CAPITAL: AUGUSTA

MARYLAND
POPULATION: 5,042,000 ✳ CAPITAL: ANNAPOLIS

MASSACHUSETTS
POPULATION: 6,074,000 ✳ CAPITAL: BOSTON

NEW HAMPSHIRE
POPULATION: 1,148,000 ✳ CAPITAL: CONCORD

NEW JERSEY
POPULATION: 7,945,000 ✳ CAPITAL: TRENTON

NEW YORK
POPULATION: 18,136,000 ✳ CAPITAL: ALBANY

PENNSYLVANIA
POPULATION: 12,072,000 ✳ CAPITAL: HARRISBURG

RHODE ISLAND
POPULATION: 989,800 ✳ CAPITAL: PROVIDENCE

VERMONT
POPULATION: 584,800 ✳ CAPITAL: MONTPELIER

VIRGINIA
POPULATION: 6,618,000 ✳ CAPITAL: RICHMOND

WEST VIRGINIA
POPULATION: 1,828,000 ✳ CAPITAL: CHARLESTON

◆ PROJECT: *Iroquois Beads* ◆

According to the custom of the native Iroquois people, a person saying something important must give the listener a gift to confirm the truth of the statement. This gift is often a string of white and purple shell beads known as wampum. Try making your own Iroquois friendship beads. Thread some coloured beads onto pieces of string and attach the strings to a length of yarn. Remember to explain the meaning of your gift to the receiver.

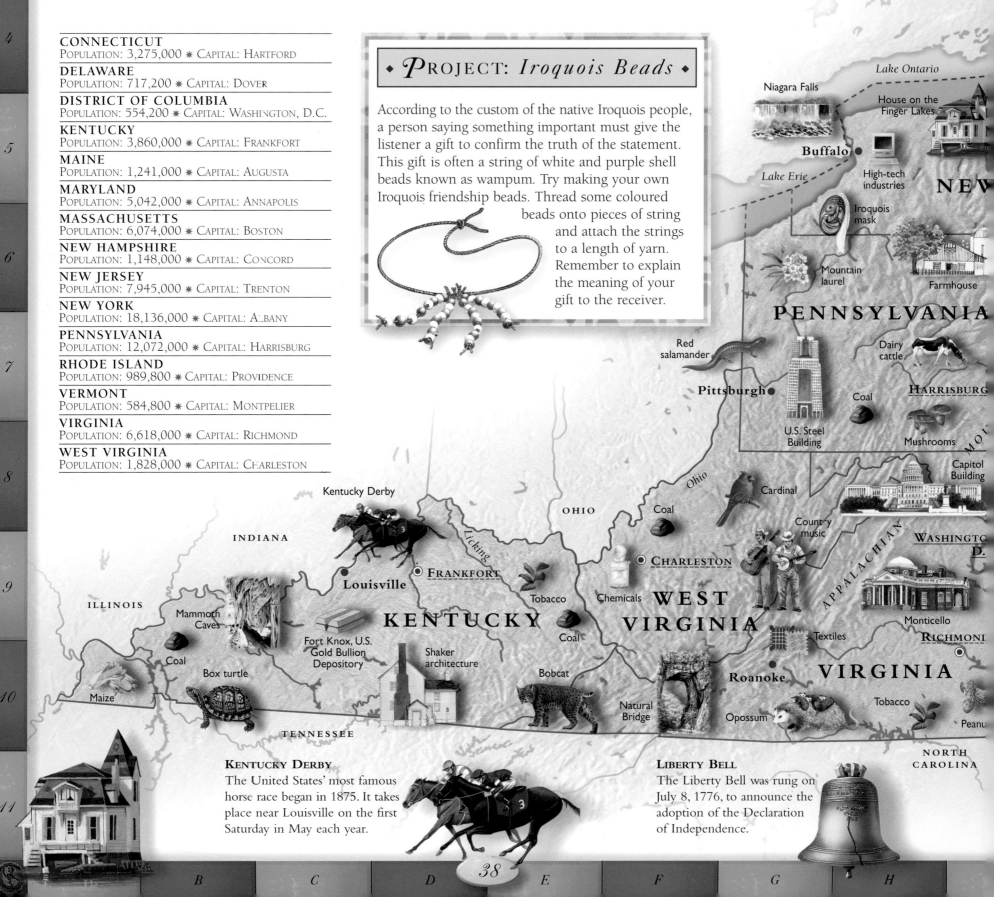

KENTUCKY DERBY
The United States' most famous horse race began in 1875. It takes place near Louisville on the first Saturday in May each year.

LIBERTY BELL
The Liberty Bell was rung on July 8, 1776, to announce the adoption of the Declaration of Independence.

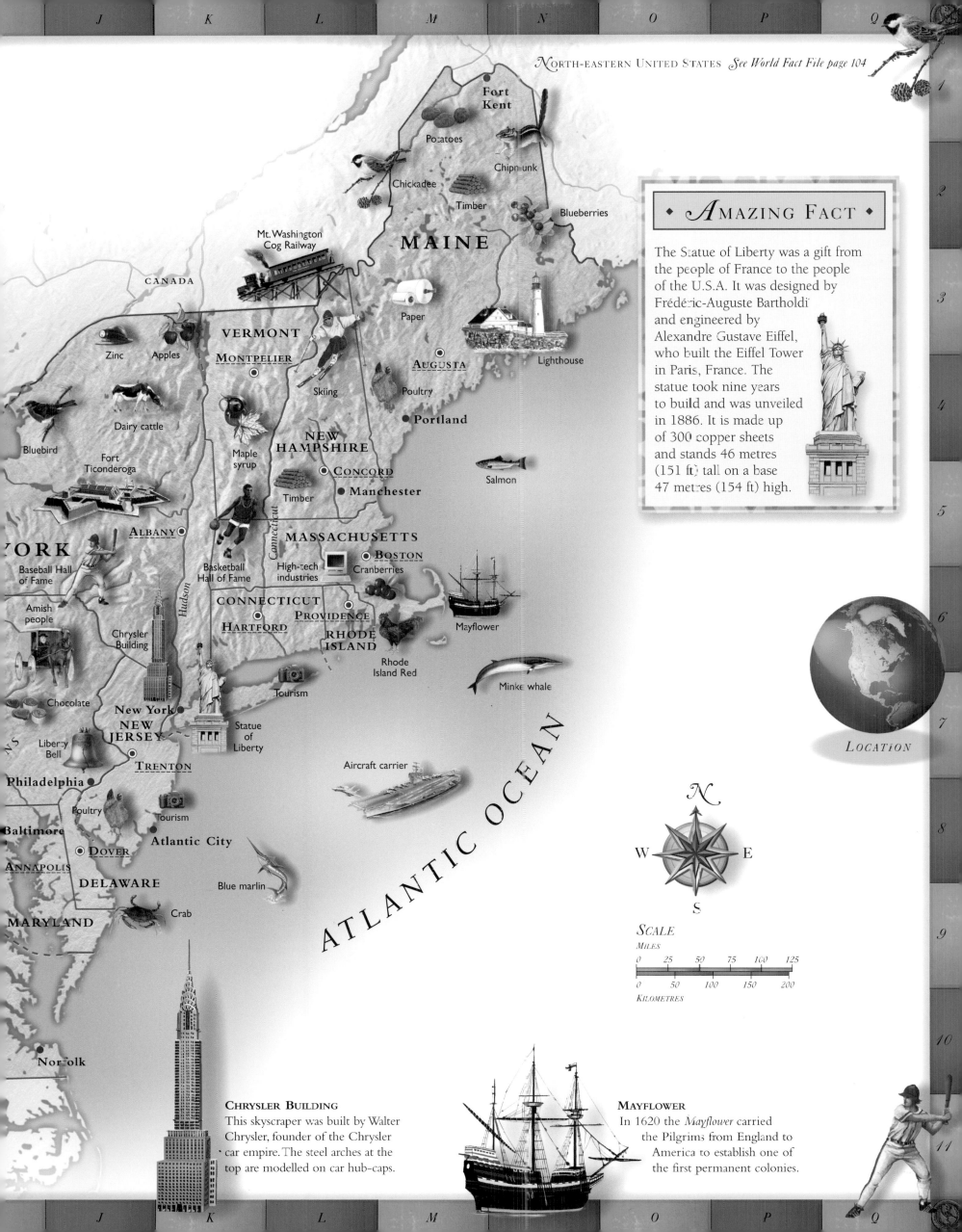

J   K   L   M   N   O   P   Q

Fort
Kent

Potatoes

Chickadee

Chipmunk

Timber

Blueberries

MAINE

Mt. Washington
Cog Railway

CANADA

Paper

Lighthouse

VERMONT

Zinc   Apples

MONTPELIER

Skiing

AUGUSTA

Poultry

Dairy cattle

Portland

Bluebird

NEW
HAMPSHIRE

Fort
Ticonderoga

Maple
syrup

Salmon

CONCORD

Manchester

Timber

ALBANY

MASSACHUSETTS

YORK

BOSTON

Baseball Hall
of Fame

Basketball
Hall of Fame

High-tech
industries

Cranberries

Amish
people

CONNECTICUT

PROVIDENCE

Mayflower

Chrysler
Building

HARTFORD

RHODE
ISLAND

Chocolate

Rhode
Island Red

Minke whale

New York

Liberty
Bell

NEW
JERSEY

Statue
of
Liberty

Tourism

Philadelphia

TRENTON

Aircraft carrier

Baltimore

Poultry

Tourism

Atlantic City

ANNAPOLIS

DOVER

DELAWARE

Blue marlin

MARYLAND

Crab

Norfolk

AMAZING FACT

The Statue of Liberty was a gift from the people of France to the people of the U.S.A. It was designed by Frédéric-Auguste Bartholdi and engineered by Alexandre Gustave Eiffel, who built the Eiffel Tower in Paris, France. The statue took nine years to build and was unveiled in 1886. It is made up of 300 copper sheets and stands 46 metres (151 ft) tall on a base 47 metres (154 ft) high.

LOCATION

ATLANTIC OCEAN

N
W   E
S

SCALE

MILES

0   25   50   75   100   125

0   50   100   150   200

KILOMETRES

CHRYSLER BUILDING

This skyscraper was built by Walter Chrysler, founder of the Chrysler car empire. The steel arches at the top are modelled on car hub-caps.

MAYFLOWER

In 1620 the *Mayflower* carried the Pilgrims from England to America to establish one of the first permanent colonies.

J   K   L   M   N   O   P   Q

Southern United States

THE SOUTHERN U.S.A. is a warm, humid region of plains, rivers, swamps and coastal lagoons. From southern Texas, a broad belt of lowland stretches around the Gulf of Mexico, across Florida and along the shores of the Atlantic Ocean. In the north-east, the coastal plains rise to plateaux and mountain ranges, including the Appalachian Mountains, which formed about 400 million years ago and are North America's oldest mountains. Mixed crop and livestock farms cover the fertile eastern and southern plains. In the west, on the dry Texas grasslands, ranch hands tend huge herds of cattle. Texas is the second biggest American state after Alaska, and its beef industry and large oil reserves have made it one of the richest parts of the country. Numerous rivers cross the southern U.S.A., including the Mississippi, one of North America's longest rivers and busiest inland waterways. Along the coast of the Gulf of Mexico and in northern Florida, these rivers have formed shallow lakes, muddy deltas and steamy swamps that are home to snakes, turtles and alligators. Florida's sunny climate and sandy beaches make it a popular holiday destination. The Walt Disney World theme park near Orlando is the world's number one tourist attraction, with more than 25 million visitors each year.

Many of the first Europeans to settle in this region came from France and Spain in the 17th century, and their descendants are called Creoles. Other French-speakers known as Cajuns arrived soon afterwards from Canada. Florida's large Spanish-speaking population includes immigrants from the island of Cuba, which lies just 217 kilometres (135 mi) south of Key West, the southernmost tip of Florida and the U.S.A.

ALABAMA
POPULATION: 4,253,000 ✳ CAPITAL: MONTGOMERY

ARKANSAS
POPULATION: 2,484,000 ✳ CAPITAL: LITTLE ROCK

FLORIDA
POPULATION: 14,166,000 ✳ CAPITAL: TALLAHASSEE

GEORGIA
POPULATION: 7,201,000 ✳ CAPITAL: ATLANTA

LOUISIANA
POPULATION: 4,342,000 ✳ CAPITAL: BATON ROUGE

MISSISSIPPI
POPULATION: 2,697,000 ✳ CAPITAL: JACKSON

NORTH CAROLINA
POPULATION: 7,195,000 ✳ CAPITAL: RALEIGH

OKLAHOMA
POPULATION: 3,278,000 ✳ CAPITAL: OKLAHOMA CITY

SOUTH CAROLINA
POPULATION: 3,673,000 ✳ CAPITAL: COLUMBIA

TENNESSEE
POPULATION: 5,256,000 ✳ CAPITAL: NASHVILLE

TEXAS
POPULATION: 18,724,000 ✳ CAPITAL: AUSTIN

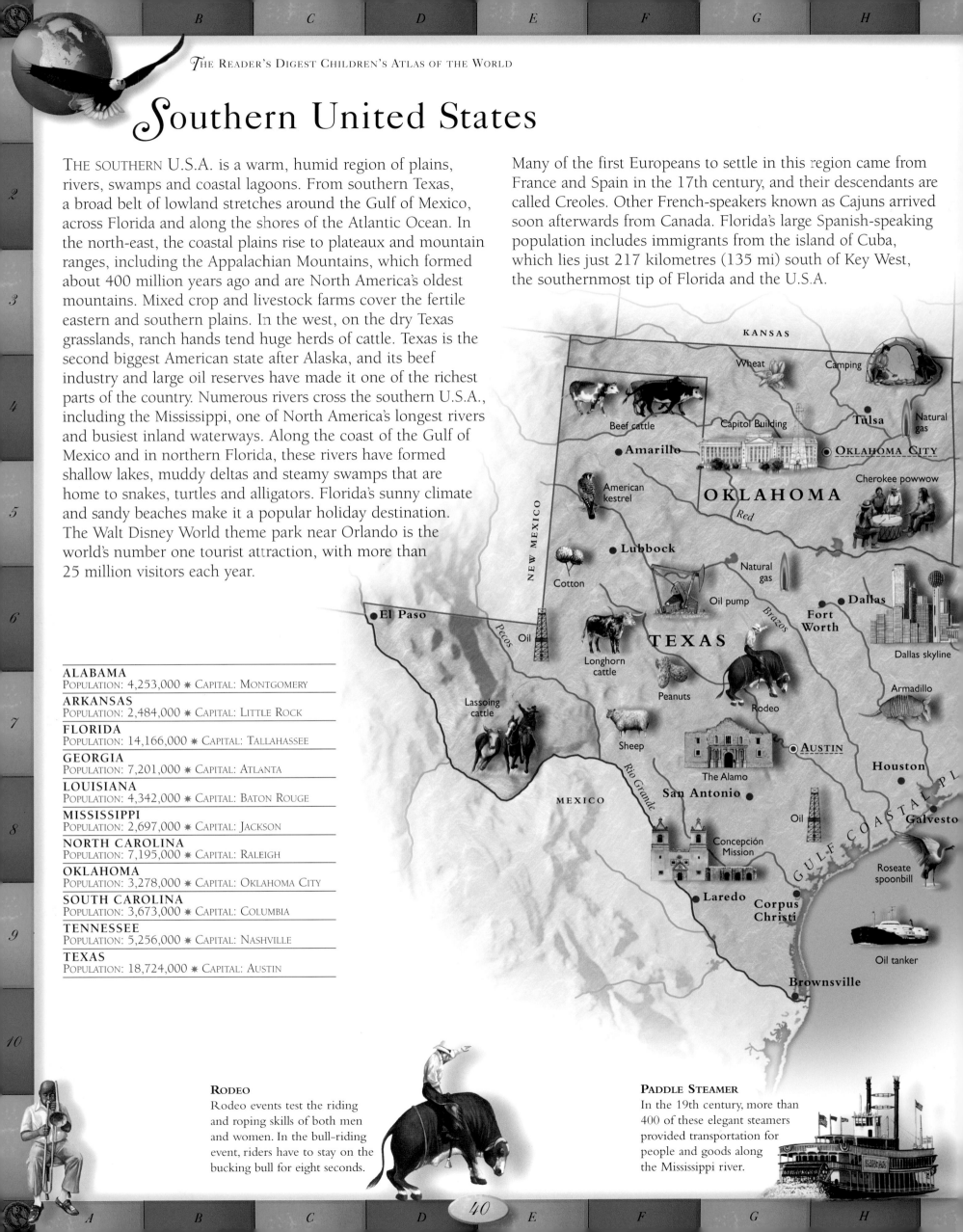

KANSAS

Wheat — Camping

Beef cattle — Capitol Building — Tulsa — Natural gas

● Amarillo — ● OKLAHOMA CITY

OKLAHOMA — Cherokee powwow

American kestrel — Red

● Lubbock — Natural gas

Cotton — Oil pump — Dallas ●

NEW MEXICO — Fort Worth

El Paso ● — Pecos — Oil — Brazos — Dallas skyline

TEXAS — Armadillo

Longhorn cattle — Peanuts — Rodeo

Lassoing cattle

Sheep — ● AUSTIN — Houston ●

The Alamo

MEXICO — Rio Grande — San Antonio ● — Oil — GULF COASTAL PL — Galveston

Concepción Mission — Roseate spoonbill

● Laredo — Corpus Christi ●

● Brownsville — Oil tanker

RODEO
Rodeo events test the riding and roping skills of both men and women. In the bull-riding event, riders have to stay on the bucking bull for eight seconds.

PADDLE STEAMER
In the 19th century, more than 400 of these elegant steamers provided transportation for people and goods along the Mississippi river.

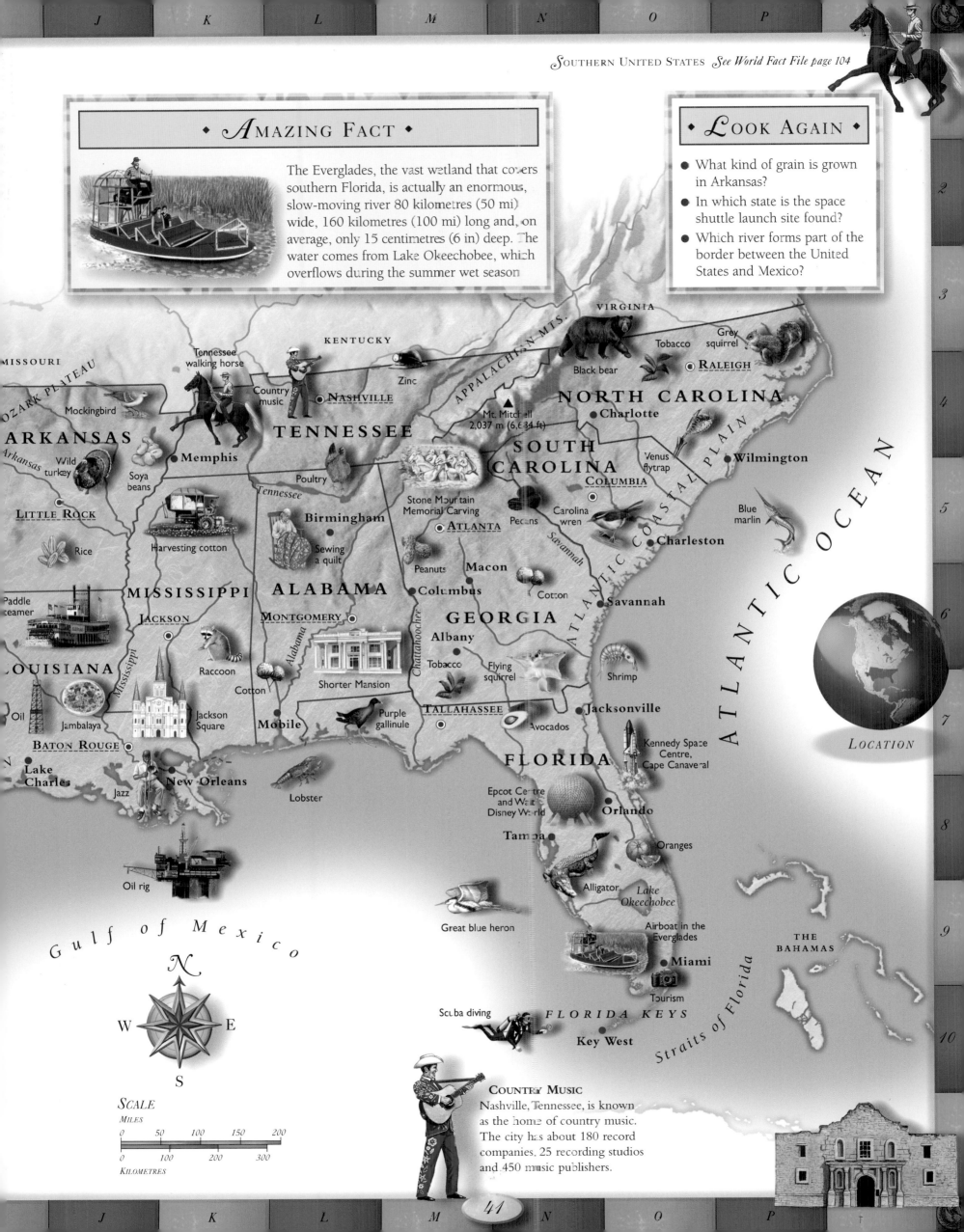

✦ Amazing Fact ✦

The Everglades, the vast wetland that covers southern Florida, is actually an enormous, slow-moving river 80 kilometres (50 mi) wide, 160 kilometres (100 mi) long and, on average, only 15 centimetres (6 in) deep. The water comes from Lake Okeechobee, which overflows during the summer wet season.

✦ Look Again ✦

- What kind of grain is grown in Arkansas?
- In which state is the space shuttle launch site found?
- Which river forms part of the border between the United States and Mexico?

VIRGINIA

KENTUCKY

MISSOURI

OZARK PLATEAU

Mockingbird

Tennessee walking horse

Country music

NASHVILLE

Zinc

APPALACHIAN MTS.

Tobacco

Grey squirrel

Black bear

RALEIGH

NORTH CAROLINA

ARKANSAS

Arkansas

Wild turkey

Memphis

Soya beans

Poultry

Tennessee

TENNESSEE

Mt. Mitchell 2,037 m (6,684 ft)

Charlotte

SOUTH CAROLINA

COLUMBIA

Venus flytrap

Wilmington

LITTLE ROCK

Rice

Harvesting cotton

Birmingham

Stone Mountain Memorial Carving

ATLANTA

Pecans

Carolina wren

Charleston

Blue marlin

ATLANTIC COASTAL PLAIN

Paddle steamer

MISSISSIPPI

ALABAMA

Sewing a quilt

Peanuts

Macon

Savannah

Cotton

Savannah

JACKSON

Raccoon

Cotton

MONTGOMERY

Shorter Mansion

GEORGIA

Columbus

Albany

Shrimp

LOUISIANA

Alabama

Chattahoochee

Tobacco

Flying squirrel

Oil

Jambalaya

Mississippi

Jackson Square

Cotton

TALLAHASSEE

Mobile

Purple gallinule

Jacksonville

Avocados

A T L A N T I C   O C E A N

BATON ROUGE

Lake Charles

Jazz

New Orleans

Lobster

FLORIDA

Kennedy Space Centre, Cape Canaveral

Epcot Centre and Walt Disney World

Orlando

LOCATION

Oil rig

Tampa

Oranges

Alligator

Lake Okeechobee

Gulf of Mexico

Great blue heron

Airboat in the Everglades

Miami

THE BAHAMAS

N
W   E
S

Tourism

FLORIDA KEYS

Scuba diving

Straits of Florida

Key West

Scale

MILES

0   50   100   150   200

0   100   200   300

KILOMETRES

Country Music

Nashville, Tennessee, is known as the home of country music. The city has about 180 record companies, 25 recording studios and 450 music publishers.

Central United States

THE CENTRAL U.S.A. consists of a vast area of lowland known as the Midwest or prairies. In the north-eastern part of this region lie the Great Lakes, the largest group of freshwater lakes in the world. Rivers and canals connect the lakes to the Atlantic Ocean and the Gulf of Mexico, forming a major transportation network. This network and the area's many natural resources, including coal and iron ore, have helped to turn the Great Lakes region into the industrial heart of the U.S.A. Factories now line the southern shores of Lake Michigan and Lake Erie, and these supply most of the country's iron, steel and cars. Unfortunately, these industries create a great deal of waste, and the Great Lakes are now badly polluted. The area south and west of the lakes was once an enormous natural grassland, roamed by millions of bison and deer, and home to Native American tribes such as the Sioux and the Comanche. Now it is one of the world's most important farming regions. Iowa lies at the centre of an area known as the Corn Belt because it produces half of the world's corn, or maize. Almost all of this maize is used to fatten the region's pigs and cattle, which provide most of the U.S.A.'s meat. Further west, on the Great Plains, is a wheat belt. Here, immense fields of wheat stretch as far as the eye can see.

ILLINOIS
POPULATION: 11,830,000 ✳ CAPITAL: SPRINGFIELD

INDIANA
POPULATION: 5,803,000 ✳ CAPITAL: INDIANAPOLIS

IOWA
POPULATION: 2,842,000 ✳ CAPITAL: DES MOINES

KANSAS
POPULATION: 2,565,000 ✳ CAPITAL: TOPEKA

MICHIGAN
POPULATION: 9,549,000 ✳ CAPITAL: LANSING

MINNESOTA
POPULATION: 4,610,000 ✳ CAPITAL: ST. PAUL

MISSOURI
POPULATION: 5,324,000 ✳ CAPITAL: JEFFERSON CITY

NEBRASKA
POPULATION: 1,637,000 ✳ CAPITAL: LINCOLN

NORTH DAKOTA
POPULATION: 641,400 ✳ CAPITAL: BISMARCK

OHIO
POPULATION: 11,150,000 ✳ CAPITAL: COLUMBUS

SOUTH DAKOTA
POPULATION: 729,000 ✳ CAPITAL: PIERRE

WISCONSIN
POPULATION: 5,123,000 ✳ CAPITAL: MADISON

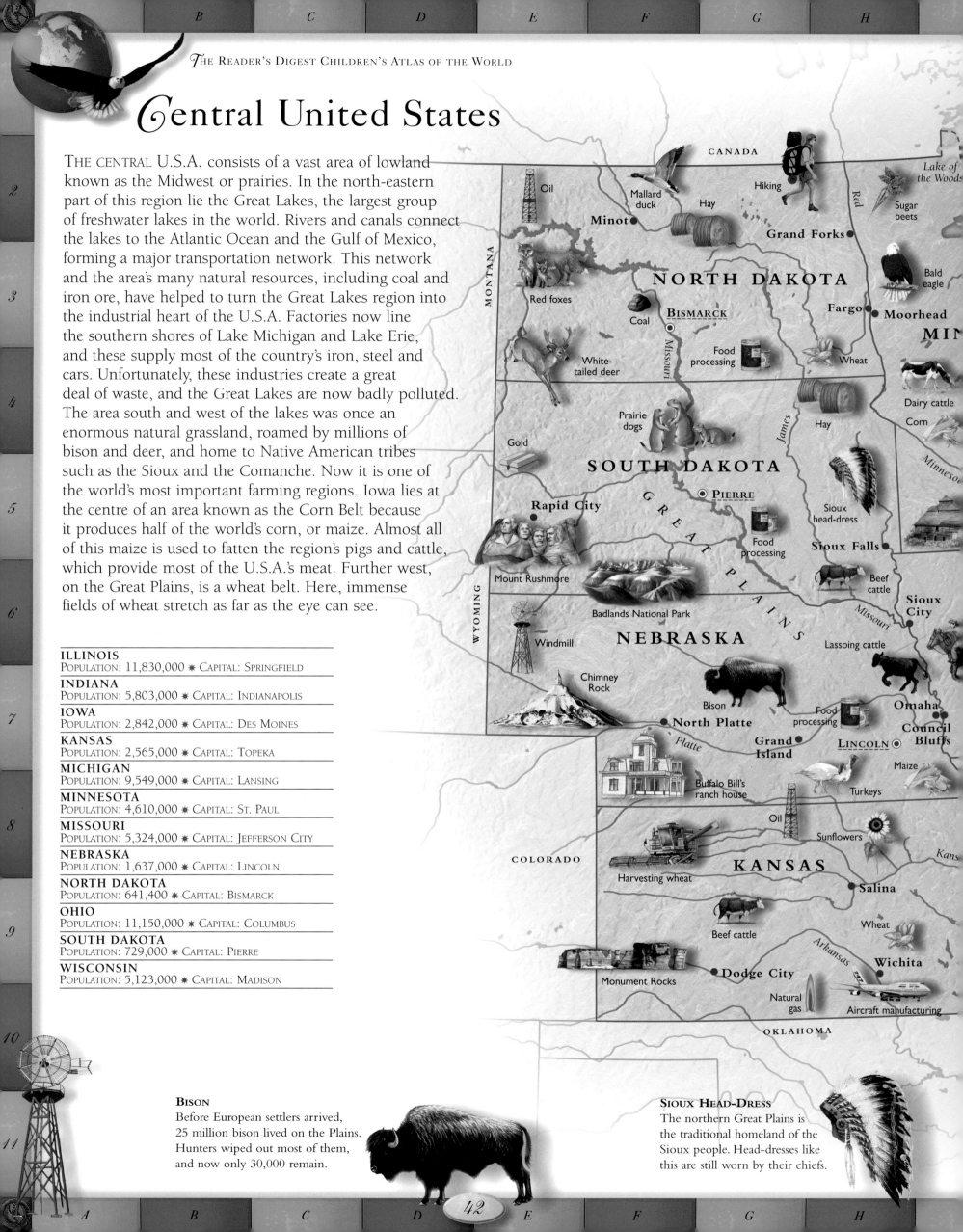

CANADA

Oil

Mallard duck

Hiking

Minot

Hay

Lake of the Woods

Sugar beets

Grand Forks

MONTANA

Red foxes

Coal

BISMARCK

Food processing

Fargo

Bald eagle

Moorhead

MIN

NORTH DAKOTA

Missouri

Wheat

Dairy cattle

Corn

White-tailed deer

Prairie dogs

James

Hay

Minneso

Gold

Rapid City

SOUTH DAKOTA

Sioux head-dress

G R E A T

PIERRE

Food processing

Sioux Falls

Mount Rushmore

P L A I N S

Beef cattle

Sioux City

Badlands National Park

Missouri

WYOMING

Windmill

NEBRASKA

Lassoing cattle

Chimney Rock

Bison

Food processing

Omaha

North Platte

Platte

Grand Island

LINCOLN

Council Bluffs

Maize

Buffalo Bill's ranch house

Turkeys

Oil

Sunflowers

COLORADO

Harvesting wheat

KANSAS

Kans

Salina

Beef cattle

Wheat

Arkansas

Wichita

Monument Rocks

Dodge City

Natural gas

Aircraft manufacturing

OKLAHOMA

BISON
Before European settlers arrived, 25 million bison lived on the Plains. Hunters wiped out most of them, and now only 30,000 remain.

SIOUX HEAD-DRESS
The northern Great Plains is the traditional homeland of the Sioux people. Head-dresses like this are still worn by their chiefs.

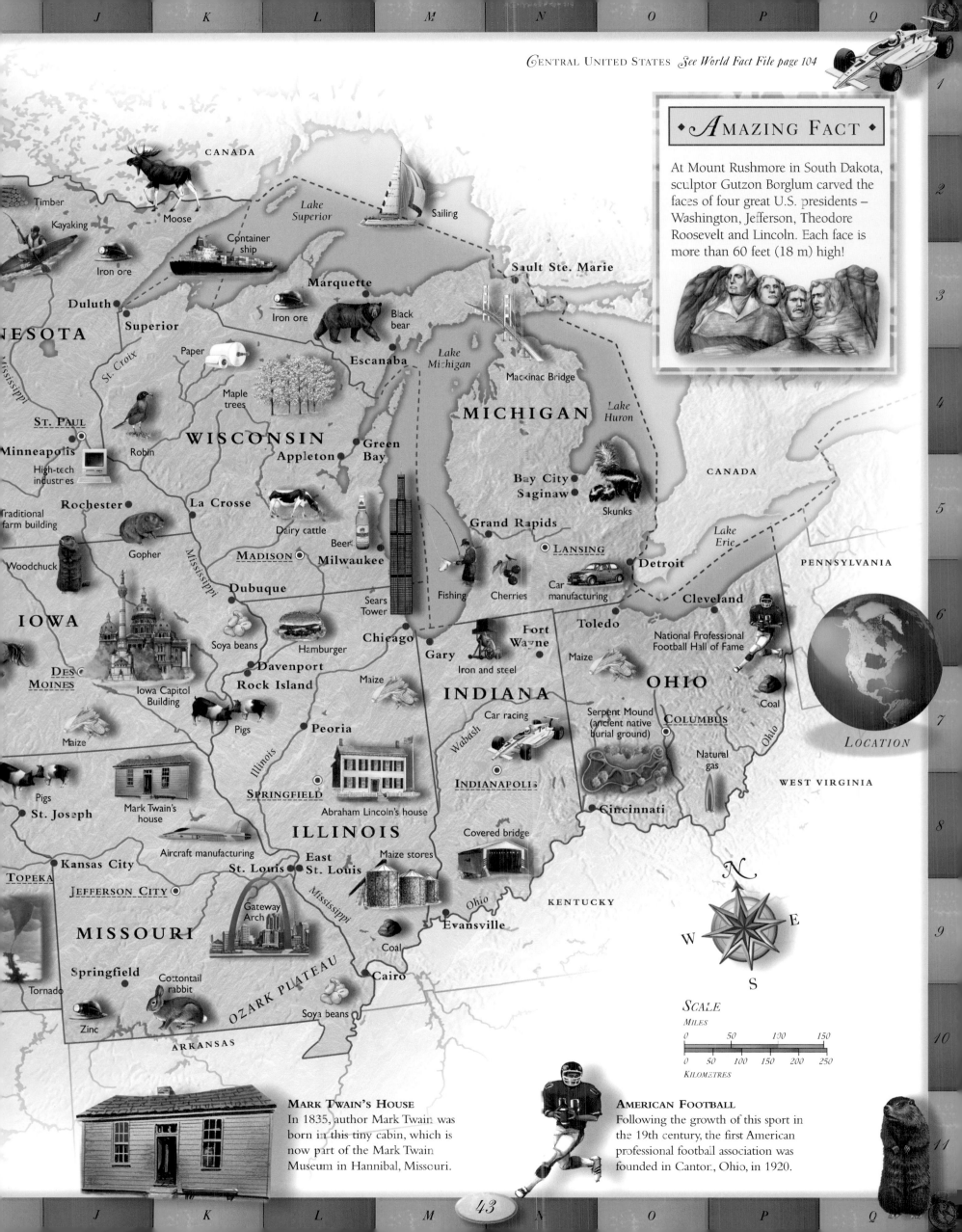

CANADA

Timber

Kayaking

Moose

Lake Superior

Iron ore

Sailing

Container ship

Duluth

Marquette

Iron ore

Black bear

Sault Ste. Marie

NESOTA

Superior

St. Croix

Paper

Escanaba

Lake Michigan

Mackinac Bridge

St. Paul

Maple trees

WISCONSIN

Minneapolis

Green Bay

MICHIGAN

Lake Huron

High-tech industries

Robin

Appleton

Bay City

CANADA

Rochester

La Crosse

Saginaw

Skunks

Traditional farm building

Dairy cattle

Grand Rapids

Gopher

MADISON

Beer

Lansing

Lake Erie

Woodchuck

Milwaukee

Car manufacturing

Detroit

PENNSYLVANIA

IOWA

Dubuque

Sears Tower

Fishing

Cherries

Cleveland

Soya beans

Chicago

Fort Wayne

Toledo

National Professional Football Hall of Fame

Coal

DES MOINES

Hamburger

Gary

Maize

Iowa Capitol Building

Davenport

Maize

Iron and steel

OHIO

Rock Island

INDIANA

Maize

Pigs

Peoria

Car racing

Serpent Mound (ancient native burial ground)

COLUMBUS

Natural gas

Pigs

St. Joseph

Illinois

SPRINGFIELD

Wabash

WEST VIRGINIA

Aircraft manufacturing

Abraham Lincoln's house

INDIANAPOLIS

Cincinnati

Kansas City

ILLINOIS

Covered bridge

TOPEKA

St. Louis

East St. Louis

Maize stores

JEFFERSON CITY

Gateway Arch

Mississippi

Ohio

KENTUCKY

MISSOURI

Evansville

Springfield

Cottontail rabbit

Coal

Cairo

Tornado

Zinc

OZARK PLATEAU

Soya beans

ARKANSAS

• AMAZING FACT •

At Mount Rushmore in South Dakota, sculptor Gutzon Borglum carved the faces of four great U.S. presidents – Washington, Jefferson, Theodore Roosevelt and Lincoln. Each face is more than 60 feet (18 m) high!

N

W E

S

SCALE

MILES

0   50   100   150

0   50   100 150 200 250

KILOMETRES

MARK TWAIN'S HOUSE
In 1835, author Mark Twain was born in this tiny cabin, which is now part of the Mark Twain Museum in Hannibal, Missouri.

AMERICAN FOOTBALL
Following the growth of this sport in the 19th century, the first American professional football association was founded in Canton, Ohio, in 1920.

Western United States

THE COLOSSAL ROCKY MOUNTAINS separate the western U.S.A. from the plains of the Midwest. Among the valleys and peaks of this spectacular range, mountain goats bound up steep rock faces and moose feed beside fast-flowing streams. There is little agriculture here, but herds of cattle graze the mountain meadows. West of the Rockies lies a series of dry plateaux, valleys and ranges. The Colorado Plateau has some of the continent's most spectacular scenery, including the world's largest gorge, the Grand Canyon. The states of Washington, Oregon and Idaho are known as the Pacific Northwest. The wet, densely forested western part of this area provides 40 per cent of the U.S.A.'s timber. The largest state in the region, California, is home to more people than any other American state. Most of the population lives in or near the coastal cities of Los Angeles and San Francisco. Inland, between the mountains of the Coast Ranges and the Sierra Nevada, farms form a patchwork of fields across the fertile, irrigated Central Valley. The most westerly state, Hawaii, lies 4,000 kilometres (2,500 mi) off the coast, in the middle of the Pacific Ocean. Hawaii consists of 132 islands, which were formed by undersea volcanoes. Several Hawaiian volcanoes still erupt, including Mauna Loa, the largest active volcano in the world.

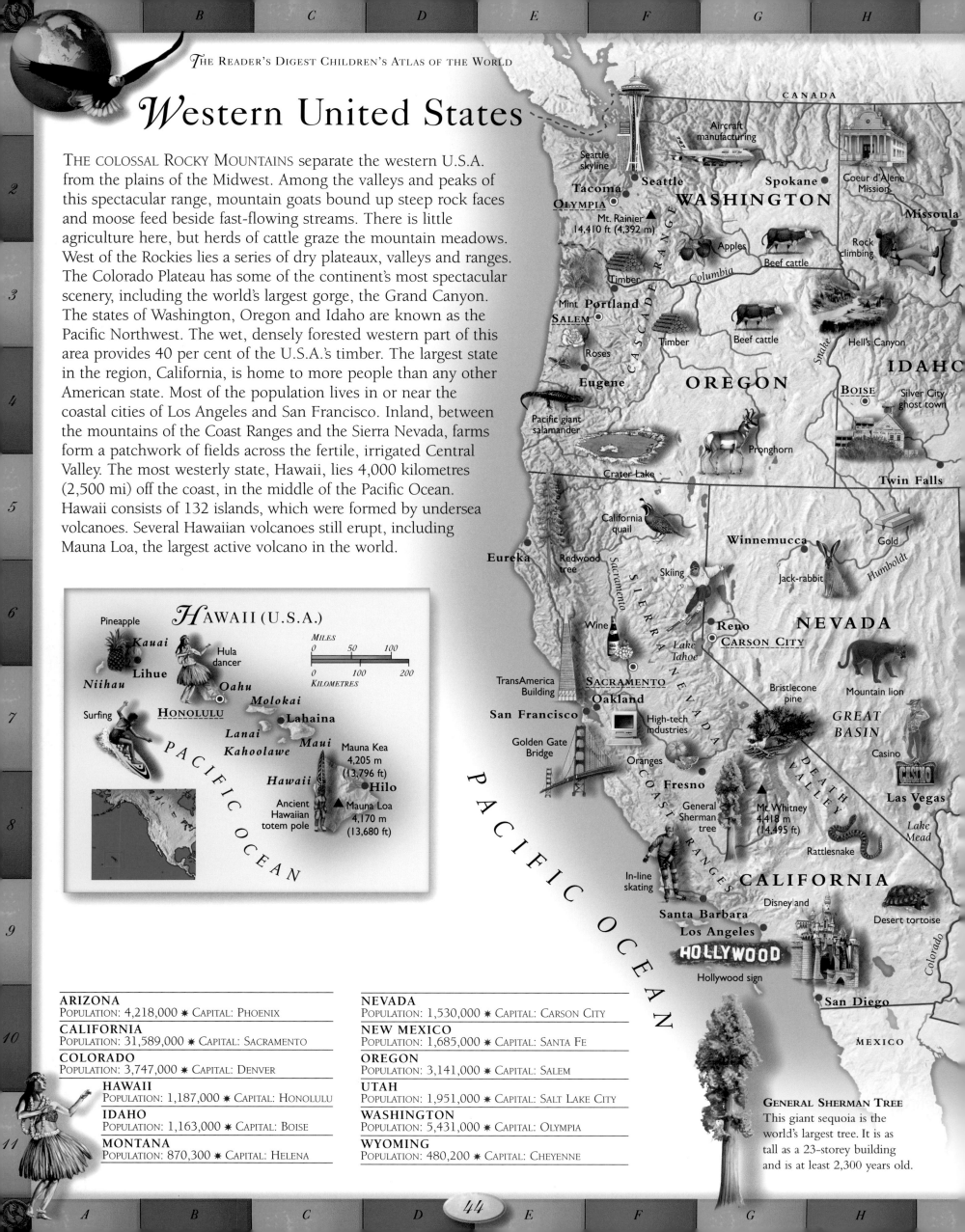

Hawaii (U.S.A.)

Pineapple
Kauai
Lihue
Niihau
Hula dancer
Oahu
HONOLULU
Molokai
Lahaina
Lanai
Kahoolawe
Maui
Surfing
Hawaii
Ancient Hawaiian totem pole
Mauna Kea 4,205 m (13,796 ft)
Mauna Loa 4,170 m (13,680 ft)
Hilo

MILES
0   50   100

KILOMETRES
0   100   200

PACIFIC OCEAN

ARIZONA
POPULATION: 4,218,000 ✳ CAPITAL: PHOENIX

CALIFORNIA
POPULATION: 31,589,000 ✳ CAPITAL: SACRAMENTO

COLORADO
POPULATION: 3,747,000 ✳ CAPITAL: DENVER

HAWAII
POPULATION: 1,187,000 ✳ CAPITAL: HONOLULU

IDAHO
POPULATION: 1,163,000 ✳ CAPITAL: BOISE

MONTANA
POPULATION: 870,300 ✳ CAPITAL: HELENA

NEVADA
POPULATION: 1,530,000 ✳ CAPITAL: CARSON CITY

NEW MEXICO
POPULATION: 1,685,000 ✳ CAPITAL: SANTA FE

OREGON
POPULATION: 3,141,000 ✳ CAPITAL: SALEM

UTAH
POPULATION: 1,951,000 ✳ CAPITAL: SALT LAKE CITY

WASHINGTON
POPULATION: 5,431,000 ✳ CAPITAL: OLYMPIA

WYOMING
POPULATION: 480,200 ✳ CAPITAL: CHEYENNE

GENERAL SHERMAN TREE
This giant sequoia is the world's largest tree. It is as tall as a 23-storey building and is at least 2,300 years old.

Map Labels

Whitewater rafting

Wheat

Oil

Natural gas

NORTH DAKOTA

Missouri

Great Falls

MONTANA

Yellowstone

HELENA

Billings

Bighorn sheep

Grizzly bear

SOUTH DAKOTA

Bighorn Canyon

Coal

Devil's Tower

Old Faithful geyser

WYOMING

Uranium

Beef cattle

Casper

Idaho Falls

Potatoes

American kestrel

Coyote

CHEYENNE

NEBRASKA

Great Salt Lake

Rock Springs

ROCKY MOUNTAINS

Stegosaur skeleton

KANSAS

Ogden

SALT LAKE CITY

Provo

Green

Skiing

Boulder

DENVER

Mormon Temple

UTAH

Arches National Park

COLORADO

Grand Junction

Colorado Springs

Pueblo

Arkansas

COLORADO PLATEAU

Cedar City

Monument Valley

Lake Powell

Mountain goat

Cumbres and Toltec Scenic Railway

Hopi buffalo dancer

Natural gas

Taos Pueblo (native village)

Appaloosa horses

Grand Canyon

Flagstaff

Navajo woman weaving

Uranium

SANTA FE

Albuquerque

Pueblo pottery

TEXAS

Saguaro cactus

ARIZONA

Zuni jewelry

NEW MEXICO

Roswell

PHOENIX

Gila

High-tech industries

Copper

Rio Grande

National Astronomy Observatory

Oil

Tucson

San Xavier de Bac Mission

Roadrunner

TEXAS

• PROJECT: *Sand-Art Jars* •

The Navajo and Pueblo people of the south-western U.S.A. make ceremonial paintings with coloured sand. After the ceremony, the paintings are erased. You can make your own coloured-sand painting in a jar.

❶ First sift the sand to make sure it is clean and fine. Divide the sand into small piles, adding a few drops of food colouring to each to make different-coloured sands. Stir the sand every few hours to dry it.

❷ When the sand is dry, slowly pour some into a clean glass jar. Then pour a layer of another colour. Keep pouring layers of different colours until the jar is full.

❸ Now make patterns by pushing a length of wire, or the end of a thin paintbrush, down the inside of the glass, between the sand and the jar. Be careful not to stir the sand! As the wire goes up and down, different colours will slide into the spaces and create designs.

❹ Finally, top off the jar with more of the coloured sand and put on the lid.

• AMAZING FACT •

Carved out by the Colorado river, the Grand Canyon is about 350 kilometres (220 mi) long and 1.6 kilometres (1 mi) deep. The rocks at its bottom are more than two billion years old!

LOCATION

N
W E
S

SCALE

MILES

0   50   100   150   200

0   100   200   300

KILOMETRES

ROADRUNNER

Roadrunners seldom fly, preferring to race along on their powerful legs. They can reach speeds of 32 kilometres per hour (20 mph).

HOPI BUFFALO DANCER

By dressing as buffalo (bison), Hopi dancers appeal to the sacred spirits of these animals to bring them health and good fortune.

Mexico, Central America and the Caribbean

MEXICO AND CENTRAL AMERICA form a land bridge between the United States and South America. At its narrowest point, this strip of land is only 80 kilometres (50 mi) wide and is split by the Panama Canal, an artificial waterway that links the Atlantic and Pacific Oceans. Mexico is more than twice the size of the seven Central American countries combined. It is dominated by a large dry plateau, and only 18 per cent of the land can be farmed. The narrow plains on the east coast are warm and humid, and contain large oil reserves. Three-quarters of Mexicans live in cities and towns, and Mexico City is one of the largest and fastest-growing cities in the world. Most of Central America is mountainous, and much of the land is covered in rainforests, where colourful parrots shriek from the tree-tops and chattering monkeys swing among branches. Although only a small proportion of Central America can be farmed, about half of the people live in rural areas and many grow their own food on small plots of land. To the east lie the Caribbean Islands, most of which are covered by tropical forests and surrounded by sandy beaches. Spain ruled much of Mexico, Central America and the Caribbean for centuries, and today most of the people speak Spanish. Their ancestors may be settlers from Europe, Native American peoples or Africans who were first brought to the region as slaves.

ANTIGUA AND BARBUDA
POPULATION: 65,200 ✱ CAPITAL: ST. JOHN'S

THE BAHAMAS
POPULATION: 256,600 ✱ CAPITAL: NASSAU

BARBADOS
POPULATION: 256,400 ✱ CAPITAL: BRIDGETOWN

BELIZE
POPULATION: 214,100 ✱ CAPITAL: BELMOPAN

COSTA RICA
POPULATION: 3,419,000 ✱ CAPITAL: SAN JOSÉ

CUBA
POPULATION: 10,938,000 ✱ CAPITAL: HAVANA

DOMINICA
POPULATION: 82,600 ✱ CAPITAL: ROSEAU

DOMINICAN REPUBLIC
POPULATION: 7,511,000 ✱ CAPITAL: SANTO DOMINGO

EL SALVADOR
POPULATION: 5,870,000 ✱ CAPITAL: SAN SALVADOR

GRENADA
POPULATION: 94,500 ✱ CAPITAL: ST. GEORGE'S

GUATEMALA
POPULATION: 10,999,000 ✱ CAPITAL: GUATEMALA

HAITI
POPULATION: 6,540,000 ✱ CAPITAL: PORT-AU-PRINCE

HONDURAS
POPULATION: 5,460,000 ✱ CAPITAL: TEGUCIGALPA

JAMAICA
POPULATION: 2,574,000 ✱ CAPITAL: KINGSTON

MEXICO
POPULATION: 93,986,000 ✱ CAPITAL: MEXICO CITY

NICARAGUA
POPULATION: 4,206,000 ✱ CAPITAL: MANAGUA

PANAMA
POPULATION: 2,681,000 ✱ CAPITAL: PANAMA

ST. KITTS–NEVIS
POPULATION: 41,000 ✱ CAPITAL: BASSETERRE

ST. LUCIA
POPULATION: 156,100 ✱ CAPITAL: CASTRIES

ST. VINCENT AND THE GRENADINES
POPULATION: 117,300 ✱ CAPITAL: KINGSTOWN

TRINIDAD AND TOBAGO
POPULATION: 1,271,000 ✱ CAPITAL: PORT-OF-SPAIN

SINGING GRASSHOPPER MOUSE
This mouse is named for its habit of squeaking or 'singing' to warn off rivals. Grasshoppers are its favourite food.

Tijuana, Mexicali, Gila monster, Tourism, Ciudad Juárez, Mexican cowboy, Saguaro cactus, Beef cattle, Singing grasshopper mouse, UNITED STATES OF AMERICA, Great white shark, Hermosillo, Chihuahua, Vampire bat, Silver, Natural gas, Rio Grande, Leatherback turtle, Gulf of Mexico, Elephant seals, Monarch butterfly, Monterrey, Cotton, Matamoros, Snapper, Lobster, Culiacán, Torreón, Ancient Toltec stone statue, Mariachi musicians, La Paz, Gold, Iron ore, Tampico, El Castillo, Chichen Itza, Maya city ruins, MEXICO, Folk dancer, Maize, Metropolitan Cathedral, Oil, Bay of Campeche, Oil, YUCATÁN PENINSULA, Common dolphins, Guadalajara, MEXICO CITY, Veracruz, Jaguar, Aztec snake carving, Soccer, Orizaba 5,700 m (18,700 ft), Great Plaza, Tikal, Belize, Tourism, Olmec stone carving, Scarlet macaw, BELMOPAN, Acapulco, Thatched corncrib, Folk costume, GUATEMALA, Eagle ray, GUATEMALA, SAN SALVADOR, EL SALVADOR, Gulf of California, Baja California, Sierra Madre Occidental, PACIFIC OCEAN

• Amazing Fact •

The saguaro cactus is found only in the deserts of north-western Mexico and the south-western United States. It grows incredibly slowly, taking 25 years to reach a height of 30 centimetres (12 in). But it can live for 200 years and grow as high as a four-storey house. Like other cacti, the saguaro survives on water stored in its stem. A fully grown saguaro may contain enough water to fill 100 bathtubs!

• Project: *Make a Mexican Piñata* •

A piñata is a pot made from papier mâché often shaped like a star or animal and filled with toys and sweets. It is a popular part of many celebrations and festivals in Mexico and Central America. Children hang the piñata from the ceiling or a tree branch and take turns trying to break it open. You can make a Mexican piñata for your next party.

❶ Cover a large balloon with strips of newspaper dipped in flour-and-water paste or white glue. Wait for this papier mâché to dry and then repeat with at least two more layers of newspaper.

❷ When the papier mâché is completely dry, cut a small hole in the top and fill the piñata with all sorts of goodies. Re-cover the hole with more papier mâché.

❸ Make star points out of cardboard as shown. Tape them to the ball using the tabs. Decorate the star with paint and coloured tissue paper.

Step 3A   Step 3B

❹ Make two small holes next to each other at the top of the piñata. Thread curved wire through one hole and out the other. Hang up the piñata and ask guests to take turns hitting it with a stick to open it.

ATLANTIC OCEAN

Queen angelfish

Tourism

THE BAHAMAS

★ NASSAU

TURKS AND CAICOS ISLANDS (U.K.)

Scuba diving

ANGUILLA (U.K.)

Traditional dancers

VIRGIN ISLANDS (U.S.A./U.K.)

ANTIGUA AND BARBUDA

HAVANA

Palm tree

San Juan

ST. KITTS–NEVIS

GUADELOUPE (FRANCE)

E Cuban crocodile

Cigars

CUBA

Bananas

SANTO DOMINGO

PUERTO RICO (U.S.A.)

MONTSERRAT (U.K.)

Tourism

DOMINICA

PORT-AU-PRINCE

DOMINICAN REPUBLIC

MARTINIQUE (FRANCE)

Cricket

HAITI

Fort-de-France

ST. LUCIA

BARBADOS

CAYMAN ISLANDS (U.K.)

★ KINGSTON

ST. VINCENT AND THE GRENADINES

Sugar cane

JAMAICA

Sailing

Fishing boat

GRENADA

Steel band

LOCATION

Caribbean Sea

NETHERLANDS ANTILLES (NETHERLANDS)

ARUBA (NETHERLANDS)

PORT-OF-SPAIN

TRINIDAD AND TOBAGO

HONDURAS

Bananas

Fishing boat

GUCIGALPA

Coffee

VENEZUELA

COLOMBIA

NICARAGUA

otton

Beef cattle

Cuna Indian

N

ANAGUA

Panama Canal

Bananas

SAN JOSÉ

PANAMA

W   E

Coffee

PANAMA

COSTA RICA

Sugar cane

Howler monkey

GREAT PLAZA, TIKAL
Tikal is an ancient city in Guatemala. It was built by the Maya between AD 75 and 900, and then mysteriously abandoned. It is now completely surrounded by jungle.

S

SCALE

MILES

0   100   200   300

0   100   200   300   400   500

KILOMETRES

South America

FROM ITS TROPICAL NORTHERN SHORE, South America stretches 7,240 kilometres (4,500 mi) southwards to the chilly, storm-battered peninsula of Cape Horn, just 1,000 kilometres (600 mi) from Antarctica. The Andes run the entire length of the continent's west coast, forming the longest mountain chain in the world. In the north, the Amazon River (the world's second-longest river) snakes eastwards from the Andes to the Atlantic Ocean, through vast rainforests that once covered more than one-third of the continent. To the south, the forests give way to the grasslands of the Gran Chaco and the Pampas. The southern tip of South America is a dry, windswept plateau known as Patagonia. South America's inhabitants include people of European, native American and African origin. Most people speak Spanish, but Portuguese is the official language in Brazil.

Continent Facts

Regional land area: 17,818,505 sq. km (6,877,943 sq. mi)
Regional population: 319,153,000
Independent countries: Argentina, Bolivia, Brazil, Chile, Colombia, Ecuador, Guyana, Paraguay, Peru, Suriname, Uruguay, Venezuela

World Records

WORLD'S LONGEST MOUNTAIN CHAIN
ANDES, WESTERN SOUTH AMERICA 7,600 KM (4,700 MI)

WORLD'S DRIEST PLACE
ATACAMA DESERT, CHILE, AVERAGE ANNUAL RAINFALL LESS THAN 0.1 MM (1/250 IN)

WORLD'S HIGHEST WATERFALL
ANGEL FALLS, VENEZUELA, 979 M (3,212 FT)

WORLD'S HIGHEST CAPITAL CITY
LA PAZ, BOLIVIA, 3,631 M (11,913 FT)

WORLD'S HIGHEST NAVIGABLE LAKE
LAKE TITICACA, PERU-BOLIVIA, 3,810 M (12,500 FT)

WORLD'S LARGEST RIVER BY VOLUME
AMAZON, PERU-BRAZIL, DISCHARGES 200,000 CUBIC M (7,100,000 CUBIC FT) PER SECOND INTO ATLANTIC OCEAN

WORLD'S LARGEST RIVER BASIN
AMAZON BASIN, NORTHERN SOUTH AMERICA, 7,045,000 SQ. KM (2,720,000 SQ. MI)

WORLD'S LARGEST LAGOON
LAGOA DOS PATOS, BRAZIL, 9,850 SQ. KM (3,803 SQ. MI)

Major Mountains and Rivers

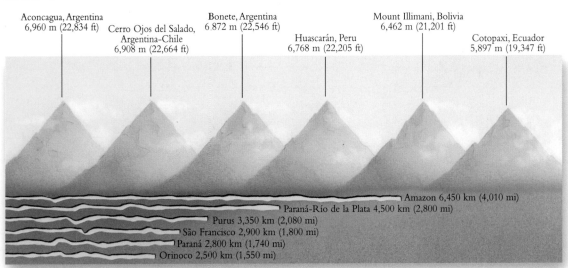

Aconcagua, Argentina 6,960 m (22,834 ft)
Cerro Ojos del Salado, Argentina-Chile 6,908 m (22,664 ft)
Bonete, Argentina 6,872 m (22,546 ft)
Huascarán, Peru 6,768 m (22,205 ft)
Mount Illimani, Bolivia 6,462 m (21,201 ft)
Cotopaxi, Ecuador 5,897 m (19,347 ft)

Amazon 6,450 km (4,010 mi)
Paraná-Río de la Plata 4,500 km (2,800 mi)
Purus 3,350 km (2,080 mi)
São Francisco 2,900 km (1,800 mi)
Paraná 2,800 km (1,740 mi)
Orinoco 2,500 km (1,550 mi)

Continent Records

HIGHEST MOUNTAIN
ACONCAGUA, ARGENTINA, 6,960 M (22,834 FT)

LOWEST POINT
VALDÉS PENINSULA, ARGENTINA, 40 M (131 FT) BELOW SEA LEVEL

LARGEST LAKE
LAKE TITICACA, PERU-BOLIVIA, 8,288 SQ. KM (3,200 SQ. MI)

LONGEST RIVER
AMAZON RIVER, PERU-BRAZIL, 6,450 KM (4,010 MI)

LARGEST COUNTRY BY AREA
BRAZIL, 8,506,663 SQ. KM (3,284,426 SQ. MI)

LARGEST COUNTRY BY POPULATION
BRAZIL, POPULATION 160,737,000

LARGEST CITY BY POPULATION
SÃO PAULO, BRAZIL, POPULATION 16,400,000

Political Map

VENEZUELA
GUYANA
SURINAME
FRENCH GUIANA (FRANCE)
COLOMBIA
GALÁPAGOS ISLANDS (ECUADOR)
ECUADOR
BRAZIL
PERU
BOLIVIA
MARTIN VAZ ISLANDS (BRAZIL)
PARAGUAY
EASTER ISLAND (CHILE)
CHILE
JUAN FERNANDEZ ISLANDS (CHILE)
URUGUAY
ARGENTINA
FALKLAND ISLANDS (U.K.)
SOUTH GEORGIA (U.K.)

◆ Amazing Fact ◆

The Atacama Desert in northern Chile is the driest place in the world. Rain showers occur only once or twice a century, and in some parts of the desert rain has never been recorded.

PHYSICAL MAP

NORTH AMERICA

AFRICA

Tropic of Cancer

Caribbean Sea

Lake Maracaibo

Orinoco

GUIANA HIGHLANDS

Amazon Delta

Gulf of Panama

LLANOS

Rio Negro

Rio Branco

GALÁPAGOS ISLANDS

Cotopaxi ▲

Amazon

Gulf of Guayaquil

AMAZON BASIN

Equator

Marañón

SELVAS

Tapajos

Xingu

Huascaran ▲

Purus

Madeira

ATLANTIC OCEAN

Tocantins

São Francisco

MATO GROSSO PLATEAU

BRAZILIAN HIGHLANDS

PACIFIC OCEAN

Lake Titicaca

▲ Mt. Illimani

Lake Poopó

GRAN CHACO

Parana

SERRA DO MAR

Tropic of Capricorn

ATACAMA DESERT

Paraguay

Cerro Ojos del Salado ▲

Uruguay

▲ Bonete

Lagoa dos Patos

Easter Island

▲ Aconcagua

A N D E S

PAMPAS

Rio de la Plata

Colorado

Blanca Bay

San Matias Gulf

PATAGONIA

VALDÉS PENINSULA

San Jorge Gulf

FALKLAND ISLANDS

Tierra del Fuego

South Georgia

CAPE HORN

Drake Passage

Antarctic Circle

ANTARCTICA

Northern South America

MOST OF NORTHERN SOUTH AMERICA is drained by the world's second longest river, the Amazon, and its more than 200 tributaries. These waterways flow through lush tropical rainforests that are home to a tenth of all the plants and animals on Earth. Sadly, the rainforests are rapidly disappearing as a growing population clears the land for farming. Every minute, an area of forest the size of five football pitches is cut down. More than a quarter of the world's rainforests lie within Brazil, the largest country in South America. Brazil has many resources, including iron ore, oil and gold. It is the continent's most industrialized country and the world's leading producer of coffee, bananas and sugar cane. North-west of Brazil lies Venezuela, a sparsely populated country that is South America's top oil producer. From Venezuela, the Andes curve southwards through Colombia, Ecuador and Peru. At the northern end of this mountain range, the climate is wet, and large coffee and banana plantations cover the hillsides. Further south, little rain falls and crops can be grown only by using water from mountain streams. On the upper slopes of the Peruvian Andes, farmers grow potatoes and wheat and raise animals, including llamas and alpacas. One thousand kilometres (600 mi) off the coast of Ecuador lie the Galápagos Islands. These volcanic islands are famous for their unusual wildlife, which includes marine iguanas and giant tortoises.

BRAZIL
POPULATION: 160,737,000 ✳ CAPITAL: BRASÍLIA

COLOMBIA
POPULATION: 36,200,000 ✳ CAPITAL: BOGOTÁ

ECUADOR
POPULATION: 10,891,000 ✳ CAPITAL: QUITO

GUYANA
POPULATION: 723,800 ✳ CAPITAL: GEORGETOWN

PERU
POPULATION: 24,087,000 ✳ CAPITAL: LIMA

SURINAME
POPULATION: 429,500 ✳ CAPITAL: PARAMARIBO

VENEZUELA
POPULATION: 21,005,000 ✳ CAPITAL: CARACAS

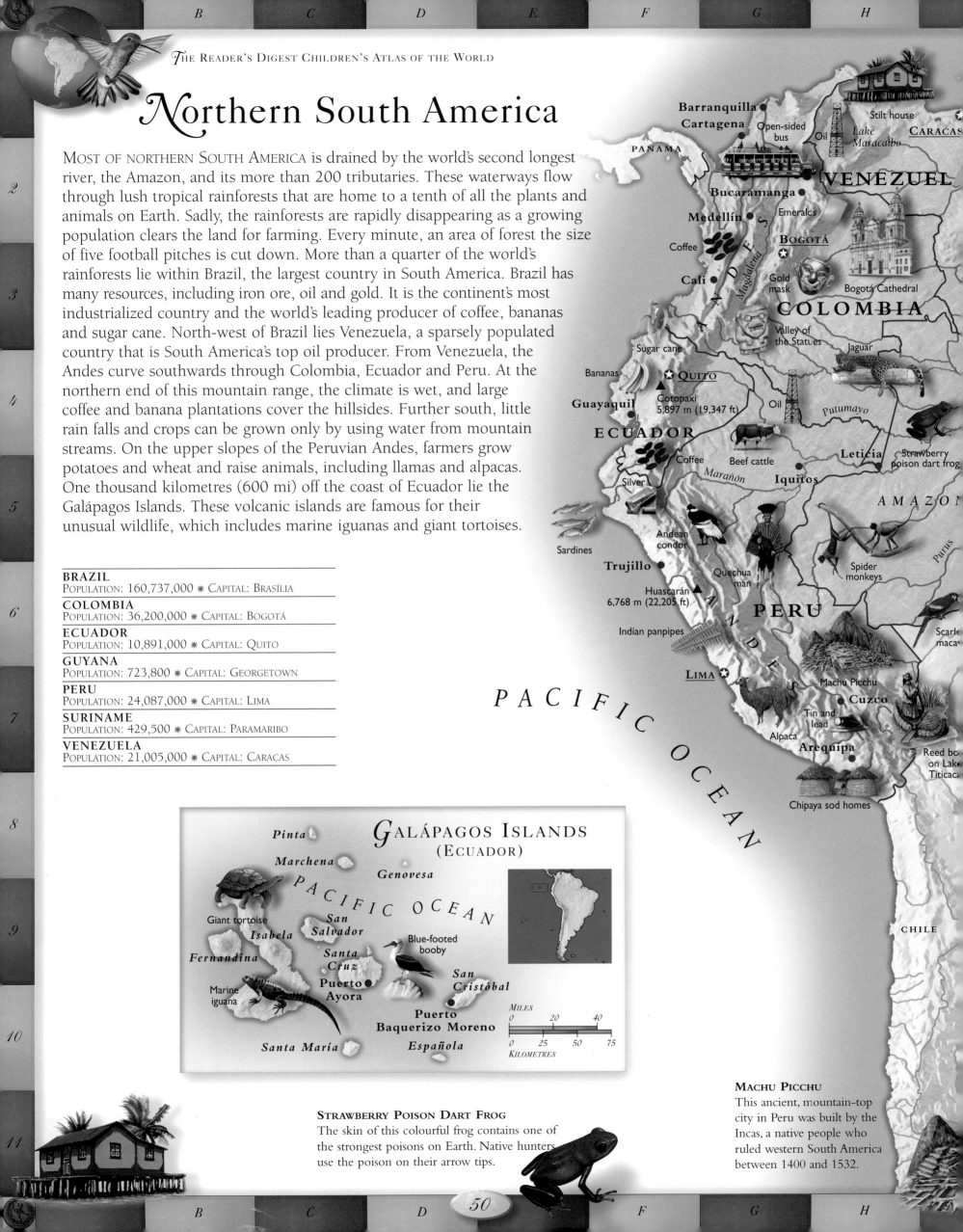

GALÁPAGOS ISLANDS
(ECUADOR)

Pinta
Marchena
Genovesa
PACIFIC OCEAN
Giant tortoise
Isabela
San Salvador
Blue-footed booby
Fernandina
Santa Cruz
Marine iguana
Puerto Ayora
San Cristóbal
Puerto Baquerizo Moreno
Santa María
Española

MILES
0   20   40

0   25   50   75
KILOMETRES

STRAWBERRY POISON DART FROG
The skin of this colourful frog contains one of the strongest poisons on Earth. Native hunters use the poison on their arrow tips.

MACHU PICCHU
This ancient, mountain-top city in Peru was built by the Incas, a native people who ruled western South America between 1400 and 1532.

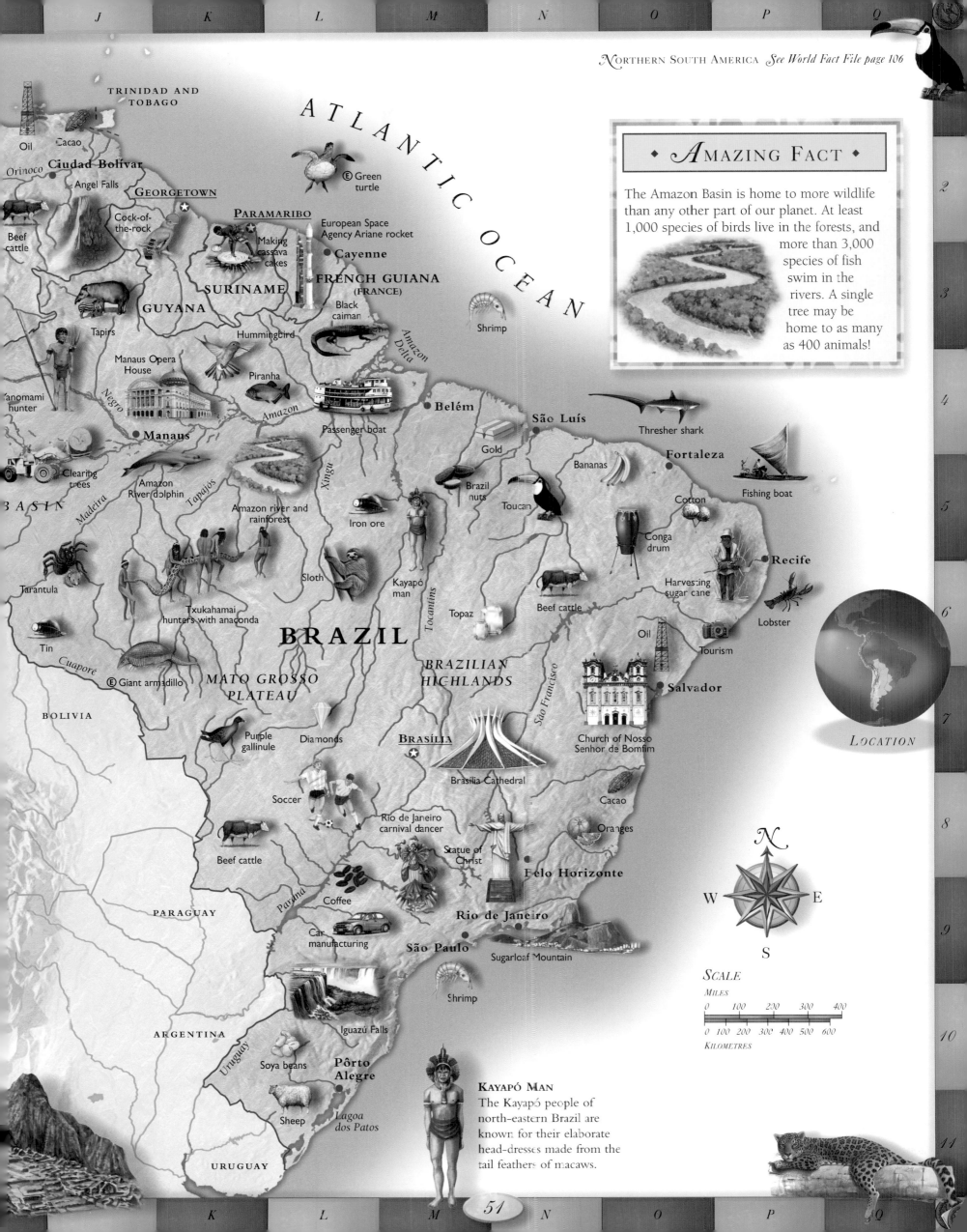

2

3

4

5

6

7

8

9

10

11

TRINIDAD AND TOBAGO

Oil

Cacao

Orinoco

Ciudad Bolívar

Angel Falls

GEORGETOWN

Beef cattle

Cock-of-the-rock

PARAMARIBO

Making cassava cakes

Cayenne

SURINAME

GUYANA

European Space Agency Ariane rocket

FRENCH GUIANA (FRANCE)

Tapirs

Hummingbird

Black caiman

Amazon Delta

Shrimp

Yanomami hunter

Manaus Opera House

Piranha

Negro

Amazon

Passenger boat

Belém

São Luís

Thresher shark

Manaus

Gold

Bananas

Fortaleza

Clearing trees

Amazon River dolphin

Madeira

Tapajós

Amazon river and rainforest

Xingu

Iron ore

Brazil nuts

Toucan

Cotton

Fishing boat

BASIN

Tarantula

Txukahamai hunters with anaconda

Sloth

Kayapó man

Conga drum

Harvesting sugar cane

Recife

Tin

Cuaporé

Ⓔ Giant armadillo

BRAZIL

Tocantins

Topaz

Beef cattle

Lobster

MATO GROSSO PLATEAU

BRAZILIAN HIGHLANDS

Oil

Tourism

BOLIVIA

Purple gallinule

Diamonds

São Francisco

Church of Nosso Senhor de Bomfim

Salvador

BRASÍLIA

Brasília Cathedral

Cacao

Soccer

Rio de Janeiro carnival dancer

Oranges

Beef cattle

Statue of Christ

Belo Horizonte

PARAGUAY

Paraná

Coffee

Car manufacturing

Rio de Janeiro

São Paulo

Sugarloaf Mountain

Uruguay

Iguazú Falls

Shrimp

ARGENTINA

Soya beans

Pôrto Alegre

Sheep

Lagoa dos Patos

URUGUAY

ATLANTIC OCEAN

Ⓔ Green turtle

◆ AMAZING FACT ◆

The Amazon Basin is home to more wildlife than any other part of our planet. At least 1,000 species of birds live in the forests, and more than 3,000 species of fish swim in the rivers. A single tree may be home to as many as 400 animals!

LOCATION

N

W **E**

S

SCALE

MILES

0   100   200   300   400

0 100 200 300 400 500 600

KILOMETRES

KAYAPÓ MAN
The Kayapó people of north-eastern Brazil are known for their elaborate head-dresses made from the tail feathers of macaws.

Southern South America

SOUTHERN SOUTH AMERICA IS SHAPED like a long, narrow triangle that tapers to a point on the southern island of Tierra del Fuego. The Andes run down the western side of the region, separating the country of Chile from its neighbours. Twenty times as long as it is wide, Chile has a variety of climates and landscapes. In the cold, wet, sparsely populated south, mountains rise steeply from the ocean, and glaciers snake through valleys. Central Chile has milder weather and many farms, vineyards and orchards. The north is very arid and includes the driest place in the world, the Atacama Desert. East of the Atacama, the Andes spread into Bolivia, one of the poorest countries in South America. From eastern Bolivia, wide plains stretch southwards through Paraguay, Uruguay and northern Argentina. Enormous herds of cattle and sheep roam the eastern and southern parts of these plains, tended by gauchos, South America's ranch hands. Argentina has more than 50 million cattle, and beef production is one of its most important industries. The country's most fertile grasslands, the Pampas, surround the capital, Buenos Aires. This city is home to one-third of the Argentinian population. In the south of the continent is a cold, barren plateau known as Patagonia. Few people live here, but the area is rich in minerals. The seas around Tierra del Fuego in the far south are often stormy. Hundreds of ships have been wrecked around Cape Horn and the Strait of Magellan.

◆ PROJECT: *Easter Island Moai* ◆

Easter Island is covered with huge statues called moai. Some are more than 9 metres (30 ft) high. The early inhabitants of Easter Island may have built the statues to honour their ancestors. You can make an Easter Island statue, too.

❶ Mix equal parts of plaster and vermiculite (both available at model shops). Stir as you add enough water to make a thick plaster. Pour the mixture into an old shoe box.

❷ When the mixture hardens, tear away the cardboard. Carve the stone using tools such as a plastic knife or an ice lolly stick.

❸ Alternatively, make your carving out of a block of modelling clay, plaster of Paris or any other modelling material.

LLAMA
A common domestic animal in South America, the llama is a relative of the camel. It is kept for its wool and is also used for carrying goods through mountainous terrain.

Map labels
BRAZIL · PERU · BOLIVIA · PARAGUAY · GRAN CHACO · ANDES · ATACAMA DESERT

Greater rhea · Beef cattle · Cotton · Chacoan peccary · Maize · Sugar cane · Polo · Maned wolf · Ranch house · Maté (tea) · Streetcar (tram) · Hydroelectricity · Presidential palace · Village musicians · Silver · Andean condor · Llamas · Giant bromelia · Tin · Zinc · Spectacled bear · Giant anteater · Gold · Timber · Motmot · Bolivian folk costume · Oil · Natural gas · Copper · Iron

Guaporé · Mamoré · Lake Titicaca · Lake Poopó · Pilcomayo · Paraná · Río Salado

Trinidad · Cochabamba · Santa Cruz · ☆ SUCRE · ★ LA PAZ · Mt. Illimani 6,462 m (21,201 ft) · Arica · Iquique · Antofagasta · Copiapó · San Miguel de Tucumán · Corrientes · ⊛ ASUNCIÓN · Cerro Ojos del Salado 6,908 m (22,664 ft) · Bonete 6,872 m (22,546 ft)

BOLIVIA

ARGENTINA
POPULATION: 34,293,000 ✳ CAPITAL: BUENOS AIRES
BOLIVIA
POPULATION: 7,896,000 ✳ CAPITALS: LA PAZ, SUCRE
CHILE
POPULATION: 14,161,000 ✳ CAPITAL: SANTIAGO
PARAGUAY
POPULATION: 5,358,000 ✳ CAPITAL: ASUNCION
URUGUAY
POPULATION: 3,223,000 ✳ CAPITAL: MONTEVIDEO

52

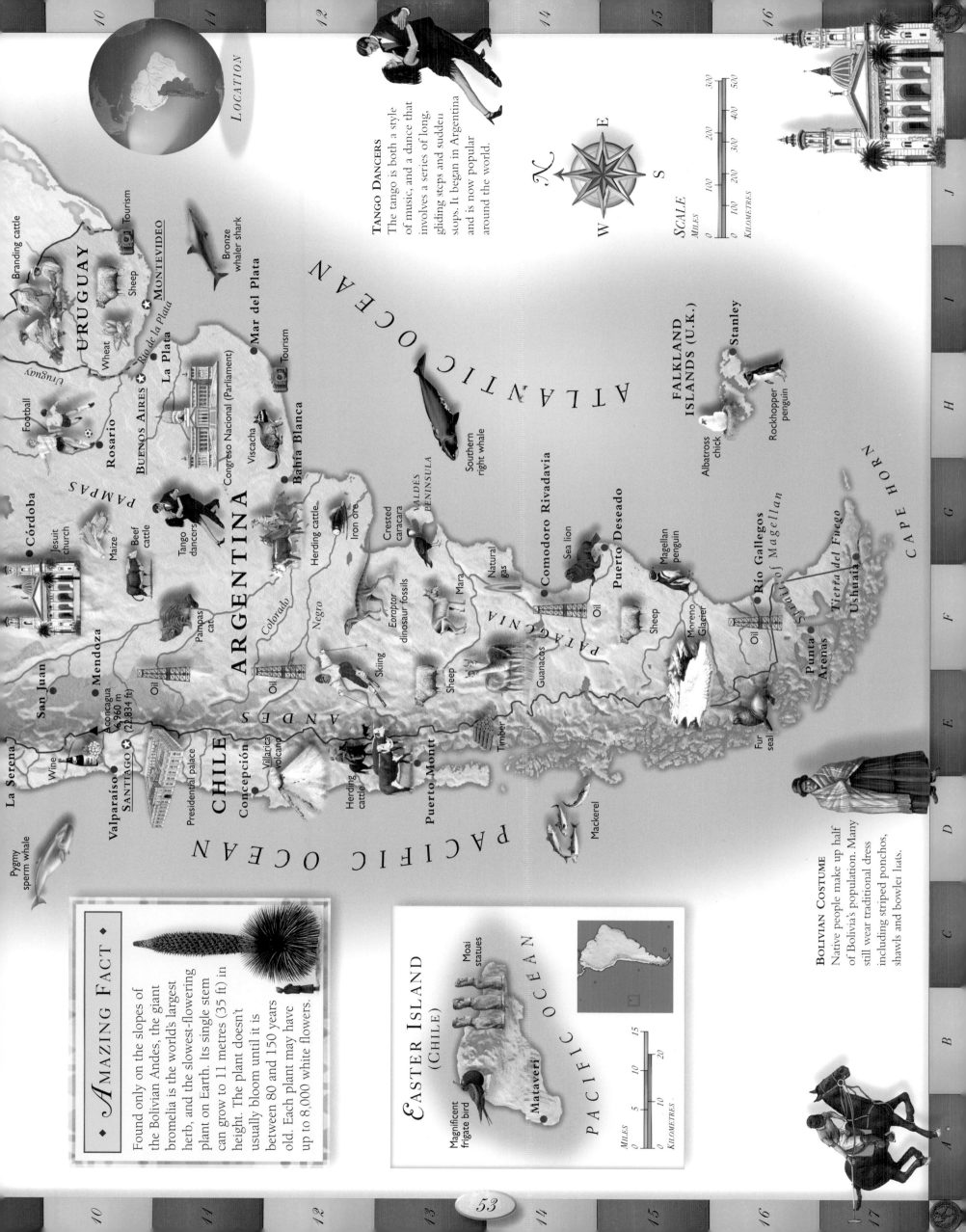

LOCATION

TANGO DANCERS

The tango is both a style of music, and a dance that involves a series of long, gliding steps and sudden stops. It began in Argentina and is now popular around the world.

N · E · S · W

SCALE

MILES   100   200   300

KILOMETRES   100   200   300   400   500

URUGUAY

Branding cattle

Tourism

Sheep

MONTEVIDEO

Bronze whaler shark

Wheat

Río de la Plata

La Plata

BUENOS AIRES

Congreso Nacional (Parliament)

Mar del Plata

Tourism

Uruguay

Football

Rosario

Viscacha

Bahía Blanca

Córdoba

PAMPAS

Jesuit church

Maize

Beef cattle

Tango dancers

ARGENTINA

Herding cattle

Iron ore

Crested caracara

VALDÉS PENINSULA

Southern right whale

ATLANTIC OCEAN

FALKLAND ISLANDS (U.K.)

Stanley

Albatross chick

Rockhopper penguin

Pampas cat

Colorado

Negro

Mara

Eoraptor dinosaur fossils

Natural gas

Sea lion

Comodoro Rivadavia

Puerto Deseado

Mendoza

San Juan

Aconcagua 6,960 m (22,834 ft)

Oil

Oil

Skiing

Guanacos

Sheep

PATAGONIA

Oil

Magellan penguin

Río Gallegos

Sheep

Oil

Moreno Glacier

Strait of Magellan

Tierra del Fuego

Ushuaia

Punta Arenas

CAPE HORN

Fur seal

La Serena

Wine

Valparaíso

SANTIAGO

Presidential palace

CHILE

Concepción

Villarica volcano

Herding cattle

Puerto Montt

Timber

Pygmy sperm whale

Mackerel

ANDES

PACIFIC OCEAN

◆ AMAZING FACT ◆

Found only on the slopes of the Bolivian Andes, the giant bromelia is the world's largest herb, and the slowest-flowering plant on Earth. Its single stem can grow to 11 metres (35 ft) in height. The plant doesn't usually bloom until it is between 80 and 150 years old. Each plant may have up to 8,000 white flowers.

EASTER ISLAND
(CHILE)

Moai statues

Magnificent frigate bird

Mataveri

PACIFIC OCEAN

MILES   0   5   10   15

KILOMETRES   0   10   20

BOLIVIAN COSTUME

Native people make up half of Bolivia's population. Many still wear traditional dress including striped ponchos, shawls and bowler hats.

Europe

EUROPE IS A SMALL, DENSELY POPULATED CONTINENT made up of many countries, each of which has its own culture and, in most cases, its own language. It is bounded by the Arctic and Atlantic Oceans in the north and west, and the Mediterranean Sea in the south. In the east, Russia's Ural Mountains separate Europe from Asia. A series of mountain ranges, including the Pyrenees, the Alps and the Carpathian Mountains, crosses Europe from east to west. South of these ranges, the land is rugged and the climate is warm and dry in summer, and mild and wet in winter. To the north, a broad band of flat land, known as the Northern European Plain, extends from the Atlantic coast to western Russia. North-western Europe has a mild, wet climate, but in the east and far north winters can be bitterly cold. Once, most of Europe was covered in forest, but over many years the trees were cleared to make way for cities, farms and industry.

CONTINENT FACTS

Regional land area: 10,354,636 sq. km (3,997,929 sq. mi) (including European Russia)
Regional population: 693,950,000 (including European Russia)
Independent countries: Albania, Andorra, Austria, Belarus, Belgium, Bosnia and Herzegovina, Bulgaria, Croatia, Czech Republic, Denmark, Estonia, Finland, France, Germany, Greece, Hungary, Iceland, Ireland, Italy, Latvia, Liechtenstein, Lithuania, Luxembourg, Macedonia, Malta, Moldova, Monaco, The Netherlands, Norway, Poland, Portugal, Romania, Russia, San Marino, Slovakia, Slovenia, Spain, Sweden, Switzerland, Ukraine, United Kingdom, Vatican City, Yugoslavia

WORLD RECORDS

WORLD'S SMALLEST COUNTRY
VATICAN CITY, 0.44 SQ. KM (0.17 SQ. MI)
WORLD'S TALLEST STALAGMITE
KRÁSNOHORSKÁ CAVE, SLOVAKIA, 32 M (105 FT)

CONTINENT RECORDS

HIGHEST MOUNTAIN
MOUNT ELBRUS, RUSSIA, 5,642 M (18,510 FT)
LOWEST POINT
VOLGA RIVER DELTA, 28 M (92 FT) BELOW SEA LEVEL
LARGEST LAKE
LAKE LADOGA, RUSSIA, 17,703 SQ. KM (6,835 SQ. MI)
LONGEST RIVER
VOLGA RIVER, RUSSIA, 3,700 KM (2,300 MI)
LARGEST COUNTRY BY AREA
EUROPEAN RUSSIA, 603,701 SQ. KM (233,089 SQ. MI)
LARGEST COUNTRY BY POPULATION
EUROPEAN RUSSIA, POPULATION 109,909,000
LARGEST CITY BY POPULATION
PARIS, FRANCE, POPULATION 9,500,000

MAJOR MOUNTAINS AND RIVERS

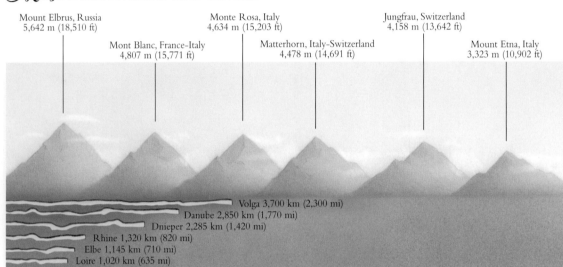

Mount Elbrus, Russia 5,642 m (18,510 ft)
Monte Rosa, Italy 4,634 m (15,203 ft)
Jungfrau, Switzerland 4,158 m (13,642 ft)
Mont Blanc, France-Italy 4,807 m (15,771 ft)
Matterhorn, Italy-Switzerland 4,478 m (14,691 ft)
Mount Etna, Italy 3,323 m (10,902 ft)

Volga 3,700 km (2,300 mi)
Danube 2,850 km (1,770 mi)
Dnieper 2,285 km (1,420 mi)
Rhine 1,320 km (820 mi)
Elbe 1,145 km (710 mi)
Loire 1,020 km (635 mi)

POLITICAL MAP

ICELAND
FAEROE ISLANDS (DENMARK)
SWEDEN
FINLAND
NORWAY
ESTONIA
UNITED KINGDOM
DENMARK
KALININGRAD OBLAST (RUSSIA)
LATVIA
LITHUANIA
RUSSIA
IRELAND
THE NETHERLANDS
BELARUS
GERMANY
BELGIUM
POLAND
LUXEMBOURG
CZECH REPUBLIC
SLOVAKIA
UKRAINE
FRANCE
AUSTRIA
1
SWITZERLAND
SLOVENIA
HUNGARY
MOLDOVA
ROMANIA
3
CROATIA
YUGOSLAVIA
4
BOSNIA and HERZEGOVINA
BULGARIA
2
5
ALBANIA
MACEDONIA
SPAIN
ITALY
PORTUGAL
GREECE
MALTA

KEY TO NUMBERED COUNTRIES

- 1 LIECHTENSTEIN
- 2 ANDORRA
- 3 MONACO
- 4 SAN MARINO
- 5 VATICAN CITY

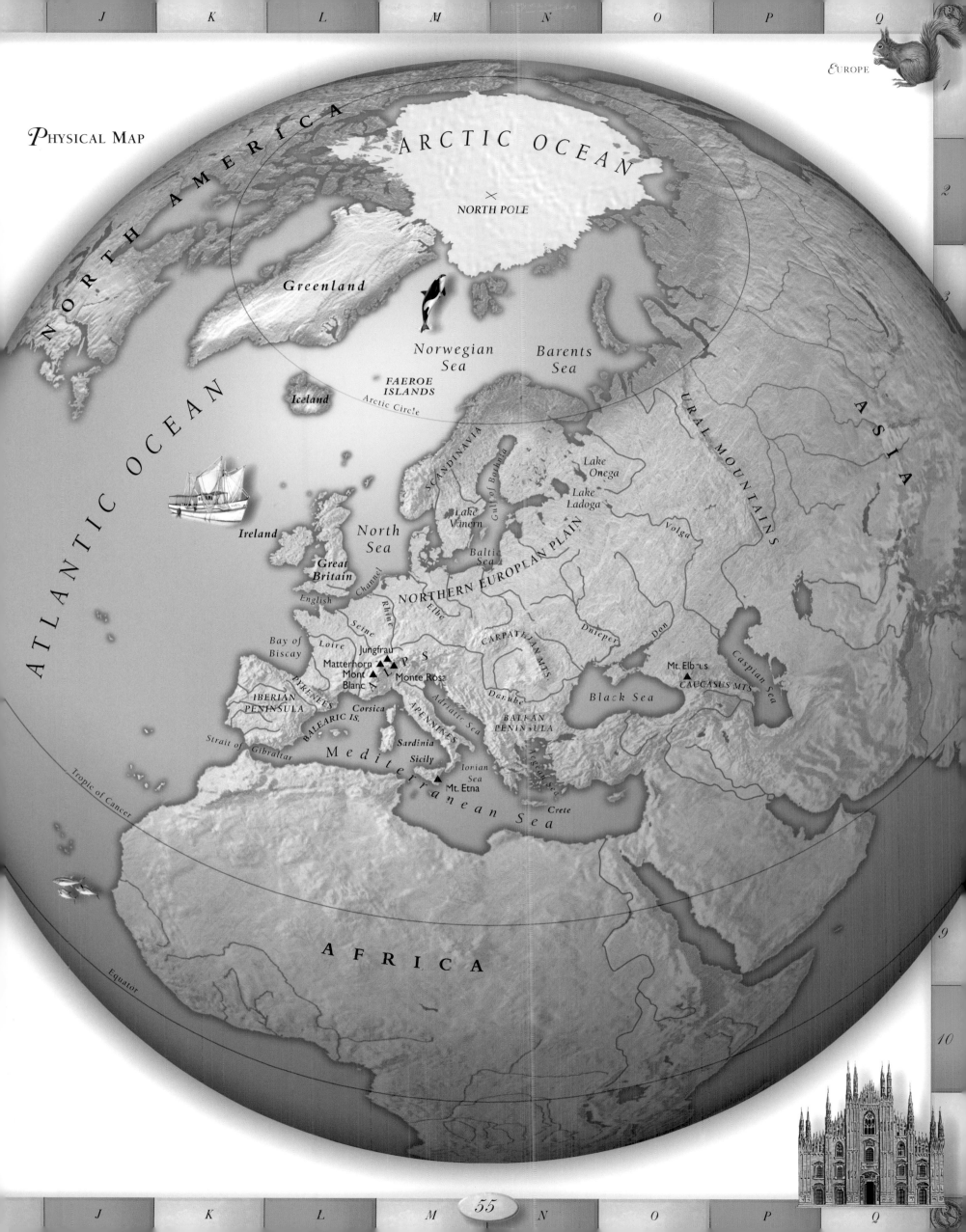

PHYSICAL MAP

NORTH AMERICA

ARCTIC OCEAN

✕
NORTH POLE

Greenland

ATLANTIC OCEAN

Norwegian
Sea

Barents
Sea

ASIA

FAEROE
ISLANDS
Arctic Circle

Iceland

URAL MOUNTAINS

SCANDINAVIA

Lake
Onega

Lake
Vänern

Gulf of Bothnia

Lake
Ladoga

Ireland

North
Sea

Baltic
Sea

Volga

Great
Britain

NORTHERN EUROPEAN PLAIN

English
Channel

Rhine

Elbe

Dnieper

Don

CARPATHIAN MTS.

Bay of
Biscay

Loire

Seine

Jungfrau

Mt. Elbrus

Caspian Sea

Matterhorn
Mont
Blanc

A L P S

Monte Rosa

Danube

CAUCASUS MTS.

PYRENEES

Black Sea

IBERIAN
PENINSULA

Corsica

Adriatic Sea

APENNINES

BALKAN
PENINSULA

BALEARIC IS.

Strait of
Gibraltar

Sardinia

Sicily

Mediterranean Sea

Ionian
Sea

Mt. Etna

Aegean Sea

Crete

Tropic of Cancer

AFRICA

Equator

The United Kingdom and the Republic of Ireland

THE UNITED KINGDOM AND THE REPUBLIC OF IRELAND occupy islands known as the British Isles. The United Kingdom (U.K.) is made up of the countries of England, Wales, Scotland and Northern Ireland, which are ruled by one government based in London but have their own cultures and educational systems, churches and regional assemblies. Scotland has its own legal and educational systems, churches and bank notes. England is a crowded country with many large cities. Almost eight million people live in London, the capital city. London is one of the world's most important centres of trade and finance and is famous for its many historic buildings. Southern and eastern England are fairly flat and fertile and their farms provide most of the U.K.'s crops. The country's most important industries are located in central England, an area known as the Midlands, and around the coalfields of the Pennine hills. To the west and north, the countryside is wet and mountainous and is used mainly for grazing animals. In the rugged, sparsely populated Scottish Highlands, red deer and sheep roam the hills and eagles soar overhead.

The Republic of Ireland occupies about 85 per cent of the island of Ireland. It is a land of green plains surrounded by coastal mountains. Most of the country's industries are located in the capital, Dublin, and the southern city of Cork.

IRELAND
POPULATION: 3,550,000 ❋ CAPITAL: DUBLIN

UNITED KINGDOM
POPULATION: 58,295,000 ❋ CAPITAL: LONDON

ENGLAND
POPULATION: 48,620,000 ❋ CAPITAL: LONDON

NORTHERN IRELAND
POPULATION: 1,640,000 ❋ CAPITAL: BELFAST

SCOTLAND
POPULATION: 5,130,000 ❋ CAPITAL: EDINBURGH

WALES
POPULATION: 2,905,000 ❋ CAPITAL: CARDIFF

◆ AMAZING FACT ◆

In the 19th century, as a hoax, the name of the Welsh village Llanfairpwllgwyngyll was lengthened to the tongue-twisting Llanfairpwllgwyngyllgogerychwyrndrobwllllantysiliogogogoch. The name means 'St. Mary's church by the pool of white hazel trees, near the rapid whirlpool, by the red cave of the Church of St. Tysilio'. In 1988 the village officially returned to using the shorter name. However, the railway station is still called by the 58-letter version.

LLANFAIRPWLLGWYNGYLLGOGERYCHWYRNDROBWLLLLANTYSILIOGOGOGOCH

◆ LOOK AGAIN ◆

● Which famous railway bridge is located near the capital of Scotland?
● Name a sport that is played in Ireland.
● What is the name of the group of islands near Land's End?

Shetland pony

Lerwick

SHETLAND ISLANDS

Cod

ORKNEY ISLANDS

Kirkwall

John o'Groats

Thurso

Red deer

Highland piper

Highland cattle

Aberdeen

Hammer throwing, Highland Games

Glamis Castle

Forth Railway Bridge

Coal

Dundee

Inverness

Urquhart Castle and Loch Ness

SCOTLAND

Dee

Capercaillie

Ben Nevis 1,343 m (4,406 ft)

GRAMPIAN MTS.

Tay

Golf

Forth

EDINBURGH

Tweed

Hadrian's Wall

Beef cattle

Oban

Salmon

Otter

Mull

Skye

Sheep

Clyde

Glasgow

Arran

Stornoway

Textiles

Lewis with Harris

HEBRIDES

North Uist

South Uist

Islay

Iona Abbey

Giant's Causeway rock formation

Oil rig

North

Haddock

Fishing trawler

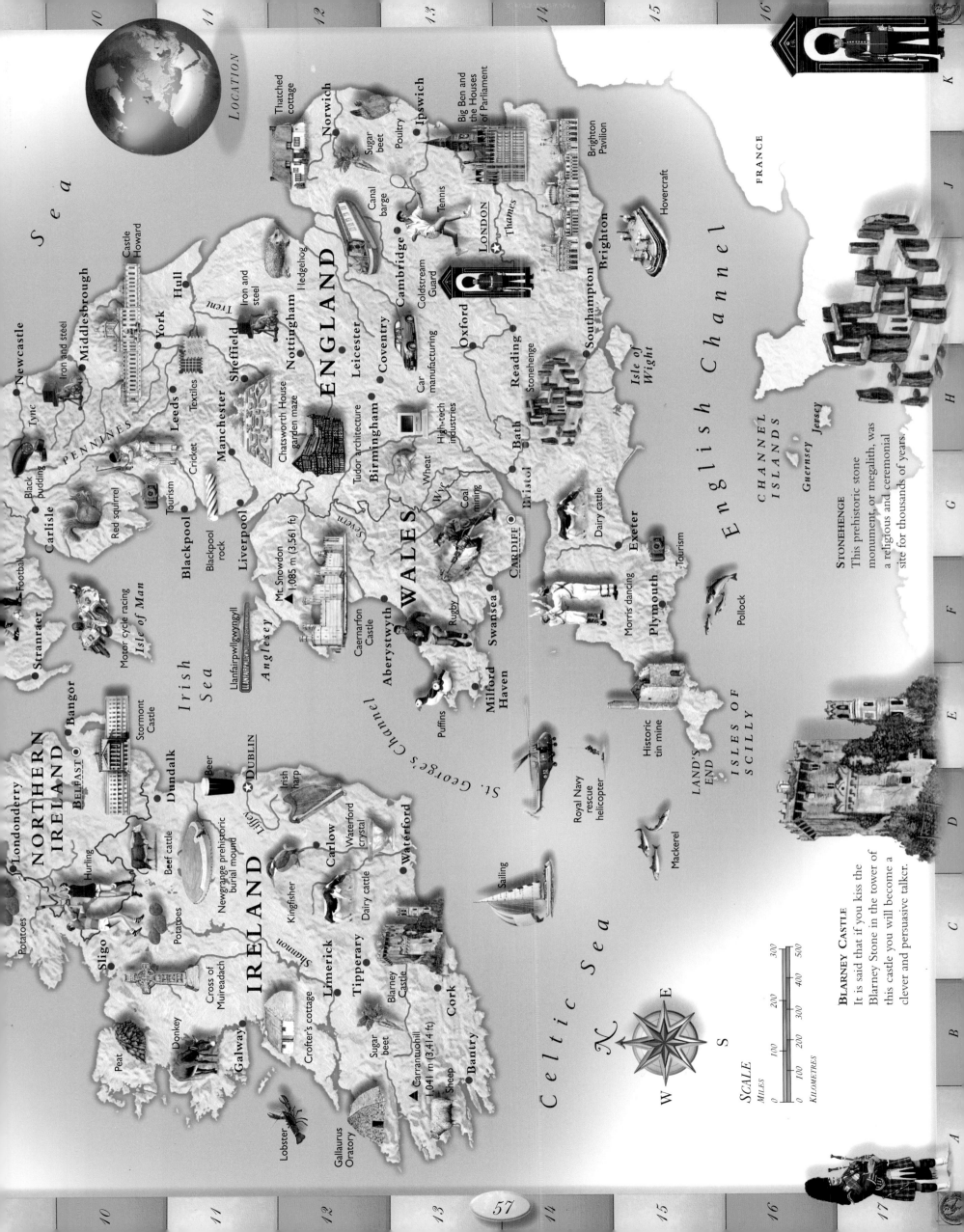

Spain and Portugal

SPAIN AND PORTUGAL OCCUPY the Iberian Peninsula, a square-shaped piece of land in south-western Europe. This peninsula is separated from the rest of the continent by the Pyrenees, a mountain range that contains the tiny country of Andorra. Most of the Iberian Peninsula consists of a huge plateau known as the Meseta, which is covered with dry grasslands, olive groves and forested hills. At the centre of the Meseta, 646 metres (2,120 ft) above sea level, lies Madrid – the largest city in Spain and the highest capital city in Europe. Spain's second-largest city, Barcelona, lies on the narrow plains of the east coast. This coastline and the nearby Balearic Islands are warm and sunny for much of the year, and in summer, crowds of holiday-makers from all over Europe sunbathe on the sandy beaches. The southern tip of Spain lies only 15 kilometres (9 mi) from Africa. Between AD 711 and the 12th century, most of Spain was ruled by the Moors, an Arabic people from North Africa, and towns such as Granada and Seville have many ornate Moorish buildings. West of Spain lies Portugal. Once the heart of a vast, worldwide empire, Portugal is now one of the poorest countries in western Europe. Olive groves and cork oak forests cover the dry, southern plains. In the many river valleys that cross the country, farmers grow grapes for wine-making. Among the best-known Portuguese wines is port, which is named after the country's second-largest city, Porto.

ANDORRA
POPULATION: 65,800 ✳ CAPITAL: ANDORRA LA VELLA
PORTUGAL
POPULATION: 10,562,000 ✳ CAPITAL: LISBON
SPAIN
POPULATION: 39,404,000 ✳ CAPITAL: MADRID

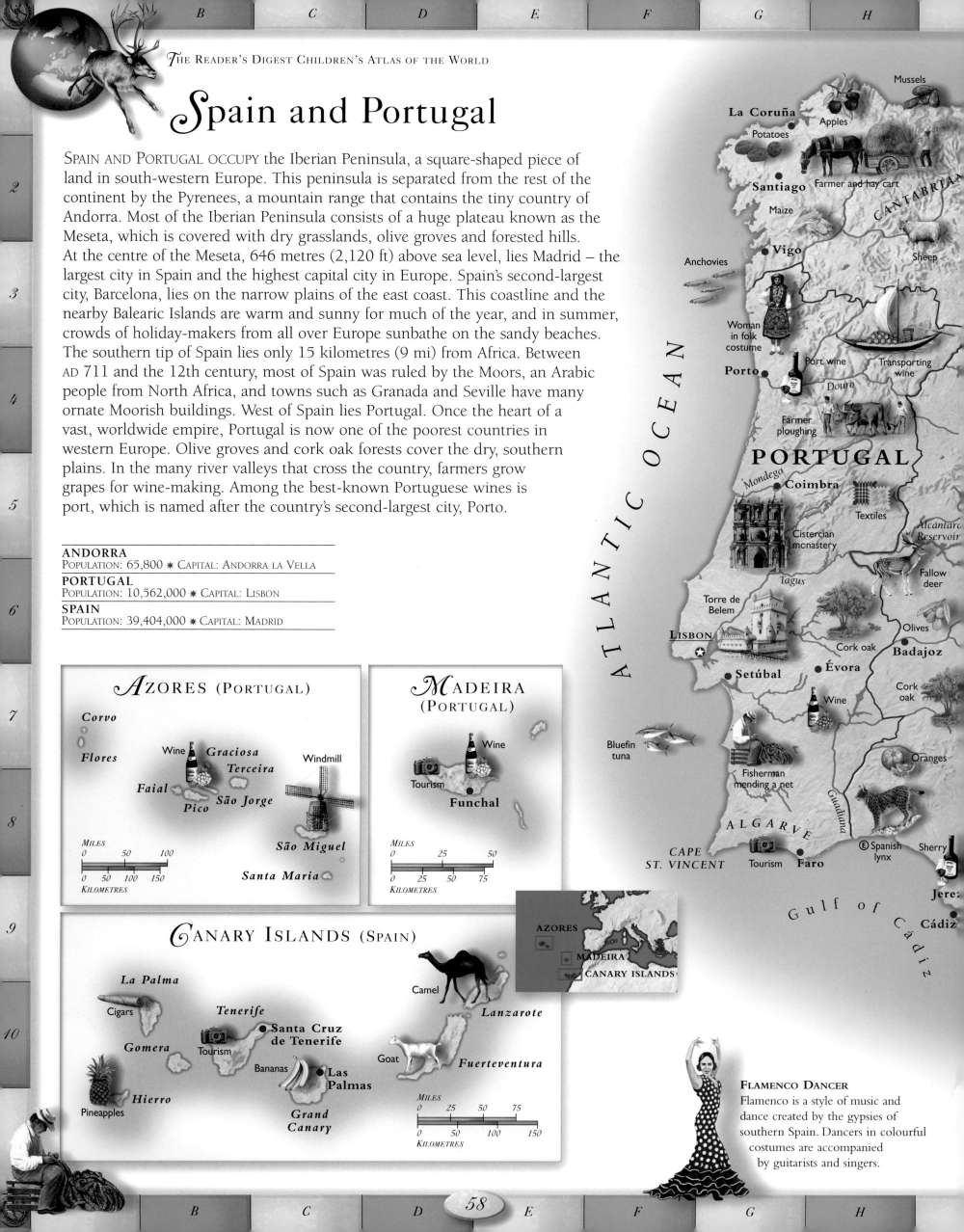

ATLANTIC OCEAN

CANTABRIAN

La Coruña
Mussels
Apples
Potatoes
Farmer and hay cart
Santiago
Maize
Vigo
Sheep
Anchovies
Woman in folk costume
Porto
Port wine
Transporting wine
Douro
Farmer ploughing
PORTUGAL
Mondego
Coimbra
Textiles
Alcantara Reservoir
Cistercian monastery
Tagus
Fallow deer
Torre de Belem
Olives
LISBON
Cork oak
Badajoz
Setúbal
Évora
Cork oak
Wine
Bluefin tuna
Fisherman mending a net
Oranges
Guadiana
ALGARVE
Spanish lynx
CAPE ST. VINCENT
Tourism
Faro
Sherry
Jerez
Cádiz
Gulf of Cádiz

AZORES (PORTUGAL)

Corvo
Flores
Wine
Graciosa
Terceira
Windmill
Faial
São Jorge
Pico
São Miguel
Santa Maria

MILES
0   50   100
0   50   100   150
KILOMETRES

MADEIRA (PORTUGAL)

Wine
Tourism
Funchal

MILES
0   25   50
0   25   50   75
KILOMETRES

AZORES
MADEIRA
CANARY ISLANDS

CANARY ISLANDS (SPAIN)

La Palma
Cigars
Tenerife
Santa Cruz de Tenerife
Camel
Lanzarote
Gomera
Tourism
Goat
Fuerteventura
Bananas
Las Palmas
Hierro
Pineapples
Grand Canary

MILES
0   25   50   75
0   50   100   150
KILOMETRES

FLAMENCO DANCER
Flamenco is a style of music and dance created by the gypsies of southern Spain. Dancers in colourful costumes are accompanied by guitarists and singers.

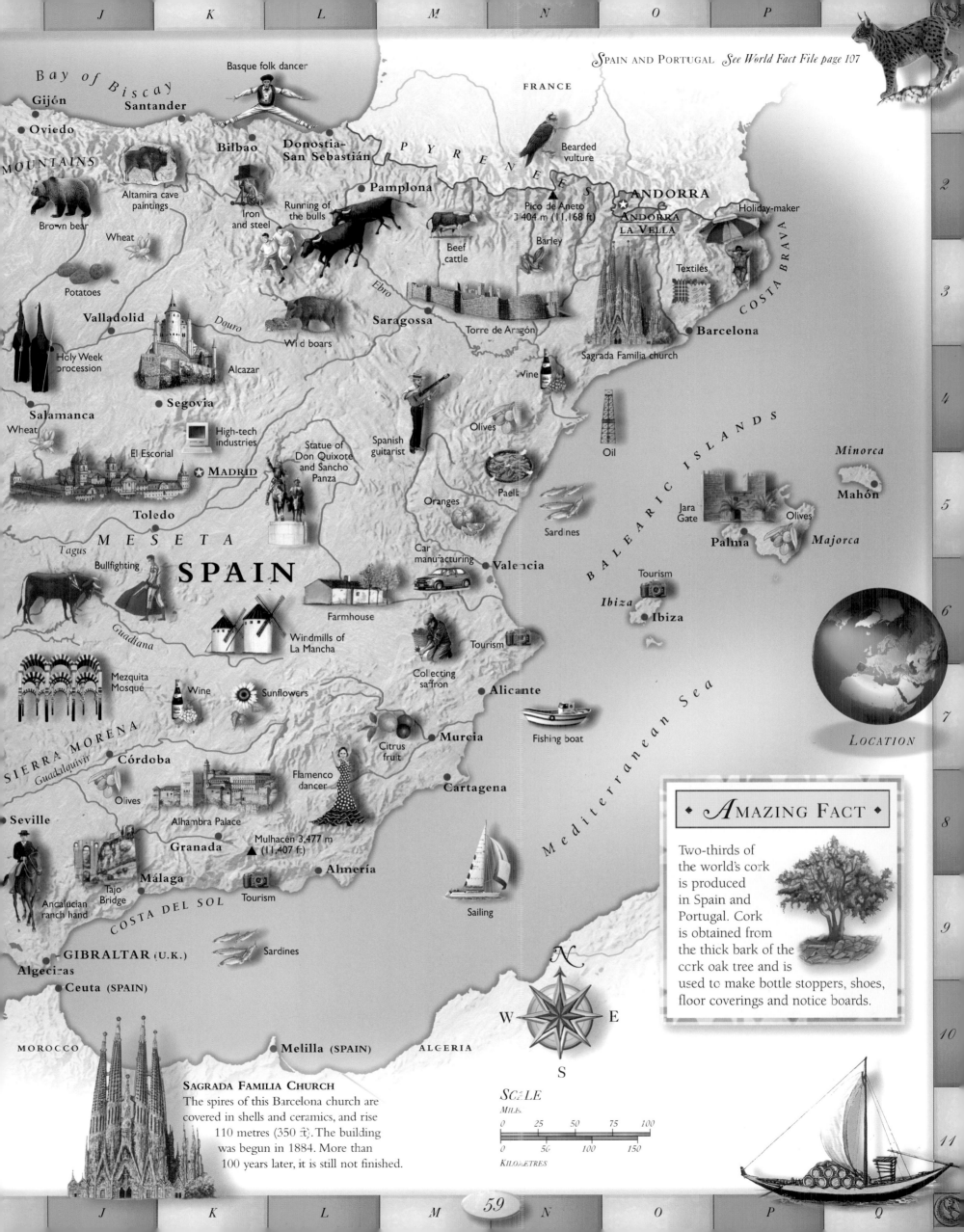

Bay of Biscay

Gijón

Santander

Oviedo

Basque folk dancer

FRANCE

Bilbao

Donostia-
San Sebastián

P Y R E N E E S

Bearded
vulture

ANDORRA

Holiday-maker

MOUNTAINS

Altamira cave
paintings

Pamplona

Running of
the bulls

Pico de Aneto
3 404 m (11,168 ft)

ANDORRA
LA VELLA

Brown bear

Iron
and steel

Beef
cattle

Barley

Textiles

COSTA BRAVA

Wheat

Ebro

Potatoes

Valladolid

Douro

Wild boars

Saragossa

Torre de Aragón

Sagrada Familia church

Barcelona

Vine

Holy Week
procession

Alcazar

Segovia

Olives

Oil

Minorca

Salamanca

High-tech
industries

Mahón

Wheat

El Escorial

MADRID

Statue of
Don Quixote
and Sancho
Panza

Spanish
guitarist

Paella

Jara
Gate

Olives

B A L E A R I C   I S L A N D S

Toledo

Tagus

M E S E T A

Sardines

Palma

Majorca

Bullfighting

Oranges

Car
manufacturing

Valencia

SPAIN

Farmhouse

Tourism

Ibiza

Ibiza

Guadiana

Windmills of
La Mancha

Collecting
saffron

Tourism

Mezquita
Mosque

Wine

Sunflowers

Alicante

SIERRA MORENA

Murcia

Fishing boat

Mediterranean Sea

Córdoba

Guadalquivir

Flamenco
dancer

Citrus
fruit

Olives

Cartagena

LOCATION

Alhambra Palace

Seville

Granada

Mulhacén 3,477 m
(11,407 ft)

Almería

Andalucian
ranch hand

Tajo
Bridge

Málaga

COSTA DEL SOL

Tourism

Sailing

GIBRALTAR (U.K.)

Algeciras

Ceuta (SPAIN)

Sardines

MOROCCO

Melilla (SPAIN)

ALGERIA

N

W   E

S

SAGRADA FAMILIA CHURCH

The spires of this Barcelona church are
covered in shells and ceramics, and rise
110 metres (350 ft). The building
was begun in 1884. More than
100 years later, it is still not finished.

SCALE

MILES

0   25   50   75   100

0   50   100   150

KILOMETRES

France

FRANCE, THE LARGEST COUNTRY in western Europe, has a varied climate and landscape. In the north, the weather is mild and wet, and much of the land is flat. As you travel south, the climate becomes warmer and the land more mountainous. Three-quarters of the population live in towns and cities, but most of the country is farmland, and France is Europe's leading farming country. The northern plains are covered in fields of wheat and sugar beet, and in central and southern France vineyards dot the hillsides – more wine is produced in France than in any other country except Italy. The area around Paris, the capital, is the most densely populated region. It is home to one-fifth of the country's population and most of its industries. Several great rivers, including the Seine and the Loire, cross France's northern and western plains. These waterways were once the country's main transport routes, and their banks are lined with historic villages and magnificent castles known as châteaux. In the south, the mountains of the Pyrenees and the Alps separate France from Spain and Italy. Among their snow-capped peaks lie popular ski resorts, and national parks that are home to eagles, marmots and goat-like antelopes called chamois. Along the Mediterranean coast there are many busy beach resorts. Near the Italian border lies Monaco, the second-smallest country in the world. Monaco is famous for its casinos and its annual Grand Prix motor race.

FRANCE
POPULATION: 58,109,000 ✳ CAPITAL: PARIS

MONACO
POPULATION: 31,500 ✳ CAPITAL: MONACO

✦ AMAZING FACT ✦

France is now connected to Great Britain by an undersea rail link known as the Channel Tunnel. The tunnel took seven years to build and includes two rail tracks. Trains take 35 minutes to pass through the tunnel. People can travel from London to Paris in about three hours.

BOULES
Boules is a bowling game that is popular in France. It is played with metal balls on a hard dirt surface.

EIFFEL TOWER
Once the tallest structure in the world, the Eiffel Tower was erected for the Paris Exhibition of 1889 by engineer Alexandre-Gustave Eiffel.

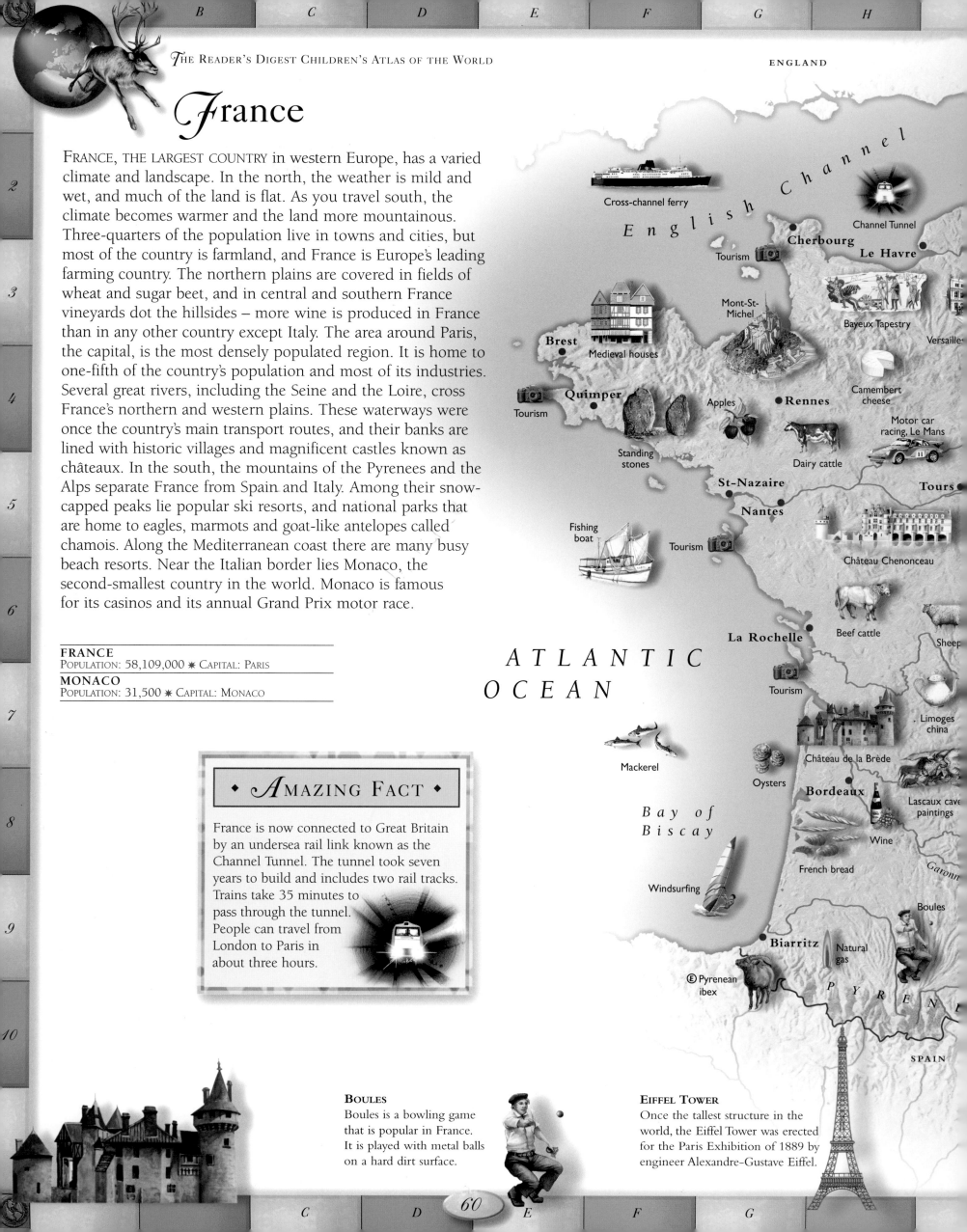

ENGLAND

English Channel

Cross-channel ferry

Channel Tunnel

Tourism
Cherbourg
Le Havre

Mont-St-Michel

Bayeux Tapestry

Versaille

Brest
Medieval houses

Camembert cheese

Quimper
Tourism

Apples
Rennes

Motor car racing, Le Mans

Standing stones

Dairy cattle

Tours

St-Nazaire

Nantes

Fishing boat

Tourism

Château Chenonceau

Beef cattle

La Rochelle

Sheep

ATLANTIC OCEAN

Tourism

Limoges china

Mackerel

Château de la Brède

Oysters

Bordeaux

Lascaux cave paintings

Bay of Biscay

Wine

French bread

Garonn

Windsurfing

Boules

Biarritz
Natural gas

Ⓔ Pyrenean ibex

PYREN

SPAIN

• PROJECT: *Cave Painting* •

The cave paintings at Lascaux were created about 15,000 years ago. Here's how you can create your own painting that will look thousands of years old.

❶ Stuff a strong paper bag with crumpled newspaper and then staple the bag closed.

❷ Mix some glue and sand and use this to paint the whole bag. When it dries it will look like a rock.

❸ Collect three or four different coloured soils. Sift out the lumps and then mix each colour with glue to make earth paints. (Add water if the paints are too thick.) Now you are ready to paint. You can paint animals living in your area, as did the artists who created the Lascaux cave paintings.

• LOOK AGAIN •

- Which cathedral lies south-west of Paris?
- Name a horned animal found in the Pyrenees.
- What kind of food is produced in Dijon?
- Which small country is located east of Nice?

LOCATION

Dunkerque
Calais
Boulogne
Mussels
Nuclear energy
Lille
Potatoes
Dieppe
Sugar beet
Amiens
Wheat
Rouen
Car manufacturing
PARIS
Fashion
Chartres Cathedral
Eiffel Tower
Seine
BELGIUM
Cafe
Reims
Champagne
Troyes
Iron ore
Iron and steel
Metz
Nancy
Wine
Nuclear energy
LUXEMBOURG
GERMANY
Coal
Strasbourg
Moselle
Folk costume
Tour de France
Chapel of Notre Dame du Haut
Gaul fort
Saône
Château de Chambord
Bourges
FRANCE
Dijon
Mustard
T.G.V. high-speed train
Doubs
Besançon
Mountain climbing
Dairy cattle
SWITZERLAND
Saône
Snail
Tungsten
Farmer with goats
Coal
Textiles
Lyon
Playing the cabrette
Marmot
Rhône
ALPS
Mont Blanc 4,807 m (15,771 ft)
St-Étienne
Chapel of St-Michel D'Aiguilhe
French bread
Wine
Chamois
Grenoble
Skiing
MASSIF CENTRALE
Geese
Hunting for truffles
Nuclear energy
Avignon
Harvesting lavender
Rhône
Durance
Perfume
ITALY
Casino, Monte Carlo
MONACO
Mackerel
Aircraft manufacturing
Toulouse
Montpellier
Pont du Gard
Cannes Film Festival
Nice
Cannes
Marseille
Tourism
Walled town of Carcassonne
Sailing
Flamingo
Water-skiing
ANDORRA
Perpignan
Solar furnace
Mediterranean Sea
Osprey
Corsica
Tourism
Ajaccio
Statue of Napoleon

TOUR DE FRANCE
France's most famous sporting event, this cycle race around the entire country covers about 4,000 kilometres (2,500 mi).

SCALE
MILES
0 25 50 75 100
0 50 100 150
KILOMETRES

N
W   E
S

The Low Countries

THE DENSELY POPULATED COUNTRIES OF the Netherlands (also called Holland), Belgium and Luxembourg are known as the Low Countries because they have no high mountains and few hills. Much of the land, including one-third of the Netherlands, actually lies below sea level. Over the centuries, local people have built large barriers known as dikes to keep the sea out, pumped water out of the marshes behind the dikes to create areas of new land called polders, and constructed thousands of kilometres of canals. Throughout the region, barges chug along these waterways, past windmills, dairy farms and colourful fields of tulips – both Belgium and the Netherlands export flowers and bulbs all over the world. The capital of the Netherlands, Amsterdam, has more than 150 canals, many of which are lined with tall, narrow, 17th-century buildings. In Belgium, canals link the country's ports to the historic cities of Bruges and Ghent, and to Brussels, the capital. Brussels is often referred to as the capital of Europe because it is the headquarters of the European Union (E.U.). South-east of Brussels lies the only high part of the Low Countries, the Ardennes. This range of forest-covered hills spreads across the northern half of Luxembourg, one of Europe's smallest countries but also one of its most important financial centres.

BELGIUM
POPULATION: 10,082,000 * CAPITAL: BRUSSELS
LUXEMBOURG
POPULATION: 404,700 * CAPITAL: LUXEMBOURG

THE NETHERLANDS
POPULATION: 15,453,000 * CAPITALS: AMSTERDAM, THE HAGUE

◆ AMAZING FACT ◆

The Low Countries have more than 8,000 kilometres (5,000 mi) of canals, which are used to transport people and goods and to drain the land. Because much of the region lies below sea level, water has to be pumped into canals built high above ground level. You could be standing in a field in the Low Countries and see a ship pass by above your head!

THE NETHERLANDS

Wheat

Natural gas

Groningen

Prehistoric hunebed (burial tomb)

Sheep

Dairy cattle

Pigs

Cycling

Folk dancers

Clogs

Beef cattle

Beef cattle

Apeldoorn

Leeuwarden

Windmill

Dairy cattle

Zuider Zee folk costume

Poultry

Arnhem

Potatoes

Tourism

Eurasian spoonbill

Football

Ameland

Harbour seals

Tourism

Dom (cathedral) tower

Fruit

Nijmegen

Terschelling

Flowers

AMSTERDAM

Amsterdam

Utrecht

Delft pottery

Vlieland

Alkmaar

Diamond cutting

Texel

Haarlem

Tulips

Herring

Alkmaar cheese market

Iron and steel

Mackerel

Rotterdam

Peace Palace

THE HAGUE

Container ship

THE ATOMIUM
The Atomium represents an iron molecule and is one of the rare remains of the World Exhibition held in Brussels in 1958.

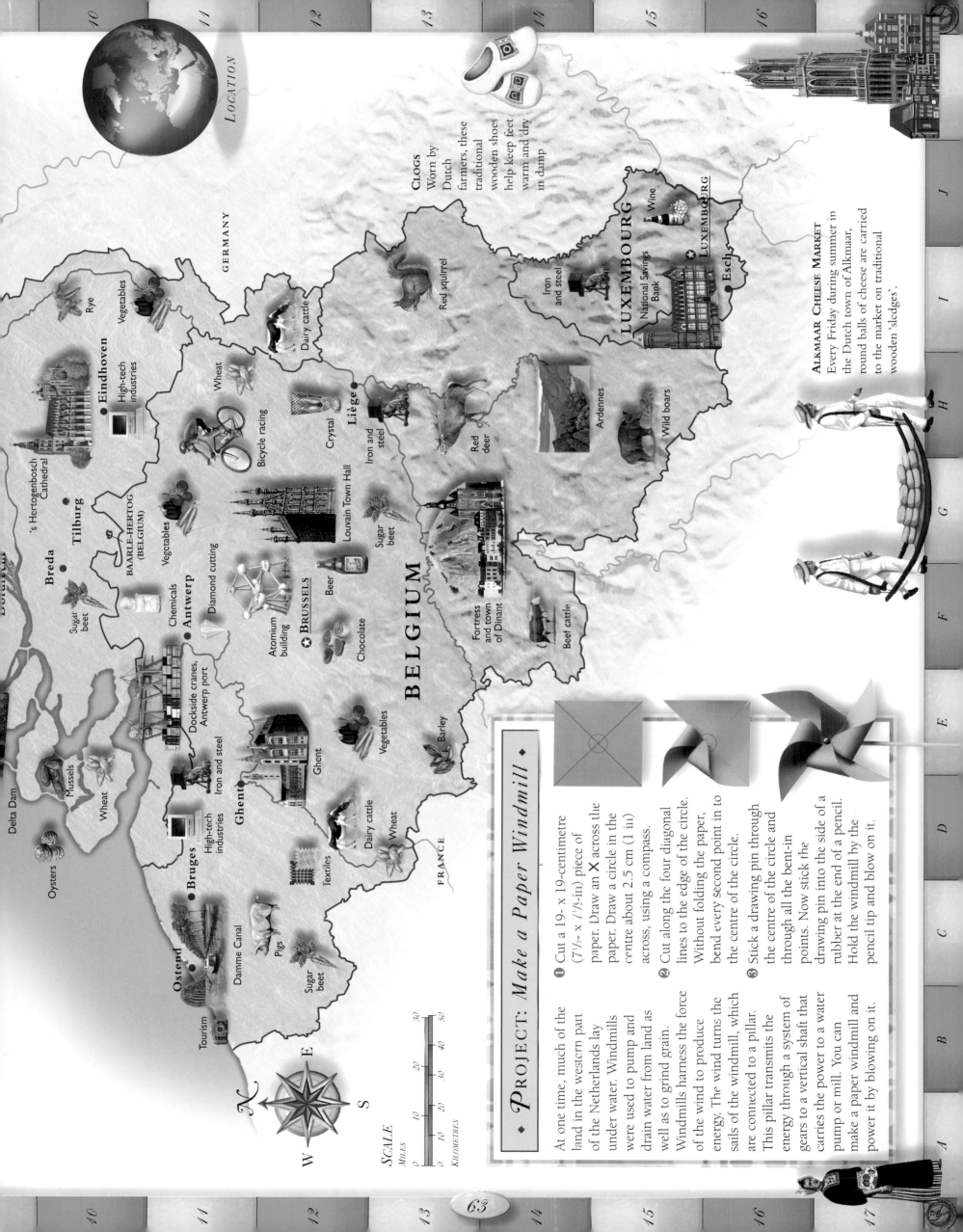

LOCATION

CLOGS
Worn by Dutch farmers, these traditional wooden shoes help keep feet warm and dry in damp

GERMANY

Red squirrel

Dairy cattle

Wheat

Eindhoven
High-tech industries

Rye

Vegetables

's Hertogenbosch Cathedral

Breda

Tilburg

BAARLE-HERTOG (BELGIUM)

Vegetables

Sugar beet

Chemicals
Antwerp

Diamond cutting

Bicycle racing

Crystal

Liège

Iron and steel

Red deer

Ardennes

Wild boars

LUXEMBOURG
National Savings Bank

Iron and steel

Wine

LUXEMBOURG

Esch

Louvain Town Hall

Beer

Atomium building

★ **BRUSSELS**

Chocolate

BELGIUM

Sugar beet

Fortress and town of Dinant

Beet cattle

Delta Dam

Oysters

Mussels

Wheat

Dockside cranes, Antwerp port

Iron and steel

Ghent

Ghent

Vegetables

Barley

High-tech industries

Bruges

Textiles

Dairy cattle

Wheat

FRANCE

Pigs

Damme Canal

Ostend

Sugar beet

Tourism

ALKMAAR CHEESE MARKET
Every Friday during summer in the Dutch town of Alkmaar, round balls of cheese are carried to the market on traditional wooden 'sledges'.

SCALE
MILES
0   10   20   30
0   10   20   30   40   50
KILOMETRES

N
W   E
S

◆ PROJECT: *Make a Paper Windmill* ◆

At one time, much of the land in the western part of the Netherlands lay under water. Windmills were used to pump and drain water from land as well as to grind grain. Windmills harness the force of the wind to produce energy. The wind turns the sails of the windmill, which are connected to a pillar. This pillar transmits the energy through a system of gears to a vertical shaft that carries the power to a water pump or mill. You can make a paper windmill and power it by blowing on it.

① Cut a 19- x 19-centimetre (7½- x 7½-in) piece of paper. Draw an **X** across the paper. Draw a circle in the centre about 2.5 cm (1 in) across, using a compass.

② Cut along the four diagonal lines to the edge of the circle. Without folding the paper, bend every second point in to the centre of the circle.

③ Stick a drawing pin through the centre of the circle and through all the bent-in points. Now stick the drawing pin into the side of a rubber at the end of a pencil. Hold the windmill by the pencil tip and blow on it.

THE READER'S DIGEST CHILDREN'S ATLAS OF THE WORLD

Western Central Europe

AFTER WORLD WAR II, GERMANY was divided into two countries: East Germany and West Germany. They were reunited in 1990, and Germany is now home to more than 80 million people, the largest population of any European country except Russia. Many of Germany's cities lie on rivers. The Rhine river connects the country's most important industrial region, the Ruhr Valley, to the ports of the Netherlands and the Swiss city of Basel. On its journey northwards, the Rhine winds past forests of spruce and fir, steep hillsides covered with vineyards, and cliffs crowned by medieval castles. From southern Germany, the spectacular Alps mountain range stretches across the countries of Switzerland and Austria, where it covers about two-thirds of the land. Throughout these mountains, roads and railways wind through narrow river valleys and cross steep passes. In summer, cows graze in the alpine meadows; in winter, skiers hurtle down the slopes. Switzerland is a peaceful country which hasn't been involved in a war since 1814. This has encouraged people from all over the world to deposit money in Swiss banks, and the country is now a leading financial centre. In Austria, many farms and industries lie on the north-eastern lowlands. This area is crossed by the Danube, Europe's second-longest river. The Danube passes through Austria's capital, Vienna – home to one-fifth of Austria's population and one of Europe's grandest cities.

AUSTRIA
POPULATION: 7,987,000 ✳ CAPITAL: VIENNA

GERMANY
POPULATION: 81,338,000 ✳ CAPITAL: BERLIN

LIECHTENSTEIN
POPULATION: 30,700 ✳ CAPITAL: VADUZ

SWITZERLAND
POPULATION: 7,085,000 ✳ CAPITAL: BERN

◆ PROJECT: *Swiss Chocolate Fondue* ◆

The Swiss eat a dish called fondue, which is often made from cheese. They dip pieces of bread in a mixture of hot melted cheese and white wine. Try making this chocolate fondue.

❶ Place 250 g (8 oz) plain chocolate pieces in a saucepan with 250 ml (8 oz) whipping cream.

❷ Ask an adult to help you warm the ingredients gently until the chocolate has melted. Beat the mixture until it becomes glossy.

❸ Let the mixture cool a little. Then spear a piece of fruit (strawberries or grapes are good) on a fork, dip it in the fondue and eat it straight away.

◆ AMAZING FACT ◆

The country of Liechtenstein is home to only 30,700 people and is just 6 kilometres (4 mi) wide. That means you could walk across it in less than two hours! The prince of Liechtenstein lives in this castle in the capital, Vaduz.

SCALE

MILES
0   25   50   75

KILOMETRES
0   25   50   75   100   125

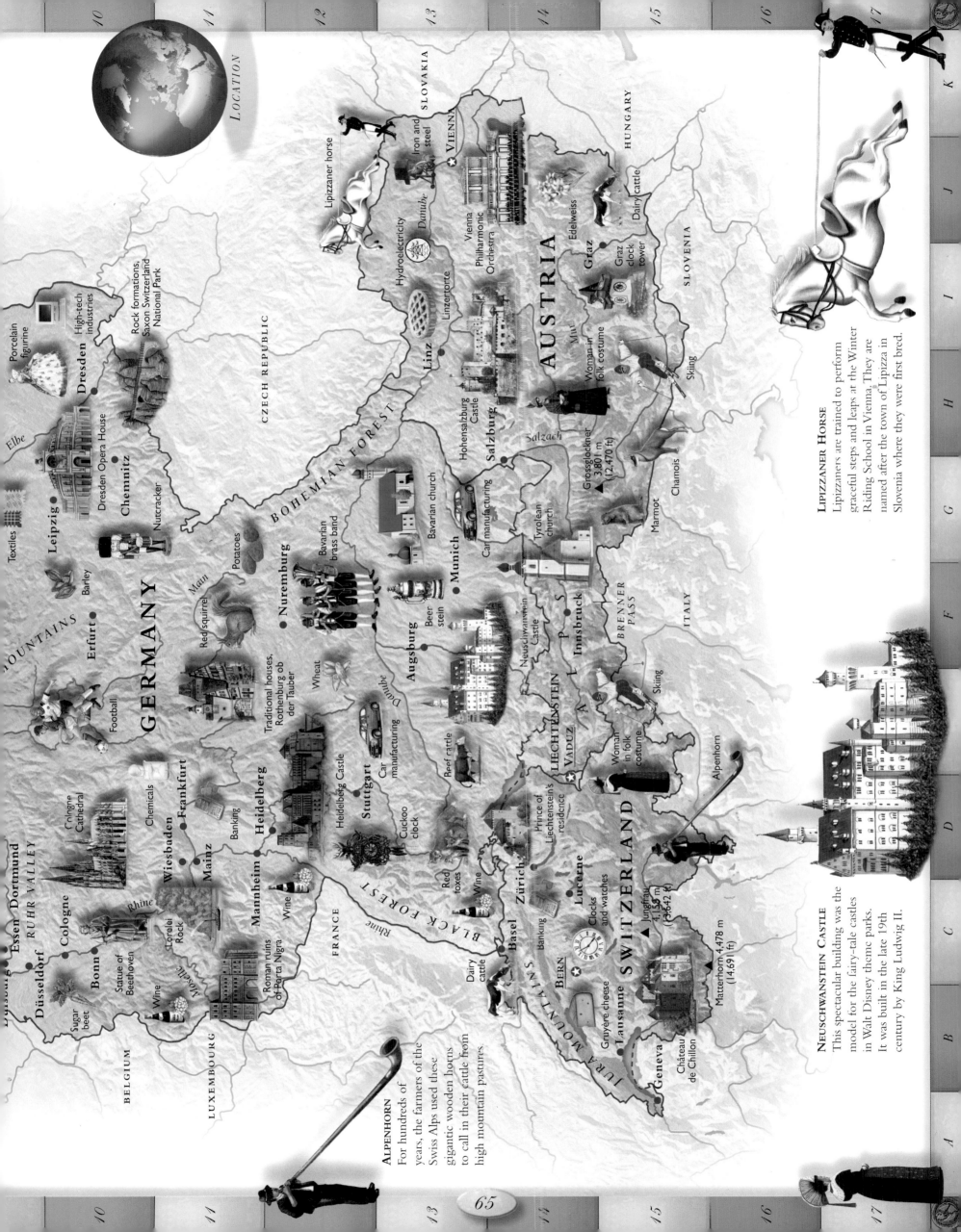

LOCATION

GERMANY

BELGIUM

LUXEMBOURG

Elbe

Porcelain figurine

High-tech industries

Dresden

Rock formations, Saxon Switzerland National Park

Dresden Opera House

Chemnitz

Nutcracker

Textiles

Leipzig

Barley

Erfurt

MOUNTAINS

Football

Red squirrel

Main

Potatoes

Traditional houses, Rothenburg ob der Tauber

Nuremburg

Bavarian brass band

Augsburg

Bavarian church

Car manufacturing

Munich

Beer stein

CZECH REPUBLIC

BOHEMIAN FOREST

Lipizzaner horse

SLOVAKIA

Iron and steel

★ **VIENNA**

Hydroelectricity

Danube

Linz

Linzertorte

Vienna Philharmonic Orchestra

Hohensalzburg Castle

Salzburg

Salzach

AUSTRIA

Mur

Woman in folk costume

Edelweiss

Graz

Graz clock tower

Dairy cattle

HUNGARY

SLOVENIA

Grossglockner ▲ 3,801 m (12,470 ft)

Chamois

Skiing

Marmot

Düsseldorf

Essen   Dortmund

RUHR VALLEY

Cologne Cathedral

Cologne

Bonn

Statue of Beethoven

Wine

Sugar beet

Moselle

Roman ruins of Porta Nigra

Lorelei Rock

Rhine

Chemicals

Frankfurt

Wiesbaden

Banking

Mainz

Mannheim

Wine

Heidelberg

Heidelberg Castle

Wheat

Stuttgart

Car manufacturing

Cuckoo clock

Beef rattle

Red foxes

Wine

BLACK FOREST

FRANCE

Rhine

Basel

Banking

Dairy cattle

BERN ★

Zürich

Lucerne

Clocks and watches

SWITZERLAND

Gruyere cheese

Lausanne

Geneva

Château de Chillon

Jungfrau 4,158 m (13,642 ft) ▲

Matterhorn 4,478 m (14,691 ft) ▲

JURA MOUNTAINS

Neuschwanstein Castle

Tyrolean church

Innsbruck

A   L   P   S

BRENNER PASS

ITALY

LIECHTENSTEIN

Prince of Liechtenstein's residence

VADUZ ★

Woman in folk costume

Skiing

Alpenhorn

ALPENHORN
For hundreds of years, the farmers of the Swiss Alps used these gigantic wooden horns to call in their cattle from high mountain pastures.

NEUSCHWANSTEIN CASTLE
This spectacular building was the model for the fairy-tale castles in Walt Disney theme parks. It was built in the late 19th century by King Ludwig II.

LIPIZZANER HORSE
Lipizzaners are trained to perform graceful steps and leaps at the Winter Riding School in Vienna. They are named after the town of Lipizza in Slovenia where they were first bred.

Italy

ITALY CONSISTS OF A LONG, boot-shaped peninsula, the large islands of Sicily and Sardinia, and about 70 smaller islands. Within Italy lie two other countries: San Marino in the east, and the Vatican City (the world's smallest country) in the city of Rome. The Vatican City is the home of the Pope, the head of the Roman Catholic Church. Most of mainland Italy is mountainous. The Alps form a great arc around the northern border, and the Apennines stretch almost the entire length of the peninsula. Between these two mountain ranges lies the Northern Plain, a flat, fertile region drained by the Po River. This plain has Italy's richest farmland and is home to the country's most important industries, including the car factories of Turin, and Milan's fashion and design houses.

Each year, more than 50 million tourists travel to Italy to visit its ancient ruins and historic cities, and the birthplace of opera, and to enjoy the sunny weather. The country's mild climate allows farmers to grow large quantities of wheat, citrus fruit, olives and grapes – Italy is the world's leading producer of olive oil and wine. Parts of Italy are regularly rocked by earthquakes, and there are active volcanoes. On the island of Sicily, Mount Etna has erupted at least 260 times since the first recorded eruption in 70 BC. About 95 kilometres (60 mi) south of Sicily lie the islands of Malta. Malta has been ruled by the Romans, Arabs, Turks, French and British. It is now an independent republic.

COLOSSEUM
This Roman stadium was built in the first century AD and used for events such as gladiator contests. It was even flooded for mock sea battles.

ITALY
POPULATION: 58,262,000 ✳ CAPITAL: ROME
MALTA
POPULATION: 369,600 ✳ CAPITAL: VALLETTA
SAN MARINO
POPULATION: 24,300 ✳ CAPITAL: SAN MARINO
VATICAN CITY
POPULATION: 830 ✳ CAPITAL: VATICAN CITY

◆ AMAZING FACT ◆
The Leaning Tower of Pisa was constructed as a bell tower between AD 1173 and 1370. Unfortunately, it was built on unstable ground, and it began to sink and tilt to one side after completion of the first three storeys. Although the tower leans about 4.5 metres (15 ft) out of line, it has recently been stabilized so that it will not fall over.

MOUNT VESUVIUS AND POMPEII
In AD 79, Mount Vesuvius erupted, burying the town of Pompeii under stone and ash. The ruins were not uncovered until the 18th century.

Map labels: SWITZERLAND, FRANCE, AUSTRIA, SLOVENIA, CROATIA, Mont Blanc 4,807 m (15,771 ft), Matterhorn 4,478 m (14,691 ft), Monte Rosa 4,634 m (15,203 ft), Skiing, Hydroelectricity, Turin, Car manufacturing, Wine, Olives, Rice, Tourism, Genoa, Fishing boat, Squid, Marble, La Spezia, Milan, Milan Cathedral, Fashion, Lake Maggiore, Lake Como, Car manufacturing, Walnuts, Leaning Tower of Pisa, Pisa, Elba, Livorno, Arno, Florence, Florence Cathedral, Chianti wine, Siena, Arezzo, Perugia, Bologna, Modena, Parmesan cheese, Parma, Parmesan cheese, Parma Baptistry, Brescia, Violin making, Skiing, Marmot, DOLOMITES, Bolzano, Pinnacles of the Dolomites, Rock climbing, Chamois, Maize, Trieste, Sugar beet, Lake Garda, Dairy cattle, Verona, Venice, Padua, Po, Rialto Bridge, Gulf of Venice, Sole, Ferrara, Wheat, Rice, Church of San Vitale, Ravenna, Rimini, SAN MARINO, Rocca Tower, San Marino, Pasta, Ancona, Wheat, APENNINES, Ligurian Sea

N W S E (compass)

LOCATION

Strait of Otranto

Adriatic Sea

Ionian Sea

Wine-making

Trulli houses

Brindisi

Crab

Bari

Octopus

Taranto

Oysters

Gulf of Taranto

Appian Way (Roman road)

Sea-horse

Potatoes

Foggia

Wall lizard

Great barracuda

Red mullet

Oil

Pescara

Goats

Olives

Wine

Cosenza

Reggio di Calabria

Sheep

Oranges

Olives

Wolf

Abbey of Monte Cassino

Football

Pizza maker

Naples

Vesuvius and the ruins of Pompeii Forum

Mt Vesuvius 1,277 m (4,190 ft)

Salerno

Tourism

Anchovies

Garfish

LIPARI ISLANDS

Stromboli

Messina

Tourism

Syracuse

SAN MARINO
The smallest republic in Europe and the oldest republic in the world. San Marino was founded in about AD 300 by Christians fleeing religious persecution.

St. Peter's Basilica, Vatican City

Sunflowers

Vatican guard

ITALY

Ischia

Capri

Tiber

Colosseum

VATICAN CITY ★ ROME

Container ship

Tyrrhenian Sea

Swordfish

Ustica

Palermo

Temple of Concordia

Mt Etna 3,323 m (10,902 ft)

Citrus fruit

Wheat

Sicily

Oil

Wine

Sardines

Mediterranean Sea

MALTA ★ VALLETTA

Tourism

Palio horse race

Giglio

CORSICA (FRANCE)

Scuba diving

Bluefin tuna

Sardines

Iron ore

Sassari

Goats

Olives

Sheep

Sardinia

Woman in folk costume

Cagliari

Tourism

Sardines

◆ PROJECT: *Making a Mosaic* ◆

A mosaic is a design made by pressing small pieces of cut stone or coloured glass into a soft plaster surface. In ancient Rome, the walls and floors of public places and private homes were decorated with mosaics. There are many colourful mosaics in the Church of San Vitale in Ravenna, which were made around AD 526–47. You can make your own mosaic using tiny pieces of coloured paper instead of stone or glass.

❶ Cut 0.5-centimetre (¼-in) squares out of several sheets of different coloured paper.

❷ On a surface of white or coloured paper, draw the outline of a simple design for your mosaic. It could be a landscape, a flower, an animal or even a portrait of a friend.

❸ To create your mosaic, carefully glue the tiny pieces of paper close together within the outlines of your design.

South-eastern Europe

THIS REGION IS OFTEN REFERRED TO as the Balkans. It lies at the edge of Europe, close to Asia, and is home to many peoples from both continents. Throughout history, disputes between countries and ethnic groups have occurred here regularly. In 1991, the republics of Slovenia, Croatia, Bosnia and Herzegovina, and Macedonia declared their independence from Yugoslavia. This led to a war that destroyed cities, farms and industries, and left thousands of people homeless. Most of south-eastern Europe is rugged and mountainous. Along the coast of Croatia, rocky slopes rise steeply from the water. Inland, forests and farms surround the peaks that spread eastwards through Yugoslavia and into Romania and Bulgaria. In Bulgaria's Balkan

Mountains, an area known as the Valley of the Roses produces more than two-thirds of the world's rose oil, an essential ingredient in most perfumes. South-eastern Europe's best farmland lies along the Danube River, which connects many of the region's towns to the ports of the Black Sea. In Greece, overgrazing by sheep and goats has stripped some of the land of trees and shrubs, but the warm climate allows farmers to grow olives, grapes, citrus fruit and wheat. Greece's sunny weather and scenic attractions bring tourists from all over the world. In Athens, home to one-third of Greece's population, rush-hour traffic roars past 2,000-year-old temples. On the Greek islands, clusters of white buildings cling to cliffs, and fishing boats drift across clear, turquoise bays.

ALBANIA
POPULATION: 3,414,000 ∗ CAPITAL: TIRANË
BOSNIA AND HERZEGOVINA
POPULATION: 3,202,000 ∗ CAPITAL: SARAJEVO
BULGARIA
POPULATION: 8,775,000 ∗ CAPITAL: SOFIA
CROATIA
POPULATION: 4,666,000 ∗ CAPITAL: ZAGREB
GREECE
POPULATION: 10,648,000 ∗ CAPITAL: ATHENS
MACEDONIA
POPULATION: 2,160,000 ∗ CAPITAL: SKOPJE
ROMANIA
POPULATION: 23,198,000 ∗ CAPITAL: BUCHAREST
SLOVENIA
POPULATION: 2,052,000 ∗ CAPITAL: LJUBLJANA
YUGOSLAVIA
POPULATION: 11,102,000 ∗ CAPITAL: BELGRADE

SCALE

LOCATION

Black Sea

Mediterranean Sea

TURKEY

TURKEY

Burgas
Shipka Memorial Church
SOFIA
Food processing
Plovdiv
Tobacco
Mt. Musala 2,925 m (9,596 ft)
Skiing
RHODOPE MTS.
Struma
Greek Orthodox monk
Ironland Steel
Thessaloniki
MACEDONIA
SKOPJE
Vardar
Morava
Goats
Cotton
Eastern Orthodox Church
Monastery, Meteora
Bitola
BITOLA
Korçë
ALBANIA
TIRANË
Maize
Copper
Shkodër
Black kite
Podgorica
Priština
Durrës
Vlorë
Inspecting carpets
Tourism
Corfu
Olives
Levkás
IONIAN ISLANDS
Zákinthos
Cephalonia
Bouzoulki
Wine
GREECE
Volos
Ruins of Delphi
Mt. Olympus 2,917 m (9,570 ft)
Patras
PELOPONNESE
Tripolis
Ruins of Olympia
King Aganemnon's gold death mask
Parthenon
ATHENS
Piraeus
Evzones guards
Khalkis
Euboea
Skyros
NORTHERN SPORADES
Sardines
Thásos
Samothráke
Alexandroúpolis
Lemnos
Wheat
Sailing
Leshos
Olives
Chios
Aegean Sea
Mackerel
Andros
Tinos
Mykonos
CYCLADES
Paros
Naxos
Tourism
Thira
Traditional church
DODECANESE
Samos
Kárpathos
Rhodes
Windmill
Bull's head sculpture, Knossos
Iráklion
Crete
Canea
Wine
Sea of Crete
Kithira
Ionian Sea
Adriatic Sea
ITALY
Cruise ship

◆ PROJECT: *Make a Cave* ◆

The Postojna Caves in Slovenia are famous for their stalactites and stalagmites. These formations took thousands of years to develop, but you can make your own cave with stalactites and stalagmites in just a few days.

❶ Draw a cave scene on the inside bottom of a shoe box. Line the outside and inside walls of the box with aluminium foil. Turn the box on its side so that the scene becomes the cave's back wall. Ask an adult to help you punch two holes close together at each end of the top of the box. Place a glass beside each end of the box.

❷ Thread two lengths of string in through holes at one end and out through holes at the other end. Make sure the strings reach the bottom of each glass and hang down a little inside the cave.

❸ Fill the glasses with hot water and stir in washing soda (sodium carbonate) until no more will dissolve, then wash your hands well. Put the ends of the strings in the glasses. Over the next few days, as the water soaks into the strings and then starts to evaporate, small salt formations will appear where the strings sag. At the same time, small mounds of salt will form where the water drips on the cave floor. Gradually, these formations will grow into stalactites and stalagmites.

BLACK KITE
These birds of prey are found throughout south-eastern Europe. At night, they roost in trees in huge flocks of as many as 100 birds.

CASTLE OF VLAD TEPES
Vlad Tepes, a 15th-century Romanian prince known as Vlad the Impaler, is said to have inspired the legend of Dracula the vampire.

EVZONES GUARDS
Wearing their traditional skirts and tasselled hats and shoes, the evzones stand guard outside the parliament in Athens.

Eastern Europe

IN RECENT YEARS, MANY POLITICAL CHANGES have occurred within this vast region. During 1990 and 1991, the republics of Latvia, Estonia, Lithuania, Belarus, Moldova and the Ukraine, all formerly part of the Soviet Union, became independent countries. In 1993, Czechoslovakia divided into two countries, the Czech Republic and Slovakia. Mountains line the borders of the Czech Republic and cover most of Slovakia, but elsewhere eastern Europe is generally flat. Wide grasslands cover central Hungary and most of the Ukraine. In Poland, rivers that rise in the southern mountains meander northwards across a wide plain of rich farmland toward coastal swamps and sand dunes. The Baltic States of Lithuania, Latvia and Estonia are covered with meadows, marshes and more than 9,000 lakes. Around the Baltic Sea, winters can be bitterly cold, and ice-breaker ships often have to clear a path between the region's ports. About two-thirds of eastern Europe's people live in cities, and many work in heavy industries such as mining, steel-making and shipbuilding. These industries have created serious pollution problems. Acid rain has destroyed forests in Poland and the Czech Republic, and people are no longer allowed to swim in some polluted lakes in Hungary. In the Ukraine and Belarus, large areas of land can no longer be farmed because they were contaminated by radioactivity after an accident at the Chernobyl nuclear power plant near Kiev in 1986. Despite this, the Ukraine remains one of the largest producers of wheat in the world.

BELARUS
POPULATION: 10,437,000 ✳ CAPITAL: MINSK

CZECH REPUBLIC
POPULATION: 10,433,000 ✳ CAPITAL: PRAGUE

ESTONIA
POPULATION: 1,625,000 ✳ CAPITAL: TALLINN

HUNGARY
POPULATION: 10,319,000 ✳ CAPITAL: BUDAPEST

LATVIA
POPULATION: 2,763,000 ✳ CAPITAL: RIGA

LITHUANIA
POPULATION: 3,876,000 ✳ CAPITAL: VILNIUS

MOLDOVA
POPULATION: 4,490,000 ✳ CAPITAL: CHIŞINĂU

POLAND
POPULATION: 38,792,000 ✳ CAPITAL: WARSAW

SLOVAKIA
POPULATION: 5,432,000 ✳ CAPITAL: BRATISLAVA

UKRAINE
POPULATION: 51,868,000 ✳ CAPITAL: KIEV

◆ LOOK AGAIN ◆

- What kind of glassware is produced in the Czech Republic?
- Name a mineral that is mined in eastern Hungary.
- Ukrainians eat a soup called borscht. What is it made of?

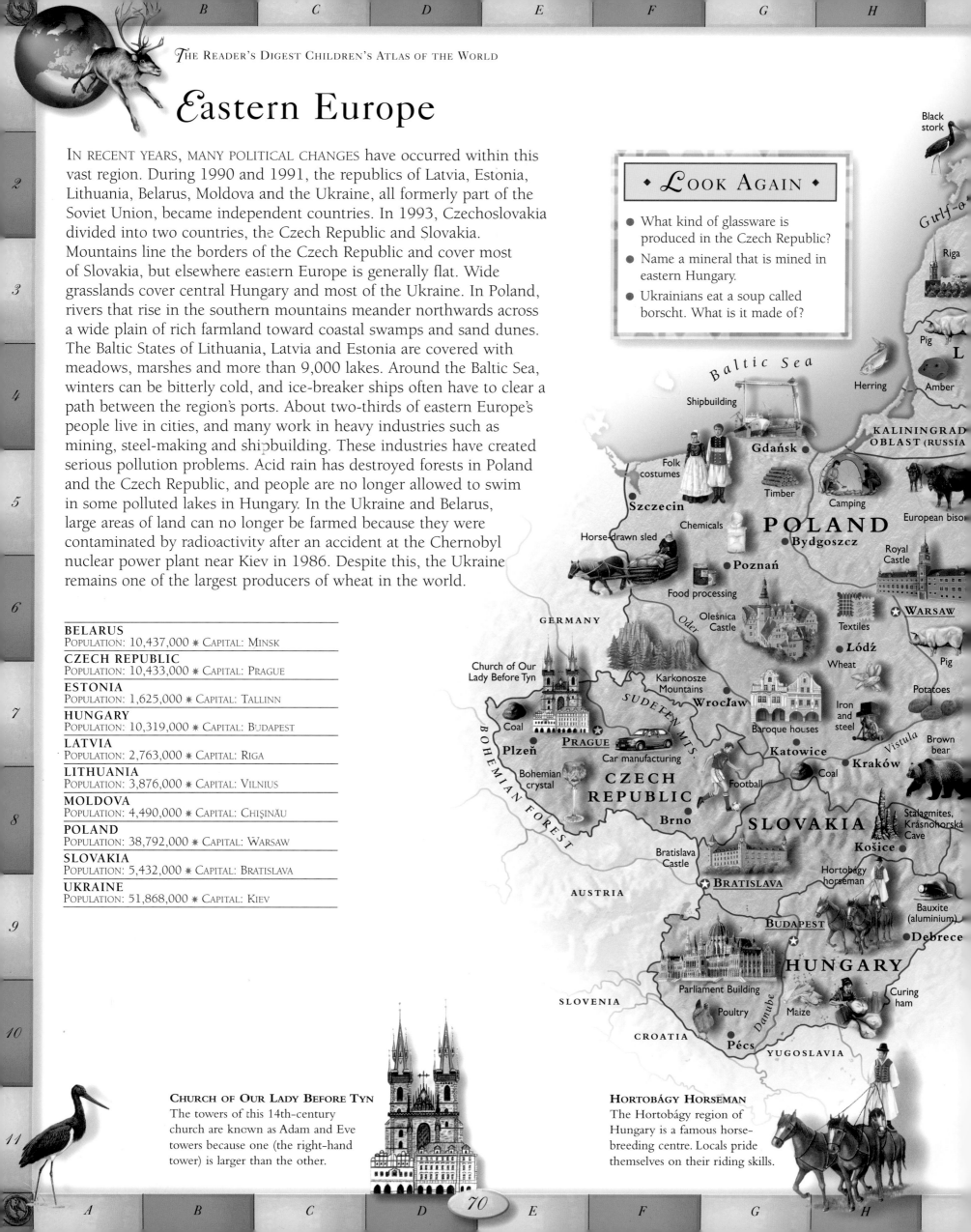

CHURCH OF OUR LADY BEFORE TYN
The towers of this 14th-century church are known as Adam and Eve towers because one (the right-hand tower) is larger than the other.

HORTOBÁGY HORSEMAN
The Hortobágy region of Hungary is a famous horse-breeding centre. Locals pride themselves on their riding skills.

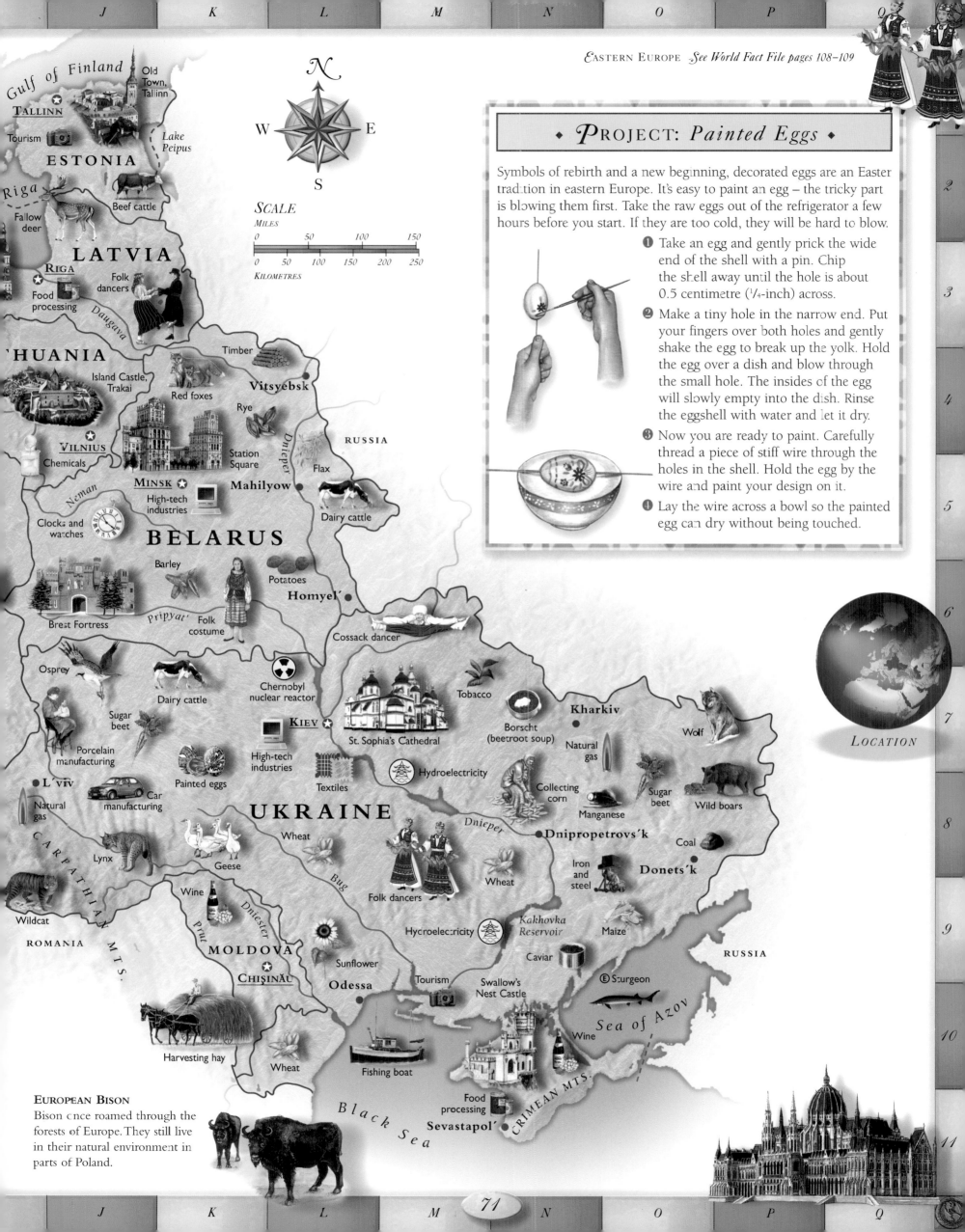

Map labels:

J K L M N O P Q

Gulf of Finland

Old Town, Tallinn

TALLINN
Tourism

ESTONIA

Lake Peipus

Riga
Fallow deer

Beef cattle

LATVIA

RIGA
Food processing

Folk dancers

Daugava

'HUANIA

Island Castle, Trakai

Timber

Red foxes

Vitsyebsk

Rye

Dnieper

RUSSIA

VILNIUS
Chemicals

Station Square

Flax

Neman

MINSK
High-tech industries

Mahilyow

Clocks and watches

BELARUS

Dairy cattle

Barley

Potatoes

Brest Fortress

Pripyat'

Folk costume

Homyel'

Cossack dancer

Osprey

Chernobyl nuclear reactor

Tobacco

Kharkiv

Dairy cattle

St. Sophia's Cathedral

Borscht (beetroot soup)

Natural gas

Wolf

Sugar beet

KIEV

High-tech industries

Collecting corn

Manganese

Sugar beet

Wild boars

Porcelain manufacturing

Textiles

Hydroelectricity

L'viv
Natural gas

Painted eggs

UKRAINE

Dnieper

Dnipropetrovs'k

Coal

Car manufacturing

Wheat

Wheat

Iron and steel

Donets'k

Lynx

Geese

Bug

Folk dancers

Wildcat

Wine

Dniester

Prut

Hydroelectricity

Kakhovka Reservoir

Maize

ROMANIA

CARPATHIAN MTS.

MOLDOVA

Sunflower

Caviar

RUSSIA

CHIŞINĂU

Odessa

Tourism

Swallow's Nest Castle

Sturgeon

Sea of Azov

Harvesting hay

Wheat

Fishing boat

Wine

Food processing

CRIMEAN MTS.

Black Sea

Sevastopol'

EUROPEAN BISON
Bison once roamed through the forests of Europe. They still live in their natural environment in parts of Poland.

SCALE

MILES
0   50   100   150

0   50   100   150   200   250
KILOMETRES

◆ PROJECT: *Painted Eggs* ◆

Symbols of rebirth and a new beginning, decorated eggs are an Easter tradition in eastern Europe. It's easy to paint an egg – the tricky part is blowing them first. Take the raw eggs out of the refrigerator a few hours before you start. If they are too cold, they will be hard to blow.

❶ Take an egg and gently prick the wide end of the shell with a pin. Chip the shell away until the hole is about 0.5 centimetre (¼-inch) across.

❷ Make a tiny hole in the narrow end. Put your fingers over both holes and gently shake the egg to break up the yolk. Hold the egg over a dish and blow through the small hole. The insides of the egg will slowly empty into the dish. Rinse the eggshell with water and let it dry.

❸ Now you are ready to paint. Carefully thread a piece of stiff wire through the holes in the shell. Hold the egg by the wire and paint your design on it.

❹ Lay the wire across a bowl so the painted egg can dry without being touched.

LOCATION

J K L M N O P Q

Northern Europe

NORTHERN EUROPE *See World Fact File page 109*

THE COUNTRIES OF NORTHERN EUROPE are often referred to as Scandinavia, although strictly speaking Scandinavia is only the wide peninsula occupied by Norway and Sweden. Another name for them is the Nordic countries. On the western side of this peninsula, fjords – spectacular, steep-sided bays formed by glaciers – and more than 150,000 islands create a maze of waterways. Inland, mountain peaks and high plateaux cover most of Norway. To the east, the marshy plains of Sweden and Finland are studded with thousands of lakes and cloaked in coniferous forests that are home to elk, brown bears and wolves. The northern half of this region has a cold climate, with long, dark, snowy winters. In the far south, the climate is more temperate and the land more fertile.

Only one-twentieth of Norway can be farmed, but more than three-quarters of Denmark is used for agriculture. The volcanic island of Iceland, which lies 1,000 kilometres (600 mi) west of Norway, has very little farmland. The island's barren interior consists mainly of volcanoes, hot springs and lava fields. Parts of Iceland are so like the surface of the moon that astronauts trained there for moon landings. Some upland areas are covered by huge sheets of ice. Vatnajökull, an ice sheet in the south-east, is larger than all the glaciers in Europe combined.

DENMARK
POPULATION: 5,199,000 ✴ CAPITAL: COPENHAGEN
FINLAND
POPULATION: 5,085,000 ✴ CAPITAL: HELSINKI
ICELAND
POPULATION: 266,000 ✴ CAPITAL: REYKJAVIK
NORWAY
POPULATION: 4,331,000 ✴ CAPITAL: OSLO
SWEDEN
POPULATION: 8,822,000 ✴ CAPITAL: STOCKHOLM

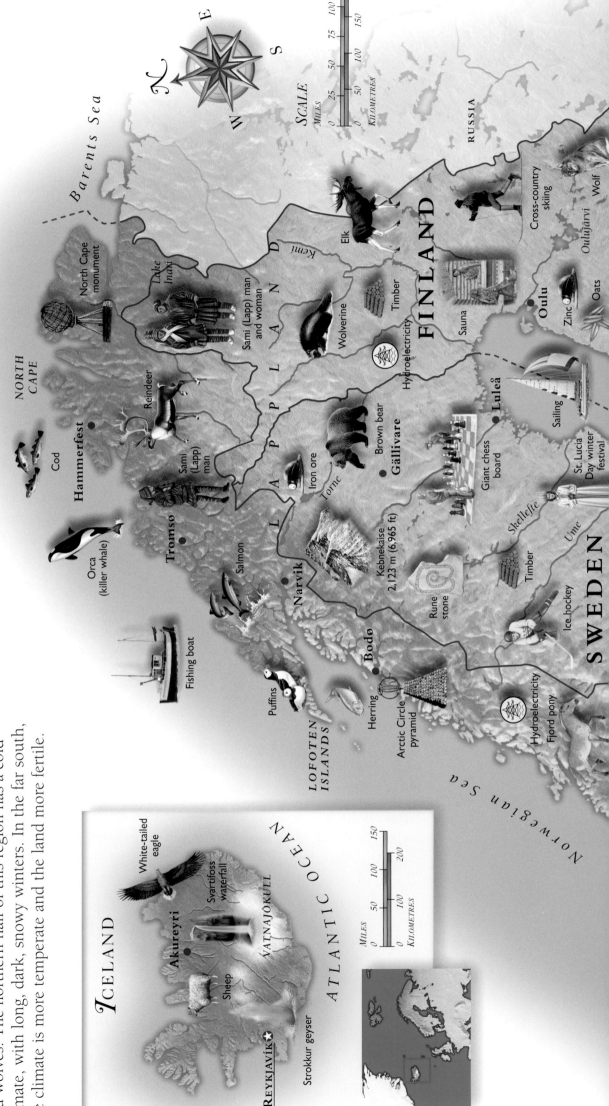

Barents Sea

North Cape monument

North Cape

NORTH CAPE

Kemi

Elk

Lake Inari

FINLAND

Sami (Lapp) man and woman

Wolverine

Timber

Cross-country skiing

Oulujärvi

Wolf

RUSSIA

Sauna

Oulu

Zinc

Oats

Hydroelectricity

Reindeer

Hammerfest

Cod

Sami (Lapp) man

LAPLAND

Iron ore

Torne

Brown bear

Gällivare

Luleå

Sailing

Tromsø

Giant chess board

St. Lucia Day winter festival

Salmon

Kebnekaise 2,123 m (6,965 ft)

Skellefte

Narvik

Rune stone

Timber

Ume

Bodø

Ice hockey

SWEDEN

Fishing boat

Puffins

LOFOTEN ISLANDS

Herring

Arctic Circle pyramid

Hydroelectricity

Fjord pony

Orca (killer whale)

Norwegian Sea

SCALE
MILES
KILOMETRES

N E S W

ICELAND

White-tailed eagle

Akureyri

Svartifoss waterfall

VATNAJÖKULL

ATLANTIC OCEAN

Sheep

REYKJAVIK ★

Strokkur geyser

MILES
KILOMETRES

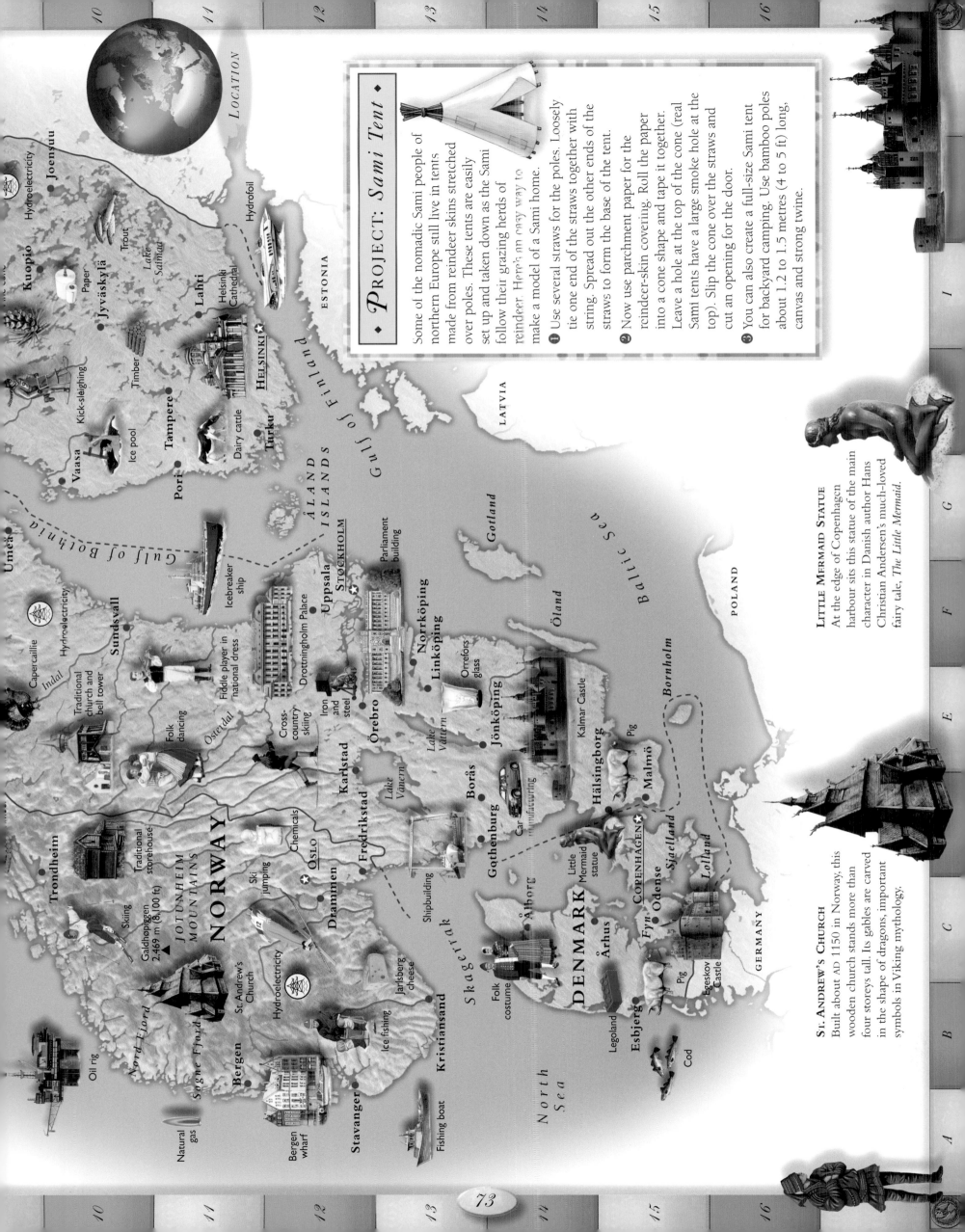

LOCATION

◆ PROJECT: Sami Tent ◆

Some of the nomadic Sami people of northern Europe still live in tents made from reindeer skins stretched over poles. These tents are easily set up and taken down as the Sami follow their grazing herds of reindeer. Here's an easy way to make a model of a Sami home.

❶ Use several straws for the poles. Loosely tie one end of the straws together with string. Spread out the other ends of the straws to form the base of the tent.

❷ Now use parchment paper for the reindeer-skin covering. Roll the paper into a cone shape and tape it together. Leave a hole at the top of the cone (real Sami tents have a large smoke hole at the top). Slip the cone over the straws and cut an opening for the door.

❸ You can also create a full-size Sami tent for backyard camping. Use bamboo poles about 1.2 to 1.5 metres (4 to 5 ft) long, canvas and strong twine.

LITTLE MERMAID STATUE
At the edge of Copenhagen harbour sits this statue of the main character in Danish author Hans Christian Andersen's much-loved fairy tale, *The Little Mermaid*.

ST. ANDREW'S CHURCH
Built about AD 1150 in Norway, this wooden church stands more than four storeys tall. Its gables are carved in the shape of dragons, important symbols in Viking mythology.

Kuopio
Joensuu
Hydroelectricity
Hydrofoil
Trout
Lake Saimaa
Paper
Jyväskylä
Lahti
Timber
Helsinki Cathedral
Kick-sleighing
ESTONIA
Vaasa
Ice pool
Tampere
Dairy cattle
Turku
HELSINKI ★
Pori
Gulf of Bothnia
Gulf of Finland
ÅLAND ISLANDS
LATVIA
Umeå
Icebreaker ship
STOCKHOLM ★
Uppsala
Parliament building
Gotland
Sundsvall
Hydroelectricity
Indal
Capercaillie
Drottningholm Palace
Fiddle player in national dress
Norrköping
Linköping
Baltic Sea
Öland
Traditional church and bell tower
Folk dancing
Österdal
Cross-country skiing
Iron and steel
Örebro
Lake Vättern
Orrefors glass
Jönköping
POLAND
Trondheim
Skiing
Traditional storehouse
Galdhøpiggen 2,469 m (8,100 ft)
JOTUNHEIM MOUNTAINS
NORWAY
Ski jumping
Karlstad
Lake Vänern
Borås
Kalmar Castle
Hälsingborg
Pig
Bornholm
Malmö
Chemicals
OSLO ★
Fredrikstad
Gothenburg
Car manufacturing
Sjælland
COPENHAGEN ★
Lolland
Drammen
Shipbuilding
Skagerrak
Ålborg
Little Mermaid statue
Odense
Fyn
DENMARK
Bergen
St. Andrew's Church
Jarlsberg cheese
Hydroelectricity
Kristiansand
Ice fishing
Århus
Pig
Esbjerg
GERMANY
Stavanger
Natural gas
Bergen wharf
Folk costume
Legoland
Eggeskov Castle
Cod
North Sea
Oil rig
Nord Fjord
Sogne Fjord
Fishing boat

Asia

THE WORLD'S BIGGEST CONTINENT, Asia stretches almost half-way around the globe and covers one-third of the Earth's land mass. It has the world's tallest mountains, the world's largest lake and the world's lowest point on land. It was the birthplace of many great religions and important civilizations, and is now home to 60 per cent of the people on Earth. Most Asians live in the east and south, where the climate is warm and wet and there are large areas of forest, fertile plains and hundreds of tropical islands. Deserts and barren mountain ranges dominate the south-west and centre of the continent. To the north, the grasslands, or steppes, of central Asia give way to the immense coniferous forests of Russia. A belt of freezing tundra extends along the continent's north coast. Russia is the world's largest country by area, but China has the world's largest population.

Continent Facts

Regional land area: 44,391,162 sq. km (17,139,445 sq. mi), excluding European Russia
Regional population: 3,516,177,000, excluding European Russia
Independent countries: Afghanistan, Armenia, Azerbaijan, Bahrain, Bangladesh, Bhutan, Brunei, Cambodia, China, Cyprus, Georgia. India, Indonesia, Iran, Iraq, Israel, Japan, Jordan, Kazakstan, Kuwait, Kyrgyzstan, Laos, Lebanon, Malaysia, Maldives, Mongolia, Myanmar (Burma), Nepal, North Korea, Oman, Pakistan, Philippines, Qatar, Russia, Saudi Arabia, Singapore, South Korea, Sri Lanka, Syria, Taiwan, Tajikistan, Thailand, Turkey, Turkmenistan, United Arab Emirates, Uzbekistan, Vietnam, Yemen

World Records

WORLD'S HIGHEST MOUNTAIN
MOUNT EVEREST, CHINA-NEPAL, 8,848 M (29,028 FT)

WORLD'S LOWEST POINT ON LAND
DEAD SEA, ISRAEL-JORDAN, 400 M (1,300 FT) BELOW SEA LEVEL

WORLD'S LARGEST LAKE BY AREA
CASPIAN SEA, CENTRAL EURASIA, 371,800 SQ. KM (143,550 SQ. MI)

WORLD'S OLDEST, DEEPEST AND LARGEST (BY VOLUME) LAKE
LAKE BAIKAL, RUSSIA, 25 MILLION YEARS OLD; 1,637 M (5,371 FT) DEEP; 23,000 CUBIC KM (5,500 CUBIC MI) OF WATER

WORLD'S LARGEST COUNTRY BY AREA
RUSSIA, 17,075,383 SQ. KM (6,592,812 SQ. MI)

WORLD'S LARGEST COUNTRY BY POPULATION
CHINA, POPULATION 1,203,097,000

WORLD'S LARGEST CITY BY POPULATION
TOKYO, JAPAN, POPULATION 26,800,000

WORLD'S LONGEST WALL
GREAT WALL OF CHINA, 3,460 KM (2,150 MI)

WORLD'S LONGEST RAILWAY LINE
TRANS-SIBERIAN, RUSSIA, 9,297 KM (5,777 MI)

Continent Records

LONGEST RIVER
CHANG (YANGTZE), 6,380 KM (3,960 MI)

Major Mountains and Rivers

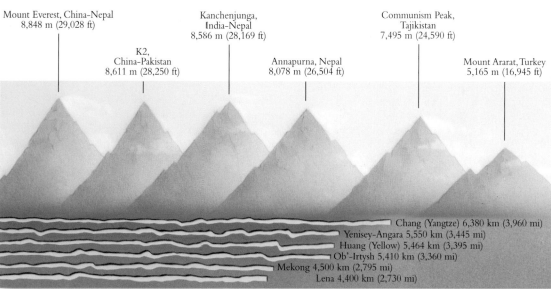

Mount Everest, China-Nepal 8,848 m (29,028 ft)
K2, China-Pakistan 8,611 m (28,250 ft)
Kanchenjunga, India-Nepal 8,586 m (28,169 ft)
Annapurna, Nepal 8,078 m (26,504 ft)
Communism Peak, Tajikistan 7,495 m (24,590 ft)
Mount Ararat, Turkey 5,165 m (16,945 ft)

Chang (Yangtze) 6,380 km (3,960 mi)
Yenisey-Angara 5,550 km (3,445 mi)
Huang (Yellow) 5,464 km (3,395 mi)
Ob'-Irtysh 5,410 km (3,360 mi)
Mekong 4,500 km (2,795 mi)
Lena 4,400 km (2,730 mi)

Political Map

RUSSIA
KAZAKSTAN
MONGOLIA
GEORGIA
UZBEKISTAN KYRGYZSTAN
TURKMENISTAN
TURKEY
TAJIKISTAN
CHINA
NORTH KOREA
CYPRUS
SYRIA
SOUTH KOREA
JAPAN
AFGHANISTAN
IRAQ
JORDAN
IRAN
PAKISTAN
NEPAL
TAIWAN
SAUDI ARABIA
OMAN
INDIA
MYANMAR (BURMA)
YEMEN
LAOS
THAILAND
PHILIPPINES
CAMBODIA
VIETNAM
SRI LANKA
MALDIVES
MALAYSIA
INDONESIA

Key to Numbered Countries

1 ARMENIA	7 QATAR
2 AZERBAIJAN	8 UNITED ARAB EMIRATES
3 LEBANON	9 BHUTAN
4 ISRAEL	10 BANGLADESH
5 KUWAIT	■ 11 SINGAPORE
■ 6 BAHRAIN	12 BRUNEI

AFRICA

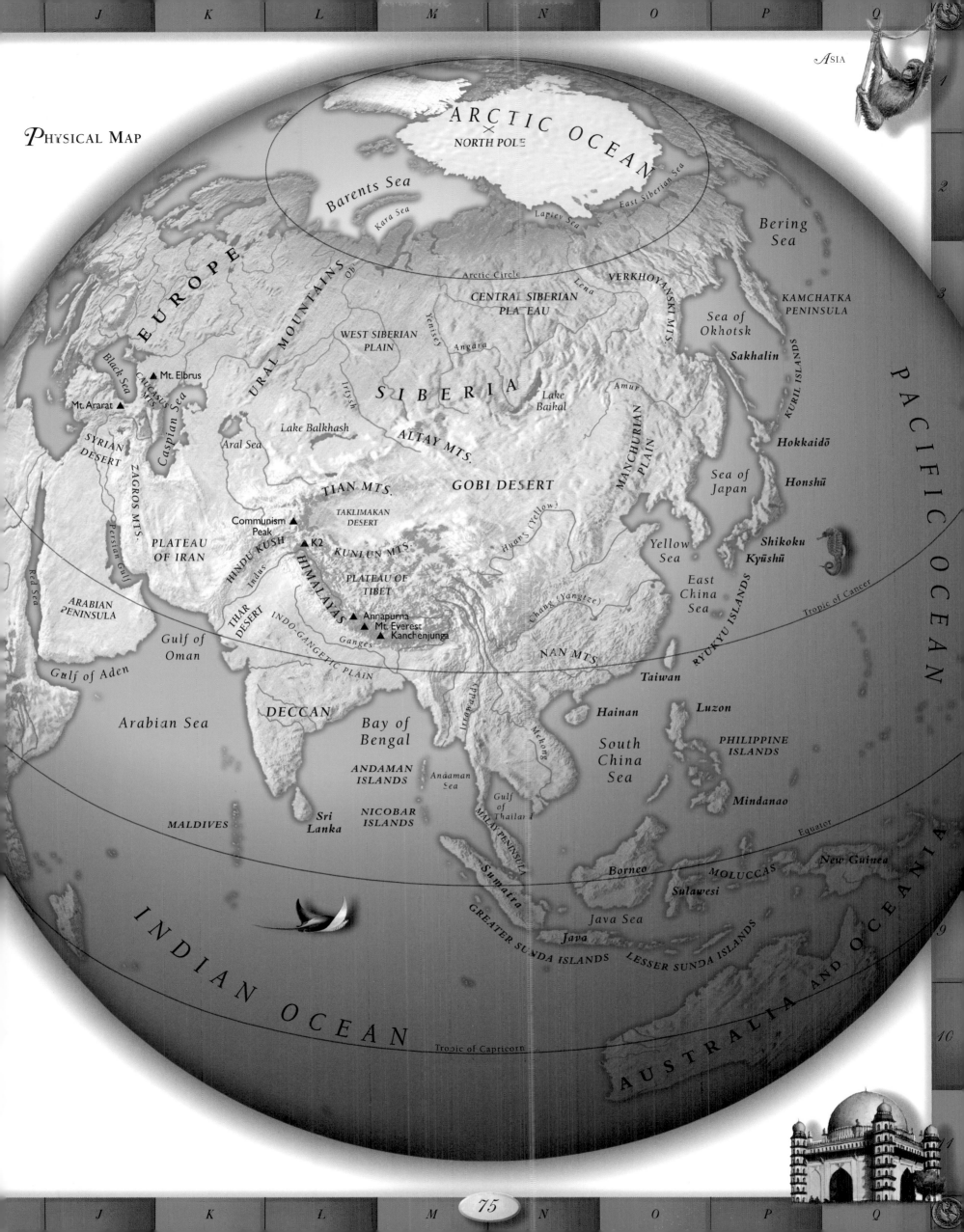

*A*SIA

PHYSICAL MAP

ARCTIC OCEAN
× NORTH POLE

Barents Sea

Kara Sea

East Siberian Sea

Laptev Sea

Bering Sea

EUROPE

URAL MOUNTAINS

Ob

Arctic Circle

Lena

VERKHOYANSKI MTS.

KAMCHATKA PENINSULA

CENTRAL SIBERIAN PLATEAU

Sea of Okhotsk

WEST SIBERIAN PLAIN

Yenisey

Angara

Sakhalin

KURIL ISLANDS

Black Sea

Mt. Elbrus ▲

CAUCASUS MTS.

Caspian Sea

SIBERIA

Amur

Lake Baikal

MANCHURIAN PLAIN

Hokkaidō

Mt. Ararat ▲

Aral Sea

Lake Balkhash

Irtysh

ALTAY MTS.

Honshū

SYRIAN DESERT

ZAGROS MTS.

TIAN MTS.

GOBI DESERT

Sea of Japan

Persian Gulf

PLATEAU OF IRAN

Communism Peak ▲

TAKLIMAKAN DESERT

Yellow Sea

Shikoku

Red Sea

HINDU KUSH

▲ K2

KUNLUN MTS.

Huang (Yellow)

Kyūshū

ARABIAN PENINSULA

Indus

HIMALAYAS

PLATEAU OF TIBET

East China Sea

RYUKYU ISLANDS

Tropic of Cancer

Gulf of Oman

THAR DESERT

▲ Annapurna
▲ Mt. Everest
▲ Kanchenjunga

Chang (Yangtze)

Gulf of Aden

INDO-GANGETIC PLAIN

Ganges

NAN MTS.

DECCAN

Arabian Sea

Bay of Bengal

Taiwan

Irrawaddy

Hainan

Luzon

South China Sea

PHILIPPINE ISLANDS

ANDAMAN ISLANDS

Andaman Sea

Mekong

MALDIVES

Sri Lanka

NICOBAR ISLANDS

MALAY PENINSULA

Gulf of Thailand

Mindanao

Equator

Sumatra

Borneo

MOLUCCAS

New Guinea

Sulawesi

Java Sea

GREATER SUNDA ISLANDS

Java

LESSER SUNDA ISLANDS

INDIAN OCEAN

PACIFIC OCEAN

AUSTRALIA AND OCEANIA

Tropic of Capricorn

Russia

RUSSIA IS THE LARGEST country in the world. It covers two-thirds of Asia and one-third of Europe, and is so wide that it has eleven time zones. When the citizens of St. Petersburg are getting ready for bed, the miners and reindeer herders who live in the remote far east are already starting their next day's work. Most of Russia has a cold climate, with mild to cool summers and cold to freezing winters. In the far north, where most of the land is tundra, winter temperatures can drop to –70°C (–94°F). South of the tundra, a wide band of coniferous woodland stretches almost all the way across the country. The Ural Mountains divide Russia into two regions. West of the Urals is European Russia, which has only one-quarter of the land, but four-fifths of the population, the largest industries and the most fertile farmland. East of the Urals, in Asia, is Siberia, a vast wilderness region that is bigger than the U.S.A. and western Europe combined.

In the southern part of this region near Mongolia lies Lake Baikal, the world's deepest lake, which holds one-fifth of the world's fresh water. Siberia is also rich in minerals, such as coal and oil. The Chukchi Peninsula in eastern Siberia is the most easterly point in Asia. It lies only 82 kilometres (50 mi) from North America. Before 1991, Russia was part of an even larger country – the Soviet Union – which also included 14 present-day countries in eastern Europe and central Eurasia.

RUSSIA
POPULATION: 149,909,000 ∗ CAPITAL: MOSCOW

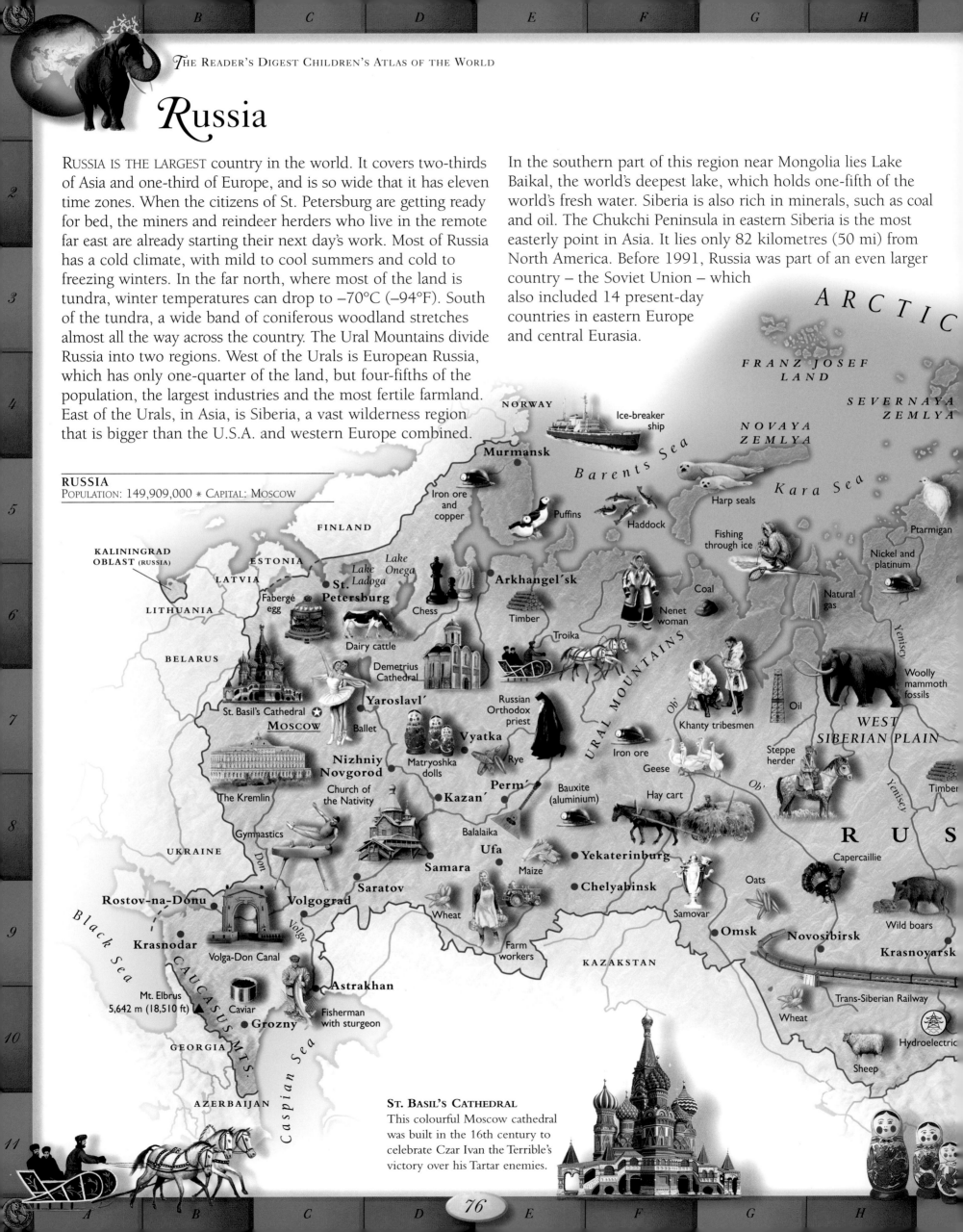

ST. BASIL'S CATHEDRAL
This colourful Moscow cathedral was built in the 16th century to celebrate Czar Ivan the Terrible's victory over his Tartar enemies.

Map labels: ARCTIC; FRANZ JOSEF LAND; SEVERNAYA ZEMLYA; NOVAYA ZEMLYA; Barents Sea; Kara Sea; NORWAY; Ice-breaker ship; Murmansk; Iron ore and copper; Puffins; Haddock; Harp seals; Fishing through ice; Ptarmigan; Nickel and platinum; Nenet woman; Coal; Natural gas; FINLAND; Lake Onega; Lake Ladoga; Chess; St. Petersburg; Fabergé egg; Arkhangel'sk; Timber; ESTONIA; LATVIA; LITHUANIA; KALININGRAD OBLAST (RUSSIA); Dairy cattle; Demetrius Cathedral; Troika; Oil; Woolly mammoth fossils; Yenisey; URAL MOUNTAINS; BELARUS; St. Basil's Cathedral; Ballet; Yaroslavl'; Russian Orthodox priest; Khanty tribesmen; WEST SIBERIAN PLAIN; MOSCOW; Vyatka; Ob'; Steppe herder; Nizhniy Novgorod; Matryoshka dolls; Rye; Iron ore; Geese; Ob'; Timber; The Kremlin; Church of the Nativity; Kazan'; Perm'; Bauxite (aluminium); Hay cart; Yenisey; Gymnastics; Balalaika; Ufa; Capercaillie; RUS; UKRAINE; Don; Samara; Maize; Yekaterinburg; Oats; Saratov; Chelyabinsk; Samovar; Wild boars; Rostov-na-Donu; Volgograd; Wheat; Omsk; Novosibirsk; Krasnoyarsk; Black Sea; Volga; Farm workers; KAZAKSTAN; Krasnodar; Volga-Don Canal; CAUCASUS MTS.; Mt. Elbrus 5,642 m (18,510 ft); Caviar; Astrakhan; Trans-Siberian Railway; Wheat; Grozny; Fisherman with sturgeon; Hydroelectric; GEORGIA; Sheep; Caspian Sea; AZERBAIJAN

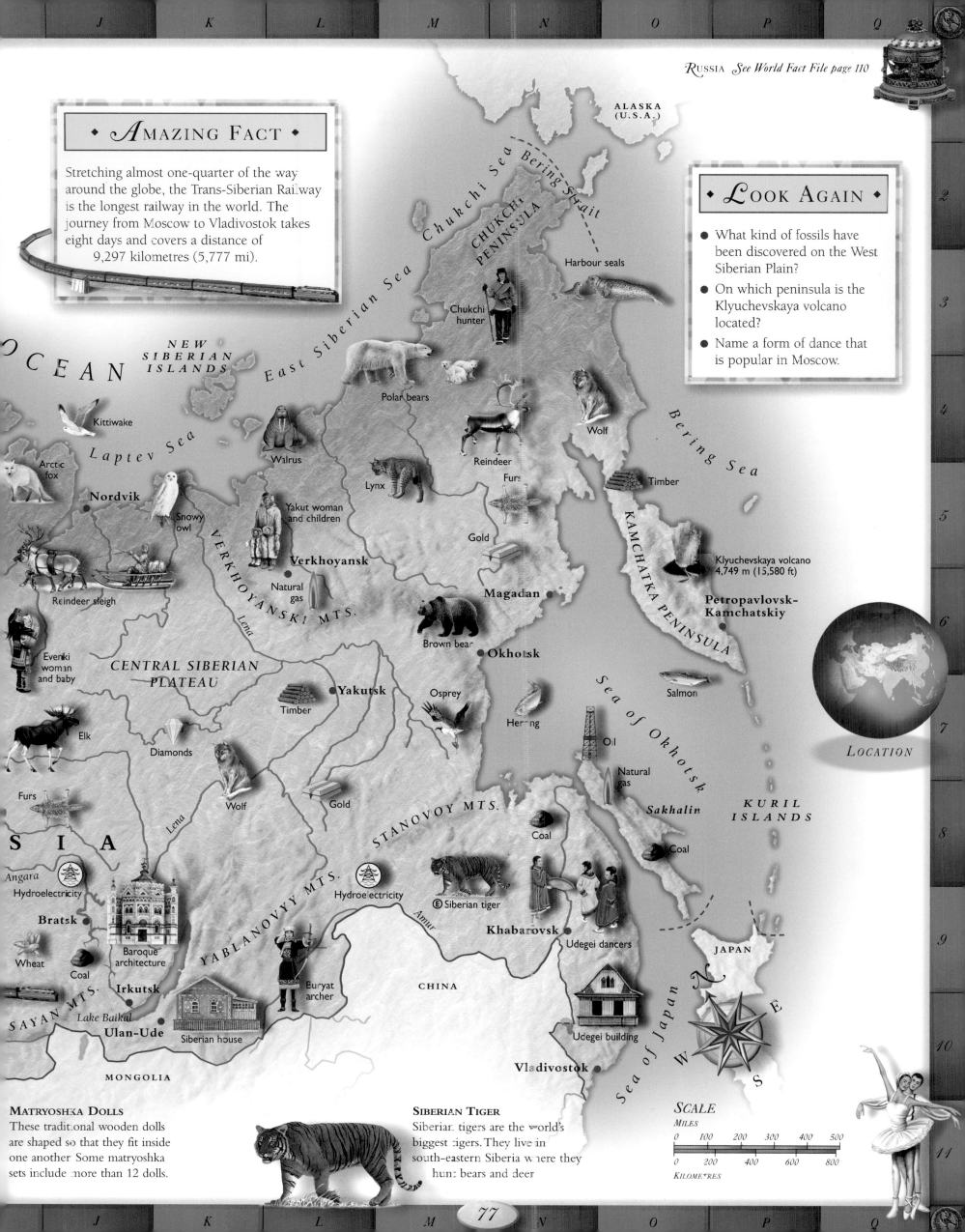

ALASKA (U.S.A.)

◆ AMAZING FACT ◆

Stretching almost one-quarter of the way around the globe, the Trans-Siberian Railway is the longest railway in the world. The journey from Moscow to Vladivostok takes eight days and covers a distance of 9,297 kilometres (5,777 mi).

◆ LOOK AGAIN ◆

- What kind of fossils have been discovered on the West Siberian Plain?
- On which peninsula is the Klyuchevskaya volcano located?
- Name a form of dance that is popular in Moscow.

Chukchi Sea

Bering Strait

CHUKCHI PENINSULA

Harbour seals

Chukchi hunter

East Siberian Sea

OCEAN

NEW SIBERIAN ISLANDS

Polar bears

Wolf

Bering Sea

Laptev Sea

Kittiwake

Walrus

Reindeer

Furs

Timber

Arctic fox

Snowy owl

Lynx

Gold

KAMCHATKA PENINSULA

Nordvik

Yakut woman and children

Klyuchevskaya volcano 4,749 m (15,580 ft)

VERKHOYANSKI MTS.

Verkhoyansk

Magadan

Petropavlovsk-Kamchatskiy

Reindeer sleigh

Natural gas

Lena

Brown bear

Eveniki woman and baby

CENTRAL SIBERIAN PLATEAU

Okhotsk

Salmon

Yakutsk

Osprey

Sea of Okhotsk

Timber

Elk

Herring

KURIL ISLANDS

Diamonds

Oil

Sakhalin

Furs

Lena

Natural gas

Wolf

Gold

STANOVOY MTS.

Coal

LOCATION

S I A

Coal

Angara

Hydroelectricity

YABLANOVYY MTS.

Hydroelectricity

Siberian tiger

Bratsk

Amur

Khabarovsk

JAPAN

Wheat

Baroque architecture

Buryat archer

Udegei dancers

Coal

Irkutsk

CHINA

Lake Baikal

Siberian house

Ulan-Ude

Udegei building

MONGOLIA

Vladivostok

Sea of Japan

MATRYOSHKA DOLLS

These traditional wooden dolls are shaped so that they fit inside one another. Some matryoshka sets include more than 12 dolls.

SIBERIAN TIGER

Siberian tigers are the world's biggest tigers. They live in south-eastern Siberia where they hunt bears and deer.

SCALE
MILES
0   100   200   300   400   500

0   200   400   600   800
KILOMETRES

Central Eurasia

EURASIA IS THE LAND MASS that contains the continents of both Europe and Asia. In central Eurasia, these two continents are separated by the narrow Bosporus strait in north-east Turkey. Central Eurasia is a dry region. Turkey's interior is hilly and barren, but its fertile coastal regions produce tea, tobacco and the world's largest crops of hazelnuts and raisins. South of Turkey lies the island of Cyprus, which is home to people of Turkish and Greek descent. Beyond Turkey's eastern border, the countries of Georgia, Armenia and Azerbaijan are flanked by

the massive Caucasus mountains. These countries are rich in minerals: at one time, Baku, the capital of Azerbaijan, supplied half of the world's oil. Across the Caspian Sea, deserts cover most of Turkmenistan, Uzbekistan and Kazakstan. Ancient trade routes between China and Europe passed through these lands, linking cities such as Samarquand and Tashkent. In the north, the desert merges with the Kirgiz Steppe, a vast grassland; in the south-east, the Tian Shan mountains cover most of Kyrgyzstan and Tajikistan. Many of central Eurasia's rivers are diverted to irrigate crops. This has lowered the levels of some lakes. The Aral Sea, once the world's fourth-largest lake, has shrunk to half its former size, stranding fishing villages and boats more than 30 kilometres (20 mi) from the shore.

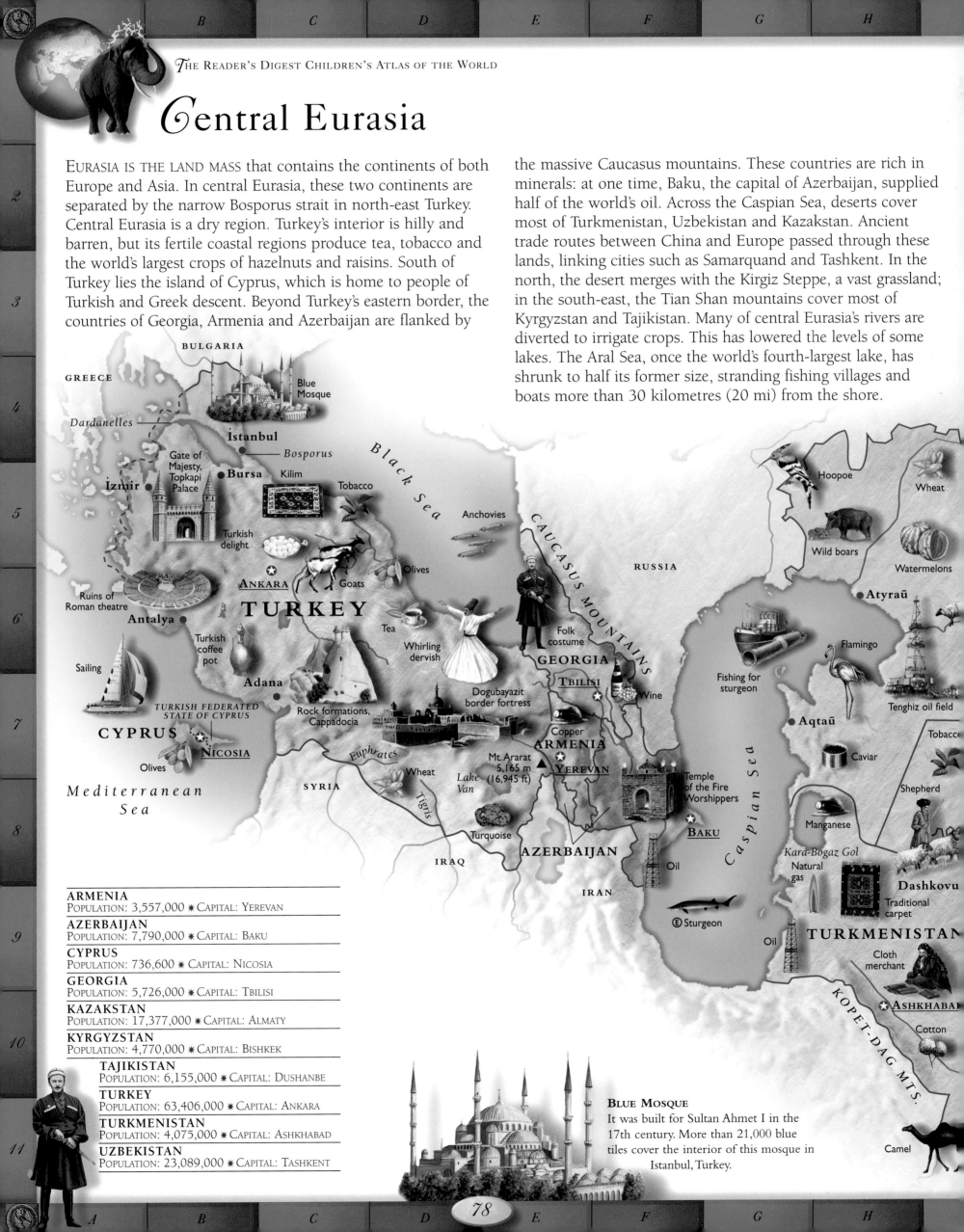

ARMENIA
POPULATION: 3,557,000 ✳ CAPITAL: YEREVAN

AZERBAIJAN
POPULATION: 7,790,000 ✳ CAPITAL: BAKU

CYPRUS
POPULATION: 736,600 ✳ CAPITAL: NICOSIA

GEORGIA
POPULATION: 5,726,000 ✳ CAPITAL: TBILISI

KAZAKSTAN
POPULATION: 17,377,000 ✳ CAPITAL: ALMATY

KYRGYZSTAN
POPULATION: 4,770,000 ✳ CAPITAL: BISHKEK

TAJIKISTAN
POPULATION: 6,155,000 ✳ CAPITAL: DUSHANBE

TURKEY
POPULATION: 63,406,000 ✳ CAPITAL: ANKARA

TURKMENISTAN
POPULATION: 4,075,000 ✳ CAPITAL: ASHKHABAD

UZBEKISTAN
POPULATION: 23,089,000 ✳ CAPITAL: TASHKENT

BLUE MOSQUE
It was built for Sultan Ahmet I in the 17th century. More than 21,000 blue tiles cover the interior of this mosque in Istanbul, Turkey.

◆ AMAZING FACT ◆

In Cappadocia in central Turkey, an eerie landscape of strange rock formations has been created by wind and water erosion. Early Christians made homes and churches inside caves cut into the rock. Some of these caves are still in use today.

◆ PROJECT: *Kilim Weaving* ◆

A kilim is a flat, woven rug traditionally made in Turkey. To make a simple kilim, you will first need to make a loom.

❶ Cut notches into the corners of a rectangular piece of cardboard. Tie a length of string to the left-hand notch and then wrap it around the cardboard, moving from left to right and leaving about one centimetre (½ in) between strings. Tie the string off on the right-hand notch.

❷ Thread wool on a darning needle and weave it under and then over the strings. If you begin the first row weaving under, begin the second

row weaving over, and so on. When you add a new piece of wool, tie it to the old piece. As you weave, push the rows tightly together.

❸ When the loom is full, turn it over so that it is face down and cut the two middle strings. Tie them together at the top and bottom edges of the weaving. Repeat with the rest of the strings.

❹ When all the strings have been cut and tied, remove the weaving from the loom. Trim the ends of the tied-off strings to make a fringe for your kilim.

Step 1 Step 2 Step 3

SNOW LEOPARD
Living high in the mountains, the snow leopard needs strong paws for rock climbing and long, thick fur to keep warm.

LOCATION

KAZAKSTAN

KIRGIZ STEPPE

UZBEKISTAN

KYRGYZSTAN

TAJIKISTAN

AFGHANISTAN

RUSSIA

CHINA

SCALE

BAYKONUR COSMODROME
Formerly a Soviet Union space centre, Baykonur is now leased from Kazakstan by Russia for use as its main space shuttle and rocket launching site.

The Middle East

THE MIDDLE EAST IS A LAND of ancient cities and vast deserts. It is home to some of the world's oldest civilizations and was the birthplace of three of the most widespread religions – Islam, Christianity and Judaism. Though there are narrow strips of fertile land on the densely populated Mediterranean coast, along the Tigris and Euphrates rivers in Iraq, and in the highlands of northern Iran and Yemen, most of this region is hot, dry and barren. Deserts extend southwards from Syria, Jordan and Israel, covering most of the Arabian Peninsula. Parts of this peninsula receive no rain for up to 10 years! Deserts also cover two-thirds of Iran. The enormous Dasht-e Kavīr salt desert in eastern Iran has almost no vegetation. Among its few inhabitants are gazelles that survive on tiny amounts of salty water. Over the centuries, the people of the Middle East have made skilful use of their limited water supplies. For thousands of years, the Tigris and Euphrates rivers have been used to water crops. Today, desalination plants on the shores of the Persian Gulf turn sea water into fresh water. The Gulf region holds half the world's reserves of oil and gas, and this has made some countries very wealthy. On average, people in the United Arab Emirates earn twice as much as people in the U.S.A. In contrast, Yemen, which has little oil, is one of the poorest countries in the world.

BAHRAIN
POPULATION: 575,900 ✳ CAPITAL: MANAMA

IRAN
POPULATION: 64,625,000 ✳ CAPITAL: TEHRAN

IRAQ
POPULATION: 20,644,000 ✳ CAPITAL: BAGHDAD

ISRAEL
POPULATION: 5,433,000 ✳ CAPITAL: JERUSALEM

JORDAN
POPULATION: 4,101,000 ✳ CAPITAL: AMMAN

KUWAIT
POPULATION: 1,817,000 ✳ CAPITAL: KUWAIT

LEBANON
POPULATION: 3,696,000 ✳ CAPITAL: BEIRUT

OMAN
POPULATION: 2,125,000 ✳ CAPITAL: MUSCAT

QATAR
POPULATION: 533,900 ✳ CAPITAL: DOHA

SAUDI ARABIA
POPULATION: 18,730,000 ✳ CAPITAL: RIYADH

SYRIA
POPULATION: 15,452,000 ✳ CAPITAL: DAMASCUS

UNITED ARAB EMIRATES
POPULATION: 2,925,000 ✳ CAPITAL: ABU DHABI

YEMEN
POPULATION: 14,728,000 ✳ CAPITAL: SANAA

✦ AMAZING FACT ✦

The Rub' al-Khali Desert, or Empty Quarter, in southern Saudi Arabia is the biggest sand desert in the world. It is as large as France and has no towns or villages. Its only inhabitants are nomadic Bedouin people.

DOME OF THE ROCK
This Muslim temple in Jerusalem backs on to the Western Wall, a site sacred to Jews. Inside the temple is a rock that some say marks the centre of the world.

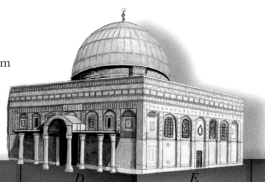

VEILED WOMAN
Traditionally, Muslim women must keep their face and hair hidden from strangers. Many wear a long black cloak and a veil or eye-mask.

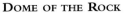

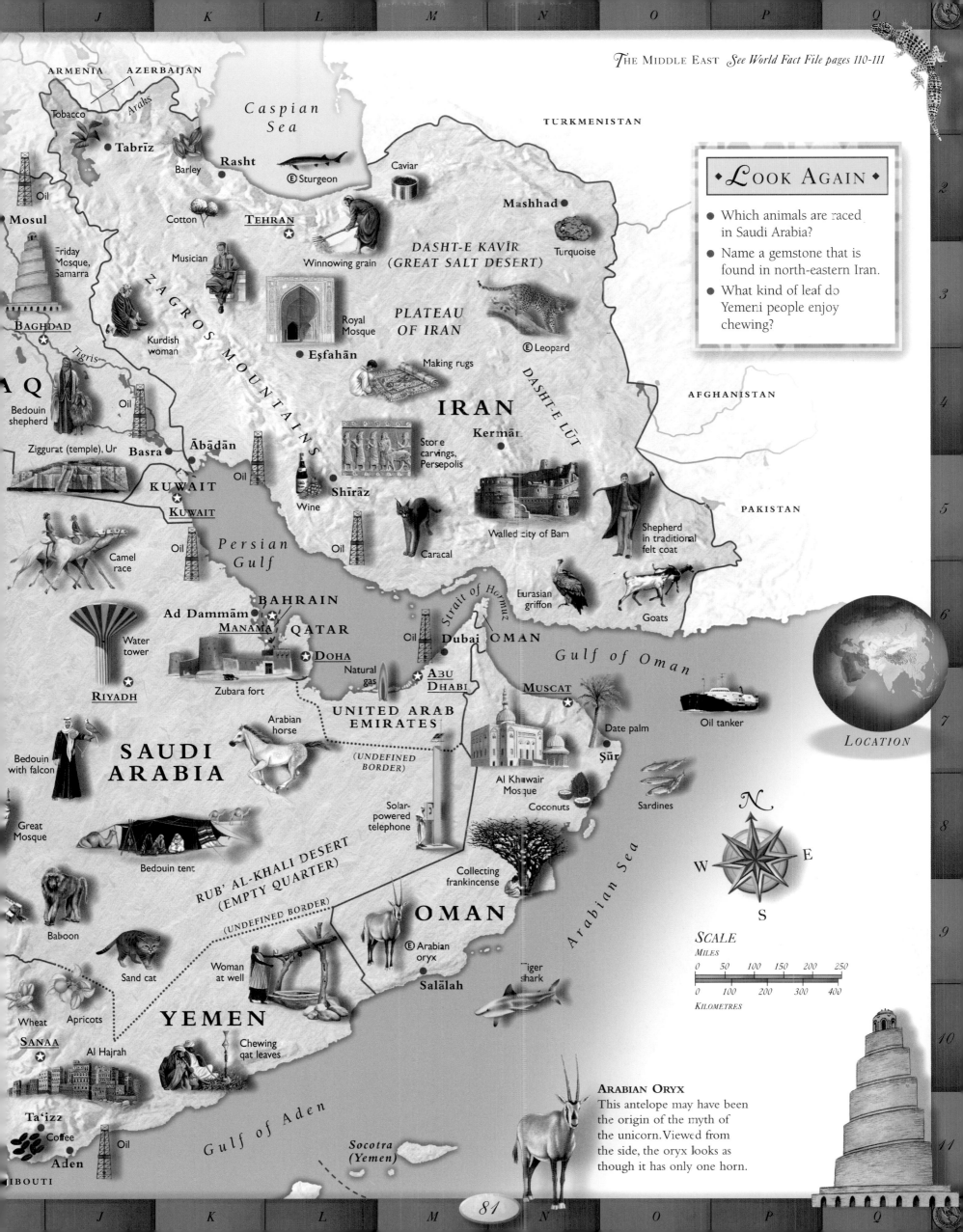

THE MIDDLE EAST *See World Fact File pages 110-111*

ARMENIA   AZERBAIJAN

Tobacco

Araks

Caspian Sea

TURKMENISTAN

Tabrīz

Barley

Rasht

Caviar

(E) Sturgeon

Oil

Mashhad

Mosul

Cotton

TEHRAN

Turquoise

Friday Mosque, Samarra

Musician

Winnowing grain

DASHT-E KAVĪR (GREAT SALT DESERT)

Royal Mosque

PLATEAU OF IRAN

BAGHDAD

Kurdish woman

ZAGROS MOUNTAINS

Eşfahān

Making rugs

IRAN

DASHT-E LŪT

Tigris

(E) Leopard

AFGHANISTAN

A Q

Bedouin shepherd

Oil

Kermān

Ziggurat (temple), Ur

Basra

Ābādān

Oil

Stone carvings, Persepolis

PAKISTAN

KUWAIT

Wine

Shīrāz

Walled city of Bam

KUWAIT

Oil

Oil

Caracal

Shepherd in traditional felt coat

Persian Gulf

Oil

Camel race

Oil

Eurasian griffon

Goats

BAHRAIN

Strait of Hormuz

Ad Dammām

Oil

Dubai

OMAN

MANAMA

QATAR

Water tower

DOHA

Natural gas

ABU DHABI

Gulf of Oman

MUSCAT

Zubara fort

UNITED ARAB EMIRATES

Al Khuwair Mosque

Date palm

Oil tanker

RIYADH

Arabian horse

(UNDEFINED BORDER)

Ṣūr

LOCATION

SAUDI ARABIA

Bedouin with falcon

Solar-powered telephone

Coconuts

Sardines

Great Mosque

Bedouin tent

RUB' AL-KHALI DESERT (EMPTY QUARTER)

Collecting frankincense

Arabian Sea

N

W   E

S

Baboon

(UNDEFINED BORDER)

OMAN

Sand cat

Woman at well

(E) Arabian oryx

Tiger shark

SCALE

MILES

0   50   100   150   200   250

Wheat

Apricots

YEMEN

Salālah

0   100   200   300   400

KILOMETRES

SANAA

Al Hajrah

Chewing qat leaves

ARABIAN ORYX

This antelope may have been the origin of the myth of the unicorn. Viewed from the side, the oryx looks as though it has only one horn.

Ta'izz

Coffee

Oil

Aden

Gulf of Aden

Socotra (Yemen)

DJIBOUTI

Southern Asia

SOUTHERN ASIA, OR THE Indian Subcontinent as it is also known, is separated from the rest of Asia by a series of massive mountain ranges. In the north-east, the mighty Himalayas, the highest mountains on Earth, tower over northern India and the two small kingdoms of Nepal and Bhutan. In the north-west, the dry, rugged Hindu Kush – the world's second-highest mountain range – spreads across central Afghanistan. South of these mountains, the land drops steeply to a wide, fertile plain that stretches from Pakistan to Bangladesh and covers most of northern India. Southern India consists of a large triangular plateau, the Deccan, fringed by narrow coastal plains. Just off the south-east coast lies the island of Sri Lanka.

Southern Asia has large areas of fertile land, valuable mineral reserves and expanding industries, but these resources barely support the region's huge population, and many people are very poor. One-fifth of the world's people live in southern Asia, and the population is growing rapidly. In India alone, almost 20 million babies are born each year. Four-fifths of southern Asians live in small villages, and most grow their own food. In India, Sri Lanka and Bangladesh, farmers rely on summer rains to water their crops. These rains are brought by winds known as monsoons. If too little rain falls, the crops fail. If too much rain falls, the crops, as well as buildings and people, can be washed away by devastating floods.

AFGHANISTAN
POPULATION: 21,252,000 ✦ CAPITAL: KABUL
BANGLADESH
POPULATION: 128,095,000 ✦ CAPITAL: DHAKA
BHUTAN
POPULATION: 1,781,000 ✦ CAPITAL: THIMPHU
INDIA
POPULATION: 936,546,000 ✦ CAPITAL: NEW DELHI
MALDIVES
POPULATION: 261,300 ✦ CAPITAL: MALE
NEPAL
POPULATION: 21,561,000 ✦ CAPITAL: KATHMANDU
PAKISTAN
POPULATION: 131,542,000 ✦ CAPITAL: ISLAMABAD
SRI LANKA
POPULATION: 18,343,000 ✦ CAPITAL: COLOMBO

✦ PROJECT: *Taj Mahal Tile* ✦

The Taj Mahal in India was built by Emperor Shah Jahan in memory of his beloved wife Mumtaz. Construction began in 1631, and it took 20,000 workers about 20 years to complete the building. It is covered in tiles of dazzling white marble. Each tile is carved with floral designs and inlaid with semi-precious stones. You can make your own paper Taj Mahal tile.
❶ Draw floral patterns on a square of white paper.
❷ Colour the patterns and then use glitter, sequins, buttons or coloured foil to fashion the jewels in the Taj Mahal's intricate designs.

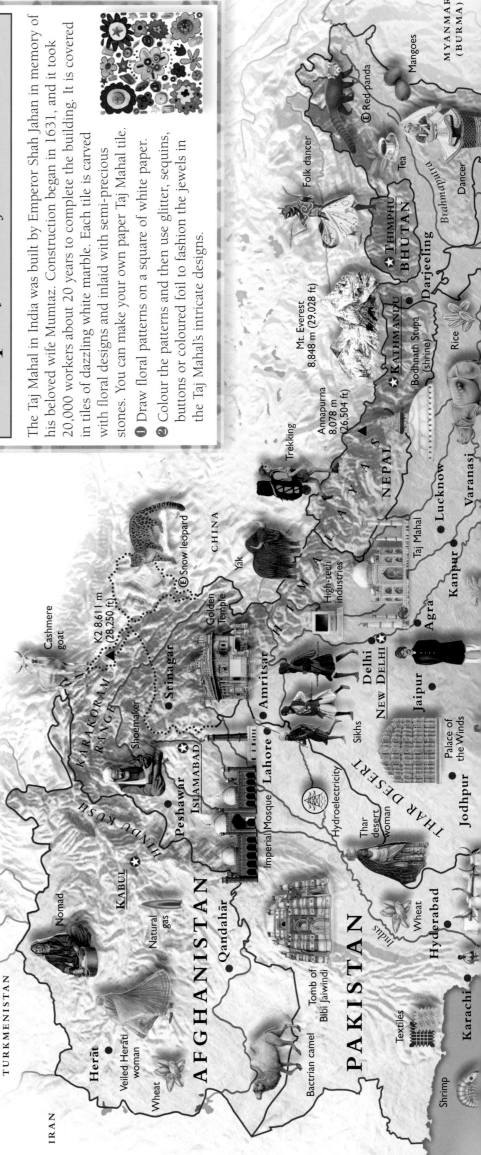

TURKMENISTAN

UZBEKISTAN

TAJIKISTAN

IRAN

Herāt
Veiled Herāti woman
Wheat
Bactrian camel
Nomad
Natural gas
Qandahār

AFGHANISTAN

KABUL

HINDU KUSH

Peshāwar
Imperial Mosque
Tomb of Bibi Jaiwindi
Textiles

PAKISTAN

ISLAMABAD
Lahore
Hydroelectricity
Thar desert woman
THAR DESERT
Wheat
Hyderabad
Karachi
Shrimp

KARAKORAM RANGE
K2 8,611 m (28,250 ft)
Shoemaker
Cashmere goat
Srinagar
Golden Temple
Amritsar
Sikhs

CHINA

Snow leopard
High-tech industries
Yak
Jaipur
Palace of the Winds
Jodhpur

Delhi
NEW DELHI

HIMALAYA
Mt. Everest 8,848 m (29,028 ft)
Annapurna 8,078 m (26,504 ft)
Trekking
Trekking

NEPAL
KATHMANDU
Bodhnath Stupa (Shrine)

Red panda
Dancer
Folk dancer

THIMPHU
BHUTAN
Darjeeling
Tea

MYANMAR (BURMA)
Mangoes

Brahmaputra

Rice

Agra
Taj Mahal
Lucknow
Kanpur
Varanasi

Indus

LOCATION

Arabian Sea

BANGLADESH

DHAKA ★

(E) Ganges dolphin

Chittagong

Transporting jute

Washing in the Ganges

Calcutta

Iron and steel

(E) Garial

Bhubaneswar

Bay of Bengal

ANDAMAN ISLANDS

NICOBAR ISLANDS

Weasel shark

Cray fisherman

Mackerel

Snake charmer

Langur monkeys

Great Stupa (shrine)

Coal

Nagpur

Bhopal

Brahman

(E) Tiger

Spice seller

Hyderabad

Bharatnatyam temple dancer

High-tech industries

Madras

Fishermen on stilts

Jaipur City Palace guard

INDIA

Cobra and mongoose

Sitar

DECCAN

Cotton

Gol Gumbaz Mosque

Cotton

Bangalore

Meenakshi Temple

SRI LANKA

Tea

Sloth bear

Jaffna

Tea

Painted elephant

Zebu cow

Millet

Panaji

Planting rice

Cricket

Blue peacock

Cinnamon

COLOMBO ★

Gateway to India

Bombay

Cochin

Trivandrum

INDIAN OCEAN

Ahmadabad

Ploughing with cattle

Pangolin

Sardines

Fishing boat

Fishing boat

N
W E
S

SCALE
MILES
0 100 200 300
0 100 200 300 400 500
KILOMETRES

◆ AMAZING FACT ◆

The Himalayas were once under the sea! About 40 million years ago the Indian land mass collided with Eurasia, pushing rocks up from the sea floor to form this vast mountain range. Fossilized seashells have been found on many Himalayan peaks.

MALDIVES

Coconut palm

MALE ★

Tourism

Magnificent frigate bird

MILES
0 100 200 300
0 200 400
KILOMETRES

FOLK DANCER

In Bhutan, dancers taking part in religious festivals wear ornate silk costumes and masks to represent gods and spirits.

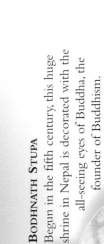

BODHNATH STUPA

Begun in the fifth century, this huge shrine in Nepal is decorated with the all-seeing eyes of Buddha, the founder of Buddhism.

PAINTED ELEPHANT

During religious processions in India, elephants are painted and then draped in colourful silks and sparkling jewels.

South-east Asia

SOUTH-EAST ASIA IS MADE UP OF a mainland peninsula and more than 20,000 islands. Throughout this hot, humid region, rugged mountains rise steeply from wide river basins and coastal plains once covered in dense rainforests. Most people live in the river valleys or near the coast, where they fish and grow food. Rice is the most important crop. On the plains, it is planted in wide, flooded fields called rice paddies. On hills and mountains, rice is grown on terraces – narrow strips of land that cover the slopes like giant staircases. In recent years, many South-east Asians have moved from the countryside to cities in search of work. Bangkok, Ho Chi Minh City, Manila and Jakarta are now among the most crowded and fastest-growing cities in the world. South-east Asia has many natural resources. Malaysia is the world's leading exporter of tin, Myanmar supplies most of the world's rubies, and oil has made Brunei one of the world's richest countries. Timber is the most widespread resource, and the region's rainforests supply more than three-quarters of the world's tropical hardwoods. But so many trees are being chopped down that several countries could soon run out of forest, and many animal and plant species are now endangered. Some countries restrict logging activities and have turned large areas of forest into magnificent national parks.

BRUNEI
POPULATION: 292,300 ∗ CAPITAL: BANDAR SERI BEGAWAN

CAMBODIA
POPULATION: 10,561,000 ∗ CAPITAL: PHNOM PENH

INDONESIA
POPULATION: 203,584,000 ∗ CAPITAL: JAKARTA

LAOS
POPULATION: 4,837,000 ∗ CAPITAL: VIENTIANE

MALAYSIA
POPULATION: 19,724,000 ∗ CAPITAL: KUALA LUMPUR

MYANMAR (BURMA)
POPULATION: 45,104,000 ∗ CAPITAL: YANGON (RANGOON)

PHILIPPINES
POPULATION: 73,266,000 ∗ CAPITAL: MANILA

SINGAPORE
POPULATION: 2,890,000 ∗ CAPITAL: SINGAPORE

THAILAND
POPULATION: 60,271,000 ∗ CAPITAL: BANGKOK

VIETNAM
POPULATION: 74,393,000 ∗ CAPITAL: HANOI

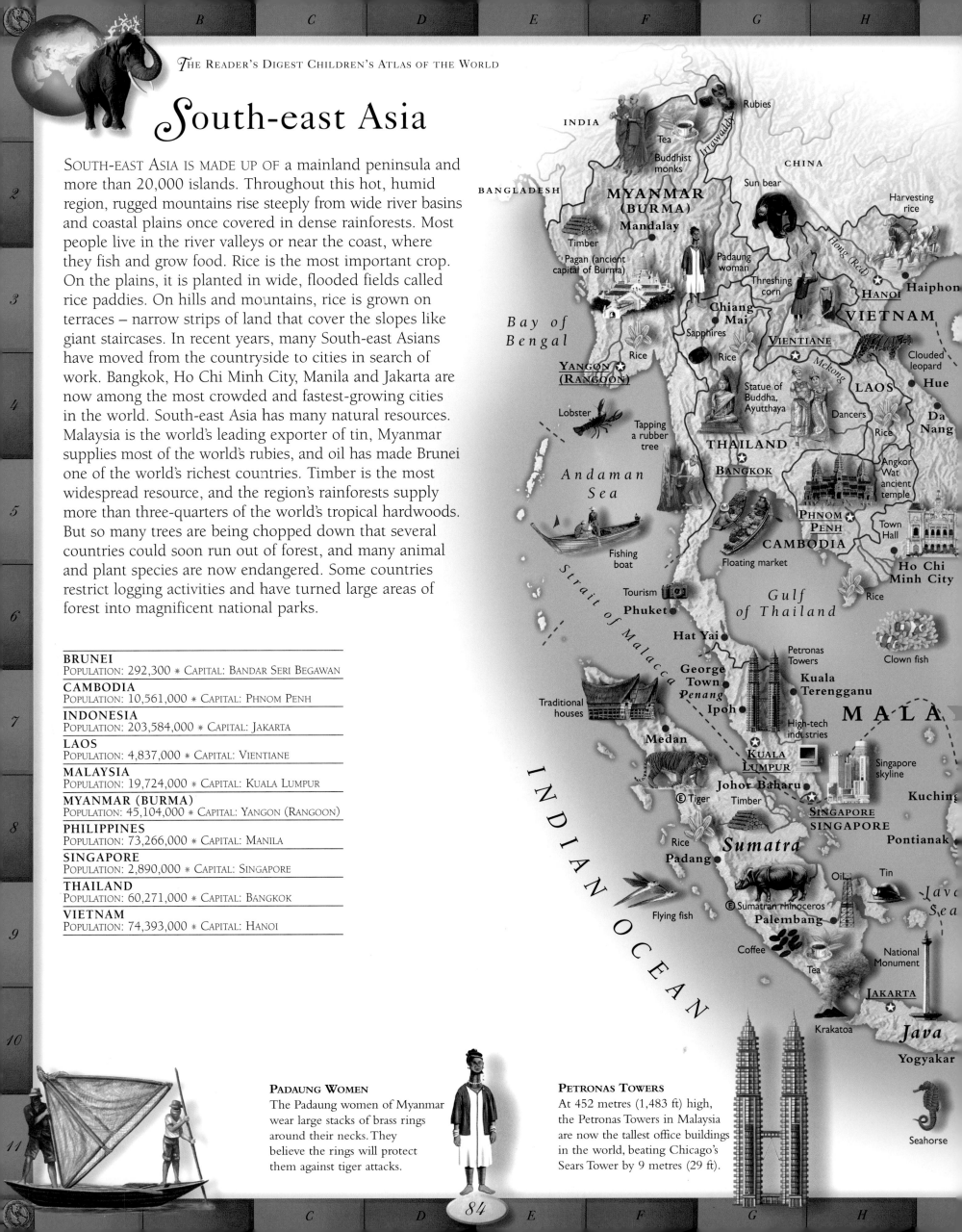

PADAUNG WOMEN
The Padaung women of Myanmar wear large stacks of brass rings around their necks. They believe the rings will protect them against tiger attacks.

PETRONAS TOWERS
At 452 metres (1,483 ft) high, the Petronas Towers in Malaysia are now the tallest office buildings in the world, beating Chicago's Sears Tower by 9 metres (29 ft).

N
W E
S

See World Fact File pages 112–113

• LOOK AGAIN •

- In which country could you shop at a floating market?
- Name a weapon used by hunters in Malaysia.
- What kind of dragon lives on an island in Indonesia?

SCALE
MILES
0 100 200 300 400
0 150 300 450 600
KILOMETRES

• PROJECT: *Erupting Volcano* •

South-east Asia has more active volcanoes than any other part of the world. The island of Java alone has 50 volcanoes that could erupt at any time. Here's a volcano that will erupt whenever you want it to.

❶ Use moist soil to model a mountain on a tray.

❷ Scoop out a hole from the top of the mountain and put in a container, such as the lid from a spray can.

❸ Pour about ¼ cup warm water into the container. Now stir in 1 tablespoon baking powder, a few drops of red food colouring and a few drops of washing-up liquid. Pour in ¼ cup vinegar and watch your volcano erupt.

Adding vinegar to the baking powder produces carbon dioxide gas. This causes pressure to build up until the volcano erupts, forcing lava suds out the top. This is similar to the pressure inside Earth's crust that causes a real volcano to erupt.

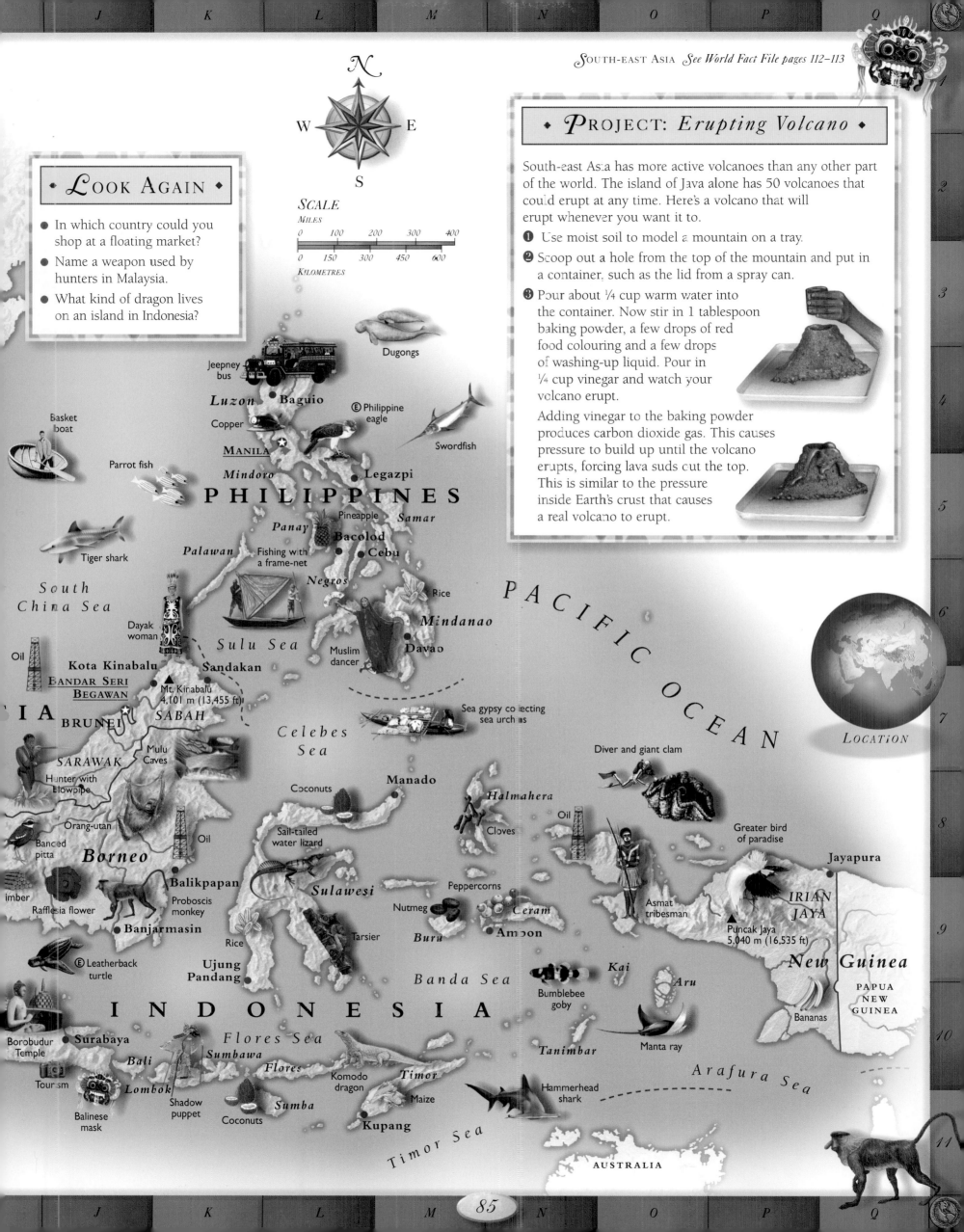

Dugongs
Jeepney bus
Luzon Baguio
Copper
ⓔ Philippine eagle
Basket boat
Manila
Parrot fish
Swordfish
Mindoro Legazpi
PHILIPPINES
Pineapple *Samar*
Panay Bacolod
Palawan Fishing with a frame-net Cebu
Tiger shark
Negros
Rice
South China Sea
Dayak woman
Mindanao
Oil *Sulu Sea* Muslim dancer Davao
Kota Kinabalu
BANDAR SERI BEGAWAN
Sandakan
▲ Mt. Kinabalu 4,101 m (13,455 ft)
BRUNEI **SABAH**
Celebes Sea
Sea gypsy collecting sea urchins
Mulu Caves
SARAWAK
Hunter with blowpipe
Diver and giant clam
Manado
Coconuts
Orang-utan
Halmahera
Banded pitta
Oil
Cloves
Borneo
Sail-tailed water lizard
Oil
Balikpapan
Greater bird of paradise
Raffia flower
Proboscis monkey
Sulawesi
Peppercorns
Asmat tribesman
Jayapura
Banjarmasin
Nutmeg
Ceram
Rice
Tarsier
Buru Ambon
IRIAN JAYA
timber
ⓔ Leatherback turtle
Ujung Pandang
▲ Puncak Jaya 5,040 m (16,535 ft)
New Guinea
Kai
INDONESIA
Banda Sea
Aru
Bumblebee goby
PAPUA NEW GUINEA
Borobudur Temple Surabaya
Flores Sea
Bananas
Tourism
Bali *Sumbawa*
Flores
Komodo dragon
Tanimbar
Manta ray
Arafura Sea
Balinese mask
Lombok
Shadow puppet
Sumba
Coconuts
Timor
Maize
Hammerhead shark
Kupang
Timor Sea
AUSTRALIA

PACIFIC OCEAN

LOCATION

Eastern Asia

EASTERN ASIA INCLUDES PART of the Asian mainland as well as several small islands. It is dominated by China, the third-largest (and most populous) country in the world. China is only slightly larger than the U.S.A., but it has more than four times as many people. Eighty per cent live in the eastern third of the country, where the climate is mild and wet, and most of the land is fertile. There are many large cities in eastern China, but most people live in villages where they raise pigs and chickens, and grow rice, wheat and vegetables. Western China is dry, rugged and sparsely populated. The south-western region – Tibet – is sometimes called the 'roof of the world' because it lies on the highest plateau on Earth and contains part of the tallest mountain range, the Himalayas. In the north, the barren Gobi Desert stretches into Mongolia, where many people are nomadic herders. On and around China's coast lie a number of rapidly developing countries and territories. South Korea and Taiwan have many thriving industries, including textile, car and electrical goods manufacturers. Macao, a tiny Portuguese colony on the south coast of China, is the world's most crowded place, with 22,150 people for every square kilometre (57,100 per sq. mi). Macao will revert to Chinese rule in 1999. Neighbouring Hong Kong, a former British colony which was given back to China in 1997, is the world's third-largest financial centre. Its modern, high-rise office buildings tower over one of Asia's busiest harbours.

CHINA
POPULATION: 1,203,097,000 ✳ CAPITAL: BEIJING
MONGOLIA
POPULATION: 2,494,000 ✳ CAPITAL: ULAANBAATAR
NORTH KOREA
POPULATION: 23,487,000 ✳ CAPITAL: P'YŎNGYANG
SOUTH KOREA
POPULATION: 45,554,000 ✳ CAPITAL: SEOUL
TAIWAN
POPULATION: 21,501,000 ✳ CAPITAL: TAIPEI

◆ AMAZING FACT ◆

The Great Wall of China stretches for 3,460 kilometres (2,150 mi) across northern China and is so large that astronauts can see it from space. It was built in the third century BC to keep out invaders from the north, then rebuilt and expanded in the 14th century AD.

KAZAKSTAN

KYRGYZSTAN

TAJIKISTAN

PAKISTAN

INDIA

NEPAL

Oil

Rice

Donkey cart

Ürümqi

TIAN SHAN

Playing the dotar

Coal

Camel train

Kashgar

Cotton

TAKLIMAKAN DESERT

Cotton

Apak Hoja Tomb

Jade

ALTUN MTS.

KUNLUN MTS.

K2 8,611 m
(28,250 ft)

PLATEAU OF TIBET

Snow leopard

Milking a yak

Tibetan monks

TIBET

HIMALAYAS

Potala Palace

Lhasa

Xiagazê

Gyangze

Mt. Everest
8,848 m
(29,028 ft)

BHUTAN

ALTAY

N

W E

S

SCALE
MILES

0   100   200   300

0   100   200   300   400   500

KILOMETRES

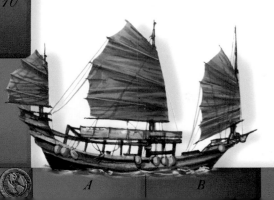

TERRACOTTA WARRIORS
Chinese emperor Qin Shi Huang had more than 6,000 life-sized clay warriors built to guard his body after his death.

GIANT PANDA
There are only 1,000 giant pandas left in the wild, and they all live in bamboo forests in central China, near Chengdu.

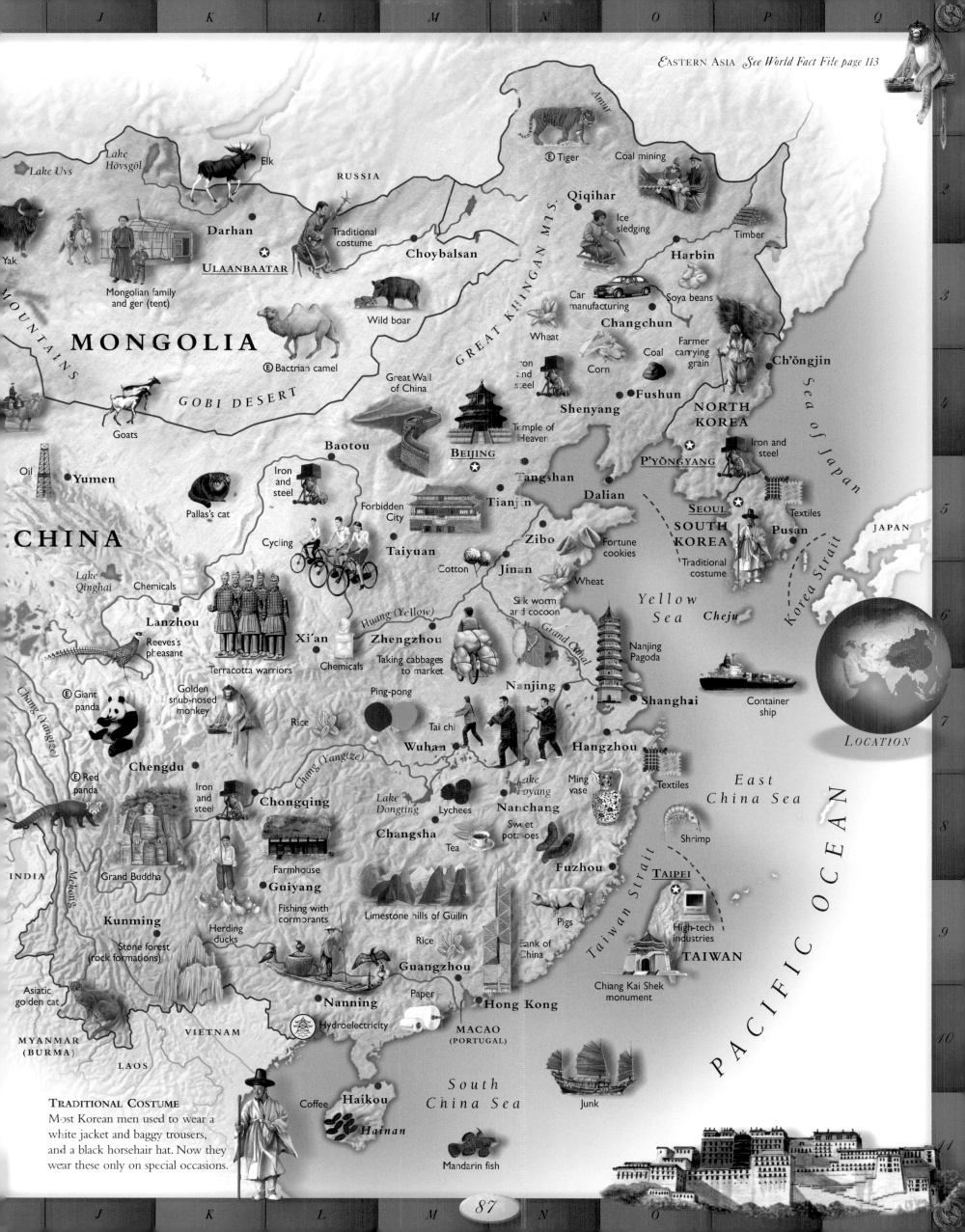

Lake Uvs
Lake Hövsgöl
Elk
Yak
RUSSIA

Tiger (E)
Coal mining
Qiqihar
Ice sledging
Timber
Harbin

Darhan
Traditional costume
Choybalsan
Car manufacturing
Soya beans

ULAANBAATAR
Changchun
Farmer carrying grain
Ch'ŏngjin

Mongolian family and ger (tent)
Wild boar
Wheat
Coal
Corn

MONGOLIA
Bactrian camel (E)
Great Wall of China
Iron and steel
Shenyang
Fushun
NORTH KOREA

GOBI DESERT
Goats
Baotou
Beijing
Temple of Heaven
Tangshan
P'YŎNGYANG
Iron and steel

Oil
Yumen
Pallas's cat
Iron and steel
Forbidden City
Tianjin
Dalian
SEOUL
SOUTH KOREA
Textiles

CHINA
Cycling
Taiyuan
Cotton
Zibo
Jinan
Fortune cookies
Wheat
Traditional costume
Pusan

Lake Qinghai
Chemicals
Terracotta warriors
Xi'an
Chemicals
Huang (Yellow)
Zhengzhou
Taking cabbages to market
Silk worm and cocoon
Grand Canal
Yellow Sea
Cheju

Lanzhou
Reeves's pheasant
Golden snub-nosed monkey
Rice
Ping-pong
Nanjing Pagoda

Giant panda (E)
Chengdu
Tai chi
Nanjing
Shanghai
Container ship

Red panda (E)
Iron and steel
Chongqing
Chang (Yangtze)
Lake Dongting
Lychees
Lake Poyang
Nanchang
Ming vase
Textiles
Hangzhou
East China Sea

Grand Buddha
Farmhouse
Guiyang
Changsha
Tea
Sweet potatoes
Fuzhou
Shrimp

INDIA
Kunming
Herding ducks
Fishing with cormorants
Limestone hills of Guilin
Rice
Bank of China
Pigs
TAIPEI
High-tech industries
TAIWAN

Stone forest (rock formations)
Asiatic golden cat
Guangzhou
Chiang Kai Shek monument

MYANMAR (BURMA)
VIETNAM
Nanning
Paper
Hydroelectricity
Hong Kong
MACAO (PORTUGAL)

LAOS
Coffee
Haikou
South China Sea
Junk

Hainan
Mandarin fish

Sea of Japan
Korea Strait
JAPAN

LOCATION

PACIFIC OCEAN

Taiwan Strait

TRADITIONAL COSTUME
Most Korean men used to wear a white jacket and baggy trousers, and a black horsehair hat. Now they wear these only on special occasions.

Japan

JAPAN CONSISTS OF A long chain of 4 main islands and more than 4,000 smaller islands that lies off the east coast of the Asian mainland. The northern half of Japan has a cold temperate climate with snowy winters and mild summers. In the south the weather is more tropical, with mild winters and a summer wet season. Most of the land is mountainous, and almost two-thirds is covered in forests. Earthquakes are common, and there are many active volcanoes. Three-quarters of the population live in cities, the largest of which are located on the large island of Honshū. Japan's capital, Tokyo, sprawls across more than 80 neighbouring towns, forming the biggest urban area in the world, and is home to almost 27 million people. So many workers commute to the city centre each day that railway stations employ guards known as 'pushers' to cram passengers into trains. Despite having little farmland, Japan manages to produce most of its food, including large quantities of rice. Fish is the country's most important resource, and the Japanese fishing fleet is the largest in the world. Although it has few other natural resources, Japan has become a major industrial power by importing raw materials and manufacturing high-quality goods. It is the world's top car manufacturer, has the world's foremost shipbuilding industry, and is a leading exporter of electronic goods.

JAPAN
POPULATION: 125,506,000 ✷ CAPITAL: TOKYO

◆ LOOK AGAIN ◆

● What kind of festival takes place in Sapporo?

● Name two kinds of shark found off the west coast of Honshū.

● Which famous mountain lies south-west of Japan's capital?

Map labels

RUSSIA
RUSSIA
RUSSIA
Salmon
Sea of Okhotsk
Dairy cattle
Ainu man
Kushiro
Coal
Brown bear
Timber
Great white shark
Pollock
Hokkaidō
Asahikawa
Rice
Sapporo snow festival
Sapporo
Mackerel
Shiogama festival
Sardines
Wakkanai
Skiing
Otaru
Hakodate
Tsugaru Strait
Dancer in traditional costume
Kokechi doll
Carp streamers
Sendai
Rebun
Rishiri
Halibut
Serows
Japanese crane
Macaques
Morioka
Sushi
Making chopsticks
Rice
Fukushima
JAPAN
Aomori
Apples
Akita
Japanese spider crab
Mako shark
Niigata
Shinano
Sado
Utsunomiya
Ninja
Sea of Japan

RYUKYU ISLANDS

East China Sea
OKINAWA ISLANDS
AMAMI ISLANDS
Rice
Long-tailed carpet shark
Karate
Tourism
Naha
Pineapple

MILES
0 25 50 75

KILOMETRES
0 50 100 150

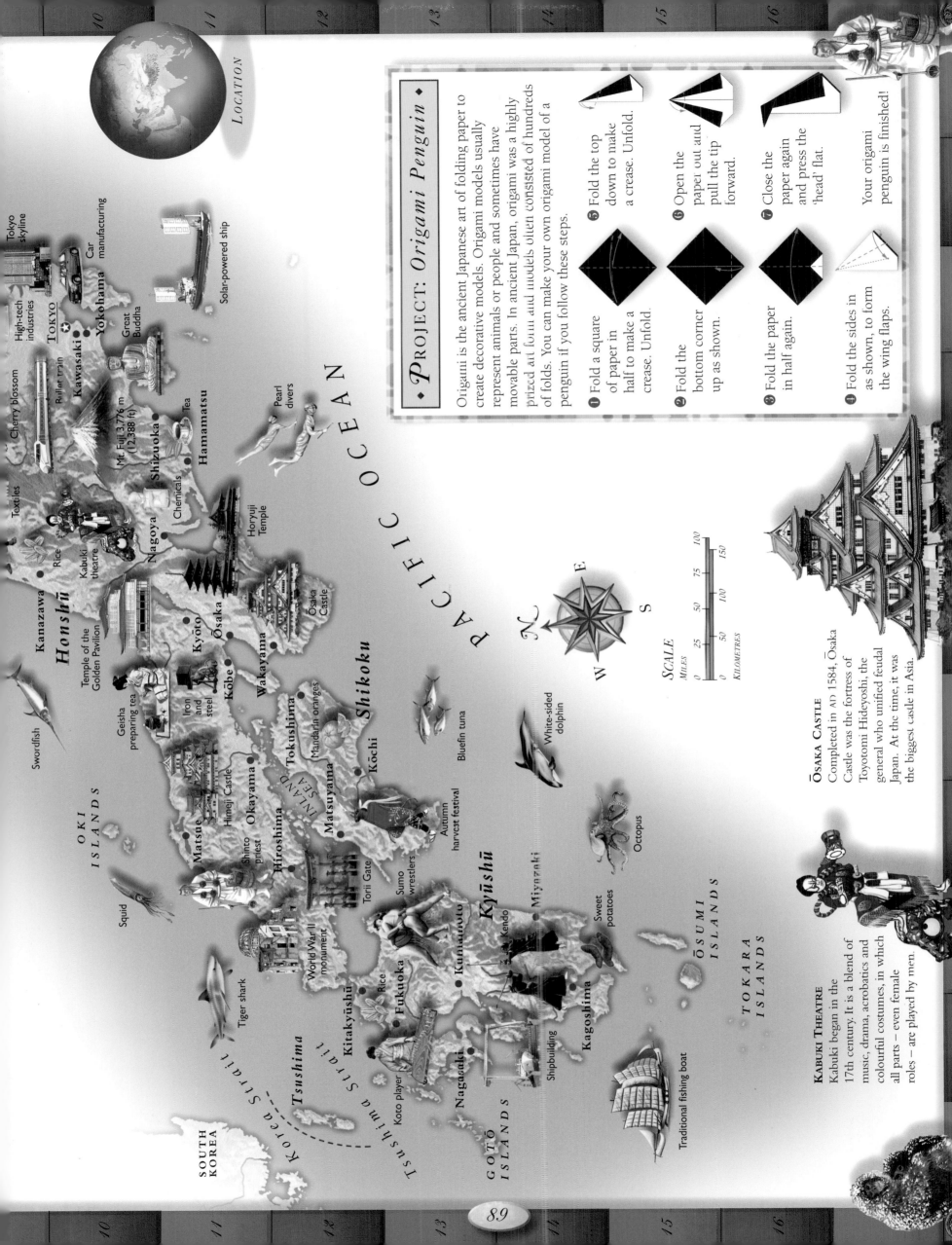

PROJECT: Origami Penguin

Origami is the ancient Japanese art of folding paper to create decorative models. Origami models usually represent animals or people and sometimes have movable parts. In ancient Japan, origami was a highly prized art form and models often consisted of hundreds of folds. You can make your own origami model of a penguin if you follow these steps.

1 Fold a square of paper in half to make a crease. Unfold.

2 Fold the bottom corner up as shown. Unfold.

3 Fold the paper in half again.

4 Fold the sides in as shown, to form the wing flaps.

5 Fold the top down to make a crease. Unfold.

6 Open the paper out and pull the tip forward.

7 Close the paper again and press the 'head' flat.

Your origami penguin is finished!

ŌSAKA CASTLE
Completed in AD 1584, Ōsaka Castle was the fortress of Toyotomi Hideyoshi, the general who unified feudal Japan. At the time, it was the biggest castle in Asia.

KABUKI THEATRE
Kabuki began in the 17th century. It is a blend of music, drama, acrobatics and colourful costumes, in which all parts — even female roles — are played by men.

PACIFIC OCEAN

LOCATION

SOUTH KOREA

Korea Strait

Tsushima Strait

Tsushima

GOTŌ ISLANDS

Kitakyūshū

Fukuoka

Nagasaki

Kumamoto

Kyūshū

Kagoshima

Miyazaki

ŌSUMI ISLANDS

TOKARA ISLANDS

Shikoku

Kōchi

Matsuyama

Tokushima

Shinto priest

World War II monument

Hiroshima

Okayama

Matsue

OKI ISLANDS

Himeji Castle

Kōbe

Wakayama

INLAND SEA

Ōsaka

Kyōto

Ōsaka Castle

Honshū

Kanazawa

Temple of the Golden Pavilion

Geisha preparing tea

Iron and steel

Nagoya

Hōryūji Temple

Shizuoka

Hamamatsu

Mt. Fuji 3,776 m (12,388 ft)

Tea

Chemicals

Kabuki theatre

Rice

Textiles

Cherry blossom

Bullet train

Kawasaki

Great Buddha

TOKYO

Yokohama

High-tech industries

Tokyo skyline

Car manufacturing

Solar-powered ship

Pearl divers

Swordfish

Squid

Tiger shark

Koto player

Traditional fishing boat

Shipbuilding

Sweet potatoes

Rice

Kendo

Sumo wrestlers

Torii Gate

Autumn harvest festival

Mandarin oranges

Bluefin tuna

Octopus

White-sided dolphin

SCALE

MILES
0   25   50   75   100

KILOMETRES
0   50   100   150

N E S W

89

Africa

THE WORLD'S SECOND-LARGEST CONTINENT, Africa is an enormous plateau surrounded by narrow coastal plains. A thick band of tropical rainforest covers much of the centre of the continent. To the north and south of this forest lie grasslands, known as savannahs, and deserts. The Sahara Desert, the biggest desert in the world, spans the entire width of northern Africa, from the Atlantic Ocean to the Red Sea, and covers an area almost as large as the U.S.A. The Kalahari and Namib deserts extend across much of the south-west. In the east, the Great Rift Valley, a series of valleys formed by cracks in Earth's crust, stretches from Syria, in Asia, to Mozambique. Africa includes 53 countries ranging from vast, mainly arid Sudan to the tiny tropical islands of the Seychelles. Arab peoples form the majority of the population in the north. The south's mainly black population is made up of hundreds of native tribes.

Major Mountains and Rivers

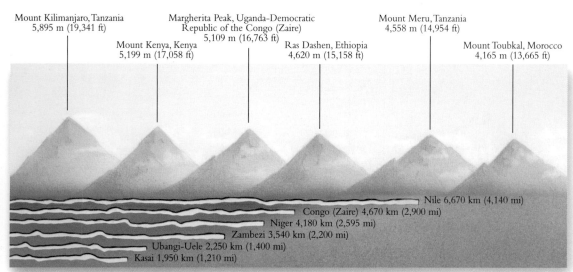

Mount Kilimanjaro, Tanzania 5,895 m (19,341 ft)

Margherita Peak, Uganda-Democratic Republic of the Congo (Zaire) 5,109 m (16,763 ft)

Mount Kenya, Kenya 5,199 m (17,058 ft)

Ras Dashen, Ethiopia 4,620 m (15,158 ft)

Mount Meru, Tanzania 4,558 m (14,954 ft)

Mount Toubkal, Morocco 4,165 m (13,665 ft)

Nile 6,670 km (4,140 mi)
Congo (Zaire) 4,670 km (2,900 mi)
Niger 4,180 km (2,595 mi)
Zambezi 3,540 km (2,200 mi)
Ubangi-Uele 2,250 km (1,400 mi)
Kasai 1,950 km (1,210 mi)

Political Map

MADEIRA (PORTUGAL)
MOROCCO
TUNISIA
CANARY ISLANDS (SPAIN)
WESTERN SAHARA
ALGERIA
LIBYA
EGYPT
MAURITANIA
MALI
NIGER
CHAD
SUDAN
ERITREA
CAPE VERDE ISLANDS
SENEGAL
GAMBIA
GUINEA-BISSAU
GUINEA
BURKINA FASO
BENIN
NIGERIA
DJIBOUTI
SIERRA LEONE
CÔTE D'IVOIRE
GHANA
TOGO
CENTRAL AFRICAN REPUBLIC
ETHIOPIA
LIBERIA
CAMEROON
SÃO TOMÉ and PRÍNCIPE
EQUATORIAL GUINEA
GABON
CONGO
DEMOCRATIC REPUBLIC OF THE CONGO (ZAIRE)
UGANDA
SOMALIA
KENYA
RWANDA
BURUNDI
ASCENSION (U.K.)
TANZANIA
SEYCHELLES
ANGOLA
COMOROS
ZAMBIA
MALAWI
MAYOTTE (FRANCE)
ST. HELENA (U.K.)
MOZAMBIQUE
MAURITIUS
NAMIBIA
ZIMBABWE
MADAGASCAR
RÉUNION (FRANCE)
BOTSWANA
SWAZILAND
LESOTHO
SOUTH AFRICA

Continent Facts

Regional land area: 30,354,852 sq. km (11,716,972 sq. mi)
Regional population: 720,702,000
Independent countries: Algeria, Angola, Benin, Botswana, Burkina Faso, Burundi, Cameroon, Cape Verde Islands, Central African Republic, Chad, Comoros, Congo, Côte d'Ivoire (Ivory Coast), Democratic Republic of the Congo (Zaire), Djibouti, Egypt, Equatorial Guinea, Eritrea, Ethiopia, Gabon, Gambia, Ghana, Guinea, Guinea-Bissau, Kenya, Lesotho, Liberia, Libya, Madagascar, Malawi, Mali, Mauritania, Mauritius, Morocco, Mozambique, Namibia, Niger, Nigeria, Rwanda, São Tomé and Príncipe, Senegal, Seychelles, Sierra Leone, Somalia, South Africa, Sudan, Swaziland, Tanzania, Togo, Tunisia, Uganda, Zambia, Zimbabwe

World Records

WORLD'S LARGEST DESERT
SAHARA DESERT, NORTHERN AFRICA, 9,269,000 SQ. KM (3,579,000 SQ. MI)

WORLD'S LONGEST RIVER
NILE RIVER, NORTHERN AFRICA, 6,670 KM (4,140 MI)

WORLD'S LARGEST ARTIFICIAL LAKE
LAKE VOLTA, GHANA, 8,482 SQ. KM (3,275 SQ. MI)

WORLD'S HIGHEST TEMPERATURE
AL-'AZĪZĪYA, LIBYA, SHADE TEMPERATURE OF 58°C (136°F) RECORDED ON SEPTEMBER 13, 1922

Continent Records

HIGHEST MOUNTAIN
KILIMANJARO, TANZANIA, 5,895 M (19,341 FT)

LOWEST POINT
LAKE ASSAL, DJIBOUTI, 152 M (500 FT) BELOW SEA LEVEL

LARGEST LAKE
LAKE VICTORIA, EAST AFRICA, 69,485 SQ. KM (26,828 SQ. MI)

LARGEST COUNTRY BY AREA
SUDAN, 2,505,825 SQ. KM (967,500 SQ. MI)

LARGEST COUNTRY BY POPULATION
NIGERIA, POPULATION 101,232,000

LARGEST CITY BY POPULATION
CAIRO, EGYPT, POPULATION 9,700,000

• Amazing Fact •

The huge volume of water that pours over Victoria Falls, on the border between Zambia and Zimbabwe, creates a deafening roar and a cloud of spray that can be seen from more than 32 kilometres (20 mi) away. Because of this, locals refer to the Falls as 'the smoke that thunders'.

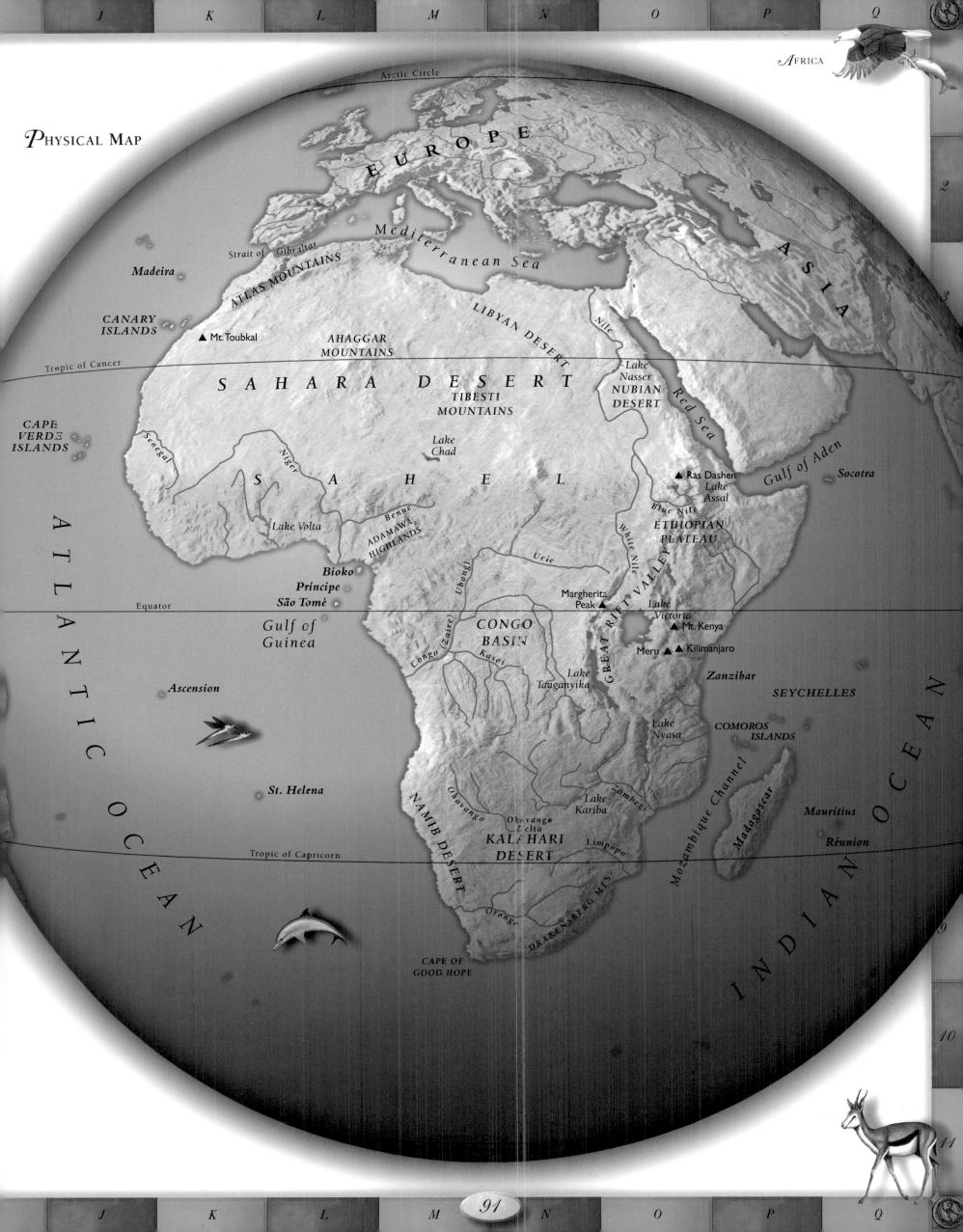

PHYSICAL MAP

E U R O P E

A S I A

Arctic Circle

Madeira

Strait of   Gibraltar

Mediterranean Sea

ATLAS MOUNTAINS

LIBYAN DESERT

CANARY ISLANDS

Nile

▲ Mt. Toubkal

AHAGGAR MOUNTAINS

Lake Nasser

NUBIAN DESERT

Red Sea

Tropic of Cancer

S A H A R A   D E S E R T

TIBESTI MOUNTAINS

CAPE VERDE ISLANDS

Senegal

Lake Chad

S   A   H   E   L

▲ Ras Dashen
Lake Assal

Gulf of Aden

Socotra

Niger

Benue

ADAMAWA HIGHLANDS

Blue Nile

ETHIOPIAN PLATEAU

Lake Volta

Ueie

White Nile

A
T
L
A
N
T
I
C

Ubangi

Bioko
Príncipe
São Tomé

Margherita Peak ▲

Lake Victoria

▲ Mt. Kenya

Equator

Gulf of Guinea

CONGO BASIN

GREAT RIFT VALLEY

Meru ▲▲ Kilimanjaro

Congo (Zaire)

Kasei

Lake Tanganyika

Zanzibar

SEYCHELLES

Ascension

Lake Nyasa

COMOROS ISLANDS

I
N
D
I
A
N

O
C
E
A
N

St. Helena

Zambezi

Lake Kariba

Mozambique Channel

Madagascar

Mauritius

O
C
E
A
N

Okavango

Okavango Delta

NAMIB DESERT

KALAHARI DESERT

Limpopo

Réunion

Tropic of Capricorn

Orange

DRAKENSBERG MTS.

CAPE OF GOOD HOPE

Northern Africa

THE SAHARA DESERT, the largest desert in the world, covers more than half of northern Africa. On its barren, rocky plains and rolling sand dunes, the heat is fierce, water is scarce and there is little land that can be farmed. Most of the people of the Sahara are nomads who move their camels, sheep and goats around the desert in search of water and pasture. The only usable fertile land north or east of the Sahara lies in the valleys of the Atlas Mountains and along the banks of the River Nile in Egypt. People have farmed the Nile valley for thousands of years, and it is now one of the most densely populated places on Earth. There is little farmland in Algeria and Libya, but both countries possess large oil and gas reserves which have helped them overcome serious poverty. South of the Sahara lies a wide belt of dry grasslands known as the Sahel. These grasslands suffer frequent droughts, and overfarming is turning some areas into desert. Further south, the Sahel gives way to the tropical rainforests of central Africa. Around the Gulf of Guinea, much of the forest has been cleared to make way for farms and large plantations where cocoa beans, coffee and cotton are grown. Oil and other minerals have been discovered in a number of Gulf countries, and this has created some wealth and industries. However, only a minority of the region's huge population benefit and most people are still very poor.

ALGERIA
POPULATION: 28,539,000 ✹ CAPITAL: ALGIERS

BENIN
POPULATION: 5,523,000 ✹ CAPITALS: COTONOU, PORTO-NOVO

BURKINA FASO
POPULATION: 10,423,000 ✹ CAPITAL: OUAGADOUGOU

CAMEROON
POPULATION: 13,521,000 ✹ CAPITAL: YAOUNDÉ

CAPE VERDE ISLANDS
POPULATION: 435,900 ✹ CAPITAL: PRAIA

CENTRAL AFRICAN REPUBLIC
POPULATION: 3,210,000 ✹ CAPITAL: BANGUI

CHAD
POPULATION: 5,587,000 ✹ CAPITAL: N'DJAMENA

CÔTE D'IVOIRE (IVORY COAST)
POPULATION: 14,791,000 ✹ CAPITALS: ABIDJAN, YAMOUSSOUKRO

DJIBOUTI
POPULATION: 421,300 ✹ CAPITAL: DJIBOUTI

EGYPT
POPULATION: 62,360,000 ✹ CAPITAL: CAIRO

EQUATORIAL GUINEA
POPULATION: 420,300 ✹ CAPITAL: MALABO

ERITREA
POPULATION: 3,579,000 ✹ CAPITAL: ASMARA

ETHIOPIA
POPULATION: 55,979,000 ✹ CAPITAL: ADDIS ABABA

GAMBIA
POPULATION: 989,300 ✹ CAPITAL: BANJUL

GHANA
POPULATION: 17,763,000 ✹ CAPITAL: ACCRA

GUINEA
POPULATION: 6,549,000 ✹ CAPITAL: CONAKRY

GUINEA-BISSAU
POPULATION: 1,125,000 ✹ CAPITAL: BISSAU

LIBERIA
POPULATION: 3,073,000 ✹ CAPITAL: MONROVIA

LIBYA
POPULATION: 5,248,000 ✹ CAPITAL: TRIPOLI

MALI
POPULATION: 9,375,000 ✹ CAPITAL: BAMAKO

MAURITANIA
POPULATION: 2,263,000 ✹ CAPITAL: NOUAKCHOTT

MOROCCO
POPULATION: 29,169,000 ✹ CAPITAL: RABAT

NIGER
POPULATION: 9,280,000 ✹ CAPITAL: NIAMEY

NIGERIA
POPULATION: 101,232,000 ✹ CAPITAL: ABUJA

SENEGAL
POPULATION: 9,007,000 ✹ CAPITAL: DAKAR

SIERRA LEONE
POPULATION: 4,753,000 ✹ CAPITAL: FREETOWN

SOMALIA
POPULATION: 7,348,000 ✹ CAPITAL: MOGADISHU

SUDAN
POPULATION: 30,120,000 ✹ CAPITAL: KHARTOUM

TOGO
POPULATION: 4,410,000 ✹ CAPITAL: LOMÉ

TUNISIA
POPULATION: 8,880,000 ✹ CAPITAL: TUNIS

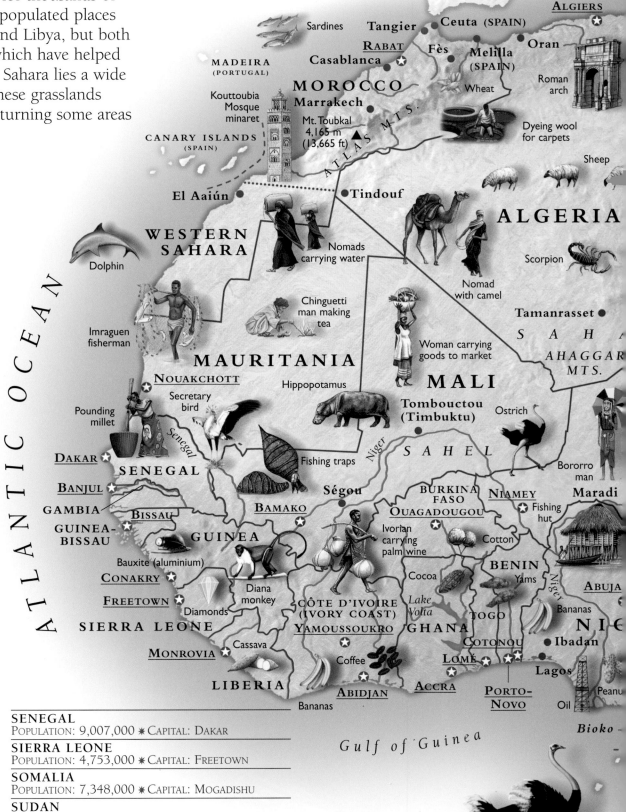

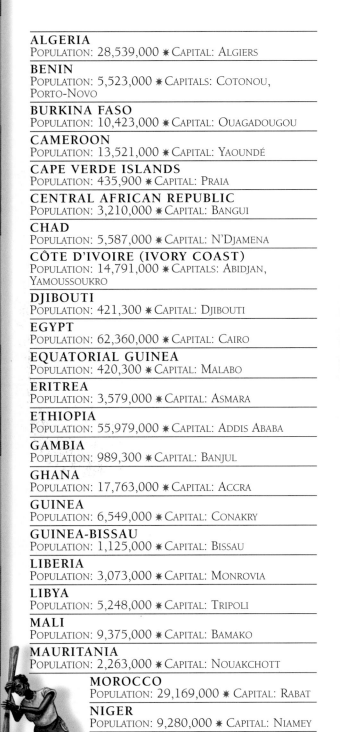

OSTRICH
The largest bird in the world, the ostrich cannot fly, but can run at up to 65 kilometres per hour (40 mph).

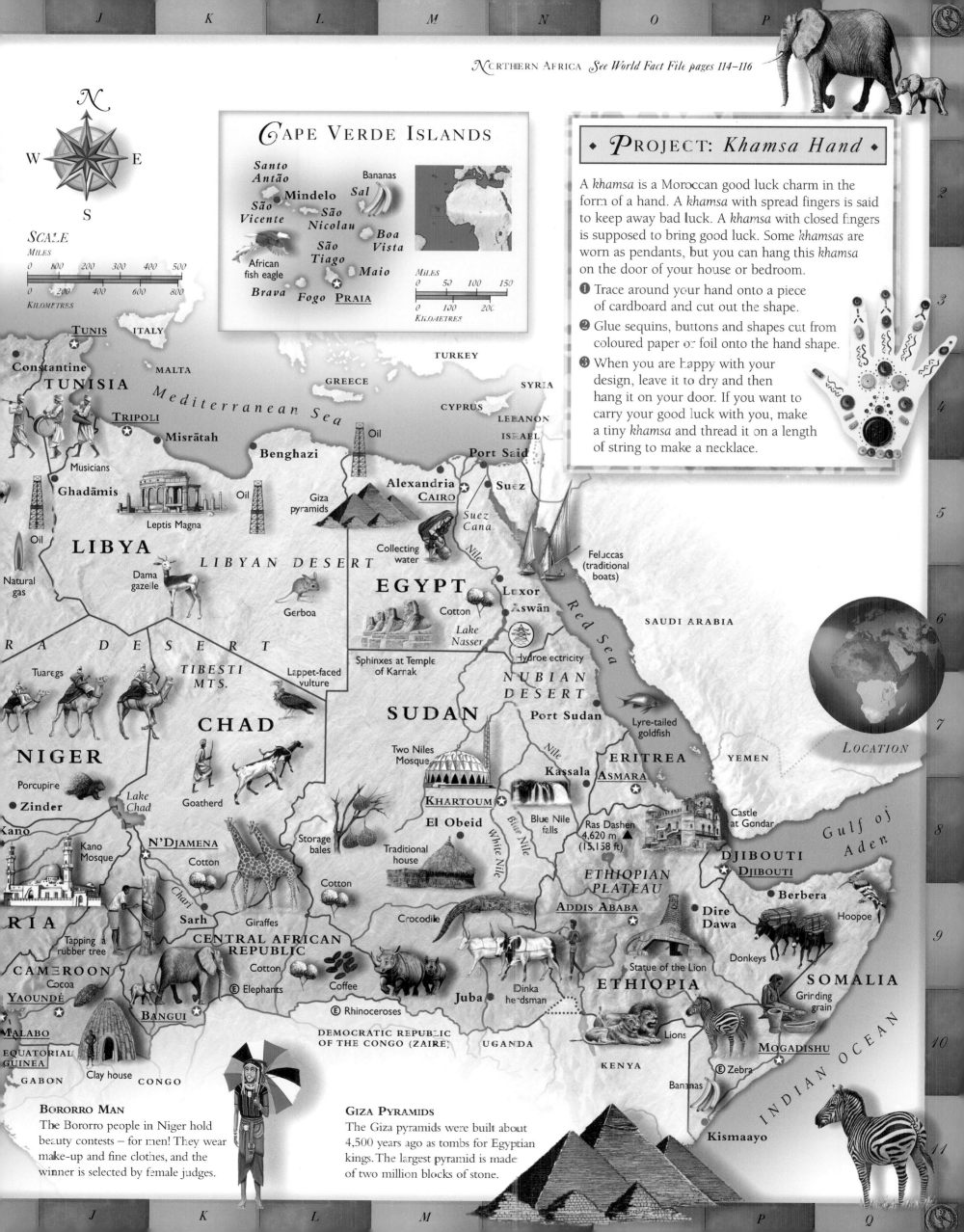

N W E S

CAPE VERDE ISLANDS

Santo Antão
Mindelo
São Vicente
São Nicolau
São Tiago
Brava
Fogo
Praia
Bananas
Sal
Boa Vista
Maio
African fish eagle

MILES
0   50   100   150
KILOMETRES
0   100   200

SCALE
MILES
0   100   200   300   400   500
0   200   400   600   800
KILOMETRES

◆ PROJECT: *Khamsa Hand* ◆

A *khamsa* is a Moroccan good luck charm in the form of a hand. A *khamsa* with spread fingers is said to keep away bad luck. A *khamsa* with closed fingers is supposed to bring good luck. Some *khamsas* are worn as pendants, but you can hang this *khamsa* on the door of your house or bedroom.

❶ Trace around your hand onto a piece of cardboard and cut out the shape.

❷ Glue sequins, buttons and shapes cut from coloured paper or foil onto the hand shape.

❸ When you are happy with your design, leave it to dry and then hang it on your door. If you want to carry your good luck with you, make a tiny *khamsa* and thread it on a length of string to make a necklace.

TUNIS   ITALY
Constantine   MALTA
TUNISIA   GREECE   TURKEY
Tripoli   Misrātah   SYRIA
Musicians   CYPRUS
Benghazi   LEBANON
Ghadāmis   Oil   ISRAEL
Mediterranean Sea   Port Said
Oil   Alexandria   Suez
Leptis Magna   CAIRO   Suez Canal
Oil   Giza pyramids   Nile
LIBYA   LIBYAN DESERT
Natural gas   Collecting water   EGYPT
Dama gazelle   Luxor
Gerboa   Cotton   Aswān
Lake Nasser   Red Sea
SAUDI ARABIA
Lappet-faced vulture   Hydroelectricity
R A   D E S E R T   Sphinxes at Temple of Karnak   NUBIAN DESERT
Tuaregs   TIBESTI MTS.   SUDAN   Port Sudan   Lyre-tailed goldfish
CHAD   ERITREA   YEMEN
NIGER   Two Niles Mosque   Kassala   ASMARA
Porcupine   Lake Chad   KHARTOUM   Blue Nile falls   Ras Dashen 4,620 m (15,158 ft)   Castle at Gondar
Zinder   Goatherd   El Obeid   Nile   Gulf of Aden
Kano   Storage bales   White Nile   Blue Nile   ETHIOPIAN PLATEAU   DJIBOUTI
Kano Mosque   Traditional house   ADDIS ABABA   DJIBOUTI
N'DJAMENA   Berbera
Cotton   Giraffes   ETHIOPIA   Dire Dawa   Hoopoe
RIA   Chari   Crocodile   Statue of the Lion
Tapping a rubber tree   Sarh   CENTRAL AFRICAN REPUBLIC   Donkeys
CAMEROON   Cotton   Coffee   Dinka herdsman   SOMALIA
Cocoa   (E) Elephants   Juba   Grinding grain
YAOUNDÉ   (E) Rhinoceroses   Lions
BANGUI   DEMOCRATIC REPUBLIC OF THE CONGO (ZAIRE)   UGANDA   MOGADISHU
MALABO   KENYA   (E) Zebra   INDIAN OCEAN
EQUATORIAL GUINEA   Clay house   Bananas
GABON   CONGO   Kismaayo

LOCATION

BORORRO MAN
The Bororro people in Niger hold beauty contests – for men! They wear make-up and fine clothes, and the winner is selected by female judges.

GIZA PYRAMIDS
The Giza pyramids were built about 4,500 years ago as tombs for Egyptian kings. The largest pyramid is made of two million blocks of stone.

Southern Africa

IN THE NORTH-WESTERN PART of this region, the Congo River and its many tributaries flow through immense tropical rainforests. Crocodiles swim the waterways, and the jungles are home to chimpanzees, gorillas and tropical birds. Most of the local people live in villages near the rivers and grow their own food on small plots of cleared land. The rainforests stretch eastwards across the continent toward the Great Rift Valley, a chain of dramatic, steep-sided valleys that runs down the eastern side of Africa. Within these valleys lie many deep lakes as well as a number of volcanoes, including Mount Kilimanjaro, Africa's highest mountain. On the valley floors and across the surrounding grassland plateaus, enormous herds of zebras, wildebeests and antelopes are hunted by lions, cheetahs and other predators. To protect the region's wildlife, many countries have created nature reserves, which attract tourists from all over the world. From the southern end of the Rift Valley, in Mozambique, high grasslands known as the veld spread westwards toward the Kalahari and Namib deserts. In South Africa the veld is an important farming region rich in mineral resources including copper, gold and diamonds. Off the coast of Mozambique lies the large island of Madagascar. Madagascar is famous for its unique wildlife, which includes many species of lemurs, unusual types of monkeys.

ANGOLA
POPULATION: 10,070,000 ✳ CAPITAL: LUANDA

BOTSWANA
POPULATION: 1,392,000 ✳ CAPITAL: GABORONE

BURUNDI
POPULATION: 6,262,000 ✳ CAPITAL: BUJUMBURA

COMOROS
POPULATION: 549,300 ✳ CAPITAL: MORONI

CONGO
POPULATION: 2,505,000 ✳ CAPITAL: BRAZZAVILLE

DEMOCRATIC REPUBLIC OF THE CONGO (ZAIRE)
POPULATION: 44,061,000 ✳ CAPITAL: KINSHASA

GABON
POPULATION: 1,156,000 ✳ CAPITAL: LIBREVILLE

KENYA
POPULATION: 28,817,000 ✳ CAPITAL: NAIROBI

LESOTHO
POPULATION: 1,993,000 ✳ CAPITAL: MASERU

MADAGASCAR
POPULATION: 13,862,000 ✳ CAPITAL: ANTANANARIVO

MALAWI
POPULATION: 9,808,000 ✳ CAPITAL: LILONGWE

MAURITIUS
POPULATION: 1,127,000 ✳ CAPITAL: PORT LOUIS

MOZAMBIQUE
POPULATION: 18,115,000 ✳ CAPITAL: MAPUTO

NAMIBIA
POPULATION: 1,652,000 ✳ CAPITAL: WINDHOEK

RWANDA
POPULATION: 8,605,000 ✳ CAPITAL: KIGALI

SÃO TOMÉ AND PRÍNCIPE
POPULATION: 140,400 ✳ CAPITAL: SÃO TOMÉ

SEYCHELLES
POPULATION: 72,700 ✳ CAPITAL: VICTORIA

SOUTH AFRICA
POPULATION: 45,095,000 ✳ CAPITALS: BLOEMFONTEIN, CAPE TOWN, PRETORIA

SWAZILAND
POPULATION: 967,000 ✳ CAPITAL: MBABANE

TANZANIA
POPULATION: 28,701,000 ✳ CAPITALS: DAR ES SALAAM, DODOMA

UGANDA
POPULATION: 19,573,000 ✳ CAPITAL: KAMPALA

ZAMBIA
POPULATION: 9,446,000 ✳ CAPITAL: LUSAKA

ZIMBABWE
POPULATION: 11,140,000 ✳ CAPITAL: HARARE

SCALE

MILES

0   100   200   300   400

0 100 200 300 400 500 600

KILOMETRES

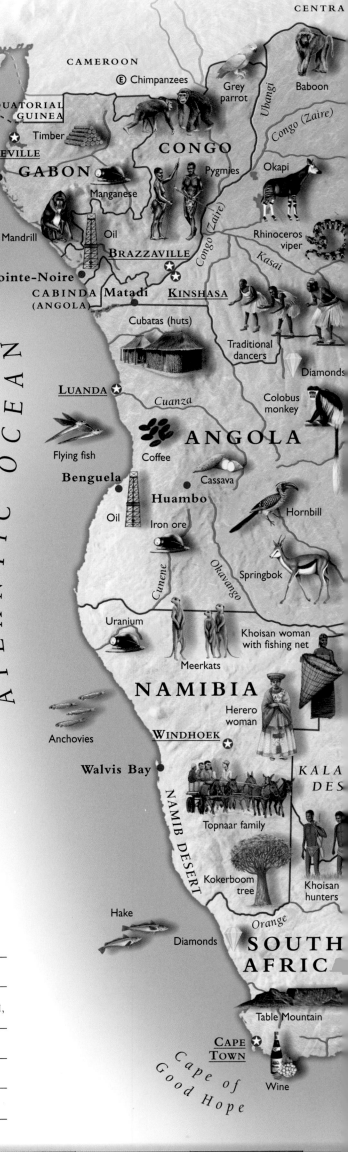

CENTRA

CAMEROON

São Tomé and Príncipe
Príncipe

E Chimpanzees

Grey parrot

Baboon

São Tomé
SÃO TOMÉ

EQUATORIAL GUINEA

Timber

Ubangi

CONGO

Congo (Zaire)

LIBREVILLE

GABON

Pygmies

Okapi

Port-Gentil

Manganese

Oil

Mandrill

BRAZZAVILLE

Congo (Zaire)

Kasai

Rhinoceros viper

Pointe-Noire

KINSHASA

CABINDA (ANGOLA)   Matadi

Cubatas (huts)

Traditional dancers

Diamonds

LUANDA

Cuanza

Colobus monkey

ANGOLA

Flying fish

Coffee

Benguela

Cassava

Huambo

Hornbill

Oil

Iron ore

ATLANTIC OCEAN

Springbok

Cunene

Okavango

Uranium

Khoisan woman with fishing net

Meerkats

NAMIBIA

Herero woman

Anchovies

WINDHOEK

Walvis Bay

KALA DES

NAMIB DESERT

Topnaar family

Kokerboom tree

Khoisan hunters

Hake

Orange

Diamonds

SOUTH AFRIC

Table Mountain

CAPE TOWN

Cape of Good Hope

Wine

CENTRAL AFRICAN REPUBLIC

African fish eagle

Tapping a rubber tree

Uele

(E) Gorilla

SUDAN

Ankole cattle

Leopard

Samburu women

ETHIOPIA

Lake Turkana

SOMALIA

DEMOCRATIC REPUBLIC OF THE CONGO (ZAIRE)

Margherita Peak 5,109 m (16,763 ft) ▲

UGANDA

KAMPALA ★

Tea

Lake Victoria

Bananas

Masai dancer

KENYA

Mt. Kenya 5,199 m (17,058 ft) ▲

★ NAIROBI

Lions

Coffee

Herding cattle

Ivory mask

RWANDA

Marabou stork

★ KIGALI

BURUNDI

Diamonds

Lomami

★ BUJUMBURA

Mwanza

Lake Tanganyika

Mt. Kilimanjaro 5,895 m (19,341 ft)

● Mombasa

Tourism

Ninga drummers

Acacia tree

TANZANIA

Zanzibar

● Mbuji-Mayi

Kananga

★ DODOMA

★ DAR ES SALAAM

Mafia

Cheetah

Coffee

Open-cast copper mining

Crowned crane

Likasi

Wildebeest

(E) Elephants

Great white shark

SEYCHELLES

Lubumbashi

Copper

Luangwa

Ruvuma

Cashew nuts

COMOROS

★ MORONI

★ VICTORIA

Cassava

Ndola

MALAWI

Lake Nyasa

Aardvark

Magnificent frigate bird

ZAMBIA

★ LILONGWE

Coconuts

MAYOTTE (FRANCE)

(E) Indri

Lozi royal barge

★ LUSAKA

Nampula

Victoria Falls

Hydroelectricity

Fishing boat

Tea

(E) Ruffed lemur

Zambezi

Lake Kariba

★ HARARE

Rice

Tourism

Black mamba

Gold

Tourism

LOCATION

ZIMBABWE

● Bulawayo

(E) Zebra

● Beira

(E) Coelacanth

Mozambique Channel

Ring-tailed lemur

● Toamasina

Giraffes

Francistown

Ruined town of Great Zimbabwe

MOZAMBIQUE

★ ANTANANARIVO

MAURITIUS

BOTSWANA

Diamonds

Limpopo

Cape buffalo

MADAGASCAR

★ PORT LOUIS

★ GABORONE

Rugby

Ndundza woman

Coffee

Streaked tenrec

RÉUNION (FRANCE)

★ PRETORIA

★ MAPUTO

Johannesburg

★ MBABANE

Sugarcane

Gold Zulus

★ BLOEMFONTEIN

SWAZILAND

Chameleon

Vaal

★ MASERU

● Durban

LESOTHO

Iron ore

Tourism

INDIAN OCEAN

East London

Cape hunting dogs

Port Elizabeth

AMAZING FACT

Over a short distance, the cheetah is the fastest animal in the world. As it pursues wildebeest, antelope and other prey across the savannah, it can reach speeds of more than 100 kilometres per hour (60 mph).

GIRAFFES

Giraffes grow to a height of 6 metres (18 ft) – taller than a single-storey house. Their height allows them to feed on leaves that other animals cannot reach.

ZULUS

The Zulu people have the largest population of any African group. In the 19th century, their kingdom covered much of what is now South Africa.

Australia and Oceania

STRETCHING FROM THE INDIAN OCEAN to the centre of the Pacific Ocean, Australia and Oceania cover a vast area of the globe. But because most of this region is ocean, it has a relatively small population. Australia is by far the largest land mass. This island is so big that it is considered a continent. Oceania consists of thousands of much smaller islands that are scattered across the Pacific Ocean to the east of Australia. They are divided into three groups: Micronesia, Melanesia and Polynesia, which includes the large islands of New Zealand. There are two main types of Pacific island: high, rugged islands that are the peaks of undersea volcanoes and submerged mountain ranges; and coral atolls – low, sandy islands formed by coral reefs growing on the tops of undersea mountains. Many of the Pacific islands are so small that they do not appear on regular maps.

Continent Facts

Regional land area: 8,507,753 sq. km (3,283,993 sq. mi)
Regional population: 28,462,000
Independent countries: Australia, Federated States of Micronesia, Fiji, Kiribati, Marshall Islands, Nauru, New Zealand, Palau, Papua New Guinea, Solomon Islands, Tonga, Tuvalu, Vanuatu, Western Samoa

World Records

WORLD'S LONGEST CORAL REEF
THE GREAT BARRIER REEF, AUSTRALIA, 2,025 KM (1,260 MI)

WORLD'S LARGEST ROCK
ULURU (AYERS ROCK), AUSTRALIA, 348 M (1,143 FT) HIGH; 2.5 KM (1.5 MI) LONG; 1.6 KM (1 MI) WIDE

WORLD'S LARGEST SAND ISLAND
FRASER ISLAND, AUSTRALIA, 120 KM (75 MI) LONG

Continent Records

HIGHEST MOUNTAIN
MOUNT WILHELM, PAPUA NEW GUINEA, 4,500 M (14,762 FT)

LOWEST POINT
LAKE EYRE, AUSTRALIA, 52 FT (16 M) BELOW SEA LEVEL

LARGEST LAKE
LAKE EYRE, AUSTRALIA, 9,324 SQ. KM (3,600 SQ. MI)

LONGEST RIVER
MURRAY-DARLING, AUSTRALIA, 3,750 KM (2,330 MI)

LARGEST COUNTRY BY AREA
AUSTRALIA, 7,686,884 SQ. KM (2,967,909 SQ. MI)

LARGEST COUNTRY BY POPULATION
AUSTRALIA, POPULATION 18,322,000

LARGEST CITY BY POPULATION
SYDNEY, AUSTRALIA, POPULATION 3,657,000

Major Mountains and Rivers

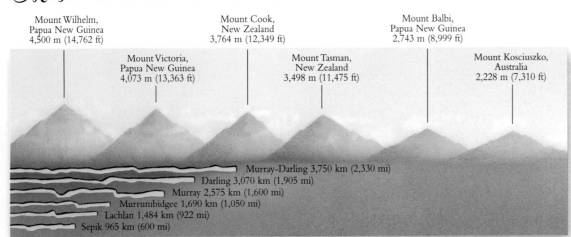

Mount Wilhelm, Papua New Guinea 4,500 m (14,762 ft)
Mount Victoria, Papua New Guinea 4,073 m (13,363 ft)
Mount Cook, New Zealand 3,764 m (12,349 ft)
Mount Tasman, New Zealand 3,498 m (11,475 ft)
Mount Balbi, Papua New Guinea 2,743 m (8,999 ft)
Mount Kosciuszko, Australia 2,228 m (7,310 ft)

Murray-Darling 3,750 km (2,330 mi)
Darling 3,070 km (1,905 mi)
Murray 2,575 km (1,600 mi)
Murrumbidgee 1,690 km (1,050 mi)
Lachlan 1,484 km (922 mi)
Sepik 965 km (600 mi)

Political Map

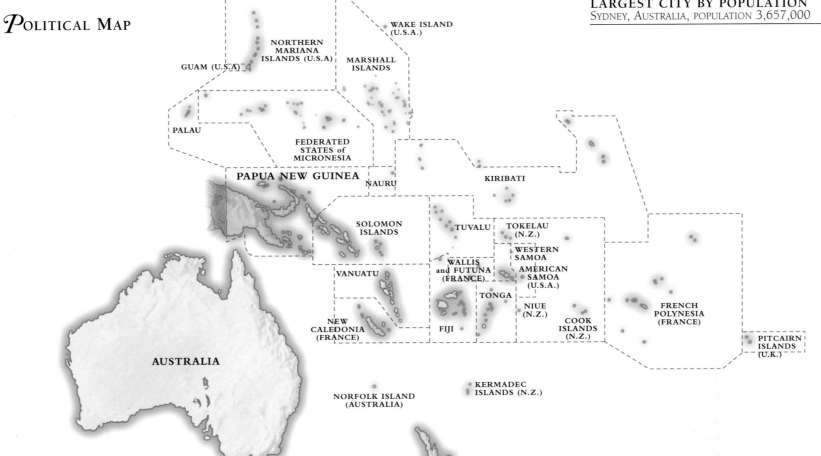

WAKE ISLAND (U.S.A.)
NORTHERN MARIANA ISLANDS (U.S.A)
GUAM (U.S.A)
MARSHALL ISLANDS
PALAU
FEDERATED STATES of MICRONESIA
PAPUA NEW GUINEA
NAURU
KIRIBATI
SOLOMON ISLANDS
TUVALU
TOKELAU (N.Z.)
WESTERN SAMOA
AMERICAN SAMOA (U.S.A.)
WALLIS and FUTUNA (FRANCE)
VANUATU
TONGA
NIUE (N.Z.)
FRENCH POLYNESIA (FRANCE)
NEW CALEDONIA (FRANCE)
FIJI
COOK ISLANDS (N.Z.)
PITCAIRN ISLANDS (U.K.)
AUSTRALIA
KERMADEC ISLANDS (N.Z.)
NORFOLK ISLAND (AUSTRALIA)
NEW ZEALAND
CHATHAM ISLANDS (N.Z.)

PHYSICAL MAP

Arctic Circle

ASIA

NORTH AMERICA

PACIFIC OCEAN

Tropic of Cancer

HAWAIIAN
ISLANDS

MARIANA
ISLANDS

MICRONESIA

MARSHALL
ISLANDS

CAROLINE ISLANDS

LINE ISLANDS

Equator

MELANESIA

GILBERT
ISLANDS

Nauru

PHOENIX
ISLANDS

MARQUESAS
ISLANDS

New
Guinea Sepik
Mt. ▲
Wilhelm

New
Britain

SOLOMON ISLANDS

▲ Mt.
Balbi

Tokelau

COOK ISLANDS

POLYNESIA

TUAMOTU
ARCHIPELAGO

Arafura
Sea

Torres Strait ▲ Mt.
Victoria

Tuvalu

CAPE
YORK
PENINSULA

SAMOA ISLANDS

SOCIETY
ISLANDS

GREAT
SANDY
DESERT

Great Barrier Reef

Coral Sea

Vanuatu

FIJI
ISLANDS

Great Dividing Range

PITCAIRN
ISLANDS

MACDONNELL
RANGES

Tonga

Australia

New
Caledonia

Tropic of Capricorn

GREAT VICTORIA
DESERT

Fraser
Island

Lake
Eyre

Great
Australian
Bight

Darling

Norfolk
Island

KERMADEC
ISLANDS

Lord Howe
Island

Lachlan

Murrumbidgee
Murray

North
Island

▲ Mt.
Kosciuszko

Tasman
Sea

New
Zealand

CHATHAM
ISLANDS

Tasmania

Mt. ▲ ▲ Mt. Cook
Tasman

South
Island

Stewart
Island

Macquarie
Island

Australia and Papua New Guinea

AUSTRALIA IS MORE THAN 30 times as big as the U.K., but its population is three times smaller. The vast, dry interior, known as the outback, consists mainly of deserts and grasslands.The outback contains mineral reserves and is used for grazing enormous numbers of sheep, but few people live there. Most Australians live in or near cities along the east, south-east and south-west coasts, where the climate is temperate and the land fertile. The far north-east is tropical, with areas of dense rainforest. The south-east is cooler, and mountain snowfalls are common. Most of Australia's native peoples, the Aborigines, live in towns and cities, but some still follow old traditions in the outback. Aborigines originally came to Australia more than 40,000 years ago, having crossed over from the island of New Guinea when it was still attached to Australia. Papua New Guinea, an Australian territory until 1975, is made up of several island chains and half the island of New Guinea. This main island is covered in jungle and surrounded by swampy plains. Most people live in small villages, where they grow food in gardens and raise animals. Many communities have little contact with the outside world and have retained their own traditions and languages. Papua New Guinea has over 700 languages – more than any other country.

AUSTRALIA
POPULATION: 18,322,000 ✳ CAPITAL: CANBERRA
PAPUA NEW GUINEA
POPULATION: 4,295,000 ✳ CAPITAL: PORT MORESBY

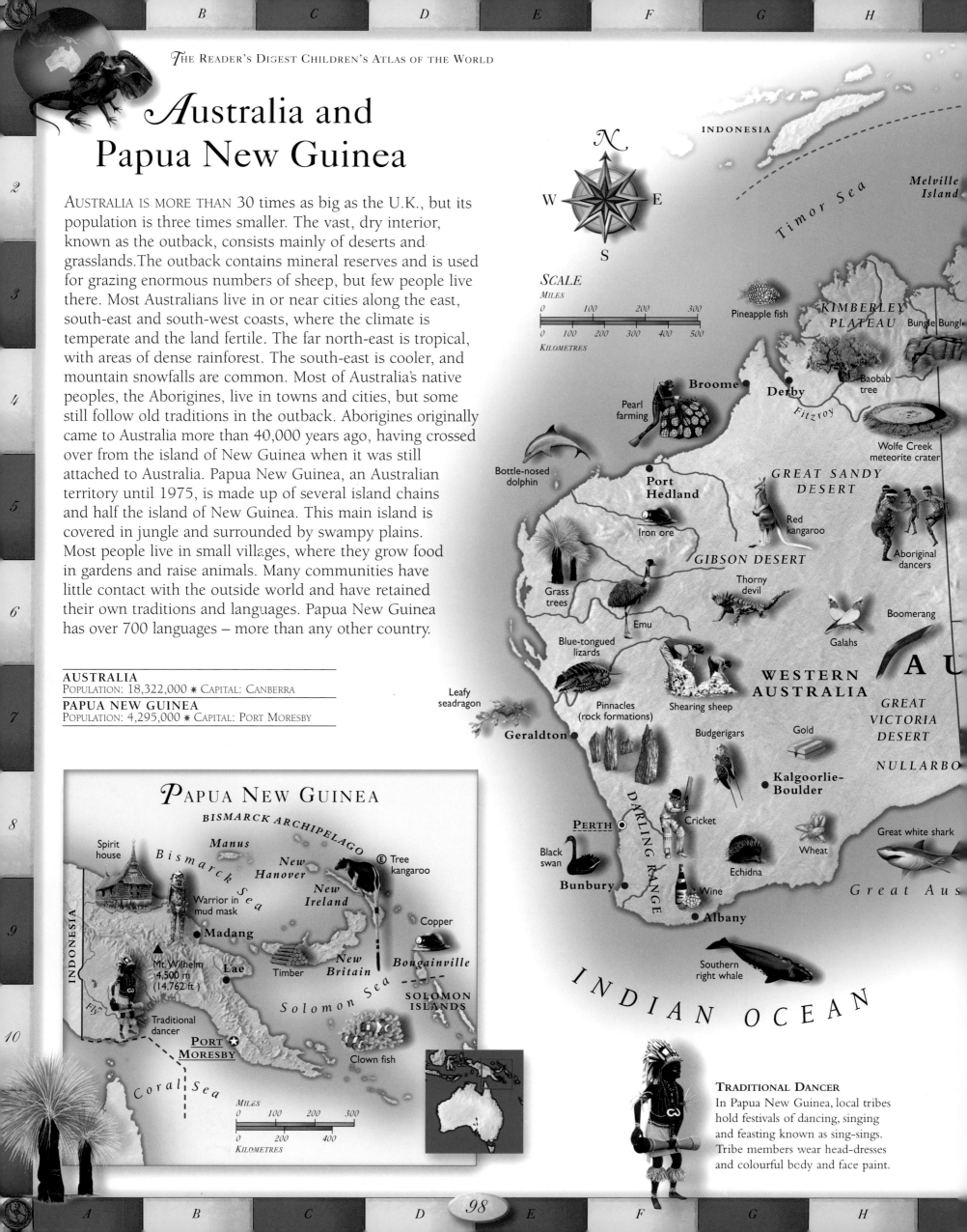

SCALE
MILES
0   100   200   300
0 100 200 300 400 500
KILOMETRES

INDONESIA

Timor Sea

Melville Island

Pineapple fish

KIMBERLEY PLATEAU

Bungle Bungle

Broome

Derby

Baobab tree

Pearl farming

Fitzroy

Wolfe Creek meteorite crater

Bottle-nosed dolphin

Port Hedland

GREAT SANDY DESERT

Red kangaroo

Iron ore

Aboriginal dancers

GIBSON DESERT

Thorny devil

Boomerang

Emu

Galahs

Blue-tongued lizards

Leafy seadragon

Pinnacles (rock formations)

Shearing sheep

WESTERN AUSTRALIA

GREAT VICTORIA DESERT

NULLARBO

AU

Geraldton

Budgerigars

Gold

Kalgoorlie-Boulder

Grass trees

Cricket

PERTH

DARLING RANGE

Black swan

Echidna

Wheat

Great white shark

Bunbury

Wine

Albany

Great Aus

Southern right whale

INDIAN OCEAN

PAPUA NEW GUINEA

BISMARCK ARCHIPELAGO

Spirit house

Manus

B i s m a r c k

New Hanover

Tree kangaroo

Warrior in mud mask

Bismarck Sea

New Ireland

INDONESIA

Madang

Mt. Wilhelm 4,500 m (14,762 ft)

Lae

Timber

New Britain

Copper

Bongainville

Fly

Traditional dancer

Solomon Sea

SOLOMON ISLANDS

PORT MORESBY

Clown fish

Coral Sea

MILES
0   100   200   300
0   200   400
KILOMETRES

TRADITIONAL DANCER
In Papua New Guinea, local tribes hold festivals of dancing, singing and feasting known as sing-sings. Tribe members wear head-dresses and colourful body and face paint.

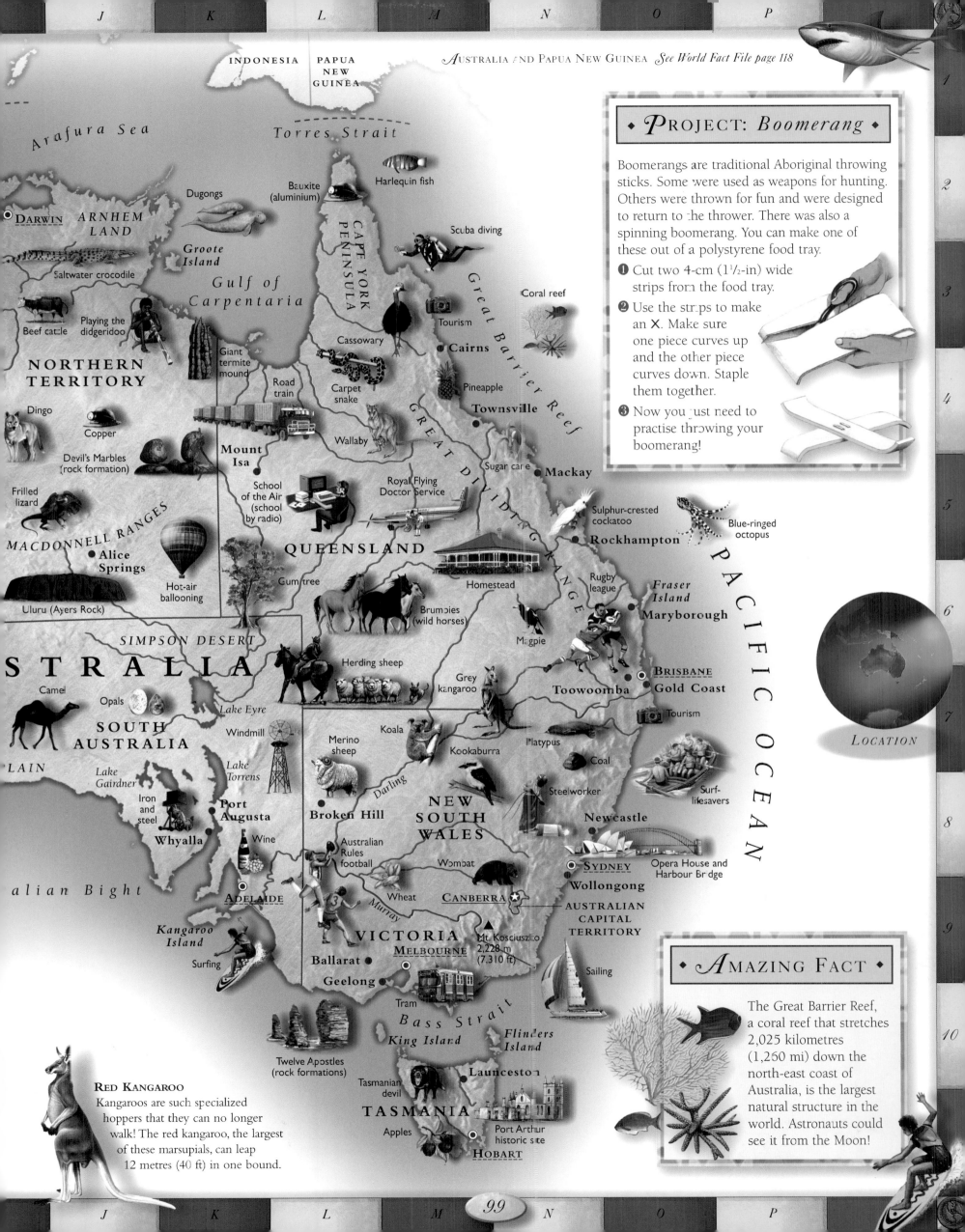

INDONESIA   PAPUA
NEW
GUINEA

Arafura Sea

Torres Strait

Harlequin fish

DARWIN   ARNHEM
LAND

Dugongs

Bauxite
(aluminium)

Groote
Island

Saltwater crocodile

*Gulf of
Carpentaria*

CAPE YORK
PENINSULA

Scuba diving

Coral reef

Beef cattle

Playing the
didgeridoo

Tourism

Cassowary

Cairns

NORTHERN
TERRITORY

Giant
termite
mound

Carpet
snake

Pineapple

Townsville

Road
train

Dingo

Copper

Road train

Wallaby

Sugar cane   **Mackay**

Devil's Marbles
(rock formation)

**Mount
Isa**

Frilled
lizard

School
of the Air
(school
by radio)

Royal Flying
Doctor Service

Sulphur-crested
cockatoo

Blue-ringed
octopus

MACDONNELL RANGES

**Alice
Springs**

Rockhampton

QUEENSLAND

Homestead

Rugby
league

*Fraser
Island*

Maryborough

Hot-air
ballooning

Gum tree

Uluru (Ayers Rock)

Brumbies
(wild horses)

Magpie

PACIFIC OCEAN

SIMPSON DESERT

STRALIA

Camel

Herding sheep

Grey
kangaroo

Toowoomba

BRISBANE
Gold Coast

Opals

Lake Eyre

Koala

Whyalla

SOUTH
AUSTRALIA

Windmill

Merino
sheep

Kookaburra

Platypus

Coal

Tourism

LOCATION

LAIN

*Lake
Gairdner*

*Lake
Torrens*

Iron
and
steel

**Port
Augusta**

Darling

NEW
SOUTH
WALES

Steelworker

Surf-
lifesavers

Broken Hill

Wine

Australian
Rules
football

Newcastle

alian Bight

ADELAIDE

Wombat

SYDNEY
Wollongong

Opera House and
Harbour Bridge

*Kangaroo
Island*

Wheat

CANBERRA

AUSTRALIAN
CAPITAL
TERRITORY

Surfing

Murray

VICTORIA

▲ Mt. Kosciuszko
2,228 m
(7,310 ft)

Sailing

MELBOURNE

Ballarat

Geelong

Tram

Bass Strait

*Flinders
Island*

Twelve Apostles
(rock formations)

King Island

Launceston

Tasmanian
devil

TASMANIA

Apples

Port Arthur
historic site

HOBART

RED KANGAROO
Kangaroos are such specialized
hoppers that they can no longer
walk! The red kangaroo, the largest
of these marsupials, can leap
12 metres (40 ft) in one bound.

◆ **PROJECT:** *Boomerang* ◆

Boomerangs are traditional Aboriginal throwing
sticks. Some were used as weapons for hunting.
Others were thrown for fun and were designed
to return to the thrower. There was also a
spinning boomerang. You can make one of
these out of a polystyrene food tray.

❶ Cut two 4-cm (1½-in) wide
strips from the food tray.

❷ Use the strips to make
an **X**. Make sure
one piece curves up
and the other piece
curves down. Staple
them together.

❸ Now you just need to
practise throwing your
boomerang!

◆ *AMAZING FACT* ◆

The Great Barrier Reef,
a coral reef that stretches
2,025 kilometres
(1,260 mi) down the
north-east coast of
Australia, is the largest
natural structure in the
world. Astronauts could
see it from the Moon!

New Zealand and the South-western Pacific

SCATTERED ACROSS A VAST EXPANSE of ocean and separated from each other by great distances, the islands of the south-western Pacific are among the most isolated places on Earth. The largest and most southerly group is New Zealand, consisting of two large islands – the North Island and the South Island – and several smaller islands. New Zealand is a modern, industrialized country. About 70 per cent of the population live on the North Island, which has several active volcanoes. Lake Taupo, New Zealand's largest lake, lies in a crater that formed when a volcano exploded. The nearby volcanoes, Ruapehu and Ngauruhoe, have erupted several times in recent years. The Southern Alps form the 'backbone' of the South Island. On their western side, temperate rainforests have grown up around a line of mighty glaciers that run down to the coast. More than half of New Zealand is used for growing crops and grazing animals – there are 20 sheep for every New Zealander! The country's original inhabitants, the Maori people, make up one-sixth of the population. Most other New Zealanders are descendants of British immigrants. Thousands of tropical islands lie to the north and east of New Zealand. Tourism is a growing industry in countries such as Fiji and Vanuatu. Some islands have developing towns with new businesses, but most islanders live in small villages. They fish for crabs, lobsters, turtles and tuna, and grow sweet potatoes and bananas. One of the most important export products is copra (dried coconut meat), which is used in making soap and candles.

FIJI
POPULATION: 772,900 ✳ CAPITAL: SUVA

NEW ZEALAND
POPULATION: 3,407,000 ✳ CAPITAL: WELLINGTON

SOLOMON ISLANDS
POPULATION: 399,200 ✳ CAPITAL: HONIARA

TONGA
POPULATION: 105,600 ✳ CAPITAL: NUKU'ALOFA

VANUATU
POPULATION: 173,600 ✳ CAPITAL: PORT VILA

WESTERN SAMOA
POPULATION: 209,400 ✳ CAPITAL: APIA

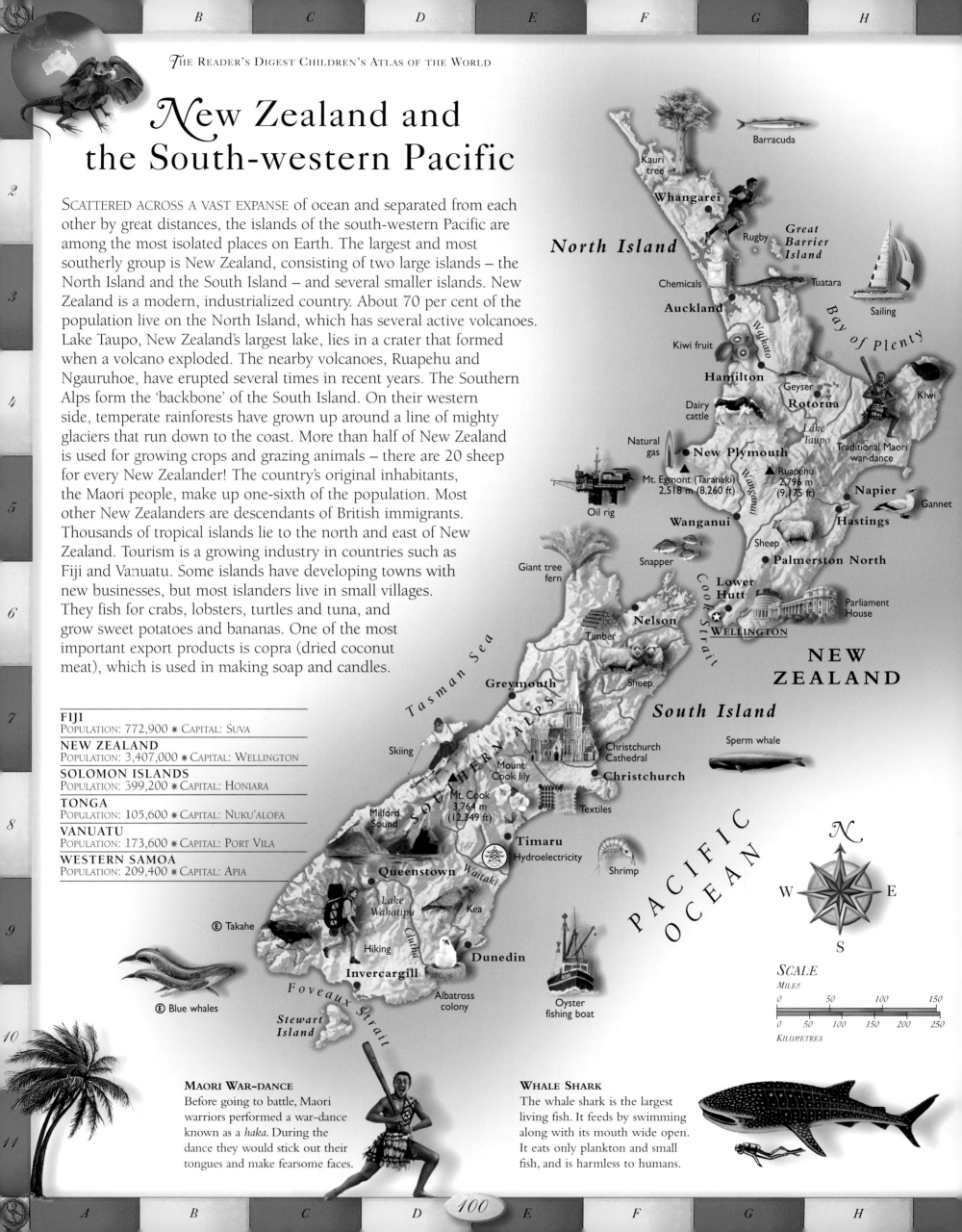

North Island

Kauri tree

Barracuda

Whangarei

Rugby

Great Barrier Island

Chemicals

Tuatara

Sailing

Auckland

Bay of Plenty

Kiwi fruit

Waikato

Hamilton

Geyser

Rotorua

Kiwi

Dairy cattle

Lake Taupo

Traditional Maori war-dance

Natural gas

New Plymouth

Napier

Gannet

Mt. Egmont (Taranaki) 2,518 m (8,260 ft)

Ruapehu 2,796 m (9,175 ft)

Hastings

Oil rig

Wanganui

Sheep

Snapper

Palmerston North

Giant tree fern

Lower Hutt

Parliament House

Nelson

Cook Strait

WELLINGTON

Timber

NEW ZEALAND

Tasman Sea

Greymouth

Sheep

South Island

Sperm whale

SOUTHERN ALPS

Skiing

Christchurch Cathedral

Mount Cook lily

Christchurch

Mt. Cook 3,764 m (12,349 ft)

Milford Sound

Textiles

Timaru

Hydroelectricity

Shrimp

(E) Takahe

Lake Wakatipu

Kea

PACIFIC OCEAN

Queenstown

Waitaki

Clutha

Hiking

Dunedin

Invercargill

Blue whales

Albatross colony

Oyster fishing boat

Foveaux Strait

Stewart Island

SCALE
MILES
0   50   100   150

0   50   100   150   200   250
KILOMETRES

N
W E
S

MAORI WAR-DANCE
Before going to battle, Maori warriors performed a war-dance known as a *haka*. During the dance they would stick out their tongues and make fearsome faces.

WHALE SHARK
The whale shark is the largest living fish. It feeds by swimming along with its mouth wide open. It eats only plankton and small fish, and is harmless to humans.

SOLOMON ISLANDS

House on stilts
Choiseul
Santa Isabel
Spotted cuscus

MILES
0   100   200
0   100   200   300
KILOMETRES

NEW GEORGIA ISLANDS
Malaita
HONIARA
Guadalcanal
Timber
San Cristóbal
Bananas
Harlequin tuskfish
Rennell
Coral Sea
SANTA CRUZ ISLANDS

SAMOA ISLANDS

WESTERN SAMOA

Coconuts
Savai'i
Sala'ilua
Making tapa cloth
Bottle-nosed dolphin

APIA
Upolu

AMERICAN SAMOA (U.S.A.)

Pago-Pago
Preparing copra
Tau
Tutuila
MANUA ISLANDS

MILES
0   25   50
0   25   50   75
KILOMETRES

Manta ray
Bluefin tuna

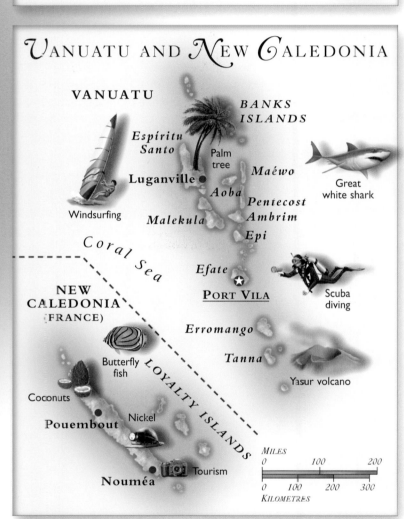

VANUATU AND NEW CALEDONIA

VANUATU

BANKS ISLANDS
Espíritu Santo
Palm tree
Maéwo
Luganville
Aoba
Great white shark
Windsurfing
Malekula
Pentecost
Ambrim
Epi

Coral Sea

NEW CALEDONIA (FRANCE)
Efate
PORT VILA
Scuba diving

Erromango
Tanna
Yasur volcano

Butterfly fish
Coconuts
Nickel
LOYALTY ISLANDS
Pouembout
Nouméa
Tourism

MILES
0   100   200
0   100   200   300
KILOMETRES

SOLOMON ISLANDS
FIJI
SAMOA ISLANDS
VANUATU AND NEW CALEDONIA
TONGA
SOCIETY ISLANDS
NEW ZEALAND

FIJI

Sugar cane
Vanua Levu
Taveuni
Koro
Tourism
Cocoa
Viti Levu
Walking on hot coals
Koro Sea
LAU GROUP
SUVA
Gau
Lakeba
Magnificent frigate bird
Moala
Coconuts
Kandavu
Angelfish

MILES
0   25   50   75
0   50   100   150
KILOMETRES

LOCATION

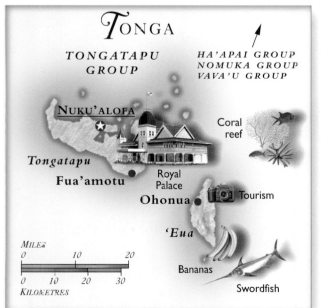

TONGA

TONGATAPU GROUP
HA'APAI GROUP
NOMUKA GROUP
VAVA'U GROUP

NUKU'ALOFA
Coral reef
Tongatapu
Fua'amotu
Royal Palace
Ohonua
Tourism
'Eua
Bananas

MILES
0   10   20
0   10   20   30
KILOMETRES

Swordfish

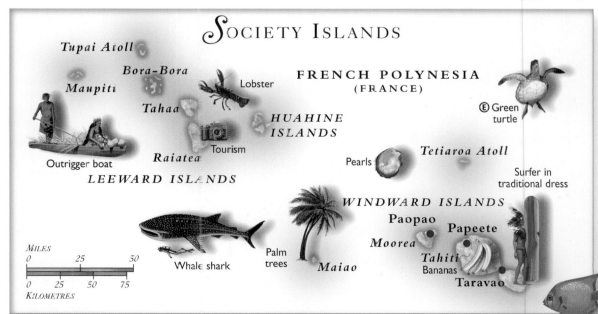

SOCIETY ISLANDS

Tupai Atoll
Bora-Bora
Lobster
FRENCH POLYNESIA (FRANCE)
Maupiti
Tahaa
HUAHINE ISLANDS
Ⓔ Green turtle
Outrigger boat
Raiatea
Tourism
Pearls
Tetiaroa Atoll
LEEWARD ISLANDS
Surfer in traditional dress
WINDWARD ISLANDS
Paopao
Whale shark
Palm trees
Moorea
Papeete
Maiao
Tahiti
Bananas
Taravao

MILES
0   25   50
0   25   50   75
KILOMETRES

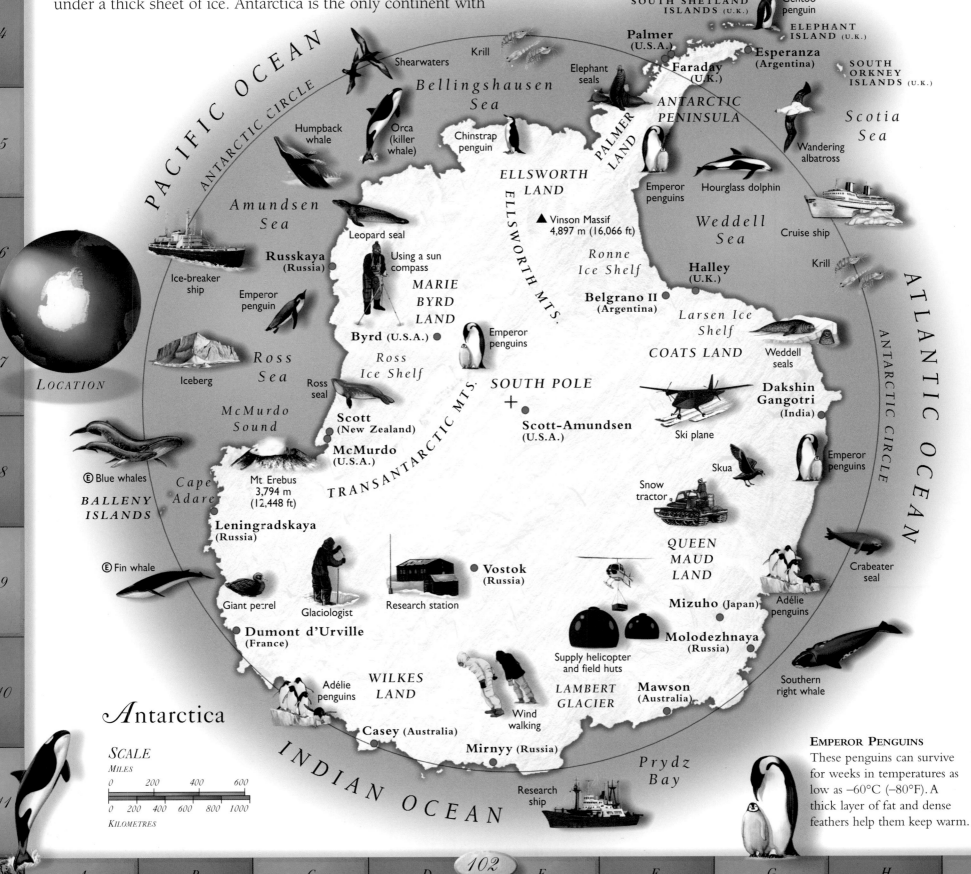

The Polar Regions

THE REGIONS THAT SURROUND the North and South poles are the coldest and windiest parts of our planet. Both are permanently covered in snow and ice, and during winter months there is little or no daylight. Antarctica is a frozen continent surrounded by ocean. The Arctic is an area of frozen ocean surrounded by continents. In winter, the Arctic ice spreads southwards, reaching North America, Europe and Asia. The northern fringes of these continents are home to native peoples who have adapted to Arctic life. They include the Saami (Lapps) of Scandinavia and the Inuit of Canada, Alaska, Greenland and Russia. A Danish territory, Greenland is the world's largest island. Most of it lies under a thick sheet of ice. Antarctica is the only continent with

no permanent population. Scientists spend part of the year at research stations, but many leave Antarctica before the cold, dark winter sets in. The continent is covered by a vast ice sheet which is three kilometres (2 mi) thick in some places. Along the coast, the ice sheet forms huge ice shelves over the ocean. Giant blocks of ice break off and float away as icebergs. Some icebergs are as large as small countries and take years to melt. There is little life in the Antarctic interior, but whales, seals and fish swim just offshore, and during the summer enormous colonies of seabirds nest along the coast and on nearby islands.

LOCATION

Antarctica

SCALE

MILES

0   200   400   600

0   200   400   600   800   1000

KILOMETRES

PACIFIC OCEAN

ANTARCTIC CIRCLE

Bellingshausen Sea

Shearwaters

Krill

Humpback whale

Orca (killer whale)

Chinstrap penguin

Amundsen Sea

Leopard seal

Using a sun compass

Russkaya (Russia)

MARIE BYRD LAND

Byrd (U.S.A.)

Emperor penguins

Ice-breaker ship

Emperor penguin

Iceberg

Ross Sea

Ross seal

Ross Ice Shelf

McMurdo Sound

Scott (New Zealand)

McMurdo (U.S.A.)

ⒺBlue whales

Cape Adare

Mt Erebus 3,794 m (12,448 ft)

BALLENY ISLANDS

Leningradskaya (Russia)

ⒺFin whale

Giant petrel

Glaciologist

Research station

Dumont d'Urville (France)

Adélie penguins

WILKES LAND

Casey (Australia)

Mirnyy (Russia)

SOUTH SHETLAND ISLANDS (U.K.)

Gentoo penguin

ELEPHANT ISLAND (U.K.)

Palmer (U.S.A.)

Esperanza (Argentina)

Elephant seals

Faraday (U.K.)

SOUTH ORKNEY ISLANDS (U.K.)

ANTARCTIC PENINSULA

PALMER LAND

ELLSWORTH LAND

Scotia Sea

Wandering albatross

Emperor penguins

Hourglass dolphin

Weddell Sea

▲ Vinson Massif 4,897 m (16,066 ft)

Ronne Ice Shelf

Cruise ship

ELLSWORTH MTS.

Halley (U.K.)

Krill

Belgrano II (Argentina)

Larsen Ice Shelf

COATS LAND

Weddell seals

TRANSANTARCTIC MTS.

SOUTH POLE +

Scott-Amundsen (U.S.A.)

Dakshin Gangotri (India)

Ski plane

Emperor penguins

Skua

ATLANTIC OCEAN

ANTARCTIC CIRCLE

Snow tractor

Vostok (Russia)

QUEEN MAUD LAND

Mizuho (Japan)

Adélie penguins

Crabeater seal

Supply helicopter and field huts

Molodezhnaya (Russia)

Wind walking

LAMBERT GLACIER

Mawson (Australia)

Southern right whale

Prydz Bay

Research ship

INDIAN OCEAN

EMPEROR PENGUINS
These penguins can survive for weeks in temperatures as low as −60°C (−80°F). A thick layer of fat and dense feathers help them keep warm.

The Arctic

SCALE

MILES

0   200   400   600

0   200   400   600   800   1000

KILOMETRES

Icebreaker ship

Bering Strait

ALASKA (U.S.A.)

Reindeer

Chukchi hunter

Arctic hare

Pevek

Ambarchik

ARCTIC CIRCLE

Oil

Chukchi Sea

Wrangel Island

East Siberian Sea

CANADA

Barrow

Prudhoe Bay

Narwhal

Walrus

NEW SIBERIAN ISLANDS

Snow goose

Beaufort Sea

Arctic tern

Grey whale

Lena

Yakut woman and children

Musk-ox

Banks Island

Skua

Ptarmigan

RUSSIA

Zinc and lead

Polar bears

Laptev Sea

Victoria Island

ARCTIC OCEAN

Nordvik

Snowmobile

QUEEN ELIZABETH ISLANDS

Snowy owl

Kittiwake

Wolf

ARCTIC CIRCLE

Walrus

SEVERNAYA ZEMLYA

Arctic fox

Resolute

NORTH POLE +

Ⓔ Beluga whale

Dudinka

Hudson Bay

Baffin Island

Ellesmere Island

Kara Sea

Natural gas

Walrus tusk carvings

FRANZ JOSEF LAND

Inuit fishing through ice

Thule

Hooded seal

Harp seals

LOCATION

Baffin Bay

Jakobshavn houses

NOVAYA ZEMLYA

CANADA

Upernavik

Svalbard reindeer

Haddock

Nenet woman

Tourism

SVALBARD (NORWAY)

GREENLAND (DENMARK)

Longyearbyen

Barents Sea

Nar'yan-Mar

Spitsbergen

Musk-ox

Inuit hunter

Harbour seals

Snowmobile

Bowhead whale

Nuuk

NORTH CAPE

Murmansk

Iceberg

Cod

Orca (killer whale)

Hammerfest

Tourism

Mt. Gunnbjørn 3,700 m (12,139 ft)

FINLAND

Julianehåb

Denmark Strait

Norwegian Sea

CAPE FAREWELL

Puffins

Sam (Lapp) man

SWEDEN

ICELAND

NORWAY

CHUKCHI HUNTER

Traditionally, Chukchi people hunted seals, walruses and whales from kayaks, using ivory-tipped harpoons. Now most hunters use rifles and travel in motorboats.

REINDEER

Huge herds of reindeer roam over the tundra in search of food. Their large hooves prevent them from sinking into the snow and help them dig through to reach plants and lichens.

World Fact File

NORTH AMERICA

CANADA

AREA: 9,976,185 sq. km
(3,851,809 sq. mi)
POPULATION: 28,435,000
CAPITAL: Ottawa
CURRENCY: 100 cents = 1 Canadian dollar (Can$)
OFFICIAL LANGUAGES: English, French
MAIN RELIGION: Christianity 72%
EXPORTS: Newsprint, wood pulp, timber, crude petroleum, machinery, natural gas, aluminium, motor vehicles and parts, telecommunications equipment

UNITED STATES OF AMERICA

AREA: 9,375,720 sq. km
(3,619,969 sq. mi)
POPULATION: 263,814,000
CAPITAL: Washington, D.C.
CURRENCY: 100 cents = 1 United States dollar (US$)
OFFICIAL LANGUAGE: English
OTHER LANGUAGE: Spanish
MAIN RELIGIONS: Christianity 86%, Judaism 2%
EXPORTS: Motor vehicles, raw materials, consumer goods, agricultural products

MEXICO

AREA: 1,972,544 sq. km
(761,600 sq. mi)
POPULATION: 93,986,000
CAPITAL: Mexico City
CURRENCY: 100 centavos = 1 Mexican peso (Mex$)
OFFICIAL LANGUAGE: Spanish
OTHER LANGUAGES: Regional languages
MAIN RELIGION: Christianity 95%
EXPORTS: Crude oil, oil products, coffee, silver, engines, motor vehicles, cotton, electronic goods

GUATEMALA

AREA: 108,889 sq. km (42,042 sq. mi)
POPULATION: 10,999,000
CAPITAL: Guatemala
CURRENCY: 100 centavos = 1 Guatemalan quetzal (Q)
OFFICIAL LANGUAGE: Spanish
OTHER LANGUAGES: Quiche, Cakchiquel, Kekchi and other regional languages
MAIN RELIGIONS: Christianity 99%, traditional Mayan religions
EXPORTS: Coffee, bananas, cotton, sugar, minerals, textiles

BELIZE

AREA: 22,966 sq. km
(8,867 sq. mi)
POPULATION: 214,100
CAPITAL: Belmopan
CURRENCY: 100 cents = 1 Belizian dollar (Bz$)
OFFICIAL LANGUAGE: English
OTHER LANGUAGES: Spanish, Maya, Garifuna
MAIN RELIGION: Christianity 92%
EXPORTS: Sugar, molasses, citrus fruit, bananas, clothing, fish products, timber

HONDURAS

AREA: 112,087 sq. km
(43,277 sq. mi)
POPULATION: 5,460,000
CAPITAL: Tegucigalpa
CURRENCY: 100 centavos = 1 lempira (L)
OFFICIAL LANGUAGE: Spanish
OTHER LANGUAGES: Regional languages
MAIN RELIGION: Christianity 97%
EXPORTS: Bananas, coffee, shrimp, lobsters, minerals, meat, timber

EL SALVADOR

AREA: 21,393 sq. km
(8,260 sq. mi)
POPULATION: 5,870,000
CAPITAL: San Salvador
CURRENCY: 100 centavos = 1 Salvadorean colón (C)
OFFICIAL LANGUAGE: Spanish
OTHER LANGUAGE: Nahuatl
MAIN RELIGION: Christianity 92%
EXPORTS: Coffee, sugar cane, shrimp

NICARAGUA

AREA: 128,410 sq. km
(49,579 sq. mi)
POPULATION: 4,206,000
CAPITAL: Managua
CURRENCY: 100 centavos = 1 gold cordoba (C$)
OFFICIAL LANGUAGE: Spanish
OTHER LANGUAGES: English, Indian
MAIN RELIGION: Christianity 100%
EXPORTS: Meat, coffee, cotton, sugar, bananas, seafood, gold

COSTA RICA

AREA: 50,899 sq. km
(19,652 sq. mi)
POPULATION: 3,419,000
CAPITAL: San José
CURRENCY: 100 centimos = 1 Costa Rican colón (C)
OFFICIAL LANGUAGE: Spanish
OTHER LANGUAGE: English
MAIN RELIGION: Christianity 95%
EXPORTS: Coffee, bananas, sugar, textiles

PANAMA

AREA: 87,177 sq. km
(33,659 sq. mi)
POPULATION: 2,681,000
CAPITAL: Panama City
CURRENCY: 100 centesimos = 1 balboa (B)

FLAGS OF THE WORLD

Next to the name of each country in this World Fact File is an illustration of that country's flag. Flags come in many different designs and colours

The First Flags

We will never know who invented flags, but we do know that about 5,000 years ago Egyptian soldiers carried into battle long poles with symbols made of cloth, wood or metal attached to the top. The soldiers hoped that these symbols would bring them good luck. At about the same time, silk banners were made in China. Both of these were early forms of flags.

National Flags

Today's national flags remind us of a country's history, religion and culture. The flags of many Islamic countries, for example, include a crescent and star, while the flags of Christian countries often include a cross. Countries with a shared history often have similar flags. For example, some countries in Central America have blue and white flags, because they were once part of the same country. The flags of several Arab countries are green, white, red and black, as these colours are the symbols of Arab unity. Every country's flag is special to the people of that country.

OFFICIAL LANGUAGE: Spanish
OTHER LANGUAGES: English, regional languages
MAIN RELIGION: Christianity 100%
EXPORTS: Bananas, shrimp, sugar, coffee, clothing

THE BAHAMAS

AREA: 13,950 sq. km (5,386 sq. mi)
POPULATION: 256,600
CAPITAL: Nassau
CURRENCY: 100 cents = 1 Bahamian dollar (B$)
OFFICIAL LANGUAGE: English
OTHER LANGUAGE: Bahamian creole
MAIN RELIGION: Christianity 95%
EXPORTS: Pharmaceuticals, cement, rum, crayfish, refined petroleum products

CUBA

AREA: 110,862 sq. km (42,804 sq. mi)
POPULATION: 10,938,000
CAPITAL: Havana
CURRENCY: 100 centavos = 1 Cuban peso (Cu$)
OFFICIAL LANGUAGE: Spanish
MAIN RELIGION: Christianity 85%
EXPORTS: Sugar, shellfish, citrus fruit, coffee, tobacco, nickel, medical products

JAMAICA

AREA: 11,580 sq. km (4,471 sq. mi)
POPULATION: 2,574,000
CAPITAL: Kingston
CURRENCY: 100 cents = 1 Jamaican dollar (J$)
OFFICIAL LANGUAGE: English
OTHER LANGUAGE: Jamaican creole
MAIN RELIGION: Christianity 61%
EXPORTS: Bauxite, sugar, bananas, rum

HAITI

AREA: 27,749 sq. km (10,714 sq. mi)
POPULATION: 6,540,000
CAPITAL: Port-au-Prince
CURRENCY: 100 centimes = 1 gourde (G)
OFFICIAL LANGUAGE: French
OTHER LANGUAGE: Haitian creole
MAIN RELIGION: Christianity 96%
EXPORTS: Clothing, coffee, sugar

DOMINICAN REPUBLIC

AREA: 48,322 sq. km (18,657 sq. mi)
POPULATION: 7,511,000
CAPITAL: Santo Domingo
CURRENCY: 100 centavos = 1 Dominican peso (RD$)
OFFICIAL LANGUAGE: Spanish
MAIN RELIGION: Christianity 95%
EXPORTS: Minerals, sugar, coffee, cocoa, gold

ANTIGUA AND BARBUDA

AREA: 443 sq. km (171 sq. mi)
POPULATION: 65,200
CAPITAL: St. John's
CURRENCY: 100 cents = 1 East Caribbean dollar (EC$)
OFFICIAL LANGUAGE: English
OTHER LANGUAGES: Regional languages
MAIN RELIGIONS: Christianity 97%, indigenous religions 3%
EXPORTS: Petroleum products, manufactured goods, machinery and transport equipment, food and livestock

ST. KITTS–NEVIS

AREA: 269 sq. km (104 sq. mi)
POPULATION: 41,000
CAPITAL: Basseterre
CURRENCY: 100 cents = 1 East Caribbean dollar (EC$)
OFFICIAL LANGUAGE: English
MAIN RELIGION: Christianity 86%
EXPORTS: Machinery, food, beverages, electronics, tobacco

DOMINICA

AREA: 749 sq. km (289 sq. mi)
POPULATION: 82,600
CAPITAL: Roseau
CURRENCY: 100 cents = 1 East Caribbean dollar (EC$)
OFFICIAL LANGUAGE: English
OTHER LANGUAGE: French patois
MAIN RELIGION: Christianity 92%
EXPORTS: Bananas, grapefruit, oranges, vegetables, soap, bay oil

ST. LUCIA

AREA: 616 sq. km (238 sq. mi)
POPULATION: 156,100
CAPITAL: Castries
CURRENCY: 100 cents = 1 East Caribbean dollar (EC$)
OFFICIAL LANGUAGE: English
OTHER LANGUAGE: French patois
MAIN RELIGION: Christianity 100%
EXPORTS: Bananas, clothing, cocoa, fruit and vegetables, coconut oil

BARBADOS

AREA: 430 sq. km (166 sq. mi)
POPULATION: 256,400
CAPITAL: Bridgetown
CURRENCY: 100 cents = 1 Barbadian dollar (Bds$)
OFFICIAL LANGUAGE: English
OTHER LANGUAGE: Barbadian creole
MAIN RELIGION: Christianity 71%
EXPORTS: Sugar, molasses, rum, other foods and beverages, chemicals, electrical components, clothing

ST. VINCENT AND THE GRENADINES

AREA: 389 sq. km (150 sq. mi)
POPULATION: 117,300
CAPITAL: Kingstown
CURRENCY: 100 cents = 1 East Caribbean dollar (EC$)
OFFICIAL LANGUAGE: English
OTHER LANGUAGE: French patois
MAIN RELIGION: Christianity 75%
EXPORTS: Bananas, taro (food plant), tennis racquets

GRENADA

AREA: 344 sq. km (133 sq. mi)
POPULATION: 94,500
CAPITAL: St. George's
CURRENCY: 100 cents = 1 East Caribbean dollar (EC$)
OFFICIAL LANGUAGE: English
OTHER LANGUAGE: French patois
MAIN RELIGION: Christianity 85%
EXPORTS: Bananas, cocoa, nutmeg, fruit and vegetables, clothing, mace (spice)

TRINIDAD AND TOBAGO

AREA: 5,128 sq. km (1,980 sq. mi)
POPULATION: 1,271,000
CAPITAL: Port-of-Spain
CURRENCY: 100 cents = 1 Trinidad and Tobago dollar (TT$)
OFFICIAL LANGUAGE: English
OTHER LANGUAGES: Hindi, French, Spanish
MAIN RELIGIONS: Christianity 60%, Hinduism 24%, Islam 6%
EXPORTS: Petroleum and petroleum products, chemicals, steel products, fertilizer, sugar, cocoa, coffee, citrus fruit, flowers

SOUTH AMERICA

COLOMBIA
AREA: 1,138,914 sq. km
(439,735 sq. mi)
POPULATION: 36,200,000
CAPITAL: Bogotá
CURRENCY: 100 centavos = 1 Colombian peso (Col$)
OFFICIAL LANGUAGE: Spanish
MAIN RELIGION: Christianity 95%
EXPORTS: Petroleum, coffee, coal, bananas, flowers

VENEZUELA
AREA: 912,050 sq. km
(352,143 sq. mi)
POPULATION: 21,005,000
CAPITAL: Caracas
CURRENCY: 100 centimos = 1 bolivar (B)
OFFICIAL LANGUAGE: Spanish
OTHER LANGUAGES: Regional languages
MAIN RELIGION: Christianity 98%
EXPORTS: Petroleum, bauxite and aluminium, steel, chemicals, agricultural products, manufactured goods

GUYANA
AREA: 214,970 sq. km
(83,000 sq. mi)
POPULATION: 723,800
CAPITAL: Georgetown
CURRENCY: 100 cents = 1 Guyanese dollar (G$)
OFFICIAL LANGUAGE: English
OTHER LANGUAGES: Regional languages
MAIN RELIGIONS: Christianity 57%, Hinduism 33%, Islam 9%
EXPORTS: Sugar, molasses, bauxite, rice, shrimp

SURINAME
AREA: 163,820 sq. km
(63,251 sq. mi)
POPULATION: 429,500
CAPITAL: Paramaribo
CURRENCY: 100 cents = 1 Surinamese guilder or florin (Sf)
OFFICIAL LANGUAGE: Dutch
OTHER LANGUAGES: English, Sranang Tongo, Hindustani, Javanese
MAIN RELIGIONS: Christianity 48%, Hinduism 27%, Islam 20%, regional religions 5%
EXPORTS: Aluminium, shrimp, fish, rice, bananas

ECUADOR
AREA: 283,561 sq. km
(109,483 sq. mi)
POPULATION: 10,891,000
CAPITAL: Quito
CURRENCY: 100 centavos = 1 sucre (S/.)
OFFICIAL LANGUAGE: Spanish
OTHER LANGUAGES: Quechua, other regional languages
MAIN RELIGION: Christianity 95%
EXPORTS: Petroleum, bananas, shrimp, cocoa, coffee

PERU
AREA: 1,285,215 sq. km
(496,222 sq. mi)
POPULATION: 24,087,000
CAPITAL: Lima
CURRENCY: 100 centavos = 1 sol (S/.)
OFFICIAL LANGUAGES: Spanish, Quechua
OTHER LANGUAGE: Aymara
MAIN RELIGION: Christianity 90%
EXPORTS: Copper, zinc, petroleum and petroleum products, lead, refined silver, coffee, cotton

BRAZIL
AREA: 8,506,663 sq. km
(3,284,426 sq. mi)
POPULATION: 160,737,000
CAPITAL: Brasília
CURRENCY: 100 centavos = 1 cruzeiro (Cr$)
OFFICIAL LANGUAGE: Portuguese
OTHER LANGUAGES: Spanish, English, French
MAIN RELIGION: Christianity 96%
EXPORTS: Iron ore, soya bean bran, bananas, orange juice, shoes, coffee, motor vehicle parts

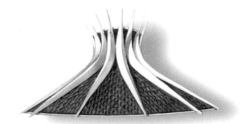

BOLIVIA
AREA: 1,098,579 sq. km
(424,162 sq. mi)
POPULATION: 7,896,000
CAPITALS: La Paz (seat of government), Sucre (legal and judicial)
CURRENCY: 100 centavos = 1 boliviano ($b)
OFFICIAL LANGUAGES: Spanish, Quechua, Aymara
MAIN RELIGION: Christianity 100%
EXPORTS: Metals, natural gas, soya beans, jewellery, timber

CHILE
AREA: 756,946 sq. km
(292,257 sq. mi)
POPULATION: 14,161,000
CAPITAL: Santiago
CURRENCY: 100 centavos = 1 Chilean peso (Ch$)
OFFICIAL LANGUAGE: Spanish
OTHER LANGUAGES: Regional languages
MAIN RELIGION: Christianity 99%
EXPORTS: Copper, other metals and minerals, timber products, fish, fruit

PARAGUAY
AREA: 406,741 sq. km
(157,043 sq. mi)
POPULATION: 5,358,000
CAPITAL: Asunción
CURRENCY: 100 centimos = 1 guarani (G)
OFFICIAL LANGUAGE: Spanish
OTHER LANGUAGE: Guarani
MAIN RELIGION: Christianity 97%
EXPORTS: Cotton, soya beans, timber, vegetable oils, meat products, coffee

ARGENTINA
AREA: 2,776,884 sq. km
(1,072,156 sq. mi)
POPULATION: 34,293,000
CAPITAL: Buenos Aires
CURRENCY: 100 centavos = 1 peso argentino
OFFICIAL LANGUAGE: Spanish
OTHER LANGUAGES: English, Italian, German, French
MAIN RELIGIONS: Christianity 94%, Judaism 2%
EXPORTS: Manufactured goods, meat, wheat, maize, oilseed

URUGUAY
AREA: 176,221 sq. km
(68,039 sq. mi)
POPULATION: 3,223,000
CAPITAL: Montevideo
CURRENCY: 100 centesimos = 1 Uruguayan peso ($Ur)
OFFICIAL LANGUAGE: Spanish
MAIN RELIGIONS: Christianity 68%, Judaism 2%
EXPORTS: Wool, textiles, beef and other animal products, leather, rice

EUROPE

UNITED KINGDOM
AREA: 244,110 sq. km
(94,251 sq. mi)
POPULATION: 58,295,000
CAPITAL: London
CURRENCY: 100 pence = 1 British pound (£)
OFFICIAL LANGUAGE: English
OTHER LANGUAGES: Welsh, Scottish Gaelic,
Irish Gaelic
MAIN RELIGIONS: Christianity 90%,
Islam 3%, Sikh 1%, Hinduism 1%,
Judaism 1%
EXPORTS: Manufactured goods, machinery,
fuels, chemicals, transport equipment

IRELAND
AREA: 68,894 sq. km
(26,600 sq. mi)
POPULATION: 3,550,000
CAPITAL: Dublin
CURRENCY: 100 pence = 1 Irish pound (£Ir)
OFFICIAL LANGUAGES: English, Irish (Gaelic)
MAIN RELIGION: Christianity 96%
EXPORTS: Chemicals, data processing
equipment, industrial machinery, livestock,
animal products

PORTUGAL
AREA: 91,642 sq. km
(35,383 sq. mi)
POPULATION: 10,562,000
CAPITAL: Lisbon
CURRENCY: 100 centavos = 1 Portuguese
escudo (Esc)
OFFICIAL LANGUAGE: Portuguese
MAIN RELIGION: Christianity 98%
EXPORTS: Clothing, shoes, machinery,
cork, paper products, animal skins

SPAIN
AREA: 504,742 sq. km
(194,881 sq. mi)
POPULATION: 39,404,000
CAPITAL: Madrid
CURRENCY: 100 centimos = 1 peseta (PTA)
OFFICIAL LANGUAGE: Castilian Spanish
OTHER LANGUAGES: Catalan, Galician, Basque
MAIN RELIGION: Christianity 99%
EXPORTS: Motor vehicles, manufactured goods,
food, machinery

ANDORRA
AREA: 482 sq. km (180 sq. mi)
POPULATION: 65,800
CAPITAL: Andorra la Vella
CURRENCIES: 100 centimes = 1 French franc (F),
100 centimos = 1 peseta (Pta)
OFFICIAL LANGUAGE: Catalan
OTHER LANGUAGES: French, Spanish
MAIN RELIGION: Christianity 95%
EXPORTS: Electricity, tobacco products, furniture

FRANCE
AREA: 551,458 sq. km
(212,918 sq. mi)
POPULATION: 58,109,000
CAPITAL: Paris
CURRENCY: 100 centimes = 1 French franc (F)
OFFICIAL LANGUAGE: French
OTHER LANGUAGES: Occitan, German, Breton,
Catalan, Arabic
MAIN RELIGIONS: Christianity 92%, Judaism 1%,
Islam 1%
EXPORTS: Machinery and transport equipment,
chemicals, food, agricultural products, iron and
steel products, textiles, clothing

MONACO
AREA: 1.5 sq. km (0.58 sq. mi)
POPULATION: 31,500
CAPITAL: Monaco
CURRENCY: 100 centimes = 1 French franc (F)
OFFICIAL LANGUAGE: French
OTHER LANGUAGES: English, Italian, Monégasque
MAIN RELIGION: Christianity 95%
EXPORTS: Pharmaceuticals, perfumes, clothing

THE NETHERLANDS
AREA: 41,525 sq. km
(16,033 sq. mi)
POPULATION: 15,453,000
CAPITALS: Amsterdam; The Hague (judicial)
CURRENCY: 100 cents = 1 Dutch
guilder (Gld)
OFFICIAL LANGUAGE: Dutch
MAIN RELIGIONS: Christianity 59%, Islam 3%
EXPORTS: Metal products, chemicals, processed
food, tobacco, agricultural products

BELGIUM
AREA: 30,513 sq. km
(11,781 sq. mi)
POPULATION: 10,082,000
CAPITAL: Brussels
CURRENCY: 100 centimes = 1 Belgian franc (BF)
OFFICIAL LANGUAGES: Dutch (Flemish), French
OTHER LANGUAGE: German
MAIN RELIGION: Christianity 100%
EXPORTS: Iron and steel, transport equipment,
tractors, diamonds, petroleum products

LUXEMBOURG
AREA: 2,587 sq. km (999 sq. mi)
POPULATION: 404,700
CAPITAL: Luxembourg
CURRENCY: 100 centimes = 1 Luxembourg
franc (Flux)
OFFICIAL LANGUAGES: Letzeburgesh,
German, French
OTHER LANGUAGE: English
MAIN RELIGION: Christianity 99%, Judaism 1%
EXPORTS: Steel products, chemicals, rubber
products, glass, aluminium

GERMANY
AREA: 356,734 sq. km
(137,735 sq. mi)
POPULATION: 81,338,000
CAPITAL: Berlin
CURRENCY: 100 pfennig = 1 Deutschmark (DM)
OFFICIAL LANGUAGE: German
MAIN RELIGION: Christianity 82%
EXPORTS: Machines and machine tools, chemicals,
motor vehicles, iron and steel products,
agricultural products, raw materials, fuels

SWITZERLAND
AREA: 41,287 sq. km
(15,941 sq. mi)
POPULATION: 7,085,000
CAPITAL: Bern
CURRENCY: 100 centimes = 1 Swiss franc (F)
OFFICIAL LANGUAGES: German, French, Italian,
Romansh
MAIN RELIGION: Christianity 92%
EXPORTS: Machinery, precision instruments,
metal products, food, textiles

LIECHTENSTEIN
AREA: 161 sq. km
(62 sq. mi)
POPULATION: 30,700
CAPITAL: Vaduz
CURRENCY: 100 centimes = 1 Swiss franc (F)
OFFICIAL LANGUAGE: German
MAIN RELIGION: Christianity 95%
EXPORTS: Machinery, dental products,
stamps, hardware, pottery

AUSTRIA

AREA: 83,851 sq. km (32,375 sq. mi)
POPULATION: 7,987,000
CAPITAL: Vienna
CURRENCY: 100 groschen = 1 Austrian schilling (S)
OFFICIAL LANGUAGE: German
MAIN RELIGION: Christianity 91%
EXPORTS: Machinery, electrical equipment, iron and steel, timber, textiles, paper products, chemicals

ITALY

AREA: 301,251 sq. km (116,313 sq. mi)
POPULATION: 58,262,000
CAPITAL: Rome
CURRENCY: Italian lira (L)
OFFICIAL LANGUAGE: Italian
OTHER LANGUAGES: German, French, Slovene
MAIN RELIGION: Christianity 98%
EXPORTS: Metals, textiles, clothing, machinery, motor vehicles, transport equipment, chemicals

SAN MARINO

AREA: 62 sq. km (24 sq. mi)
POPULATION: 24,300
CAPITAL: San Marino
CURRENCY: Italian lira (L)
OFFICIAL LANGUAGE: Italian
MAIN RELIGION: Christianity 95%
EXPORTS: Building stone, lime, timber, chestnuts, wheat, wine, baked goods, animal skins, ceramics

VATICAN CITY

AREA: 0.44 sq. km (0.17 sq. mi)
POPULATION: 830
CAPITAL: Vatican City
CURRENCY: Vatican lira (VLit)
OFFICIAL LANGUAGES: Italian, Latin
MAIN RELIGION: Christianity 100%
EXPORTS: None

MALTA

AREA: 316 sq. km (122 sq. mi)
POPULATION: 369,600
CAPITAL: Valletta
CURRENCY: 100 cents = 1 Maltese lira (Lm)
OFFICIAL LANGUAGES: Maltese, English
MAIN RELIGION: Christianity 98%
EXPORTS: Machinery and transport equipment, clothing, shoes, printed matter

SLOVENIA

AREA: 20,251 sq. km (7,819 sq. mi)
POPULATION: 2,052,000
CAPITAL: Ljubljana
CURRENCY: 100 stotins = 1 tolar (SlT)
OFFICIAL LANGUAGE: Slovenian
OTHER LANGUAGE: Serbo-Croatian
MAIN RELIGIONS: Christianity 96%, Islam 1%
EXPORTS: Motor vehicles, furniture, machinery, manufactured goods, chemicals, textiles, food, raw materials

CROATIA

AREA: 56,537 sq. km (21,829 sq. mi)
POPULATION: 4,666,000
CAPITAL: Zagreb
CURRENCY: 100 lipa = 1 Croatian kuna (HRK)
OFFICIAL LANGUAGE: Serbo-Croatian
MAIN RELIGIONS: Christianity 88%, Islam 1%
EXPORTS: Machinery and transport equipment, other manufactured goods, chemicals, food, livestock, raw materials, fuels and lubricants

BOSNIA AND HERZEGOVINA

AREA: 51,750 sq. km (19,904 sq. mi)
POPULATION: 3,202,000
CAPITAL: Sarajevo
CURRENCY: 100 paras = 1 dinar (D)
OFFICIAL LANGUAGE: Serbo-Croatian
MAIN RELIGIONS: Christianity 50%, Islam 40%
EXPORTS: Timber, furniture

YUGOSLAVIA

AREA: 102,173 sq. km (39,449 sq. mi)
POPULATION: 11,102,000
CAPITAL: Belgrade
CURRENCY: 100 paras = 1 Yugoslav dinar (YD)
OFFICIAL LANGUAGE: Serbo-Croatian
OTHER LANGUAGES: Albanian, Hungarian
MAIN RELIGIONS: Christianity 70%, Islam 19%
EXPORTS: Textiles, leather goods, machinery

ROMANIA

AREA: 237,500 sq. km (91,699 sq. mi)
POPULATION: 23,198,000
CAPITAL: Bucharest
CURRENCY: 100 bani = 1 leu (L)
OFFICIAL LANGUAGE: Romanian
OTHER LANGUAGES: Hungarian, German
MAIN RELIGION: Christianity 82%
EXPORTS: Metals and metal products, mineral products, textiles, electrical equipment, transport equipment

BULGARIA

AREA: 110,912 sq. km (42,823 sq. mi)
POPULATION: 8,775,000
CAPITAL: Sofia
CURRENCY: 100 stotinki = 1 Lev (Lv)
OFFICIAL LANGUAGE: Bulgarian
MAIN RELIGIONS: Christianity 85%, Islam 13%, Judaism 1%
EXPORTS: Machinery, agricultural products, manufactured goods, fuels, minerals, raw materials, metals

ALBANIA

AREA: 28,749 sq. km (11,100 sq. mi)
POPULATION: 3,414,000
CAPITAL: Tiranë
CURRÉNCY: 100 qindarka = 1 lek (L)
OFFICIAL LANGUAGE: Albanian
OTHER LANGUAGE: Greek
MAIN RELIGIONS: Islam 70%, Christianity 30%
EXPORTS: Asphalt, metals and metallic ores, electricity, crude oil, fruit and vegetables, tobacco

MACEDONIA

AREA: 25,714 sq. km (9,928 sq. mi)
POPULATION: 2,160,000
CAPITAL: Skopje
CURRENCY: 100 paras = 1 denar
OFFICIAL LANGUAGE: Macedonian
OTHER LANGUAGES: Albanian, Turkish, Serbo-Croatian
MAIN RELIGIONS: Christianity 67%, Islam 30%
EXPORTS: Manufactured goods, machinery and transport equipment, raw materials, food, livestock, beverages, tobacco, chemicals

GREECE

AREA: 131,945 sq. km (50,944 sq. mi)
POPULATION: 10,648,000
CAPITAL: Athens
CURRENCY: 100 lepta = 1 drachma (Dr)
OFFICIAL LANGUAGE: Greek
OTHER LANGUAGES: English, French
MAIN RELIGION: Christianity 98%
EXPORTS: Manufactured goods, food, fuels

ESTONIA

AREA: 45,100 sq. km (17,413 sq. mi)
POPULATION: 1,625,000
CAPITAL: Tallinn
CURRENCY: 100 cents = 1 Estonian kroon (EEK)
OFFICIAL LANGUAGE: Estonian
OTHER LANGUAGES: Latvian, Lithuanian, Russian
MAIN RELIGION: Christianity 100%
EXPORTS: Textiles, food, motor vehicles, metals

LATVIA

AREA: 63,701 sq. km
(24,595 sq. mi)
POPULATION: 2,763,000
CAPITAL: Riga
CURRENCY: 100 santims = 1 lat (Ls)
OFFICIAL LANGUAGE: Latvian
OTHER LANGUAGES: Lithuanian, Russian
MAIN RELIGION: Christianity 100%
EXPORTS: Oil products, timber, metals, dairy
products, furniture, textiles

LITHUANIA

AREA: 65,201 sq. km
(25,174 sq. mi)
POPULATION: 3,876,000
CAPITAL: Vilnius
CURRENCY: 100 centas = 1 litas (Lt)
OFFICIAL LANGUAGE: Lithuanian
OTHER LANGUAGES: Polish, Russian
MAIN RELIGION: Christianity 100%
EXPORTS: Electronics, petroleum products,
food, chemicals

BELARUS

AREA: 207,599 sq. km
(80,154 sq. mi)
POPULATION: 10,437,000
CAPITAL: Minsk
CURRENCY: Belarussian rubel (BR)
OFFICIAL LANGUAGE: Belarussian
OTHER LANGUAGE: Russian
MAIN RELIGION: Christianity 68%
EXPORTS: Machinery and transport
equipment, chemicals, food

POLAND

AREA: 312,758 sq. km
(120,756 sq. mi)
POPULATION: 38,792,000
CAPITAL: Warsaw
CURRENCY: 100 groszy = 1 zloty (Zl)
OFFICIAL LANGUAGE: Polish
MAIN RELIGION: Christianity 95%
EXPORTS: Machinery and transport equipment,
manufactured goods, food, fuels

CZECH REPUBLIC

AREA: 78,866 sq. km
(30,450 sq. mi)
POPULATION: 10,433,000
CAPITAL: Prague
CURRENCY: 100 haleru = 1 koruna (Kc)
OFFICIAL LANGUAGE: Czech
OTHER LANGUAGE: Slovak
MAIN RELIGION: Christianity 47%
EXPORTS: Manufactured goods, machinery and
transport equipment, chemicals, fuels, minerals,
metals, agricultural products

SLOVAKIA

AREA: 49,011 sq. km (18,923 sq. mi)
POPULATION: 5,432,000
CAPITAL: Bratislava
CURRENCY: 100 haleru = 1 koruna (Sk)
OFFICIAL LANGUAGE: Slovak
OTHER LANGUAGE: Hungarian
MAIN RELIGION: Christianity 72%
EXPORTS: Machinery and transport equipment,
chemicals, fuels, minerals and
metals, agricultural products

UKRAINE

AREA: 603,701 sq. km
(233,089 sq. mi)
POPULATION: 51,868,000
CAPITAL: Kiev
CURRENCY: Karbovanets (Kb)
OFFICIAL LANGUAGE: Ukrainian
OTHER LANGUAGES: Russian, Romanian,
Polish, Hungarian
MAIN RELIGIONS: Christianity 90%, Judaism 2%
EXPORTS: Coal, electricity, metals, chemicals,
machinery and transport equipment,
grain, meat

HUNGARY

AREA: 93,030 sq. km
(35,919 sq. mi)
POPULATION: 10,319,000
CAPITAL: Budapest
CURRENCY: 100 filler = 1 forint (Ft)
OFFICIAL LANGUAGE: Hungarian
MAIN RELIGION: Christianity 92%
EXPORTS: Raw materials, machinery and
transport equipment, manufactured goods,
food, agriculture, fuels, energy

MOLDOVA

AREA: 33,701 sq. km
(13,012 sq. mi)
POPULATION: 4,490,000
CAPITAL: Chişinău
CURRENCY: 100 bani = 1 leu (L)
OFFICIAL LANGUAGE: Moldovian
OTHER LANGUAGES: Russian, Gagauz
MAIN RELIGIONS: Christianity 99%, Judaism 1%
EXPORTS: Food, wine, tobacco, textiles, shoes,
machinery, chemicals

ICELAND

AREA: 102,828 sq. km
(39,702 sq. mi)
POPULATION: 266,000
CAPITAL: Reykjavík
CURRENCY: 100 aurar = 1 Icelandic krona (IKr)
OFFICIAL LANGUAGE: Icelandic

MAIN RELIGION: Christianity 99%
EXPORTS: Fish and fish products, animal
products, minerals

NORWAY

AREA: 400,906 sq. km
(154,790 sq. mi)
POPULATION: 4,331,000
CAPITAL: Oslo
CURRENCY: 100 ore = 1 Norwegian krone (NKr)
OFFICIAL LANGUAGE: Norwegian
OTHER LANGUAGES: Lappish, Finnish
MAIN RELIGION: Christianity 91%
EXPORTS: Petroleum and petroleum products,
metals and metal products, fish and fish products,
chemicals, natural gas, ships

SWEDEN

AREA: 449,792 sq. km
(173,665 sq. mi)
POPULATION: 8,822,000
CAPITAL: Stockholm
CURRENCY: 100 ore = 1 Swedish krona (SKr)
OFFICIAL LANGUAGE: Swedish
OTHER LANGUAGES: Lapp, Finnish
MAIN RELIGION: Christianity 96%
EXPORTS: Machinery, motor vehicles, paper
products, pulp and wood, iron and steel products,
chemicals, petroleum and petroleum products

FINLAND

AREA: 337,032 sq. km
(130,128 sq. mi)
POPULATION: 5,085,000
CAPITAL: Helsinki
CURRENCY: 100 pennia = 1 markka (FmK)
OFFICIAL LANGUAGES: Finnish, Swedish
OTHER LANGUAGES: Lapp, Russian
MAIN RELIGION: Christianity 90%
EXPORTS: Paper and pulp, machinery, chemicals,
metals, timber

DENMARK

AREA: 43,069 sq. km
(16,629 sq. mi)
POPULATION: 5,199,000
CAPITAL: Copenhagen
CURRENCY: 100 ore = 1 Danish krone (DKr)
OFFICIAL LANGUAGE: Danish
OTHER LANGUAGES: Faroese, Greenlandic, German
MAIN RELIGION: Christianity 93%
EXPORTS: Meat and meat products, dairy products,
transport equipment, ships, fish, chemicals,
industrial machinery

ASIA

RUSSIA
AREA: 17,075,383 sq. km
(6,592,812 sq. mi)
POPULATION: 149,909,000
CAPITAL: Moscow
CURRENCY: 100 copecks = 1 rouble (R)
OFFICIAL LANGUAGE: Russian
MAIN RELIGIONS: Christianity 75%, Islam,
Buddhism
EXPORTS: Petroleum and petroleum products,
natural gas, timber and timber products, metals,
chemicals, manufactured goods

TURKEY
AREA: 780,574 sq. km
(301,380 sq. mi)
POPULATION: 63,406,000
CAPITAL: Ankara
CURRENCY: 100 kurus = 1 Turkish lira (TL)
OFFICIAL LANGUAGE: Turkish
OTHER LANGUAGES: Kurdish, Arabic
MAIN RELIGION: Islam 99%
EXPORTS: Manufactured goods, food,
mining products

CYPRUS
AREA: 9,251 sq. km (3,572 sq. mi)
POPULATION: 736,600
CAPITAL: Nicosia
CURRENCY: 100 cents = 1 Cypriot pound (£C);
100 kurus = 1 Turkish lira (TL)
OFFICIAL LANGUAGES: Greek, Turkish
OTHER LANGUAGE: English
MAIN RELIGIONS: Christianity 78%, Islam 18%
EXPORTS: Citrus fruit, potatoes, grapes, wine,
cement, clothing, shoes

GEORGIA
AREA: 69,699 sq. km
(26,911 sq. mi)
POPULATION: 5,726,000
CAPITAL: Tbilisi
CURRENCY: Lari
OFFICIAL LANGUAGE: Georgian
OTHER LANGUAGES: Russian, Armenian, Azeri
MAIN RELIGIONS: Christianity 83%, Islam 11%
EXPORTS: Citrus fruit, tea, wine, machinery,
metals, textiles, chemicals, fuel re-exports

ARMENIA
AREA: 29,800 sq. km
(11,506 sq. mi)
POPULATION: 3,557,000
CAPITAL: Yerevan
CURRENCY: 100 luma = 1 dram
OFFICIAL LANGUAGE: Armenian
OTHER LANGUAGE: Russian
MAIN RELIGION: Christianity 94%
EXPORTS: Gold and jewellery, aluminium,
transport equipment, electrical equipment

AZERBAIJAN
AREA: 86,599 sq. km
(33,436 sq. mi)
POPULATION: 7,790,000
CAPITAL: Baku
CURRENCY: 100 gopik = 1 manat
OFFICIAL LANGUAGE: Azerbaijani
OTHER LANGUAGES: Russian, Armenian
MAIN RELIGIONS: Islam 94%, Christianity 5%
EXPORTS: Oil, gas, chemicals, oil field equipment,
textiles, cotton

KAZAKSTAN
AREA: 2,715,097 sq. km
(1,048,300 sq. mi)
POPULATION: 17,377,000
CAPITAL: Almaty
CURRENCY: 100 teins = 1 tenge
OFFICIAL LANGUAGE: Kazak
OTHER LANGUAGE: Russian
MAIN RELIGIONS: Islam 47%, Christianity 46%
EXPORTS: Oil, metals, chemicals, grain, wool,
meat, coal

UZBEKISTAN
AREA: 449,601 sq. km
(173,591 sq. mi)
POPULATION: 23,089,000
CAPITAL: Tashkent
CURRENCY: Som
OFFICIAL LANGUAGE: Uzbek
OTHER LANGUAGES: Russian, Tajik
MAIN RELIGIONS: Islam 88%, Christianity 9%
EXPORTS: Cotton, gold, natural gas, mineral
fertilizer, metals, textiles, food

TURKMENISTAN
AREA: 488,098 sq. km
(188,455 sq. mi)
POPULATION: 4,075,000
CAPITAL: Ashkhabad
CURRENCY: 100 tenge = 1 manat
OFFICIAL LANGUAGE: Turkmen
OTHER LANGUAGES: Russian, Uzbek
MAIN RELIGIONS: Islam 87%, Christianity 11%
EXPORTS: Natural gas, cotton, petroleum products,
electricity, textiles, carpets

KYRGYZSTAN
AREA: 198,500 sq. km
(76,641 sq. mi)
POPULATION: 4,770,000
CAPITAL: Bishkek
CURRENCY: 100 tiyin = 1 som
OFFICIAL LANGUAGE: Kyrgyz
OTHER LANGUAGE: Russian
MAIN RELIGION: Islam 70%
EXPORTS: Wool, chemicals, cotton, metals, shoes,
machinery, tobacco

TAJIKISTAN
AREA: 143,100 sq. km
(55,251 sq. mi)
POPULATION: 6,155,000
CAPITAL: Dushanbe
CURRENCY: 100 copecks = 1 Tajik rouble (TR)
OFFICIAL LANGUAGE: Tajik
OTHER LANGUAGE: Russian
MAIN RELIGION: Islam 85%
EXPORTS: Cotton, aluminium, fruit and
vegetables, textiles

SYRIA
AREA: 185,180 sq. km
(71,498 sq. mi)
POPULATION: 15,452,000
CAPITAL: Damascus
CURRENCY: 100 piastres = 1 Syrian pound (£S)
OFFICIAL LANGUAGE: Arabic
OTHER LANGUAGES: Kurdish, Armenian, Aramaic,
Circassian, French
MAIN RELIGIONS: Islam 90%, Christianity 10%
EXPORTS: Petroleum, textiles, cotton, fruit and
vegetables, wheat, barley, chickens

IRAQ

AREA: 437,521 sq. km
(168,927 sq. mi)
POPULATION: 20,644,000
CAPITAL: Baghdad
CURRENCY: 1,000 fils = 1 Iraqi dinar (ID)
OFFICIAL LANGUAGES: Arabic, Kurdish (in
Kurdish regions)
OTHER LANGUAGES: Assyrian, Armenian
MAIN RELIGIONS: Islam 97%, Christianity 3%
EXPORTS: Crude oil and refined products,
fertilizer, sulphur

IRAN

AREA: 1,647,064 sq. km
(635,932 sq. mi)
POPULATION: 64,625,000
CAPITAL: Tehran
CURRENCY: 100 dinars = 1 rial (R)
OFFICIAL LANGUAGE: Farsi (Persian)
OTHER LANGUAGES: Turkic, Kurdish
MAIN RELIGION: Islam 99%
EXPORTS: Petroleum, carpets, fruit, nuts,
animal skins

LEBANON

AREA: 10,228 sq. km (3,949 sq. mi)
POPULATION: 3,696,000
CAPITAL: Beirut
CURRENCY: 100 piastres = 1 Lebanese pound (£L)
OFFICIAL LANGUAGES: Arabic, French
OTHER LANGUAGES: Armenian, English
MAIN RELIGIONS: Islam 70%, Christianity 30%
EXPORTS: Agricultural products, chemicals,
textiles, metals, jewellery

ISRAEL

AREA: 20,699 sq. km (7,992 sq. mi)
POPULATION: 5,433,000
CAPITAL: Jerusalem
CURRENCY: 100 new agorot = 1 Israeli shekel (IS)
OFFICIAL LANGUAGE: Hebrew, Arabic
OTHER LANGUAGES: English
MAIN RELIGIONS: Judaism 82%, Islam 14%,
Christianity 2%
EXPORTS: Machinery, cut diamonds, chemicals,
textiles, agricultural products, metals

JORDAN

AREA: 89,549 sq. km
(34,575 sq. mi)
POPULATION: 4,101,000
CAPITAL: Amman
CURRENCY: 1,000 fils = 1 Jordanian dinar (JD)
OFFICIAL LANGUAGE: Arabic
OTHER LANGUAGE: English
MAIN RELIGIONS: Islam 92%, Christianity 8%
EXPORTS: Phosphates, fertilizer, potash,
agricultural products, manufactured goods

SAUDI ARABIA

AREA: 2,240,350 sq. km
(865,000 sq. mi)
POPULATION: 18,730,000
CAPITAL: Riyadh
CURRENCY: 100 halalas = 1 Saudi riyal (SR)
OFFICIAL LANGUAGE: Arabic
MAIN RELIGION: Islam 100%
EXPORTS: Petroleum and petroleum products

KUWAIT

AREA: 17,819 sq. km (6,880 sq. mi)
POPULATION: 1,817,000
CAPITAL: Kuwait
CURRENCY: 1,000 fils = 1 Kuwaiti dinar (KD)
OFFICIAL LANGUAGE: Arabic
OTHER LANGUAGE: English
MAIN RELIGIONS: Islam 85%, Christianity 8%,
Hinduism and Parsi 2%
EXPORTS: Oil

BAHRAIN

AREA: 661 sq. km (255 sq. mi)
POPULATION: 575,900
CAPITAL: Manama
CURRENCY: 1,000 fils = 1 Bahraini dinar (BD)
OFFICIAL LANGUAGE: Arabic
OTHER LANGUAGES: English, Farsi, Urdu
MAIN RELIGION: Islam 100%
EXPORTS: Petroleum and petroleum
products, aluminium

QATAR

AREA: 11,395 sq. km (4,400 sq. mi)
POPULATION: 533,900
CAPITAL: Doha
CURRENCY: 100 dirhams = 1 Qatari riyal (QR)
OFFICIAL LANGUAGE: Arabic
OTHER LANGUAGE: English
MAIN RELIGION: Islam 95%
EXPORTS: Petroleum products, steel, fertilizer

UNITED ARAB EMIRATES

AREA: 77,701 sq. km
(30,000 sq. mi)
POPULATION: 2,925,000
CAPITAL: Abu Dhabi
CURRENCY: 100 fils = 1 Emirian dirham (Dh)
OFFICIAL LANGUAGE: Arabic
OTHER LANGUAGES: Persian, English, Hindi, Urdu
MAIN RELIGION: Islam 96%
EXPORTS: Crude oil, natural gas, dried fish, dates

OMAN

AREA: 212,380 sq. km
(82,000 sq. mi)
POPULATION: 2,125,000
CAPITAL: Muscat
CURRENCY: 1,000 baiza = 1 Omani rial (RO)
OFFICIAL LANGUAGE: Arabic
OTHER LANGUAGES: English, Baluchi, Urdu,
Indian languages
MAIN RELIGIONS: Islam 86%, Hinduism 13%
EXPORTS: Petroleum, fish, copper, textiles

YEMEN

AREA: 527,969 sq. km
(203,849 sq. mi)
POPULATION: 14,728,000
CAPITAL: Sanaa
CURRENCY: 100 fils = 1 Yemeni rial
OFFICIAL LANGUAGE: Arabic
MAIN RELIGION: Islam 99%
EXPORTS: Crude oil, cotton, coffee, animal skins,
vegetables, dried and salted fish

AFGHANISTAN

AREA: 649,507 sq. km
(250,775 sq. mi)
POPULATION: 21,252,000
CAPITAL: Kabul
CURRENCY: 100 puls = 1 afghani (AF)
OFFICIAL LANGUAGES: Afghan, Persian, Pashto
OTHER LANGUAGES: Uzbek, Turkmen
MAIN RELIGIONS: Islam 99%, Hinduism and Judaism 1%
EXPORTS: Fruit, nuts, hand-woven carpets, wool, cotton, animal skins, precious and semi-precious gemstones

PAKISTAN

AREA: 803, 944 km
(310,403 sq. mi)
POPULATION: 131,542,000
CAPITAL: Islamabad
CURRENCY: 100 paisa = 1 Pakistani rupee (PRe)
OFFICIAL LANGUAGES: Urdu, English
OTHER LANGUAGES: Punjabi, Sindhi, Pashto, Baluchi
MAIN RELIGION: Islam 97%
EXPORTS: Cotton, textiles, clothing, rice, leather, carpets

INDIA

AREA: 3,095,472 sq. km
(1,195,063 sq. mi)
POPULATION: 936,546,000
CAPITAL: New Delhi
CURRENCY: 100 paisa = 1 Indian rupee (Re)
OFFICIAL LANGUAGES: Hindi, English
OTHER LANGUAGES: Hindustani, Bengali, Telugu, Marathi, Tamil, Urdu, Gujarati, Malayalam, Kannada, Oriya, Punjabi, Assamese, Kashmiri, Rajasthani, Sindhi, Sanskrit
MAIN RELIGIONS: Hinduism 80%, Islam 14%, Christianity 3%
EXPORTS: Clothing, gemstones and jewellery, engineering equipment, chemicals, leather goods, cotton yarn, fabric

NEPAL

AREA: 140,798 sq. km
(54,362 sq. mi)
POPULATION: 21,561,000
CAPITAL: Kathmandu
CURRENCY: 100 paisa = 1 Nepalese rupee (NR)
OFFICIAL LANGUAGE: Nepali
MAIN RELIGIONS: Hinduism 90%, Buddhism 5%, Islam 3%
EXPORTS: Carpets, clothing, leather goods, jute (fibre) goods, grain

BHUTAN

AREA: 41,440 sq. km
(16,000 sq. mi)
POPULATION: 1,781,000
CAPITAL: Thimphu
CURRENCY: 100 chetrum = 1 ngultrum (Nu); Indian currency is also legal tender
OFFICIAL LANGUAGE: Dzongkha
OTHER LANGUAGES: Tibetan and Nepali
MAIN RELIGIONS: Buddhism 75%, Hinduism 25%
EXPORTS: Timber, handicrafts, cement, fruit, electricity, gemstones, spices

BANGLADESH

AREA: 142,776 sq. km
(55,126 sq. mi)
POPULATION: 128,095,000
CAPITAL: Dhaka
CURRENCY: 100 poisha = 1 taka (Tk)
OFFICIAL LANGUAGE: Bengali
OTHER LANGUAGE: English
MAIN RELIGIONS: Islam 83%, Hinduism 16%, Buddhism and Christianity 1%
EXPORTS: Garments, jute (fibre) and jute goods, leather, shrimp

MALDIVES

AREA: 298 sq. km (115 sq. mi)
POPULATION: 261,300
CAPITAL: Male
CURRENCY: 100 laris = 1 rufiyaa (Rf)
OFFICIAL LANGUAGE: Divehi (Maldivian)
OTHER LANGUAGE: English
MAIN RELIGION: Islam 100%
EXPORTS: Fish, clothing

SRI LANKA

AREA: 65,610 sq. km
(25,332 sq. mi)
POPULATION: 18,343,000
CAPITAL: Colombo
CURRENCY: 100 cents = 1 Sri Lankan rupee (SLRe)
OFFICIAL LANGUAGES: Sinhala, Tamil
OTHER LANGUAGE: English
MAIN RELIGIONS: Buddhism 69%, Hinduism 15%,

Christianity 8%, Islam 8%
EXPORTS: Textiles, tea, diamonds and other precious gemstones, petroleum products, rubber products, agricultural products, marine products

MYANMAR (BURMA)

AREA: 678,034 sq. km
(261,789 sq. mi)
POPULATION: 45,104,000
CAPITAL: Yangon (Rangoon)
CURRENCY: 100 pyas = 1 kyat (K)
OFFICIAL LANGUAGE: Burmese
MAIN RELIGIONS: Buddhism 89%, Christianity 4%, Islam 4%
EXPORTS: Pulses and beans, rice, timber

LAOS

AREA: 236,799 sq. km
(91,428 sq. mi)
POPULATION: 4,837,000
CAPITAL: Vientiane
CURRENCY: 100 ats = 1 kip (K)
OFFICIAL LANGUAGE: Lao
OTHER LANGUAGES: French, English
MAIN RELIGIONS: Buddhism 60%, animism 34%, Christianity 2%
EXPORTS: Electricity, timber products, coffee, tin, textiles

VIETNAM

AREA: 337,912 sq. km
(130,468 sq. mi)
POPULATION: 74,393,000
CAPITAL: Hanoi
CURRENCY: 100 xu = 1 dong (D)
OFFICIAL LANGUAGE: Vietnamese
OTHER LANGUAGES: French, Chinese, English, Khmer, tribal languages
MAIN RELIGIONS: Buddhism 55%, Christianity 7%, Taoism, indigenous religions, Islam
EXPORTS: Petroleum, rice, agricultural products, marine products, coffee

THAILAND

AREA: 513,998 sq. km
(198,455 sq. mi)
POPULATION: 60,271,000
CAPITAL: Bangkok
CURRENCY: 100 satangs = 1 baht (B)
OFFICIAL LANGUAGE: Thai
OTHER LANGUAGES: English, Chinese, Malay
MAIN RELIGIONS: Buddhism 95%, Islam 4%
EXPORTS: Machinery, manufactured goods, agricultural products, fish

CAMBODIA

AREA: 181,036 sq. km (69,898 sq. mi)
POPULATION: 10,561,000
CAPITAL: Phnom Penh
CURRENCY: 100 sen = 1 riel (CR)
OFFICIAL LANGUAGE: Khmer
OTHER LANGUAGE: French
MAIN RELIGIONS: Buddhism 95%, Islam 2%
EXPORTS: Timber, rubber, soya beans, sesame

MALAYSIA
AREA: 333,403 sq. km (128,727 sq. mi)
POPULATION: 19,724,000
CAPITAL: Kuala Lumpur
CURRENCY: 100 sen = 1 ringgit (M$)
OFFICIAL LANGUAGE: Malay
OTHER LANGUAGES: English, Mandarin, Tamil, Hakka, regional languages
MAIN RELIGIONS: Islam 53%, Buddhism 17%, Confucianism 12%, Christianity 9%, Hinduism 7%
EXPORTS: Electronic equipment, petroleum and petroleum products, palm oil, timber and timber products, rubber, textiles

PHILIPPINES
AREA: 299,536 sq. km (115,551 sq. mi)
POPULATION: 73,266,000
CAPITAL: Manila
CURRENCY: 100 centavos = 1 Philippine peso (P)
OFFICIAL LANGUAGES: Filipino, English
OTHER LANGUAGES: Regional languages
MAIN RELIGIONS: Christianity 92%, Islam 5%, Buddhism 3%
EXPORTS: Electronics, textiles, coconut products, copper, fish

SINGAPORE
AREA: 583 sq. km (225 sq. mi)
POPULATION: 2,890,000
CAPITAL: Singapore
CURRENCY: 100 cents = 1 Singapore dollar (S$)
OFFICIAL LANGUAGES: Chinese, Malay, Tamil, English
MAIN RELIGIONS: Buddhism 28%, Islam 15%, Christianity 13%, Taoism 13%, Hinduism 5%
EXPORTS: Computer equipment, rubber and rubber products, petroleum products, telecommunications equipment

BRUNEI

AREA: 5,765 sq. km (2,226 sq. mi)
POPULATION: 292,300
CAPITAL: Bandar Seri Begawan
CURRENCY: 100 sen = 1 Bruneian dollar (B$)
OFFICIAL LANGUAGE: Malay
OTHER LANGUAGES: English, Chinese
MAIN RELIGIONS: Islam 63%, Buddhist 14%, Christianity 8%, indigenous religions
EXPORTS: Crude oil, liquefied natural gas, petroleum products

INDONESIA
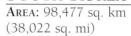
AREA: 2,019,358 sq. km (779,675 sq. mi)
POPULATION: 203,584,000
CAPITAL: Jakarta
CURRENCY: 100 sen = 1 Indonesian rupiah (Rp)
OFFICIAL LANGUAGE: Bahasa Indonesia
OTHER LANGUAGES: English, Dutch, Javanese, regional languages
MAIN RELIGIONS: Islam 87%, Christianity 9%, Hinduism 2%, Buddhism 1%
EXPORTS: Manufactured goods, fuels, food, raw materials

CHINA
AREA: 9,583,000 sq. km (3,700,000 sq. mi)
POPULATION: 1,203,097,000
CAPITAL: Beijing
CURRENCY: 100 fen = 1 yuan (Y)
OFFICIAL LANGUAGE: Mandarin
OTHER LANGUAGES: Cantonese, Shanghainese, Fuzhou, Hokkien-Taiwanese
MAIN RELIGIONS: Daoism (Taoism) 20%, Buddhism 6%
EXPORTS: Textiles, clothing, shoes, toys, machinery, weapons

MONGOLIA
AREA: 1,565,000 sq. km (604,247 sq. mi)
POPULATION: 2,494,000
CAPITAL: Ulaanbaatar
CURRENCY: 100 mongos = 1 tugrik (Tug)
OFFICIAL LANGUAGE: Khalkha Mongol
OTHER LANGUAGES: Turkic, Russian, Chinese
MAIN RELIGIONS: Buddhism 95%, Islam 4%
EXPORTS: Copper, livestock, animal products, cashmere, wool, animal skins, metals

NORTH KOREA

AREA: 120,717 sq. km (46,609 sq. mi)
POPULATION: 23,487,000
CAPITAL: P'yŏngyang
CURRENCY: 100 chon = 1 North Korean won (NKW)
OFFICIAL LANGUAGE: Korean
MAIN RELIGIONS: Chondogya 14%, Buddhism 2%, Christianity 1%
EXPORTS: Minerals, metal products, agricultural and fishery products, manufactured goods

SOUTH KOREA
AREA: 98,477 sq. km (38,022 sq. mi)
POPULATION: 45,554,000
CAPITAL: Seoul
CURRENCY: 100 chon = 1 South Korean won (W)
OFFICIAL LANGUAGE: Korean
OTHER LANGUAGE: English
MAIN RELIGIONS: Christianity 49%, Buddhism 47%, Confucianism 3%
EXPORTS: Electronic and electrical equipment, machinery, steel, motor vehicles, ships, textiles, clothing, shoes, fish

TAIWAN
AREA: 35,967 sq. km (13,887 sq. mi)
POPULATION: 21,501,000
CAPITAL: Taipei
CURRENCY: 100 cents = 1 New Taiwan dollar (NT$)
OFFICIAL LANGUAGE: Mandarin
OTHER LANGUAGES: Fukien, Hakka
MAIN RELIGIONS: Buddhism 43%, Daoism (Taoism) 21%, Christianity 7%, Confucianism
EXPORTS: Electrical machinery, electronic goods, textiles, shoes, food, timber products

JAPAN
AREA: 371,973 sq. km (143,619 sq. mi)
POPULATION: 125,506,000
CAPITAL: Tokyo
CURRENCY: 100 sen = 1 yen (¥)
OFFICIAL LANGUAGE: Japanese
MAIN RELIGIONS: Shinto and Buddhism 84%
EXPORTS: Machinery, motor vehicles, consumer electronics

AFRICA

MOROCCO
AREA: 446,550 sq. km
(172,413 sq. mi)
POPULATION: 29,169,000
CAPITAL: Rabat
CURRENCY: 100 centimes = 1 Moroccan dirham (DH)
OFFICIAL LANGUAGE: Arabic
OTHER LANGUAGES: Berber, French
MAIN RELIGIONS: Islam 99%, Christianity 1%
EXPORTS: Food, beverages, consumer goods, phosphates

ALGERIA
AREA: 2,378,907 sq. km
(918,497 sq. mi)
POPULATION: 28,539,000
CAPITAL: Algiers
CURRENCY: 100 centimes = 1 Algerian dinar (DA)
OFFICIAL LANGUAGE: Arabic
OTHER LANGUAGES: French, Berber
MAIN RELIGIONS: Islam 99%, Christianity and Judaism 1%
EXPORTS: Petroleum, natural gas

TUNISIA
AREA: 164,149 sq. km
(63,378 sq. mi)
POPULATION: 8,880,000
CAPITAL: Tunis
CURRENCY: 1,000 milliemes = 1 Tunisian dinar (TD)
OFFICIAL LANGUAGE: Arabic
OTHER LANGUAGES: French, Berber
MAIN RELIGIONS: Islam 98%, Christianity 1%, Judaism 1%
EXPORTS: Agricultural products, chemicals

LIBYA
AREA: 1,759,540 sq. km
(679,360 sq. mi)
POPULATION: 5,248,000
CAPITAL: Tripoli
CURRENCY: 1,000 dirhams = 1 Libyan dinar (LD)
OFFICIAL LANGUAGE: Arabic
OTHER LANGUAGES: Italian, English
MAIN RELIGION: Islam 97%
EXPORTS: Crude oil, refined petroleum products, natural gas

CAPE VERDE ISLANDS
AREA: 4,033 sq. km (1,557 sq. mi)
POPULATION: 435,900
CAPITAL: Praia
CURRENCY: 100 centavos = 1 Cape Verdean escudo (CVEsc)
OFFICIAL LANGUAGE: Portuguese
OTHER LANGUAGE: Cape Verde creole
MAIN RELIGION: Christianity 97%
EXPORTS: Fish, bananas, animal skins

EGYPT
AREA: 1,002,071 sq. km
(386,900 sq. mi)
POPULATION: 62,360,000
CAPITAL: Cairo
CURRENCY: 100 piastres = 1 Egyptian pound (£E)
OFFICIAL LANGUAGE: Arabic
OTHER LANGUAGES: English, French
MAIN RELIGIONS: Islam 94%, Christianity 6%
EXPORTS: Crude oil and petroleum products, cotton, textiles, metal products, chemicals

MAURITANIA
AREA: 1,030,807 sq. km
(397,955 sq. mi)
POPULATION: 2,263,000
CAPITAL: Nouakchott
CURRENCY: 5 khoums = 1 ouguiya (UM)
OFFICIAL LANGUAGES: Hasaniya Arabic, Wolof
OTHER LANGUAGES: French, Pular, Soninke
MAIN RELIGION: Islam 100%
EXPORTS: Iron ore, fish, fish products

MALI
AREA: 1,239,709 sq. km
(478,652 sq. mi)
POPULATION: 9,375,000
CAPITAL: Bamako
CURRENCY: 100 centimes = 1 CFA franc (CFAF)
OFFICIAL LANGUAGE: French
OTHER LANGUAGES: Regional languages
MAIN RELIGIONS: Islam 90%, indigenous religions 9%, Christianity 1%
EXPORTS: Cotton, livestock, gold

BURKINA FASO
AREA: 274,201 sq. km
(105,869 sq. mi)
POPULATION: 10,423,000
CAPITAL: Ouagadougou
CURRENCY: 100 centimes = 1 CFA franc (CFAF)
OFFICIAL LANGUAGE: French
OTHER LANGUAGES: Tribal languages
MAIN RELIGIONS: Islam 50%, indigenous religions 40%, Christianity 10%
EXPORTS: Cotton, gold, animal products

NIGER
AREA: 1,188,999 sq. km
(459,073 sq. mi)
POPULATION: 9,280,000
CAPITAL: Niamey
CURRENCY: 100 centimes = 1 CFA franc (CFAF)
OFFICIAL LANGUAGE: French
OTHER LANGUAGES: Hausa, Djerma
MAIN RELIGIONS: Islam 80%, indigenous religions 14%, Christianity 1%
EXPORTS: Uranium ore, livestock, cowpeas, onions

CHAD
AREA: 1,283,998 sq. km
(495,752 sq. mi)
POPULATION: 5,587,000
CAPITAL: N'Djamena
CURRENCY: 100 centimes = 1 CFA franc (CFAF)
OFFICIAL LANGUAGES: French, Arabic
OTHER LANGUAGES: Sara, Sango
MAIN RELIGIONS: Islam 50%, Christianity 25%, indigenous religions and animism 25%
EXPORTS: Cotton, cattle, textiles, fish

SUDAN
AREA: 2,505,825 sq. km
(967,500 sq. mi)
POPULATION: 30,120,000
CAPITAL: Khartoum
CURRENCY: 100 piastres = 1 Sudanese pound (£S)
OFFICIAL LANGUAGE: Arabic
OTHER LANGUAGES: Nubian, Ta Bedawie, Nilotic, Nilo-Hamitic, regional languages, English
MAIN RELIGIONS: Islam 70%, indigenous religions 25%, Christianity 5%
EXPORTS: Gum, livestock, cotton, sesame, peanuts

ERITREA
AREA: 117,599 sq. km
(45,405 sq. mi)
POPULATION: 3,579,000
CAPITAL: Asmara
CURRENCY: 100 cents = 1 birr (Br)
OFFICIAL LANGUAGES: Arabic, Tigrinya, Tigre
OTHER LANGUAGES: African languages
MAIN RELIGIONS: Islam 50%, Christianity 50%
EXPORTS: Salt, animal skins, oilseed

ETHIOPIA

AREA: 1,221,897 sq. km
(471,775 sq. mi)
POPULATION: 55,979,000
CAPITAL: Addis Ababa
CURRENCY: 100 cents = 1 birr (Br)
OFFICIAL LANGUAGE: Amharic
OTHER LANGUAGES: African languages,
Arabic, English
MAIN RELIGIONS: Islam 50%, Christianity 40%,
animism 10%
EXPORTS: Coffee, leather products, gold

DJIBOUTI

AREA: 22,999 sq. km
(8,880 sq. mi)
POPULATION: 421,300
CAPITAL: Djibouti
CURRENCY: 100 centimes = 1 Djiboutian
franc (DF)
OFFICIAL LANGUAGES: French, Arabic
OTHER LANGUAGES: Somali, Afar
MAIN RELIGIONS: Islam 94%, Christianity 6%
EXPORTS: Animal skins, coffee

SOMALIA

AREA: 637,539 sq. km
(246,154 sq. mi)
POPULATION: 7,348,000
CAPITAL: Mogadishu
CURRENCY: 100 cents = 1 Somali shilling (So.Sh.)
OFFICIAL LANGUAGE: Somali
OTHER LANGUAGES: Arabic, Italian, English
MAIN RELIGION: Islam 99%
EXPORTS: Bananas, livestock, fish, animal skins

SENEGAL

AREA: 197,161 sq. km
(76,124 sq. mi)
POPULATION: 9,007,000
CAPITAL: Dakar
CURRENCY: 100 centimes = 1 CFA franc (CFAF)
OFFICIAL LANGUAGE: French
OTHER LANGUAGES: Regional languages
MAIN RELIGIONS: Islam 92%, indigenous
religions 6%, Christianity 2%
EXPORTS: Fish, peanuts, petroleum products,
phosphates, cotton

GAMBIA

AREA: 10,368 sq. km (4,003 sq. mi)
POPULATION: 989,300
CAPITAL: Banjul
CURRENCY: 100 butut = 1 dalasi (D)
OFFICIAL LANGUAGE: English
OTHER LANGUAGES: African languages
MAIN RELIGIONS: Islam 90%, Christianity 9%,
indigenous religions 1%
EXPORTS: Peanuts, fish, palm kernels

GUINEA-BISSAU

AREA: 36,125 sq. km
(13,948 sq. mi)
POPULATION: 1,125,000
CAPITAL: Bissau
CURRENCY: 100 centavos = 1 Guinea-Bissauan
peso (PG)
OFFICIAL LANGUAGE: Portuguese
OTHER LANGUAGES: Criolo, African languages
MAIN RELIGIONS: Indigenous religions 65%,
Islam 30%, Christianity 5%
EXPORTS: Cashews, fish, peanuts, palm kernels

GUINEA

AREA: 245,856 sq. km
(94,925 sq. mi)
POPULATION: 6,549,000
CAPITAL: Conakry
CURRENCY: 100 centimes = 1 Guinean franc (FG)
OFFICIAL LANGUAGE: French
OTHER LANGUAGES: Tribal languages
MAIN RELIGIONS: Islam 85%, Christianity 8%,
indigenous religions 7%
EXPORTS: Bauxite, alumina, diamonds, gold,
coffee, pineapples, bananas, palm kernels

SIERRA LEONE

AREA: 71,740 sq. km
(27,699 sq. mi)
POPULATION: 4,753,000
CAPITAL: Freetown
CURRENCY: 100 cents = 1 leone (Le)
OFFICIAL LANGUAGE: English
OTHER LANGUAGES: Mende, Temne, Krio
MAIN RELIGIONS: Islam 60%, indigenous
religions 30%, Christianity 10%
EXPORTS: Diamonds and other minerals, coffee,
cocoa, fish

LIBERIA

AREA: 111,370 sq. km
(43,000 sq. mi)
POPULATION: 3,073,000
CAPITAL: Monrovia
CURRENCY: 100 cents = 1 Liberian dollar (L$)
OFFICIAL LANGUAGE: English
OTHER LANGUAGES: Niger-Congo languages
MAIN RELIGIONS: Indigenous religions 70%,
Islam 20%, Christianity 10%
EXPORTS: Iron ore, rubber, timber, coffee

CÔTE D'IVOIRE (IVORY COAST)

AREA: 322,463 sq. km
(124,503 sq. mi)
POPULATION: 14,791,000
CAPITALS: Abidjan (seat of government),
Yamoussoukro (official)
CURRENCY: 100 centimes = 1 CFA franc (CFAF)
OFFICIAL LANGUAGE: French
OTHER LANGUAGES: Regional languages
MAIN RELIGIONS: Islam 60%, indigenous
religions 25%, Christianity 12%
EXPORTS: Cocoa, coffee, timber, petroleum, cotton,
bananas, pineapples, palm oil

GHANA

AREA: 238,539 sq. km
(92,100 sq. mi)
POPULATION: 17,763,000
CAPITAL: Accra
CURRENCY: 100 pesewas = 1 cedi (C)
OFFICIAL LANGUAGE: English
OTHER LANGUAGES: African languages
MAIN RELIGIONS: Indigenous religions 38%, Islam
30%, Christianity 24%
EXPORTS: Cocoa, gold, timber, tuna, bauxite,
aluminium

TOGO

AREA: 56,599 sq. km
(21,853 sq. mi)
POPULATION: 4,410,000
CAPITAL: Lomé
CURRENCY: 100 centimes = 1 CFA franc (CFAF)
OFFICIAL LANGUAGE: French
OTHER LANGUAGES: Regional languages
MAIN RELIGIONS: Indigenous religions 70%,
Christianity 20%, Islam 10%
EXPORTS: Phosphates, cotton, cocoa, coffee

THE READER'S DIGEST CHILDREN'S ATLAS OF THE WORLD

BENIN
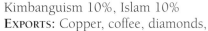
AREA: 112,621 sq. km
(43,483 sq. mi)
POPULATION: 5,523,000
CAPITALS: Cotonou (de facto), Porto-Novo (legal)
CURRENCY: 100 centimes = 1 CFA franc (CFAF)
OFFICIAL LANGUAGE: French
OTHER LANGUAGES: Fon, Yoruba, regional languages
MAIN RELIGIONS: Indigenous religions 70%, Islam 15%, Christianity 15%
EXPORTS: Cotton, crude oil, palm products, cocoa

NIGERIA
AREA: 923,773 sq. km
(356,669 sq. mi)
POPULATION: 101,232,000
CAPITAL: Abuja
CURRENCY: 100 kobo = 1 naira (₦)
OFFICIAL LANGUAGE: English
OTHER LANGUAGES: Regional languages
MAIN RELIGIONS: Islam 50%, Christianity 40%, indigenous religions 10%
EXPORTS: Oil, cocoa, rubber

CAMEROON
AREA: 475,501 sq. km
(183,591 sq. mi)
POPULATION: 13,521,000
CAPITAL: Yaoundé
CURRENCY: 100 centimes = 1 CFA franc (CFAF)
OFFICIAL LANGUAGES: English, French
OTHER LANGUAGES: African languages
MAIN RELIGIONS: Indigenous religions 51%, Christianity 33%, Islam 16%
EXPORTS: Petroleum products, timber, cocoa beans, aluminium, coffee, cotton

EQUATORIAL GUINEA
AREA: 28,037 sq. km
(10,825 sq. mi)
POPULATION: 420,300
CAPITAL: Malabo
CURRENCY: 100 centimes = 1 CFA franc (CFAF)
OFFICIAL LANGUAGE: Spanish
OTHER LANGUAGES: Pidgin English, regional languages
MAIN RELIGION: Christianity 85%
EXPORTS: Coffee, timber, cocoa

CENTRAL AFRICAN REPUBLIC
AREA: 622,374 sq. km
(240,376 sq. mi)
POPULATION: 3,210,000
CAPITAL: Bangui
CURRENCY: 100 centimes = 1 CFA franc (CFAF)
OFFICIAL LANGUAGE: French
OTHER LANGUAGES: Sangho, Arabic, Hunsa, Swahili
MAIN RELIGIONS: Christianity 50%, indigenous religions 24%, Islam 15%
EXPORTS: Diamonds, timber, cotton, coffee, tobacco

SÃO TOMÉ AND PRÍNCIPE
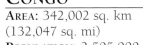
AREA: 963 sq. km (372 sq. mi)
POPULATION: 140,400
CAPITAL: São Tomé
CURRENCY: 100 centavos = 1 dobra (Db)
OFFICIAL LANGUAGE: Portuguese
MAIN RELIGION: Christianity 100%
EXPORTS: Cocoa, copra (dried coconut flesh), coffee, palm oil

GABON

AREA: 265,001 sq. km
(102,317 sq. mi)
POPULATION: 1,156,000
CAPITAL: Libreville
CURRENCY: 100 centimes = 1 CFA franc (CFAF)
OFFICIAL LANGUAGE: French
OTHER LANGUAGES: African languages
MAIN RELIGIONS: Christianity 60%, animism 40%, Islam 1%
EXPORTS: Crude oil, timber, manganese, uranium

CONGO

AREA: 342,002 sq. km
(132,047 sq. mi)
POPULATION: 2,505,000
CAPITAL: Brazzaville
CURRENCY: 100 centimes = 1 CFA franc (CFAF)
OFFICIAL LANGUAGE: French
OTHER LANGUAGES: African languages
MAIN RELIGIONS: Christianity 50%, animism 48%, Islam 2%
EXPORTS: Crude oil, timber, sugar, cocoa, coffee, diamonds

DEMOCRATIC REPUBLIC OF THE CONGO (ZAIRE)

AREA: 2,344,872 sq. km
(905,356 sq. mi)
POPULATION: 44,061,000
CAPITAL: Kinshasa
CURRENCY: 100 makuta = 1 new zaire (NZ)
OFFICIAL LANGUAGE: French
OTHER LANGUAGES: Lingala, Swahili, Kingwana, Kikongo, Tshiluba
MAIN RELIGIONS: Christianity 70%,

Kimbanguism 10%, Islam 10%
EXPORTS: Copper, coffee, diamonds, crude oil

UGANDA

AREA: 236,037 sq. km
(91,134 sq. mi)
POPULATION: 19,573,000
CAPITAL: Kampala
CURRENCY: 100 cents = 1 Ugandan shilling (USh)
OFFICIAL LANGUAGE: English
OTHER LANGUAGES: Luganda, Swahili, Bantu and other regional languages
MAIN RELIGIONS: Christianity 66%, indigenous religions 18%, Islam 16%
EXPORTS: Coffee, cotton, tea

KENYA

AREA: 582,646 sq. km (224,960 sq. mi)
POPULATION: 28,817,000
CAPITAL: Nairobi
CURRENCY: 100 cents = 1 Kenyan shilling (KSh)
OFFICIAL LANGUAGES: English, Swahili
OTHER LANGUAGES: Indigenous languages
MAIN RELIGIONS: Christianity 66%, indigenous religions 26%
EXPORTS: Tea, coffee, petroleum products

RWANDA

AREA: 26,338 sq. km (10,169 sq. mi)
POPULATION: 8,605,000
CAPITAL: Kigali
CURRENCY: 100 centimes = 1 Rwandan franc (RF)
OFFICIAL LANGUAGES: Kinyarwanda, French
OTHER LANGUAGE: Kiswahili
MAIN RELIGIONS: Christianity 74%, indigenous religions 25%, Islam 1%
EXPORTS: Coffee, tea, minerals

BURUNDI

AREA: 10,759 sq. miles (27,866 sq. km)
POPULATION: 6,262,000
CAPITAL: Bujumbura
CURRENCY: 100 centimes = 1 Burundi franc (FBu)
OFFICIAL LANGUAGES: Kirundi, French
OTHER LANGUAGE: Swahili
MAIN RELIGIONS: Christianity 67%, indigenous religions 32%, Islam 1%
EXPORTS: Coffee, tea, cotton, animal skins

TANZANIA

AREA: 945,091 sq. km (364,900 sq. mi)
POPULATION: 28,701,000
CAPITALS: Dar es Salaam (seat of government), Dodoma (official)

CURRENCY: 100 cents = 1 Tanzanian shilling (TSh)
OFFICIAL **L**ANGUAGES: Swahili, English
MAIN **R**ELIGIONS: Christianity 45%, Islam 35%, indigenous religions 20%
EXPORTS: Coffee, cotton, tobacco, tea, cashew nuts, sisal (fibre)

ANGOLA

AREA: 1,246,699 sq. km
(481,351 sq. mi)
POPULATION: 10,070,000
CAPITAL: Luanda
CURRENCY: 100 lwei = 1 kwanza (Kz)
OFFICIAL **L**ANGUAGE: Portuguese
OTHER **L**ANGUAGES: Bantu and other African languages
MAIN **R**ELIGIONS: Christianity 53%, indigenous religions 47%
EXPORTS: Oil, diamonds, refined petroleum products, gas, coffee, sisal (fibre), fish and fish products, timber, cotton

ZAMBIA

AREA: 752,615 sq. km
(290 585 sq. mi)
POPULATION: 9,446,000
CAPITAL: Lusaka
CURRENCY: 100 ngwee = 1 Zambian kwacha (ZK)
OFFICIAL **L**ANGUAGE: English
OTHER **L**ANGUAGES: Regional languages
MAIN **R**ELIGIONS: Christianity 75%, indigenous religions 23%, Islam and Hinduism 1%
EXPORTS: Copper, zinc, cobalt, lead, tobacco

ZIMBABWE

AREA: 390,624 sq. km
(150,820 sq. mi)
POPULATION: 11,140,000
CAPITAL: Harare
CURRENCY: 100 cents = 1 Zimbabwean dollar (Z$)
OFFICIAL **L**ANGUAGE: English
OTHER **L**ANGUAGES: Regional languages
MAIN **R**ELIGIONS: Syncretic (part Christianity, part indigenous religions) 50%, Christianity 25%, indigenous religions 24%
EXPORTS: Tobacco, manufactured goods, gold, textiles

MALAWI

AREA: 118,485 sq. km
(45,747 sq. mi)
POPULATION: 9,808,000
CAPITAL: Lilongwe
CURRENCY: 100 tambala = 1 Malawian kwacha (MK)
OFFICIAL **L**ANGUAGES: English, Chichewa
OTHER **L**ANGUAGES: Regional languages
MAIN **R**ELIGIONS: Christianity 75%, Islam 20%, indigenous religions 5%
EXPORTS: Tobacco, tea, sugar, coffee, peanuts, timber products

MOZAMBIQUE

AREA: 771,421 sq. km (297,846 sq. mi)
POPULATION: 18,115,000
CAPITAL: Maputo
CURRENCY: 100 centavos = 1 metical (Mt)
OFFICIAL **L**ANGUAGE: Portuguese
OTHER **L**ANGUAGES: Regional languages
MAIN **R**ELIGIONS: Indigenous religions 60%, Christianity 30%, Islam 10%
EXPORTS: Shrimp, cashews, cotton, sugar, copra (dried coconut flesh), citrus fruit

NAMIBIA

AREA: 824,451 sq. km
(318,321 sq. mi)
POPULATION: 1,652,000
CAPITAL: Windhoek
CURRENCY: 100 cents = 1 South African rand (R)
OFFICIAL **L**ANGUAGE: English
OTHER **L**ANGUAGES: Afrikaans, German, regional languages
MAIN **R**ELIGION: Christianity 90%
EXPORTS: Diamonds, copper, gold, zinc, lead, uranium, cattle, processed fish

BOTSWANA

AREA: 569,582 sq. km
(219,916 sq. mi)
POPULATION: 1,392,000
CAPITAL: Gaborone
CURRENCY: 100 thebe = 1 pula (P)
OFFICIAL **L**ANGUAGE: English
OTHER **L**ANGUAGE: Setswana
MAIN **R**ELIGIONS: Indigenous religions 50%, Christianity 50%
EXPORTS: Diamonds, copper and nickel, meat

SOUTH AFRICA

AREA: 1,221,043 sq. km
(471,445 sq. mi)
POPULATION: 45,095,000
CAPITALS: Bloemfontein (judicial), Cape Town (legislative), Pretoria (administrative)
CURRENCY: 100 cents = 1 rand (R)
OFFICIAL **L**ANGUAGES: Afrikaans, English, Xhosa, Zulu and other regional languages
MAIN **R**ELIGIONS: Christianity 67%, Hinduism, Islam
EXPORTS: Gold, diamonds and other minerals and metals, food, chemicals

SWAZILAND

AREA: 17,366 sq. km (6,705 sq. mi)
POPULATION: 967,000
CAPITAL: Mbabane
CURRENCY: 100 cents = 1 lilangeni (E)
OFFICIAL **L**ANGUAGES: English, Swazi
MAIN **R**ELIGIONS: Christianity 60%, indigenous religions 40%
EXPORTS: Sugar, wood pulp, cotton, asbestos

LESOTHO

AREA: 30,344 sq. km (11,716 sq. mi)
POPULATION: 1,993,000
CAPITAL: Maseru
CURRENCY: 100 lisente = 1 loti (L)
OFFICIAL **L**ANGUAGES: English, Sesotho
OTHER **L**ANGUAGES: Zulu, Xhosa
MAIN **R**ELIGIONS: Christianity 80%, indigenous religions 20%
EXPORTS: Wool, mohair, wheat, cattle, peas, beans, maize, animal skins, baskets

COMOROS

AREA: 1,862 sq. km (719 sq. mi)
POPULATION: 549,300
CAPITAL: Moroni
CURRENCY: 100 centimes = 1 Comoran franc (CF)
OFFICIAL **L**ANGUAGES: Arabic, French
OTHER **L**ANGUAGE: Comoran
MAIN **R**ELIGIONS: Islam 86%, Christianity 14%
EXPORTS: Vanilla, cloves, perfume oil, copra

MADAGASCAR

AREA: 587,042 sq. km
(226,657 sq. mi)
POPULATION: 13,862,000
CAPITAL: Antananarivo
CURRENCY: 100 centimes = 1 Malagasy franc (FMG)
OFFICIAL **L**ANGUAGES: French, Malagasy
MAIN **R**ELIGIONS: Indigenous religions 52%, Christianity 41%, Islam 7%
EXPORTS: Coffee, vanilla, cloves, shellfish, sugar, petroleum products

SEYCHELLES

AREA: 277 sq. km (107 sq. mi)
POPULATION: 72,700
CAPITAL: Victoria
CURRENCY: 100 cents = 1 Seychelles rupee (SR)
OFFICIAL **L**ANGUAGES: English, French
OTHER **L**ANGUAGE: Seychelles creole
MAIN **R**ELIGION: Christianity 98%
EXPORTS: Fish, cinnamon, copra (dried coconut flesh), petroleum products

MAURITIUS

AREA: 1,865 sq. km (720 sq. mi)
POPULATION: 1,127,000
CAPITAL: Port Louis
CURRENCY: 100 cents = 1 Mauritian rupee (MauR)
OFFICIAL **L**ANGUAGE: English
OTHER **L**ANGUAGES: Mauritian creole, French, Hindi, Urdu, Hakka, Bojpoori
MAIN **R**ELIGIONS: Hinduism 52%, Christianity 26%, Islam 17%
EXPORTS: Textiles, sugar, light manufactured goods

AUSTRALIA AND OCEANIA

AUSTRALIA
AREA: 7,686,884 sq. km (2,967,909 sq. mi)
POPULATION: 18,322,000
CAPITAL: Canberra
CURRENCY: 100 cents = 1 Australian dollar ($A)
OFFICIAL LANGUAGE: English
OTHER LANGUAGES: Aboriginal languages
MAIN RELIGION: Christianity 76%
EXPORTS: Coal, gold, meat, wool, wheat, machinery and transport equipment

PAPUA NEW GUINEA
AREA: 461,693 sq. km (178,260 sq. mi)
POPULATION: 4,295,000
CAPITAL: Port Moresby
CURRENCY: 100 toea = 1 kina (K)
OFFICIAL LANGUAGES: English, pidgin English, Motu
OTHER LANGUAGES: Regional languages
MAIN RELIGIONS: Christianity 66%, indigenous religions 34%
EXPORTS: Gold, copper ore, oil, timber, palm oil, coffee, cocoa, lobster

NEW ZEALAND
AREA: 268,676 sq. km (103,736 sq. mi)
POPULATION: 3,407,000
CAPITAL: Wellington
CURRENCY: 100 cents = 1 New Zealand dollar (NZ$)
OFFICIAL LANGUAGE: English
OTHER LANGUAGE: Maori
MAIN RELIGION: Christianity 67%
EXPORTS: Wool, lamb, mutton, beef, fish, cheese, chemicals, forestry products, fruit and vegetables, manufactured goods

SOLOMON ISLANDS
AREA: 29,785 sq. km (11,500 sq. mi)
POPULATION: 399,200
CAPITAL: Honiara
CURRENCY: 100 cents = 1 Solomon Islands dollar (SI$)
OFFICIAL LANGUAGE: English
OTHER LANGUAGE: Melanesian pidgin
MAIN RELIGIONS: Christianity 96%, indigenous religions 4%
EXPORTS: Fish, timber, palm oil, cocoa, copra (dried coconut flesh)

WESTERN SAMOA
AREA: 2,850 sq. km (1,100 sq. mi)
POPULATION: 209,400
CAPITAL: Apia
CURRENCY: 100 sene = 1 tala (WS$)
OFFICIAL LANGUAGES: Samoan (Polynesian), English
MAIN RELIGION: Christianity 99%
EXPORTS: Coconut oil and cream, taro (food plant), copra (dried coconut flesh), cocoa

VANUATU
AREA: 14,763 sq. km (5,700 sq. mi)
POPULATION: 173,600
CAPITAL: Port Vila
CURRENCY: 100 centimes = 1 vatu (VT)
OFFICIAL LANGUAGES: English, French
OTHER LANGUAGE: Bislama
MAIN RELIGIONS: Christianity 77%, indigenous religions 8%
EXPORTS: Copra, beef, cocoa, timber, coffee

FIJI
AREA: 18,272 sq. km (7,055 sq. mi)
POPULATION: 772,900
CAPITAL: Suva
CURRENCY: 100 cents = 1 Fijian dollar (F$)
OFFICIAL LANGUAGE: English
OTHER LANGUAGES: Fijian, Hindustani
MAIN RELIGIONS: Christianity 52%, Hinduism 38%, Islam 8%
EXPORTS: Sugar, clothing, gold, processed fish, timber

TONGA
AREA: 699 sq. km (270 sq. mi)
POPULATION: 105,600
CAPITAL: Nuku'alofa
CURRENCY: 100 seniti = 1 pa'anga (T$)
OFFICIAL LANGUAGES: Tongan, English
MAIN RELIGION: Christianity 70%
EXPORTS: Squash (vegetable), vanilla, fish, root crops, coconut oil

KIRIBATI
AREA: 717 sq. km (277 sq. mi)
POPULATION: 79,400
CAPITAL: Tarawa
CURRENCY: 100 cents = 1 Australian dollar ($A)
OFFICIAL LANGUAGE: English
OTHER LANGUAGE: Gilbertese
MAIN RELIGION: Christianity 94%
EXPORTS: Copra (dried coconut flesh), seaweed, fish

MARSHALL ISLANDS
AREA: 181 sq. km (70 sq. mi)
POPULATION: 56,200
CAPITAL: Majuro
CURRENCY: 100 cents = 1 United States dollar (US$)
OFFICIAL LANGUAGE: English
OTHER LANGUAGES: Marshallese, Japanese
MAIN RELIGION: Christianity 98%
EXPORTS: Coconut oil, fish, livestock, coffee

FEDERATED STATES OF MICRONESIA
AREA: 689 sq. km (266 sq. mi)
POPULATION: 123,000
CAPITAL: Palikir
CURRENCY: 100 cents = 1 United States dollar (US$)
OFFICIAL LANGUAGE: English
OTHER LANGUAGES: Regional languages
MAIN RELIGION: Christianity 97%
EXPORTS: Fish, copra (dried coconut flesh), bananas, black pepper

NAURU
AREA: 22 sq. km (8.5 sq. mi)
POPULATION: 10,150
CAPITAL: None. Government offices in Yaren district
CURRENCY: 100 cents = 1 Australian dollar ($A)
OFFICIAL LANGUAGE: Nauruan
OTHER LANGUAGE: English
MAIN RELIGION: Christianity 100%
EXPORT: Phosphates

PALAU
AREA: 495 sq. km (191 sq. mi)
POPULATION: 16,700
CAPITAL: Koror
CURRENCY: 100 cents = 1 United States dollar (US$)
OFFICIAL LANGUAGE: English
OTHER LANGUAGES: Palauan, Sonsorolese, Angaur, Japanese, Tobi
MAIN RELIGIONS: Christianity 67%, Modekngei religion 33%
EXPORTS: Shellfish, tuna, copra, handicrafts

TUVALU
AREA: 23 sq. km (9 sq. mi)
POPULATION: 10,000
CAPITAL: Funafuti Island
CURRENCY: 100 cents = 1 Tuvaluan dollar ($T) or 1 Australian dollar ($A)
OFFICIAL LANGUAGES: Tuvaluan, English
MAIN RELIGION: Christianity 97%
EXPORTS: Copra (dried coconut flesh)

Territories and Dependencies

The countries listed below govern land outside their national borders. These areas of land are known as territories or dependencies. Some territories are governed directly by the country to which they belong. Others receive only protection and financial assistance, and have their own governments and laws. Some major territories are listed here.

United States of America

American Samoa: South Pacific Ocean; 197 sq. km (76 sq. mi); population 57,400
Guam: Western Pacific Ocean; 541 sq. km (209 sq. mi); population 153,400
Midway: Central Pacific Ocean; 5 sq. km (2 sq. mi); no permanent population
Northern Mariana Islands: North Pacific Ocean; 477 sq. km (184 sq. mi); population 51,000
Puerto Rico: Caribbean Sea; 113 sq. km (70 sq. mi); population 3,813,000
Virgin Islands of the United States: Caribbean Sea; 345 sq. km (133 sq. mi); population 97,250
Wake Island: North Pacific Ocean; 7.7 sq. km (3 sq. mi); population 300

United Kingdom

Anguilla: Caribbean Sea; 91 sq. km (35 sq. mi); population 7,100
Bermuda: North Atlantic Ocean; 52 sq. km (20 sq. mi); population 61,700
British Indian Ocean Territory: Indian Ocean; 60 sq. km (23 sq. mi); no permanent population
British Virgin Islands: Caribbean Sea; 153 sq. km (59 sq. mi); population 13,000
Cayman Islands: Caribbean Sea; 306 sq. km (118 sq. mi); population 33,200
Falkland Islands and Dependencies (South Georgia and South Sandwich Islands): South Atlantic Ocean; 16,240 sq. km (6,270 sq. mi); population 2,350
Gibraltar: Southern Spain; 6 sq. km (2.25 sq. mi); population 31,900
Guernsey: English Channel; 78 sq. km (30 sq. mi); population 64,400
Isle of Man: Irish Sea; 572 sq. km (221 sq. mi); population 72,800
Jersey: English Channel; 116 sq. km (45 sq. mi); population 86,700
Montserrat: Caribbean Sea; 104 sq. km (40 sq. mi); population 12,700

Pitcairn Islands: South Pacific Ocean; 47 sq. km (18 sq. mi); population 60
St. Helena and Dependencies (Ascension Island and Tristan da Cunha): South Atlantic Ocean; 308 sq. km (119 sq. mi); population 6,770
Turks and Caicos Islands: Caribbean Sea; 430 sq. km (166 sq. mi); population 13,900

Portugal

Macao: South coast of China; 16 sq. km (6 sq. mi); population 490,900

France

French Guiana: Northern South America; 90,976 sq. km (35,126 sq. mi); population 145,300
French Polynesia: South Pacific Ocean; 3,265 sq. km (1,261 sq. mi); population 220,000
Guadeloupe: Caribbean Sea; 1,507 sq. km (582 sq. mi); population 408,800
Martinique: Caribbean Sea; 1,101 sq. km (425 sq. mi); population 394,800
Mayotte: Mozambique Channel, Africa; 373 sq. km (144 sq. mi); population 97,100
New Caledonia: South Pacific Ocean; 19,081 sq. km (7,367 sq. mi); population 184,600
Réunion: Indian Ocean; 2,510 sq. km (969 sq. mi); population 666,000
St-Pierre and Miquelon: North Atlantic Ocean; 241 sq. km (93 sq. mi); population 6,760
Wallis and Futuna Islands: South Pacific Ocean; 275 sq. km (106 sq. mi); population 14,500

The Netherlands

Aruba: Caribbean Sea; 179 sq. km (69 sq. mi); population 66,000
Netherlands Antilles: Caribbean Sea; 961 sq. km (371 sq. mi); population 203,500

Norway

Jan Mayen Island: North Atlantic Ocean; 373 sq. km (144 sq. mi); no permanent population
Svalbard: Arctic Ocean; 62,052 sq. km (23,958 sq. mi); population 2,910

Denmark

Faeroe Islands: North Atlantic Ocean; 1,399 sq. km (540 sq. mi); population 48,500
Greenland: North Atlantic Ocean; 2,175,000 sq. km (840,000 sq. mi); population 57,700

Australia

Christmas Island: Indian Ocean; 135 sq. km (52 sq. mi); population 890
Cocos (Keeling) Islands: Indian Ocean; 23 sq. km (9 sq. mi); population 600
Heard and McDonald Islands: Indian Ocean; 293 sq. km (113 sq. mi); no permanent population
Norfolk Island: South Pacific Ocean; 34 sq. km (13 sq. mi); population 2,760

New Zealand

Cook Islands: South Pacific Ocean; 238 sq. km (92 sq. mi); population 19,300
Niue: South Pacific Ocean; 259 sq. km (100 sq. mi); population 1,840
Tokelau: South Pacific Ocean; 10 sq. km (4 sq. mi); population 1,500

Disputed Territories

Gaza Strip (Palestine): Middle East; disputed by Israel and Palestine, Palestinian interim self-government; 378 sq. km (146 sq. mi); population 813,300
Kashmir: Southern Asia; disputed by India and Pakistan; 138,992 sq. km (53,665 sq. mi); population 7,718,700
Turkish Federated State of Cyprus: Mediterranean Sea; disputed by Turkey and Cyprus; 3,424 sq. km (1,322 sq. mi); population 135,400
West Bank (Palestine): Middle East; disputed by Israel and Palestine, Palestinian interim self-government; 5,640 sq. km (2,100 sq. mi); population 1,320,000
Western Sahara: Northwestern Africa; disputed by Morocco and separatist movement; 266,001 sq. km (102,703 sq. mi); population 217,250

Glossary

acid rain ~ Rain that has combined with pollution in the atmosphere to form an acid. Acid rain can kill plants and damage buildings.

adaptation ~ A change that occurs in a plant's structure or in an animal's body or behaviour to allow it to cope better with its environment.

agriculture ~ The use of land to grow crops and raise animals. Agriculture is another word for farming.

altitude ~ The height of a place or object above sea level.

ancestor ~ A member of a person's family who lived a long time ago.

Antarctic Circle ~ A line of latitude at 66.5° south which marks the boundary of Earth's southern polar region. South of this line there is continuous daylight in midsummer and continuous darkness in midwinter.

archipelago ~ A large group of islands.

Arctic Circle ~ A line of latitude at 66.5° north which marks the boundary of Earth's northern polar region. North of this line there is continuous daylight in midsummer and continuous darkness in midwinter.

arid ~ Having low rainfall and, as a result, little vegetation. Very arid areas are called deserts.

atoll ~ A low, ring-shaped, sandy island enclosing a lagoon. An atoll is usually formed by the growth of a coral reef on top of an undersea mountain.

axis ~ An imaginary line through the centre of the Earth around which the planet rotates.

basin ~ 1. A wide, bowl-shaped dip in the landscape.
2. An area of land that is drained by a river and its tributaries.

bay ~ A body of water partly enclosed by land.

bight ~ A curve or recess in a stretch of coastline that forms a large bay.

border ~ A line that separates one country from another.

canal ~ An artificial waterway created to carry water for irrigation or shipping.

canyon ~ A deep, steep-sided valley formed by a river.

cape ~ A piece of land that juts out into a lake or sea.

capital ~ The city where a state or country's government is located. Sometimes a country has more than one capital, because parts of its government are located in different cities.

cartographer ~ A person who makes maps. The art of making maps is known as cartography.

channel ~ A narrow stretch of water between two land masses.

climate ~ The pattern of weather that occurs in a place over an extended period of time. Earth can be divided into a number of climatic zones.

compass ~ 1. An instrument with a magnetic needle that indicates the direction north.
2. An arrow or similar icon that indicates the direction north on a map.

coniferous ~ Coniferous trees are evergreen trees that produce seeds inside cones and usually have thin, needle-shaped or scaly leaves.

continent ~ One of Earth's seven major land masses: Europe, Asia, Africa, North America, South America, Australia and Antarctica.

coral ~ A rocky material formed by the skeletons of tiny marine creatures, especially corals.

crop ~ A plant that is grown in large quantities by farmers. Crops include foods such as cereals and vegetables as well as other plants such as cotton and tobacco.

crust ~ The hard, thin rocky layer that covers the Earth's surface. The crust has split into sections called plates.

culture ~ The shared traditions and way of life of a people.

currency ~ The kind of money used in a country.

dam ~ A wall or barrier built across a river to hold back the water and create an artificial lake called a reservoir.

deciduous ~ Deciduous trees shed their leaves every year, usually in autumn. The tree remains bare during winter but grows new leaves in spring.

deforestation ~ The cutting down of forest trees for timber, or to clear land for farming or building.

delta ~ A fan-shaped area formed when soil and silt carried by a river collect at the river mouth.

dependency ~ A region or land mass governed by another country.

descendants ~ The offspring of a person, including his or her children, grandchildren and so on.

desert ~ A dry area with low rainfall and sparse vegetation that is adapted to withstand drought.

earthquake ~ A shaking of the ground caused by movement of part of the Earth's crust.

ecosystem ~ A community of plants and animals and the environment to which they are adapted.

endangered ~ An animal or plant species that is in danger of becoming extinct.

environment ~ The natural surroundings of a community of plants and animals, particularly the shape of the land, the climate and the soil.

Equator ~ An imaginary line that circles the globe midway between the North and South poles. The Equator divides the world into the Northern and Southern hemispheres.

ethnic group ~ A group of people sharing the same origin, language and culture.

evergreen ~ An evergreen tree is a tree that bears leaves all year round.

evolution ~ A process of gradual change, especially in living things.

exports ~ Goods that are sold to other countries.

extinct ~ An extinct species of animal or plant is one that no longer exists because all the individual animals or plants of that kind have died.

federation ~ A group of independent states or territories that agree to become one country.

fertile ~ Fertile land is land with good soil. Plants grow well in fertile land if there is good rainfall or irrigation.

fjord ~ A deep, steep-sided valley gouged out by a glacier and later flooded by the sea to form a narrow inlet.

forestry ~ The science of using and managing forest resources.

fossil ~ The remains or traces of a prehistoric plant or animal, usually found between layers of rock.

fossil fuel ~ Fuel found deep underground that formed from the decayed remains of prehistoric plants and animals. The most common fossil fuels are coal, oil and natural gas.

gazetteer ~ An index of place names.

geyser ~ A natural spring that spouts a column of hot water and steam.

glacier ~ A large mass of ice that moves slowly down the side of a mountain or along a valley and is constantly replenished by snow falling on top of the mountain.

gorge ~ A deep, steep-sided, rocky valley.

grassland ~ A large area of land covered with grass plants.

Greenwich Meridian ~ An imaginary line that extends from the North Pole to the South Pole through Greenwich, England, and that marks 0° longitude.

gulf ~ A large bay.

hemisphere ~ One half of the world. The Earth is divided into Northern and Southern hemispheres by the Equator, and into Eastern and Western hemispheres by the Greenwich Meridian (0°) and the 180° line, an imaginary line that is 180° east or west of the Greenwich Meridian.

high-tech industries ~ Industries that produce electronic goods such as computers.

hydroelectricity ~ Electricity produced using the power of running water.

iceberg ~ A large block of ice floating in the sea. Icebergs break off the ends of glaciers and ice sheets. The part of an iceberg below the surface of the sea is usually eight times as big as the part above the surface.

ice-cap ~ A permanent sheet of ice and snow covering an area. Ice-caps are found in polar regions and on some high mountain tops.

immigrant ~ A person who has settled in a country but originally came from another country.

independent ~ Not governed by another country.

inlet ~ A narrow bay.

irrigation ~ The process of providing water to farmland by artificial means, such as pumping water from rivers, lakes and dams, or diverting water through channels and pipes.

island ~ An area of land surrounded by water.

■

kingdom ~ A country whose ruler or head of state is a king or queen.

■

lagoon ~ 1. A shallow area of salt water separated from the sea by a strip of land. 2. Inland bodies of water that were previously part of a river.

land mass ~ A large area of land not covered by water.

latitude ~ Distance north or south of the Equator measured in degrees.

livestock ~ Animals, such as cattle and sheep, raised by farmers.

longitude ~ Distance east or west of the Greenwich Meridian measured in degrees.

■

marsh ~ An area of wet land where plants adapted to water grow. Also called a swamp or wetland.

manufacturing ~ The making of useful products from raw materials.

migration ~ The movement of people or animals to another country or region. Many animals migrate to find food or avoid severe weather.

mineral ~ A natural substance occurring in the Earth's crust that is neither plant nor animal. Well-known minerals include chalk, clay and many metals.

■

native people ~ The original human inhabitants of a region or country.

nomad ~ A person who does not live in one place but continually moves around. Nomads often move in search of food and water for themselves and their animals.

North Pole ~ *See* **pole**.

■

oasis ~ A patch of land in a desert where there is water and more vegetation than elsewhere.

■

peninsula ~ A long strip of land that extends outwards from a larger land mass and is almost surrounded by water.

plain ~ An area of flat or rolling land with shallow river valleys.

plantation ~ An area of land where a particular tree crop is grown. Such crops include forest trees, rubber trees and coconut palms.

plate ~ One of the sections of the Earth's crust.

plateau ~ An area of flat or rolling land with deep river valleys, gorges and canyons.

pole ~ Points on the Earth's surface that represent the ends of the axis around which our planet is constantly rotating. The North Pole is the most northern point on Earth. The South Pole is the most southern point. The regions around the poles are known as the polar regions.

population ~ 1. The people who live in a place. 2. The total number of people living in a place.

populous ~ A populous country is a country with a large population.

principality ~ A country whose ruler or head of state is a prince or princess.

■

radioactive ~ Giving out invisible rays of high-energy particles. Some natural substances, such as uranium, are radioactive.

rainforest ~ A type of dense forest that grows in regions of high rainfall.

range ~ 1. A chain of mountains. 2. An area of open grassland where animals graze.

raw materials ~ Natural substances that can be turned into useful products. Examples include timber, coal and coffee beans. Raw materials are also known as resources.

reef ~ A ridge of rock, sand or coral lying just below the surface of the sea.

republic ~ A country led by an elected representative called a president.

reservoir ~ An artificial lake created to store water, usually by building a dam across a river.

resources ~ Substances or materials that occur naturally in a place and are of value to the area's inhabitants. Resources that can never be used up, such as water and waves, are called renewable resources. Resources that will eventually be used up, such as coal and other minerals, are known as non-renewable resources.

river basin ~ An area of land drained by a river and its tributaries.

rural ~ Relating to the countryside. The term rural industries means agricultural industries.

■

savannah ~ Open grassland with scattered trees. Most savannahs are found in tropical areas that have a distinct summer wet season.

scale ~ On a map, an indication of how distances on the map relate to actual distances.

scrub ~ An area of land covered with shrubs and low trees.

sea level ~ The average height of the surface of the sea, which is used as a base point for measuring altitude.

South Pole ~ *See* **pole**.

species ~ Animals or plants of the same type.

steppe ~ A large, grassy plain, usually without trees, as found in parts of eastern Europe and central Asia.

strait ~ A narrow strip of water that connects two larger bodies of water.

swamp ~ An area of wet land containing plants adapted to growing in water. Also called a marsh or wetland.

■

technology ~ The use of scientific knowledge to carry out tasks or solve problems. Using machines in industry is an example of technology.

temperate ~ Neither hot nor cold. Most of the Earth's temperate regions are located between the tropics and the polar regions.

territory ~ 1. A large area of land. 2. All the land and sea governed by a country or state. 3. A region or land mass governed by another country.

textiles ~ Woven or knitted fabrics.

time zone ~ A region in which everyone uses the same time. The world is divided into 24 time zones. The time in each zone is usually one hour earlier than in the zone to the east.

trade ~ The exchange of goods, usually by buying and selling.

tributary ~ A stream or river that flows into a larger stream or river.

Tropic of Cancer/Capricorn ~ *See* **tropics**.

tropics ~ 1. The hot, wet regions of the Earth that lie near the Equator. 2. Either of two lines of latitude: the Tropic of Cancer, at 23.5° north, and the Tropic of Capricorn, at 23.5° south. Because the Earth is tilted at an angle of 23.5°, these lines mark the point at which the Sun is directly overhead in summer.

tundra ~ A cold, barren area where much of the soil is frozen and the vegetation consists only of mosses, lichens and other small plants adapted to withstand intense cold. Tundra is found near the Arctic Circle and on mountain tops.

■

urban ~ Relating to cities. A country's urban population is the number of people that live in its cities.

■

valley ~ A long, narrow gap between hills or mountains along which a river usually flows.

vegetation ~ The community of plants that is characteristic of a particular region.

volcano ~ A mountain that has been built up from lava, molten rock that erupts through a hole in the Earth's crust.

■

wetland ~ An area of wet land containing plants adapted to growing in water. Also called a swamp or marsh.

woodland ~ An area of land covered with widely spaced trees and shrubs.

Index and Gazetteer

A

Ābādān Iran 81 K5
Aberdeen Scotland, U.K. 56 H7
Abidjan Côte d'Ivoire 92 G9
Abu Dhabi United Arab Emirates 81 M7
Abuja Nigeria 92 I9
Acapulco Mexico 46 F9
Accra Ghana 92 G9
Aconcagua (mountain) Argentina 49 M7, 53 E10
Adamawa Highlands Cameroon 91 L5
Adana Turkey 78 C7
Adare, Cape Antarctica 102 B8
Ad Dammām Saudi Arabia 81 K6
Addis Ababa Ethiopia 93 O9
Adelaide South Australia, Australia 99 K9
Aden Yemen 81 J11
Aden, Gulf of Arabia/eastern Africa 75 J7, 81 K11, 91 Q5, 93 Q8
Adriatic Sea southern Europe 55 M7, 67 I10, 69 C9
Aegean Sea Greece/Turkey 55 N7, 69 H12
Afghanistan 31 L5, 74 B9, 82, 112
Africa (continent) 29, 90–95, 114–117
Agra India 82 E8
Ahaggar Mountains Algeria 91 L3, 92 H6
Ahmadabad India 83 D9
airports 24
Ajaccio Corsica, France 61 O11
Akita Japan 88 H6
Aktyubinsk Kazakstan 79 I5
Akureyri Iceland 72 B5
Alabama (river) Alabama, U.S.A. 41 L6
Alabama (state) U.S.A. 41
Åland Islands Finland 73 G12
Alaska (state) U.S.A. 30 E3, 32 B8, 34
Alaska, Gulf of Alaska, U.S.A. 28 E4, 33 J4, 34 E7
Alaska Range Alaska, U.S.A. 34 E6
Albania 31 K5, 54 D10, 69, 108
Albany Georgia, U.S.A. 41 M6
Albany New York, U.S.A. 39 K5
Albany Western Australia, Australia 98 F9
Albany (river) Ontario, Canada 36 G5
Alberta (province) Canada 35
Ålborg Denmark 73 C14
Albuquerque New Mexico, U.S.A. 45 L8
Alcántara Reservoir Spain 58 I5
Aleppo Syria 80 G2
Aleutian Islands Alaska, U.S.A. 28 D4, 29 Q4, 33 J3, 34 A6
Aleutian Trench Pacific Ocean 29 P4
Alexandria Egypt 93 M5
Alexandroúpolis Greece 69 I11
Algarve Portugal 58 G8
Algeciras Spain 59 I9
Algeria 31 J5, 90 B8, 92–93, 114
Algiers Algeria 92 I3
Al Ḩudaydah Yemen 81 I10
Alicante Spain 59 M7
Alice Springs Northern Territory, Australia 99 J5
Alkmaar Netherlands 62 F7
Almaty Kazakstan 79 M9
Almería Spain 59 L8
Alps (mountain range) Central Europe 29 J4, 55 L7, 61 M7, 65 E14, 66 C6
Altay Mountains Asia 75 M4, 87 I2
Altun Mountains China 86 H5
Amami Islands Japan 88 B6
Amarillo Texas, U.S.A. 40 F4
Amazon (river) Brazil 28 H7, 49 N4, 51 L4
Amazon Basin Brazil 28 H7, 49 M4, 50 H5
Amazon Delta Brazil 49 O4, 51 M4
Ambarchik Russia 103 N3
Ambon Indonesia 85 N9
Ambrim (island) Vanuatu 101 J6
Ameland (island) Netherlands 62 I4
American Samoa (island group) Polynesia 31 Q7, 96 E9, 101 P2, 119
America, United States of see United States of America
Amiens France 61 J2
Amman Jordan 80 G4
Amritsar India 82 E7
Amsterdam Island Indian Ocean 29 M8, 31 M8
Amsterdam Netherlands 62 G7
Amu Dar'ya (river) Central Asia 79 J10
Amundsen Sea Pacific Ocean, Antarctica 102 C6
Amur (river) China/Russia 29 O4, 75 O4, 77 M9, 87 N1
Anchorage Alaska, U.S.A. 34 E6
Ancona Italy 66 G9
Andaman Islands India 29 M6, 31 M6, 75 L7, 83 J13
Andaman Sea Indian Ocean 84 E5
Andes (mountain range) South America 28 G7, 28 H8, 49 L4, 50 G3, 50 G6, 52 F7, 53 E12
Andorra 31 J5, 54 C10, 59, 107
Andorra la Vella Andorra 59 O2
Ándros (island) Greece 69 H13
Aneto, Pico de (mountain) Spain 59 N2
Angara (river) Russia 29 N4, 75 M4, 77 I8
Anglesey (island) Wales, U.K. 57 F12
Angola 31 K7, 90 C10, 94, 117
Anguilla (island) Caribbean Sea 30 H6, 32 G10, 47 O6, 119
animals 18–19, 20
Ankara Turkey 78 C6
An Nafūd Desert Saudi Arabia 80 H5
Annapolis Maryland, U.S.A. 39 I8
Annapurna (mountain) Nepal 75 L6, 82 G7
Antalya Turkey 78 B6
Antananarivo Madagascar 95 O7
Antarctica (continent) 28–29, 102
Antarctic Peninsula Antarctica 28 H11, 102 F5
Anticosti Island Québec, Canada 37 M8
Antigua and Barbuda 30 H6, 32 G10, 47, 105
Antilles (island group) Caribbean Sea 28 G6, 33 O8
Antilles, Netherlands see Netherlands Antilles
Antofagasta Chile 52 D7
Antwerp Belgium 63 F11
Aoba (island) Vanuatu 101 K5
Aomori Japan 88 H5
Apeldoorn Netherlands 62 I8
Apennines (mountain range) Italy 55 M7, 66 F8
Apia Western Samoa 101 N2
Appalachian Mountains U.S.A. 28 G5, 33 O7, 38 H9, 41 M4
Appleton Wisconsin, U.S.A. 43 L5
Aqtaū Kazakstan 78 G7
Arabian Peninsula south-western Asia 29 L6, 75 I6
Arabian Sea Arabia/India 29 L6, 75 J7, 81 N9, 83 A9
Arad Romania 68 F6
Arafura Sea Australia/Indonesia 85 P10, 97 J8, 99 J1
Araks (river) Asia 81 J1
Aral Sea Kazakstan/Uzbekistan 29 L5, 75 K4, 79 I7
Ararat, Mt. Turkey 75 J4, 78 E7
Arctic Ocean 29, 31, 33, 35, 55, 75, 76–77, 103
Ardennes Belgium 63 G13
Arequipa Peru 50 H7
Arezzo Italy 66 F8
Argentina 30 H8, 48 C10, 52–53, 106
Argentine Basin Atlantic Ocean 28 H9
Århus Denmark 73 C15
Arica Chile 52 D5
Arizona (state) U.S.A. 45
Arkansas (river) U.S.A. 41 I5, 42 H9, 45 M7
Arkansas (state) U.S.A. 41
Arkhangel'sk Russia 76 E6
Armenia 31 L5, 74 B9, 78, 110
Arnhem Netherlands 62 I8
Arnhem Land Northern Territory, Australia 99 J2
Arno (river) Italy 66 E8
Aru (island group) Indonesia 85 O10
Aruba (island) Caribbean Sea 47 N9, 119
Asahikawa Japan 88 I3
Ascension (island) Atlantic Ocean 29 J7, 31 J7, 90 B10, 91 K7, 119
Ashkhabad Turkmenistan 78 H10
Asia (continent) 29, 74–89, 110–113
Asīr (province) Saudi Arabia 80 I 9
Asmara Eritrea 93 O8
Assal, Lake Djibouti 91 O5
Astrakhan Russia 76 C10
Asunción Paraguay 52 H7
Aswān Egypt 93 N6
Atacama Desert Chile 49 M6, 52 E7
Athabasca, Lake Alberta/Saskatchewan, Canada 35 K8
Athens Greece 69 G13
Atlanta Georgia, U.S.A. 41 M5
Atlantic City New Jersey, U.S.A. 39 J8
Atlantic Coastal Plain U.S.A. 41 N6
Atlantic-Indian Basin Indian Ocean 29 L9
Atlantic Ocean 24, 30–31, 33, 37, 41, 47, 49, 51, 53, 58, 60, 72, 91, 92, 94, 102
Atlas Mountains Morocco 29 J5, 91 K3
Atyraū Kazakstan 78 H6
Auckland New Zealand 100 G3
Auckland Islands New Zealand 29 P9, 31 P9
Augsburg Germany 65 F13
Augusta Maine, U.S.A. 39 M4
Austin Texas, U.S.A. 40 G7
Australia 29 O8, 31 O8, 96 B10, 96–99, 97 J9, 118
Australian Capital Territory Australia 99 N9
Austria 31 K4, 54 D10, 65, 108
Avignon France 61 L9
Azerbaijan 31 L5, 74 B9, 78, 110
Azores (island group) Atlantic Ocean 29 I5, 31 I5, 58
Azov, Sea of Russia/Ukraine 71 O10

B

Baarle-Hertog (Belgian enclave) Netherlands 63 H10
Bacolod Philippines 85 L5
Badajoz Spain 58 H6
Baffin Bay Canada/Greenland 28 H2, 33 N2, 35 O4, 103 K7
Baffin Island North-west Territories, Canada 28 G2, 33 N3, 35 O5, 103 K6
Baghdad Iraq 81 I3
Baguio Philippines 85 L4
Bahamas, The 28 H5, 30 H5, 32 E10, 33 P8, 47, 105
Bahía Blanca Argentina 53 G12
Bahrain 31 L5, 74 B10, 81, 111
Baikal, Lake Russia 29 N4, 75 N4, 77 J10
Baja California (peninsula) Mexico 46 B5
Baku Azerbaijan 78 F8
Balbi, Mt. Papua New Guinea 97 L8
Balearic Islands Spain 55 L7, 59 O5
Bali (island) Indonesia 85 J10
Balikpapan Indonesia 85 K8
Balkan Mountains south-eastern Europe 68 H9
Balkan Peninsula eastern Europe 55 N7
Balkans 68–69
Balkhash, Lake Kazakstan 29 M4, 75 L4, 79 M8
Ballarat Victoria, Australia 99 L9
Balleny Islands Pacific Ocean, Antarctica 102 A8
Baltic Sea northern Europe 55 M6, 64 H6, 70 G4, 73 F15
Baltimore Maryland, U.S.A. 39 I8
Bamako Mali 92 F8
Bandar Seri Begawan Brunei 85 J7
Banda Sea south-western Asia 85 M10
Bangalore India 83 E13
Bangkok Thailand 84 G5
Bangladesh 31 M5, 74 C10, 83, 112
Bangor Ireland 57 E10
Bangui Central African Republic 93 K10
Banja Luka Bosnia and Herzegovina 68 C7
Banjarmasin Indonesia 85 J9
Banjul Gambia 92 D8
Banks Island North-west Territories, Canada 33 M2, 35 J4, 103 K4
Banks Islands Vanuatu 101 K5
Bantry Ireland 57 B13
Baotou China 87 L5
Barbados 30 H6, 32 G11, 47, 105
Barbuda see Antigua and Barbuda
Barcelona Spain 59 O3
Barents Sea Arctic Ocean 29 K3, 55 N4, 72 I4, 75 L2, 76 F5, 103 O8
Bari Italy 67 J12
Barranquilla Colombia 50 G1
Barrow Alaska, U.S.A. 103 L3
Basel Switzerland 65 C14
Basra Iraq 81 K4
Bass Strait Australia 99 M10
Bath England, U.K. 57 H14
Baton Rouge Louisiana, U.S.A. 41 J7
Bay City Michigan, U.S.A. 43 N5
Beaufort Sea Arctic Ocean 33 L2, 34 H4, 103 K4
Beijing China 87 M5
Beira Mozambique 95 L7
Beirut Lebanon 80 G3
Belarus 31 K4, 54 E9, 71, 109
Belcher Islands Canada 36 I4
Belém Brazil 51 M4
Belfast Ireland 57 E10
Belgium 31 J4, 54 C10, 63, 107
Belgrade Yugoslavia 68 E7
Belgrano II (research centre) Antarctica 102 F6
Belize 30 G6, 32 D11, 46, 104
Belize City Belize 46 I8
Bellingshausen Sea Pacific Ocean, Antarctica 102 D5
Belmopan Belize 46 I9
Belo Horizonte Brazil 51 N8
Bengal, Bay of India/south-eastern Asia 29 M6, 75 L7, 83 H11, 84 E3
Benghazi Libya 93 K4
Benguela Angola 94 G6
Benin 31 J6, 90 B9, 92, 116
Ben Nevis (mountain) Scotland, U.K. 56 E7
Benue (river) Cameroon/Nigeria 91 M5
Berbera Somalia 93 P9
Bergen Norway 73 A11
Bering Sea Pacific Ocean 29 P4, 33 J3, 75 P2, 77 O4
Bering Strait Arctic Ocean/Pacific Ocean 29 Q3, 34 D4, 77 N2, 103 L2
Berlin Germany 64 H8
Bermuda (island) Atlantic Ocean 28 H5, 30 H5, 32 E10, 33 Q7, 119
Bern Switzerland 65 C14
Besançon France 61 M5
Bhopal India 83 E10
Bhubaneswar India 83 H11
Bhutan 31 M5, 74 C10, 82, 112
Biarritz France 60 G9
Bilbao Spain 59 K2
Billings Montana, U.S.A. 45 K3
Bioko (island) Equatorial Guinea 91 L6, 93 I10
Birmingham England, U.K. 57 H12
Birmingham Tennessee, U.S.A. 41 L5
birth rate 22, 23
Biscay, Bay of Spain 55 L6, 59 J1, 60 F8
Bishkek Kyrgyzstan 79 M9
Bismarck North Dakota, U.S.A. 42 F3
Bismarck Archipelago (island group) Papua New Guinea 98 B8
Bismarck Sea Papua New Guinea 98 B8
Bissau Guinea-Bissau 92 E8
Bitola Macedonia 69 F10
Black Forest Germany 65 C13
Blackpool England, U.K. 57 G11
Black Sea Asia/Europe 29 K5, 55 O7, 69 K9, 71 L11, 75 J4, 76 A9, 78 D4
Blanca Bay Argentina 49 M8
Blanc, Mont (mountain) France/Italy 55 L7, 61 M7, 66 C5
Bloemfontein South Africa 95 J10
Blue Nile (river) Ethiopia/Sudan 91 O5, 93 N8
Bodø Norway 72 E7
Bogotá Colombia 50 G3
Bohemian Forest Czech Republic/Germany 65 G12, 70 E8
Boise Idaho, U.S.A. 44 H4
Bolivia 30 H7, 48 C9, 52, 106
Bologna Italy 66 F7
Bolzano Italy 66 G5
Bombay India 83 D11
Bonete (mountain) Argentina 49 M7
Bonn Germany 65 C10
Bora-Bora (island) French Polynesia 101 M9
Borås Sweden 73 D13
Bordeaux France 60 H8
Borneo (island) south-eastern Asia 29 N7, 75 O8, 85 J8
Bornholm (island) Denmark 73 E15
Bosna (river) Bosnia and Herzegovina 68 D7
Bosnia and Herzegovina 31 K4, 54 D10, 68, 108
Bosporus (channel) Turkey 78 B4
Boston Massachusetts, U.S.A. 39 L5
Bothnia, Gulf of Finland/Sweden 55 N5, 73 F10
Botswana 31 K8, 90 C11, 94–95, 117
Bougainville (island) Papua New Guinea 98 D9
Boulder Colorado, U.S.A. 45 L6
Boulogne France 61 J1
Bourges France 61 J5
Bouvet Island Atlantic Ocean 29 J9, 31 J9
Brahmaputra (river) China/India 82 I8
Branco, Rio (river) Brazil 49 M4
Brasília Brazil 51 M7
Braşov Romania 68 I7
Bratislava Slovakia 70 G9
Bratsk Russia 77 J9
Brazil 30 H7, 48 D8, 51, 106
Brazilian Highlands (mountain range) Brazil 28 H7, 49 O5, 51 M6
Brazos (river) Texas, U.S.A. 40 G6
Brazzaville Congo 94 G3
Breda Netherlands 63 F10
Bremen Germany 64 D7
Brenner Pass Austria/Italy 65 F15
Brescia Italy 66 E6
Brest France 60 E4
Brighton England, U.K. 57 I14
Brindisi Italy 67 J13
Brisbane Queensland, Australia 99 O7
Bristol England, U.K. 57 G14
British Columbia (province) Canada 34
British Indian Ocean Territory Indian Ocean 31 M7, 119
British Isles western Europe 29 J4, 55 L6, 56–57
British Virgin Islands Caribbean Sea 32 F10, 47 O7, 119
Brno Czech Republic 70 F8
Broken Hill New South Wales, Australia 99 L8
Brooks Range Alaska, U.S.A. 28 E2, 33 K2, 34 F4
Broome Western Australia, Australia 98 G4
Brownsville Texas, U.S.A. 40 G10
Bruges Belgium 63 C11
Brunei 31 N6, 74 D11, 85, 113
Brunswick Germany 64 F8
Brussels Belgium 63 F12
Bucaramanga Colombia 50 G2
Bucharest Romania 68 I8
Budapest Hungary 70 G9
Buenos Aires Argentina 53 H10
Buffalo New York, U.S.A. 38 H5
Bujumbura Burundi 95 K3
Bukhara Uzbekistan 79 J10
Bulawayo Zimbabwe 95 J7
Bulgaria 31 K5, 54 D10, 68–69, 108
Bunbury Western Australia, Australia 98 F9
Burgas Bulgaria 69 J9
Burkina Faso 31 J6, 90 B9, 92, 114
Burma see Myanmar
Bursa Turkey 78 B5
Buru (island) Indonesia 85 M9
Burundi 31 K7, 90 D10, 95, 116
Bydgoszcz Poland 70 G5
Byrd (research centre) Antarctica 102 D7

C

Cabinda Angola 94 G4
Cádiz Spain 58 I9
Cádiz, Gulf of Spain 58 H9
Cagliari Sardinia, Italy 67 B12
Caicos Islands see Turks and Caicos Islands
Cairo Egypt 93 M5
Cairo Illinois, U.S.A. 43 L9
Calais France 61 J1
Calcutta India 83 I10
Calgary Alberta, Canada 35 J10
Cali Colombia 50 G3
California (state) U.S.A. 44
California, Gulf of Mexico 33 L8, 46 C6
Cambodia 31 N6, 74 D10, 84, 113
Cambridge England, U.K. 57 J13
Cameroon 31 K6, 90 C9, 93, 116
Campbell Island New Zealand 31 P9
Campeche, Bay of Mexico 33 N9, 46 G8
Canada 30 G4, 32 D9, 34–37, 104
Canadian Shield Canada 28 G4, 33 M4
Canary Islands Atlantic Ocean 29 J5, 31 J5, 58, 90 B8, 91 K3, 92 E5
Canberra Australian Capital Territory, Australia 99 N9
Canea Crete, Greece 69 H15
Cannes France 61 N9
Cantabrian Mountains Spain 59 H2
Cape Town South Africa 94 H11
Cape Verde Islands 29 I6, 31 I6, 90 A8, 91 J4, 93, 114
Cape York Peninsula Queensland, Australia 97 K8, 99 L3
Capri (island) Italy 67 G12
Caracas Venezuela 50 I1
Cardiff Wales, U.K. 57 G14
Caribbean Sea Atlantic Ocean 28 G6, 33 O9, 47 K8, 49 L2
Carlisle England, U.K. 57 G9
Carlow Ireland 57 D12
Carolina, North (state) U.S.A. see North Carolina
Carolina, South (state) U.S.A. see South Carolina
Caroline Islands Federated States of Micronesia 29 O6, 97 K6
Carpathian Mountains eastern Europe 29 K4, 55 N6, 68 I6, 71 J8
Carpentaria, Gulf of Northern Territory/Queensland, Australia 99 K3
Carrantuohill (mountain) Ireland 57 A13
Carson City Nevada, U.S.A. 44 G6
Cartagena Colombia 50 G2
Cartagena Spain 59 M8
cartographers 9
Casablanca Morocco 92 G4
Cascade Range U.S.A. 44 F3
Casey (research centre) Antarctica 102 D10
Casper Wyoming, U.S.A. 45 L4
Caspian Sea (lake) Asia/Europe 29 L5, 55 P6, 76 C11, 78 G8, 81 K1
Caucasus Mountains Asia/Europe 55 O7, 75 J4, 76 B9, 78 E5

Cayenne French Guyana 51 L3
Cayman Islands Caribbean Sea 47 J8, 119
Cebu Philippines 85 L5
Cedar City Utah, U.S.A. 45 I7
Celebes Sea south-eastern Asia 85 L7
Celtic Sea Ireland 57 B14
Central African Republic 31 K5, 90 C9, **93**, 116
Central Pacific Basin northern Pacific Ocean 29 P6
Central Siberian Plateau Russia 29 N3, 75 N3, 77 J6
Cephalonia (island) Greece 69 E13
Ceram (island) Indonesia 85 N9
Ceuta (Spanish enclave) north-western Africa 59 J10, 92 G3
Ch'ŏngjin North Korea 87 P4
Chad 31 K6, 90 C9, **93**, 114
Chad, Lake Central Africa 91 M4, 93 J8
Chang (river) China 29 N5, 75 N6, 87 I7, 87 L8
Changchun Mongolia 87 O3
Changsha China 87 M8
Channel Islands English Channel 29 J4, 57 G16
Chardzhou Turkmenistan 79 J10
Chari (river) Chad 93 K9
Charleston South Carolina, U.S.A. 41 O5
Charleston West Virginia, U.S.A. 38 F9
Charlotte North Carolina, U.S.A. 41 N4
Charlottetown Prince Edward Island, Canada 37 M9
Chatham Islands New Zealand 29 Q9, 96 E11, 97 N11
Chattahoochee (river) Alabama/Georgia, U.S.A. 41 M6
Cheju (island) South Korea 87 P6
Chelyabinsk Russia 76 E9
Chemnitz Germany 65 G10
Chengdu China 87 K7
Cherbourg 60 G2
Cheyenne Wyoming, U.S.A. 45 L5
Chiang Mai Thailand 84 G3
Chicago Illinois, U.S.A. 43 M6
Chihuahua Mexico 46 D5
Chile 30 F8, 48 C9, **52–53**, 105
China 31 N5, 74 D9, **86–87**, 113
Chios (island) Greece 69 I13
Chisinău Moldova 71 K9
Chittagong Bangladesh 83 J10
chlorofluorocarbons 27
Choiseul (island) Solomon Islands 101 J2
Chongqing China 87 K8
Choybalsan Mongolia 87 M2
Christchurch New Zealand 100 F8
Christmas Island Indian Ocean 29 N7, 31 N7, 119
Chukchi Peninsula Russia 77 N2
Chukchi Sea Arctic Ocean 29 Q3, 33 K2, 77 M2, 103 M3
Churchill Manitoba, Canada 35 M8
Churchill (river) Manitoba, Canada 35 M8, 37 M6
Cincinnati Ohio, U.S.A. 43 N8
Ciudad Bolívar 51 J2
Ciudad Juárez Mexico 46 D5
Cleveland Ohio, U.S.A. 43 P6
climate 11, **16–17**
Clipperton Island Pacific Ocean 28 F6, 30 F6
Cluj-Napoca Romania 68 H6
Clutha (river) New Zealand 100 D9
Clyde (river) Scotland, U.K. 56 F8
Coast Mountains British Columbia, Canada 33 K5, 34 G9
Coast Ranges North America 33 K6, 44 F8
Coats Land Antarctica 102 F7
Cochabamba Bolivia 52 F5
Cochin India 83 E14
Cocos (Keeling) Islands Indian Ocean 29 N7, 31 N7, 119
Coimbra Portugal 58 G5
collisions, plate 14–15
Cologne Germany 65 C10
Colombia 30 H6, 48 C7, **50**, 106
Colombo Sri Lanka 83 F15
Colorado (river) Argentina 49 M7, 53 F12
Colorado (river) Mexico/U.S.A. 28 F5, 33 L7, 44 I9
Colorado (state) U.S.A. **45**
Colorado Plateau Arizona, U.S.A. 45 I7
Colorado Springs Colorado, U.S.A. 45 M6
Columbia South Carolina, U.S.A. 41 N5
Columbia (river) Canada/U.S.A. 44 G3
Columbia, District of (capital territory) U.S.A. **38**
Columbus Georgia, U.S.A. 41 M6
Columbus Ohio, U.S.A. 43 O7
Communism Peak (mountain) Tajikistan 75 L5, 79 L11
Comodoro Rivadavia Argentina 53 F14
Como, Lake Italy 66 E5
Comoros 29 L7, 31 L7, 90 D10, 91 P7, **95**, 117
compass points 10
Conakry Guinea 92 E8
Concepción Chile 53 D11
Concord New Hampshire, U.S.A. 39 L5
Congo 31 K7, 116, 90 C9, **94**, 116
Congo (river) Central Africa 29 K7, 91 M6, 94 H2
Congo Basin Congo/Democratic Republic of the Congo 29 K7, 91 M6
Congo, Democratic Republic of the *see* Democratic Republic of the Congo
Connecticut (river) U.S.A. 39 L5
Connecticut (state) U.S.A. **39**
Constanța Romania 68 J8
Constantine Algeria 93 I4
continents 6, 15
Cook Islands Polynesia 28 E8, 30 E7, 96 F9, 97 P8, 119
Cook, Mt. New Zealand 97 M11
Cook Strait New Zealand 100 G6
Copenhagen Denmark 73 D15
Copiapó Chile 52 E8
Coral Sea Pacific Ocean 29 P7, 97 L9, 98 B10, 101 K3
Córdoba Argentina 53 G9
Córdoba Spain 59 J7
Corfu (island) Greece 69 E12
Cork Ireland 57 B13
Corpus Christi Texas, U.S.A. 40 G9
Corrientes Argentina 52 H8
Corsica (island) France 55 M7, 61 O10, 67 C9
Corvo (island) Azores 58 A7
Cosenza Italy 67 I14
Costa Brava Spain 59 P3
Costa del Sol Spain 59 J9
Costa Rica 30 G6, 32 D11, **47**, 104
Côte d'Ivoire 31 J6, 90 B9, **92**, 115
Cotonou Benin 92 H9
Cotopaxi (volcano) Ecuador 49 L3, 50 F4
Council Bluffs Iowa, U.S.A. 42 I7
Coventry England, U.K. 57 H13
Craiova Romania 68 H8
Crete (island) Greece 55 N8, 69 H15
Crete, Sea of Greece 69 H15
Crimean Mountains Ukraine 71 N11
Croatia 31 K4, 54 D10, **68**, 108
Crozet Islands Indian Ocean 29 L9, 31 L9
Cuanza (river) Angola 94 G5
Cuba 30 G6, 32 D10, **47**, 105
Culiacán Mexico 46 D6
Cunene (river) Angola/Namibia 94 G6
Cuzco Peru 50 H7
Cyclades (island group) Greece 69 H14
Cyprus 31 K5, 74 B9, **78**, 110
Cyprus, Turkish Federated State of *see* Turkish Federated State of Cyprus
Czech Republic 31 K4, 54 D10, **70**, 109

D

Dakar Senegal 92 D7
Dakota, North *see* North Dakota
Dakota, South *see* South Dakota
Dakshin Gangotri (research centre) Antarctica 102 G8
Dalian China 87 O5
Dallas Texas, U.S.A. 40 H6
Dalmatia Croatia 68 B8
Damascus Syria 80 G3
Da Nang Vietnam 84 I4
Danube (river) Europe 29 K4, 55 N7, 65 E13, 65 J13, 68 E7, 68 H8, 70 G10
Dardanelles (channel) Turkey 78 B4
Darhan Mongolia 87 K2
Dar es Salaam Tanzania 95 M4
Darjeeling India 82 H8
Darling (river) New South Wales, Australia 29 O8, 97 K10, 99 M8
Darling Range Western Australia, Australia 99 F8
Darwin Northern Territory, Australia 99 I2
Dashkovuz Turkmenistan 78 I9
Dasht-e Kavir (desert) Iran 81 M3
Dasht-e Lūt (desert) Iran 81 N4
Daugava (river) eastern Europe 71 J3
Davao Philippines 85 M6
Davenport Iowa, U.S.A. 43 K6
Davis Strait Greenland/Canada 28 H2, 35 P4, 103 J8
Dawson Yukon Territory, Canada 34 G6
Dawson Creek British Columbia, Canada 34 I9
Dead Sea (salt lake) Israel/Jordan 80 G4
Death Valley California, U.S.A. 44 H8
Debrecen Hungary 70 H9
Deccan (plateau) India 29 M6, 75 L7, 83 E11
Dee (river) Scotland, U.K. 56 G7
Delaware (state) U.S.A. **39**
Delhi India 82 E8
Democratic Republic of the Congo 31 K7, 90 C9, **94–95**, 116
Denmark 31 K4, 54 C9, **73**, 109
Denmark Strait Greenland/Iceland 103 L9
Denver Colorado, U.S.A. 45 L6
Derby Western Australia, Australia 98 G4
deserts 17, 18, 26
Des Moines Iowa, U.S.A. 43 J7
Detroit Michigan, U.S.A. 43 O5
developed and developing countries 23
Dhaka Bangladesh 83 I9
Dieppe France 61 I2
Dijon France 61 L5
Dinaric Alps (mountain range) Bosnia and Herzegovina/Croatia 68 C8
Dire Dawa Ethiopia 93 O9
District of Columbia U.S.A. **38**
Djibouti 31 L6, 90 D9, **93**, 115
Djibouti Djibouti 93 P8
Dnieper (river) eastern Europe 29 K4, 55 N6, 71 L4, 71 M8
Dniester (river) Moldova/Ukraine 71 K9
Dnipropetrovs'k Ukraine 71 N8
Dodecanese (island group) Greece 69 J14
Dodge City Kansas, U.S.A. 42 G9
Dodoma Tanzania 95 L4
Doha Qatar 81 L6
Dolomites (mountain range) Italy 66 F5
Dominica 30 H6, 32 G11, **47**, 105
Dominican Republic 30 H6, 32 E10, **47**, 105
Donets'k Ukraine 71 O8
Dongting, Lake China 87 M8
Donostia–San Sebastián Spain 59 L2
Don (river) Russia 55 O6, 76 C8
Dordrecht Netherlands 63 F9
Dortmund Germany 65 C9
Doubs (river) France 61 L5
Douro (river) Portugal 58 H4, 59 K3
Dover Delaware, U.S.A. 39 J8
Drakensberg Mountains Lesotho/South Africa 91 N9, 95 J10
Drake Passage (channel) Atlantic Ocean/Pacific Ocean 49 M10
Drammen Norway 73 C12
Drava (river) eastern Europe 68 C6
Dresden Germany 65 I10
Dubai United Arab Emirates 81 M6
Dublin Ireland 57 D11
Dubrovnik Croatia 68 D9
Dubuque Iowa, U.S.A. 43 K6
Dudinka Russia 103 P6
Duisburg Germany 65 C9
Duluth Minnesota, U.S.A. 43 J3
Dumont d'Urville (research centre) Antarctica 102 B9
Dundalk Ireland 57 D11
Dundee Scotland, U.K. 56 G7
Dunedin New Zealand 100 D9
Dunkerque France 61 J1
Durance (river) France 61 M8
Durban South Africa 95 K10
Durrës Albania 69 E10
Dushanbe Tajikistan 79 K11
Düsseldorf Germany 65 C9
Dvina (river) Europe 29 L3

E

Earth 12–15
earthquakes 14–15
East China Sea China 29 O5, 75 O6, 87 P8, 88 A6
Easter Island Pacific Ocean 28 F8, 30 F8, 48 A9, 49 J7
East London South Africa 95 J10
East Pacific Rise Pacific Ocean 28 F9
East St. Louis Illinois, U.S.A. 43 L8
East Siberian Sea Arctic Ocean 29 P3, 75 O2, 77 L4, 103 N4
Ebro (river) Spain 59 L3
ecosystems 18–19
Ecuador 30 G7, 48 B8, **50**, 106
Edinburgh Scotland, U.K. 56 G8
Edmonton Alberta, Canada 35 J10
Efate (island) Vanuatu 101 J6
Egmont, Mt. New Zealand 100 F5
Egypt 31 K5, 90 D8, **93**, 114
Eindhoven Netherlands 63 H10
El Aaiún Western Sahara 92 F5
Elba (island) Italy 66 D9
Elbe (river) Germany 55 M6, 64 F7, 65 H9
Elbrus, Mt. Russia 55 O7, 75 J4, 76 B10
Ellesmere Island North-west Territories, Canada 28 G2, 33 N2, 35 L1, 103 K5
Ellsworth Land Antarctica 102 E5
Ellsworth Mountains Antarctica 102 E6
El Obeid Sudan 93 M8
El Paso Texas, U.S.A. 40 D6
El Salvador 30 G6, 32 D11, **46**, 104
Empty Quarter (desert) Saudi Arabia 81 K9
Ems (river) Germany 64 C8
energy supplies 20–21
England U.K. 57
English Channel France/U.K. 55 L6, 57 G16, 60 F2
environment 18–19, **26–27**
Epi (island) Vanuatu 101 J6
Equator 9
Equatorial Guinea 31 K6, 90 C9, **93**, 116
Erebus, Mt. (volcano) Antarctica 102 C8
Erfurt Germany 65 F10
Erie, Lake Canada/U.S.A. 33 O6, 36 G10, 38 G5, 43 P5
Eritrea 31 L6, 90 D8, **93**, 114
Erromango (island) Vanuatu 101 K7
Esbjerg Denmark 73 B15
Escanaba Michigan, U.S.A. 43 M4
Esch Luxemburg 63 I16
Eşfahān Iran 81 L4
Española (island) Galápagos Islands, Ecuador 50 D10
Esperanza (research centre) Antarctica 102 G4
Espíritu Santo (island) Vanuatu 101 K5
Essen Germany 65 C9
Estonia 31 K4, 54 D9, **71**, 108
Ethiopia 31 L6, 90 D9, **93**, 115
Ethiopian Plateau Ethiopia 91 O5, 93 O8
Etna, Mt. (volcano) Sicily, Italy 55 M8, 67 G16
'Eua (island) Tonga 101 K11
Eugene Oregon, U.S.A. 44 E4
Euboea (island) Greece 69 G12
Euphrates (river) south-western Asia 29 L5, 78 C7, 80 H2
Eureka California, U.S.A. 44 E5
Europe (continent) 107–109, 29, **54–73**
European Plain Europe 29 K4, 55 M6
Evansville Indiana, U.S.A. 43 M9
Everest, Mt. China/Nepal 75 L6, 82 H7, 86 G8
Évora Portugal 58 H7
Exeter England, U.K. 57 G15
Eyre, Lake South Australia, Australia 29 O8, 97 K9, 99 K7

F

Faeroe Islands Atlantic Ocean 29 J4, 31 J3, 54 B8, 55 M4, 119
Faial (island) Azores 58 B8
Fairbanks Alaska, U.S.A. 34 F6
Falkland Islands Atlantic Ocean 28 H9, 30 H9 48 C11, 49 N9, 53 H16, 119
Faraday (research centre) Antarctica 102 F4
Farewell, Cape Greenland 103 J9
Fargo North Dakota, U.S.A. 42 H3
Faro Portugal 58 G8
faults 15
Federated States of Micronesia 31 O6, 96 C8, 118
Fernandina (island) Galápagos Islands, Ecuador 50 B9
Ferrara Italy 66 F7
Fès Morocco 92 G4
Feuilles (river) Québec, Canada 37 J3
Fiji 29 P8, 31 P7, 96 E9, 97 N9, **101**, 118
Finland 31 K3, 54 D8, **72–73**, 109
Finland, Gulf of Baltic Sea 71 I1, 73 H12
Fitzroy (river) Western Australia, Australia 98 G4
Flagstaff Arizona, U.S.A. 45 J8
Flanders (region) Belgium 63 C12
Flinders Island Tasmania, Australia 99 N10
Florence Italy 66 F8
Flores (island) Azores 58 A7
Flores (island) Indonesia 85 L10
Flores Sea Indonesia 85 K10
Florida (state) U.S.A. **41**
Florida Keys (island group) Florida, U.S.A. 41 N10
Florida, Straits of Cuba/U.S.A. 41 O10
Foggia Italy 67 I11
forests 18, 19, 26
Fortaleza Brazil 51 O5
Fort-de-France Martinique 47 P7
Forth (river) Scotland, U.K. 56 F8
Fort Kent Maine, U.S.A. 39 M1
Fort Wayne Indiana, U.S.A. 43 N6
Fort Worth Texas, U.S.A. 40 H6
fossil fuels 20, 27
Foveaux Strait New Zealand 100 C10
France 31 J4, 54 C10, **60–61**, 107
Francistown Botswana 95 J8
Frankfort Kentucky, U.S.A. 38 D9
Frankfurt Germany 65 D11
Franz Josef Land (island group) Russia 28 K2, 76 G4, 103 N7
Fraser (river) British Columbia, Canada 34 H10
Fraser Island Queensland, Australia 97 L9, 99 O6
Fredericton New Brunswick, Canada 37 L9
Fredrikstad Norway 73 C12
Freetown Sierra Leone 92 E9
French Guiana South America 30 H6, 48 D7, 51 L3, 119
French Polynesia Polynesia 30 E7, 96 G9, 101 O9, 119
Fresno California, U.S.A. 44 G8
Frisian Islands, West Netherlands 62 G5
Fua'amotu Tonga 101 J10
Fuerteventura (island) Canary Islands 58 D10
Fuji, Mt. Japan 89 H10
Fukuoka Japan 89 B13
Fukushima Japan 88 I8
Funchal Madeira 58 D8
Fundy, Bay of Canada 37 L10
Fushun China 87 O4
Futuna Islands *see* Wallis and Futuna Islands
Fuzhou China 87 O8
Fyn (island) Denmark 73 C15

G

Gabon 31 K7, 90 C9, **94**, 116
Gaborone Botswana 95 J8
Gairdner, Lake South Australia, Australia 99 J8
Galápagos Islands Ecuador 28 G7, 30 G7, 33 N11, 48 B8, 49 K4, 50 D8
Galați Romania 68 J7
Galdhøpiggen (mountain) Norway 73 C10
Gällivare Sweden 72 G7
Galveston Texas, U.S.A. 40 I8
Galway Ireland 57 B11
Gambia 31 J6, 90 B9, **92**, 115
Ganges (river) India 29 M5, 75 L6, 82 H9
Garonne (river) France 60 I8
Gary Indiana, U.S.A. 43 M6
Gaspé Peninsula Québec, Canada 37 L8
Gau (island) Fiji 101 O7
Gaza Gaza Strip 80 F4
Gaza Strip south-western Asia 80 F4, 119
gazetteers 10
Gdańsk Poland 70 G4
Geelong Victoria, Australia 99 L9
Geneva Switzerland 65 A15

Genoa Italy 66 D7
Genovesa (island) Galápagos Islands, Ecuador 50 D8
Georgetown Guyana 51 K2
George Town Malaysia 84 G7
Georgia 31 L5, 74 B9, **78**, 110
Georgia (state) U.S.A. **41**
Geraldton Western Australia, Australia 98 E7
Germany 31 K4, 54 C9, **64–65**, 107
Ghadāmis Libya 93 J5
Ghana 31 J6, 90 B9, **92**, 115
Ghent Belgium 63 D11
Gibraltar Mediterranean Sea 31 J5, 59 J9, 119
Gibraltar, Strait of Morocco/Spain 55 K7, 91 K3
Gibson Desert Western Australia, Australia 98 G5
Giglio (island) Italy 67 E9
Gijón Spain 59 I1
Gila (river) Arizona/New Mexico, U.S.A. 45 J9
Gilbert Islands Kiribati 29 Q7, 97 N7
Glasgow Scotland, U.K. 56 F8
global warming 27
Gobi Desert Central Asia 29 N5, 75 M5, 87 K4
Gold Coast Queensland, Australia 99 O7
Gomera (island) Canary Islands 58 B10
Good Hope, Cape of South Africa 29 K8, 91 M9, 94 H11
Gothenburg Sweden 73 D13
Gotland (island) Sweden 73 G14
Gotō Islands Japan 89 A13
Gough Island Atlantic Ocean 29 J9, 31 J9
Graciosa (island) Azores 58 B7
Grampian Mountains Scotland 56 F7
Granada Spain 59 K8
Gran Chaco Argentina 28 H8, 49 N6, 52 G8
Grand Canal China 87 N6
Grand Canary (island) Canary Islands 58 C10
Grande, Rio (river) Mexico/U.S.A. 28 F5, 33 M8, 40 F8, 45 L9, 46 F6
Grand Forks North Dakota, U.S.A. 42 H2
Grand Island Nebraska, U.S.A. 42 G7
Grand Junction Colorado, U.S.A. 45 K6
Grand Rapids Michigan, U.S.A. 43 N5
Graz Germany 65 I15
Great Australian Bight Australia 29 N8, 97 K10, 98 H9
Great Barrier Island New Zealand 100 G3
Great Barrier Reef (coral reef) Queensland, Australia 97 K8, 99 M3
Great Basin western U.S.A. 33 L6, 44 H7
Great Bear Lake North-west Territories, Canada 28 F2, 33 L3, 35 I6
Great Britain *see* United Kingdom
Great Dividing Range Queensland, Australia 29 O8, 97 K9, 99 M4
Greater Antilles (island group) Caribbean Sea 28 G6, 33 O8
Greater Sunda Islands Indonesia 75 N9
Great Falls Montana, U.S.A. 45 J2
Great Khingan Mountains China/Mongolia 87 M4
Great Lakes North America 28 G4
Great Plains U.S.A. 28 F4, 33 L5, 42 F5
Great Rift Valley south-eastern Africa/south-western Asia 29 K7, 91 O6
Great Salt Desert Iran 81 M3
Great Salt Lake Utah, U.S.A. 33 L6, 45 I5
Great Sandy Desert Western Australia, Australia 29 O8, 97 J9, 98 G5
Great Slave Lake North-west Territories, Canada 28 F2, 33 M4, 35 J7
Great Victoria Desert Western Australia, Australia 29 N8, 97 J9, 98 H7
Greece 31 K5, 54 D11, **69**, 108
Green (river) western U.S.A. 45 K6
Green Bay Wisconsin, U.S.A. 43 L4
Greenland (island) Arctic Ocean 28 I2, 30 I2, 33 O2, 55 L3, 103 K8, 119
Greenland Sea Arctic Ocean 29 J2
Greenwich meridian 9
Grenada 30 H6, 32 G11, **47**, 105
Grenadines, The *see* St. Vincent and the Grenadines
Grenoble France 61 M7
Greymouth New Zealand 100 E7
grid system 9, 10
Groningen Netherlands 62 J5
Groote Island Northern Territory, Australia 99 K3
Grossglockner (mountain) Switzerland 65 G14
Grozny Russia 76 B10
Guadalajara Mexico 46 E8
Guadalcanal (island) Solomon Islands 101 K3
Guadalquivir (river) Spain 59 I8
Guadeloupe (island) Caribbean Sea 30 H6, 32 G10, 47 P7, 119
Guadiana (river) Portugal/Spain 58 H8, 59 J6
Guam (island) Micronesia 29 O6, 31 O6, 96 C7, 119
Guangzhou China 87 M9
Guaporé (river) Bolivia/Brazil 51 J6, 52 G3
Guatemala 30 G6, 32 D11, **46**, 104
Guatemala City Guatemala 46 H9
Guayaquil Ecuador 50 F4
Guayaquil, Gulf of Ecuador/Peru 49 K4
Guernsey (island) English Channel 57 G16, 119
Guiana, French *see* French Guiana
Guiana Highlands (mountain range) South America 28 H6, 49 M3
Guinea 31 J6, 90 B9, **92**, 115
Guinea-Bissau 31 J6, 90 B9, **92**, 115
Guinea, Equatorial *see* Equatorial Guinea
Guinea, Gulf of Central Africa 29 J7, 91 L6, 92 G10
Guiyang China 87 K9
Gulf Coastal Plain U.S.A. 40 H8
Guyana 30 H6, 48 C7, **51**, 106
Guyana Basin Atlantic Ocean 28 H6
Gyangze China 86 H8

H

Haarlem Netherlands 62 F7
Hague, The Netherlands 62 E8
Haikou China 87 L11
Hainan (island) China 75 O7, 87 L11
Haiphong Vietnam 84 H3
Haiti 32 E11, **47**, 105
Hakodate Japan 88 H5
Halifax Nova Scotia, Canada 37 M10
Halley (research centre) Antarctica 102 F6
Halmahera (island) Indonesia 85 N8
Hälsingborg Sweden 73 D15
Hamamatsu Japan 89 G11
Hambo Angola 94 G5
Hamburg Germany 64 E7
Hamilton New Zealand 100 G4
Hammerfest Norway 72 G4, 103 N9
Hangzhou China 87 O7
Hannover Germany 64 E8
Hanoi Vietnam 84 H3
Happy Valley-Goose Bay Newfoundland, Canada 37 N6
Harare Zimbabwe 95 K7
Harbin Mongolia 87 O2
Harrisburg Pennsylvania, U.S.A. 38 I7
Hartford Connecticut, U.S.A. 39 K6
Harz Mountains Germany 64 E9
Hastings New Zealand 100 H5
Hat Yai Thailand 84 G6
Havana Cuba 47 J7
Hawaii (state) U.S.A. 32 B10, **44**, 44 C8
Hawaiian Islands Pacific Ocean 28 E5, 33 I6, 97 P5
Heard and McDonald Islands Indian Ocean 29 M9, 31 M9, 119
Hearst Ontario, Canada 36 G6
Hebrides (island group) Scotland, U.K. 56 D6
Heidelberg Germany 65 D12
Hejaz Saudi Arabia 80 G5
Helena Montana, U.S.A. 45 I2
Helsinki Finland 73 I11
hemispheres 9
Herāt Afghanistan 82 B6
Hermosillo Mexico 46 C5
Herzegovina *see* Bosnia and Herzegovina
Hierro (island) Canary Islands 58 A11
Hilo Hawaii, U.S.A. 44 C8
Himalayas (mountain range) southern Asia 29 M5, 75 L6, 82 F7, 86 F7
Hindu Kush (mountain range) Afghanistan/Pakistan 29 M5, 75 K6, 82 D6
Hiroshima Japan 89 D12
Hobart Tasmania, Australia 99 M11
Ho Chi Minh City Vietnam 84 H5
Hokkaidō (island) Japan 29 O5, 75 P4, 88 I2
Holland *see* Netherlands
Homyel' Belarus 71 L6
Honduras 30 G6, 32 D11, **47**, 104
Hong (river) China/Vietnam 84 H3
Hong Kong China 87 M10
Honiara Solomon Islands 101 K3
Honolulu Hawaii, U.S.A. 44 B7
Honshū (island) Japan 29 O5, 75 P5, 89 F10
Hormuz, Strait of Iran/Oman 81 M6
Horn, Cape Chile 49 M9, 53 G17
Houston Texas, U.S.A. 40 H8
Hövsgöl Lake Mongolia 87 J2
Huahine Islands French Polynesia 101 N10
Huambo Angola 94 G4
Huang (river) China 29 N5, 75 N5, 87 L6
Huascarán (mountain) Peru 49 L5, 50 F6
Hudson (river) New York, U.S.A. 39 K6
Hudson Bay Canada 28 G4, 33 N4, 35 N7, 36 G2, 103 I6
Hudson Strait Canada 35 O6, 37 K1
Hue Vietnam 84 H4
Hull England, U.K. 57 I11
Humboldt (river) Nevada, U.S.A. 44 H6
Hungary 31 K4, 54 D10, **70**, 109
Huron, Lake Canada/U.S.A. 33 O6, 36 G9, 43 O4
Hyderabad India 83 F12
Hyderabad Pakistan 82 C9

I

Iaşi Romania 68 J5
Ibadan Nigeria 92 H9
Iberian Peninsula western Europe 55 K7, **58–59**
Ibiza Ibiza, Spain 59 O6
Ibiza (island) Spain 59 O6
Iceland 29 J2, 31 J3, 54 A8, 55 L4, **72**, 109
Idaho (state) U.S.A. **44–45**
Idaho Falls Idaho, U.S.A. 45 J4
Ijsselmeer (artificial lake) Netherlands 62 G6
Illimani, Mt. Bolivia 49 M5, 52 E5
Illinois (river) Illinois, U.S.A. 43 L7
Illinois (state) U.S.A. **43**
Inari, Lake Finland 72 H5
Indal (river) Sweden 73 E10
India 31 M6, 74 C10, **82–83**, 112
Indiana (state) U.S.A. **43**
Indianapolis Indiana, U.S.A. 43 N7
Indian Ocean 29, 31, 75, 83, 84, 91, 93, 95, 98, 102
Indo-Gangetic Plain Bangladesh/northern India 75 L6
Indonesia 31 N7, 74 D11, **84–85**, 113
Indus (river) Asia 29 M5, 75 K6, 82 C8
Inland Sea Japan 89 D12
Innsbruck Switzerland 65 F14
Invercargill New Zealand 100 C10
Inverness Scotland, U.K. 56 F6
Ionian Islands Greece 69 E13
Ionian Sea Greece/Italy 55 M7, 67 J15, 69 F15
Iowa (state) U.S.A. **43**
Ipoh Malaysia 84 G7
Ipswich England, U.K. 57 K13
Iquique Chile 52 D6
Iquitos Ecuador 50 G5
Iráklion Crete, Greece 69 H15
Iran 31 L5, **81**, 111
Iran, Plateau of Iran 75 K5, 81 M3
Iraq 31 L5, **80–81**, 111
Ireland 29 J4, 31 J4, 54 B9, 55 L5, **57**, 107
Ireland, Northern *see* Northern Ireland
Irian Jaya Indonesia 85 P9
Irish Sea Ireland/U.K. 57
Irkutsk Russia 77 J10
Irrawaddy (river) Burma 75 M7, 84 G2
Irtysh (river) northern Asia 29 M4, 75 L4, 79 N5
Isabela (island) Galápagos Islands, Ecuador 50 C9
Ischia (island) Italy 67 G12
Ishim (river) Kazakstan/Russia 79 L5
Islamabad Pakistan 82 D6
islands 14, 15
Islay (island) Scotland, U.K. 56 D8
Israel 31 K5, 74 B10, **80**, 111
Istanbul Turkey 78 B4
Italy 31 K5, 54 D11, **66–67**, 108
Ivory Coast *see* Côte d'Ivoire
Ivujivik Québec, Canada 37 I1
Izmir Turkey 78 A5

J

Jackson Missippi, U.S.A. 41 K6
Jacksonville Florida, U.S.A. 41 N7
Jaffna Sri Lanka 83 F14
Jaipur India 82 E8
Jakarta Indonesia 84 H10
Jamaica 30 G6, 32 D11, **47**, 105
James (river) North Dakota/South Dakota, U.S.A. 42 G4
James Bay Canada 36 H5
Jan Mayen Island Arctic Ocean 29 J2, 31 J3, 119
Japan 31 O5, 74 E9, **88–89**, 113
Japan, Sea of eastern Asia 29 O5, 75 O5, 77 O10, 87 P4, 88 E8
Java (island) Indonesia 29 N7, 75 N9, 84 H10
Java Sea Indonesia 75 N9, 84 I9
Java Trench Indian Ocean 29 N7
Jayapura Indonesia 85 Q8
Jeddah Saudi Arabia 80 H8
Jefferson City Missouri, U.S.A. 43 K9
Jérez Spain 58 I9
Jersey (island) English Channel 57 H17, 119
Jerusalem Israel 80 G4
Jinan China 87 N5
Jodhpur India 82 D9
Joensuu Finland 73 J10
Johannesburg South Africa 95 J9
John o'Groats Scotland, U.K. 56 G5
Johnston Atoll (island) Polynesia 29 Q6, 31 P6
Johor Baharu Malaysia 84 G8
Jönköping Sweden 73 E14
Jordan 31 L5, 74 B10, **80**, 111
Jotunheim Mountains Norway 73 C11
Juan Fernandez Islands Pacific Ocean 28 G8, 30 F8, 48 B10
Juba Sudan 93 N10
Julianehåb Greenland 103 J9
Juneau Alaska, U.S.A. 34 G8
Jungfrau (mountain) Switzerland 55 M6, 65 B15
Jura Mountains Switzerland 65 B14
Jyväskylä Finland 73 I10

K

K2 (mountain) China 75 L5, 82 E6, 86 F6
Kabul Afghanistan 82 C6
Kagoshima Japan 89 C14
Kahoolawe (island) Hawaii, U.S.A. 44 C7
Kai (island group) Indonesia 85 O9
Kakhovka Reservoir Ukraine 71 N9
Kalahari Desert Botswana 29 K8, 91 N8, 94 I8
Kalgoorlie-Boulder Western Australia, Australia 99 G8
Kaliningrad Oblast Russia 54 D9, 70 H4
Kamchatka Pensinsula Russia 75 P3, 77 O5
Kampala Uganda 95 L2
Kananga Democratic Republic of the Congo 95 I4
Kanazawa Japan 89 F9
Kanchenjunga (mountain) China 75 M6
Kandavu (island) Fiji 101 N8
Kangaroo Island South Australia, Australia 99 K9
Kano Nigeria 93 I8
Kanpur India 82 F9
Kansas (river) Kansas, U.S.A. 42 I8
Kansas (state) U.S.A. **42**
Kansas City Missouri, U.S.A. 43 J8
Kara-Bogaz Gol (bay) Turkmenistan 78 G8
Karachi Pakistan 82 B9
Karakoram Range Central Asia 82 D5
Karakumsiy Canal Turkmenistan 79 I11
Kara Sea Russia 29 L3, 75 M2, 76 G5, 103 N6
Kariba, Lake Zambia/Zimbabwe 91 N8, 95 J7
Karlstad Sweden 73 D12
Kárpathos (island) Greece 69 J15
Kasai (river) Angola/Democratic Republic of the Congo 29 K7, 91 M6, 94 H3
Kashgar China 86 F4
Kashmir southern Asia 119
Kassala Sudan 93 N8
Kathmandu Nepal 82 H8
Katowice Poland 70 G7
Kauai (island) Hawaii, U.S.A. 44 A6
Kawasaki Japan 89 I10
Kazakstan 31 M4, 74 B9, **78–79**, 110
Kazan' Russia 76 D8
Kebnekaise (mountain) Sweden 72 F7
Keeling Islands Indian Ocean 29 N7, 31N7, 119
Kemi (river) Finland 72 I6
Kentucky (state) U.S.A. **38**
Kenya 31 K7, 90 D9, **95**, 116
Kenya, Mt. Kenya 91 O6, 95 M3
Kerguélen Islands Indian Ocean 29 M9, 31 M9
Kermadec Islands Polynesia 29 P8, 31 Q8, 96 E10, 97 N10
Kermadec Trench Pacific Ocean 29 Q8
Kermān Iran 81 N4
Key West Florida, U.S.A. 41 N10
Khabarovsk Russia 77 N9
Kharkiv Ukraine 71 N7
Khartoum Sudan 93 N8
Kiel Germany 64 F6
Kiev Ukraine 71 L7
Kigali Rwanda 95 K3
Kilimanjaro, Mt. (volcano) Tanzania 91 O6, 95 M3
Kimberley Plateau Western Australia, Australia 98 H3
Kinabalu, Mt. Malaysia 85 K7
King Island Tasmania, Australia 99 M10
Kingston Jamaica 47 L8
Kinshasa Democratic Republic of the Congo 94 G4
Kirgiz Steppe Kazakstan 29 L4, 79 J6
Kiribati 30 E7, 31 Q7, 96 E8, 118
Kirkwall Orkney, Scotland, U.K. 56 G4
Kismaayo Somalia 93 O11
Kitakyūshūsh Japan 89 C12
Kíthera (island) Greece 69 G14
Kōbe Japan 89 F11
Kōchi Japan 89 E12
Kodiak Island Alaska, U.S.A. 34 D7
Kopet-Dag Mountains Iran/Turkmenistan 78 H10
Korcë Albania 69 E11
Korea, North *see* North Korea
Korea, South *see* South Korea
Korea Strait Japan/South Korea 87 P6, 89 A12
Koro (island) Fiji 101 O7
Koro Sea Fiji 101 O7
Kosciuszko, Mt. New South Wales, Australia 97 L10, 99 M9
Košice Slovakia 70 H8
Kota Kinabalu Malaysia 85 J7
Kraków Poland 70 H7
Krasnodar Russia 76 B9
Krasnoyarsk Russia 76 I9
Kristiansand Norway 73 B13
Kuala Lumpur Malaysia 84 G7
Kuala Terengganu Malaysia 84 G7
Kuching Malaysia 84 I8
Kumamoto Japan 89 C13
Kunlun Mountains China 29 M5, 75 L5, 86 G5
Kunming China 87 J9
Kuopio Finland 73 I9
Kupang Indonesia 85 L11
Kuril Islands eastern Asia 29 O4, 75 P4, 77 P8
Kuril Trench Pacific Ocean 29 P4
Kushiro Japan 88 J3
Kuwait 31 L5, 74 B10, **81**, 111
Kuwait Kuwait 81 K5
Kyōto Japan 89 F11
Kyrgyzstan 31 M5, 74 C9, **79**, 110
Kyūshū (island) Japan 75 P5, 89 C13

L

Labrador (region) Newfoundland, Canada 33 P4, **37**
Labrador Sea Canada/Greenland 28 H4, 33 P3, 37 M3
Laccadive Islands Arabian Sea 29 M6, 31 M6
Lachlan (river) New South Wales, Australia 97 K10
La Coruña Spain 58 G1

La Crosse Wisconsin, U.S.A. 43 K5
Ladoga, Lake Russia 55 N5, 76 C6
Lae Papua New Guinea 98 B9
la Gaspésie, Péninsule de (peninsula) Québec, Canada 37 L8
Lagos Nigeria 92 H9
Lahaina Hawaii, U.S.A. 44 C7
Lahore Pakistan 82 D7
Lahti Finland 73 I11
Lakeba (island) Fiji 101 P7
Lake Charles Louisiana, U.S.A. 41 I7
Lambert Glacier Antarctica 102 E10
Lanai (island) Hawaii, U.S.A. 44 C7
Land's End (cape) England, U.K. 57 E15
Lansing Michigan, U.S.A. 43 N5
Lanzarote (island) Canary Islands 58 E10
Lanzhou China 87 K6
Laos 31 N6, 74 D10, **84**, 112
La Palma (island) Canary Islands 58 B10
La Paz Bolivia 52 E5
La Paz Mexico 46 C7
Lapland northern Europe 72 G6
La Plata Argentina 53 H10
Laptev Sea Russia 29 N3, 75 N2, 77 J5, 103 O5
Laredo Texas, U.S.A. 40 F9
large-scale maps 8
La Rochelle France 60 H6
Larsen Ice Shelf Antarctica 102 F7
La Serena Chile 53 D9
Las Palmas Canary Islands 58 C10
La Spezia Italy 66 E7
Las Vegas Nevada, U.S.A. 44 H8
Latakia Syria 80 G2
latitude 9
Latvia 31 K4, 54 D9, **71** , 109
Lau Group (island group) Fiji 101 P7
Launceston Tasmania, Australia 99 M10
Lausanne Switzerland 65 B15
Lavia 109
Lebanon 31 K5, 74 B10, **80**, 111
Leeds England, U.K. 57 H11
Leeuwarden Netherlands 62 H5
Leeward Islands French Polynesia 101 M10
Legazpi Philippines 85 L5
Le Havre France 60 I3
Leicester England, U.K. 57 H12
Leipzig Germany 65 G10
Lek (river) Netherlands 62 G9
Lemnos (island) Greece 69 H11
Lena (river) Russia 29 N3, 29 N4, 75 N3, 77 K6, 77 K8, 103 O4
Leningradskaya (research centre) Antarctica 102 B8
Lerwick Shetland, Scotland, U.K. 56 H3
Lesbos (island) Greece 69 I12
Lesotho 31 K8, 90 D11, **95**, 117
Lesser Antilles (island group) Caribbean Sea 28 G6, 33 Q8
Lesser Sunda Islands Indonesia 75 O9
Leticia Colombia 50 H5
Levkas (island) Greece 69 E12
Lewis with Harris (island) Hebrides, Scotland, U.K. 56 D5
Lhasa China 86 H7
Liberia 31 J6, 90 B9, **92**, 115
Libreville Gabon 94 F2
Libya 31 K5, 90 C8, **93**, 114
Libyan Desert Libya 91 M3, 93 K5
Licking (river) Kentucky, U.S.A. 38 D9
Liechtenstein 31 K4, 54 C10, **65**, 107
Liège Belgium 63 H12
life expectancy 22
Liffey (river) Ireland 57 D11
Ligurian Sea Italy 66 C8
Lihue Hawaii, U.S.A. 44 A6
Likasi Democratic Republic of the Congo 95 J5
Lille France 61 J1
Lilongwe Malawi 95 L6
Lima Peru 50 G7
Limerick Ireland 57 B12
Limpopo (river) southern Africa 91 N8, 95 K8
Lincoln Nebraska, U.S.A. 42 H7
Line Islands Kiribati 28 E5, 97 P6
Linköping Sweden 73 E13
Linz Austria 65 H13
Lipari Islands Italy 67 G14
Lisbon Portugal 58 G6
lithospheric plates 14–15
Lithuania 31 K4, 54 D9, **71**, 109
Little Rock Arkansas, U.S.A. 41 J5
Liverpool England, U.K. 57 G11
Livorno Italy 66 E8
Ljubljana Slovenia 68 B6
Llanos Colombia/Venezuela 28 H6, 49 L4
Łódź Poland 70 H6
Lofoten Islands Norway 72 D6
Logan, Mt. Alaska, U.S.A. 33 K3, 34 F7
Loire (river) France 55 L6, 61 I5
Lomami (river) Democratic Republic of the Congo 95 J3
Lombok (island) Indonesia 85 K10
Lomé Togo 92 H9
London England, U.K. 57 I14
London Ontario, Canada 36 G10
Londonderry Northern Ireland, U.K. 57 D9
longitude 9
Longyearbyen Svalbaard 103 N8
Lord Howe Island Australia 97 L10
Los Angeles California, U.S.A. 44 G9
Louisiana (state) U.S.A. **41**
Louisville Kentucky, U.S.A. 38 C9
Low Countries 62–63
Lower Hutt New Zealand 100 G6
Loyalty Islands southern Pacific Ocean 101 K7
Lualaba (river) Democratic Republic of the Congo 95 J3
Luanda Angola 94 G5
Luangwa (river) Zambia 95 K6
Lubbock Texas, U.S.A. 40 F5
Lübeck Germany 64 F7
Lubumbashi Democratic Republic of the Congo 95 J5
Lucerne Switzerland 65 C14
Lucknow India 82 F9
Luganville Vanuatu 101 K5
Luleå Sweden 72 G8
Lusaka Zambia 95 J6
Luxembourg 31 J4, 54 C10, **63**, 107
Luxembourg Luxembourg 63 I15
Luxor Egypt 93 N6
Luzon (island) Philippines 29 N6, 75 O7, 85 K4
L'vov Ukraine 71 I8
Lyon France 61 L7

M

Maas (river) Germany/Netherlands 63 I9
Macao (Portuguese territory) south-eastern China 31 N6, 87 M10, 119
MacDonnell Ranges Northern Territory, Australia 97 J9, 99 I5
Macedonia 31 K5, 54 D10, **69**, 108
Mackay Queensland, Australia 99 N5
Mackenzie (river) North-west Territories, Canada 28 F2, 33 L3, 34 I6
Mackenzie Mountains North-west Territories, Canada 34 H6
McKinley, Mt. Alaska, U.S.A. 33 K3, 34 E5
McMurdo (research centre) Antarctica 102 C8
McMurdo Sound Antarctica 102 B8
Macon Georgia, U.S.A. 41 M6
Macquarie Island Pacific Ocean 29 P9, 31 P9, 97 M11
Madagascar 29 L8, 31 L7, 90 D11, 91 P8, **95**, 117
Madang Papua New Guinea 98 B9
Madeira (island group) Atlantic Ocean 31 J5, 58, 90 A7, 91 K3, 92 E4
Madeira (river) Bolivia/Brazil 49 M5, 51 J5
Madison Wisconsin, U.S.A. 43 L5
Madras India 83 F13
Madrid Spain 59 K5
Maéwo (island) Vanuatu 101 K5
Mafia (island) Tanzania 95 M4
Magadan Russia 77 N6
Magdalena (river) Colombia 50 G3
Magdeburg Germany 64 G9
Magellan, Strait of Chile 53 F16
magma 14
Maggiore, Lake Italy/Switzerland 66 D5
Mahilyow Belarus 70 L5
Mahón Minorca, Spain 59 Q5
Maiao (island) French Polynesia 101 O11
Main (river) Germany 65 F11
Maine (state) U.S.A. **39**
Mainz Germany 65 D11
Majorca (island) Spain 59 P5
Malabo Equatorial Guinea 93 J10
Malacca, Strait of south-eastern Asia 84 E6
Málaga Spain 59 J9
Malaita (island) Solomon Islands 101 K2
Malawi 31 K7, 90 D10, **95**, 117
Malay Peninsula south-eastern Asia 75 N8
Malaysia 31 N6, 74 D11, **84–85**, 113
Maldives 29 M6, 31 M6, 74 C11, 75 K8, **83**, 112
Malekula (island) Vanuatu 101 K6
Male Maldives 83 C14
Mali 31 J6, 90 B8, **92**, 114
Malmö Sweden 73 D15
Malta 31 K5, 54 D11, **67**, 108
Mamoré (river) Bolivia 52 F4
Manado Indonesia 85 M8
Managua Nicaragua 47 I10
Manama Bahrain 81 L6
Manaus Brazil 51 J4
Manchester England, U.K. 57 G11
Manchester New Hampshire, U.S.A. 39 L5
Manchurian Plain China 75 O5
Mandalay Myanmar 84 F2
Manila Philippines 85 L4
Man, Isle of Irish Sea 57 I10, 119
Manitoba (province) Canada **35**
Mannheim Germany 65 D11
Manua Islands American Samoa 101 Q3
Manus (island) Papua New Guinea 98 B8
maps **8–11**
Maputo Mozambique 95 K9
Maracaibo, Lake Venezuela 49 L3, 50 H2
Maradi Niger 92 I8
Marañón (river) Peru 49 L4, 50 G5
Marchena (island) Galápagos Islands, Ecuador 50 C8
Mar del Plata Argentina 53 H11
Margherita Peak (volcano) Uganda 91 N6, 95 K2
Mariana Islands Micronesia 29 O6, 97 K5
Mariana Islands, Northern Micronesia 31 O6, 96 C7, 119
Mariana Trench Pacific Ocean 29 O6
Marie Byrd Land Antarctica 102 D6
Marquesas Islands French Polynesia 97 Q7
Marquette Michigan, U.S.A. 43 L3
Marrakech Morocco 92 G4
Marseille France 61 L9
Marshall Islands 29 P6, 31 P6, 96 D7, 97 M6, 118
Martinique (island) Caribbean Sea 30 H6, 32 G11, 47 P7, 119
Martin Vaz Islands southern Atlantic Ocean 29 I8, 31 I8, 48 E9
Maryborough Queensland, Australia 99 O6
Maryland (state) U.S.A. **38–39**
Maseru Lesotho 95 J10
Mashhad Iran 81 N2
Massachusetts (state) U.S.A. **39**
Matadi Democratic Republic of the Congo 94 G4
Matamoros Mexico 46 F6
Mato Grosso Plateau Brazil 49 N5, 51 K7
Matsue Japan 89 D11
Matsuyama Japan 89 D12
Matterhorn (mountain) Switzerland 55 M6, 65 B15, 66 C5
Maui (island) Hawaii, U.S.A. 44 C7
Mauna Kea (mountain) Hawaii, U.S.A. 44 C7
Mauna Loa (mountain) Hawaii, U.S.A. 44 C8
Maupiti (island) French Polynesia 101 M9
Mauritania 31 J5, 90 B8, **92**, 114
Mauritius 29 L8, 31 L8, 90 E11, 91 Q8, **95**, 117
Mawson (research centre) Antarctica 102 F10
Mayotte (island) Indian Ocean 29 L7, 31 L7, 90 D10, 95 N5, 119
Mbabane Swaziland 95 K9
Mbuji-Mayi Democratic Republic of the Congo 95 I4
Mead, Lake Arizona/Nevada, U.S.A. 44 I8
Mecca Saudi Arabia 80 H8
Medan Indonesia 84 F7
Medellín Colombia 50 G2
Medina 80 H7
Mediterranean Sea Africa/Europe 29 J5, 55 L7, 59 N8, 64 M10, 67 E16, 69 J16, 80 E3, 91 M2, 93 K4
Mekong (river) Asia 29 N6, 75 N7, 84 H4, 87 J9
Melanesia Pacific Ocean 29 O7, 97 L7
Melbourne Victoria, Australia 99 M9
Melilla (Spanish enclave) north-western Africa 59 L10, 92 H4
Melville Island Northern Territory, Australia 98 I2
Memphis Tennessee, U.S.A. 41 K5
Mendoza Argentina 53 E10
meridians 9
Meru, Mt. Tanzania 91 O6
Meseta Spain 59 J5
Messina Sicily, Italy 67 H15
Metz France 61 M3
Meuse (river) western Europe 61 L3, 63 H13
Mexicali Mexico 46 B4
Mexico 30 G5, 32 D10, **46**, 104
Mexico City Mexico 46 F8
Mexico, Gulf of Mexico/U.S.A. 28 G5, 33 N8, 41 J9, 46 G6
Miami Florida, U.S.A. 41 O9
Michigan (state) U.S.A. **43**
Michigan, Lake U.S.A. 33 N6, 36 F8, 43 M4
Micronesia Pacific Ocean 29 P6, 97 K6
Micronesia, Federated States of *see* Federated States of Micronesia
Mid-Atlantic Ridge Atlantic Ocean 28 I5, 29 J7
Middle America Trench Pacific Ocean 28 F6
Middlesbrough England, U.K. 57 H10
Mid-Indian Basin Indian Ocean 29 M7
Mid-Indian Ridge Indian Ocean 29 M7
Mid-Pacific Mountains (submarine mountains) Pacific Ocean 29 P6
Midway Islands Polynesia 29 Q5, 31 Q5, 119
Milan Italy 66 D6
Milford Haven Wales, U.K. 57 E13
Milwaukee Wisconsin, U.S.A. 43 M5
Mindanao (island) Philippines 75 P8, 85 M6
Mindoro (island) Philippines 85 L5
minerals 14, 20
Minneapolis Minnesota, U.S.A. 43 J4
Minnesota (river) Minnesota, U.S.A. 42 I5
Minnesota (state) U.S.A. **42–43**
Minorca (island) Spain 59 Q5
Minot North Dakota, U.S.A. 42 F2
Minsk Belarus 71 K5
Miquelon (island) Canada 28 H4, 30 H4, 37 O9, 119
Mirnyy (research centre) Antarctica 102 E11
Misrātah Libya 93 K4
Mississippi (river) U.S.A. 28 G5, 33 N6, 41 J7, 43 I4, 43 L9, 43 K6
Mississippi (state) U.S.A. **41**
Missoula Montana, U.S.A. 44 I2
Missouri (river) U.S.A. 28 G4, 33 M6, 42 F4, 42 H6, 45 J2
Missouri (state) U.S.A. **43**
Mistassini, Lac (lake) Québec, Canada 37 J7
Mitchell, Mt. North Carolina, U.S.A. 41 N4
Miyazaki Japan 89 C14
Mizuho (research centre) Antarctica 102 G9
Moala (island) Fiji 101 O8
Mobile Alabama, U.S.A. 41 L7
Modena Italy 66 F7
Mogadishu Somalia 93 P10
Moldova 31 K4, 54 E10, **71**, 109
Molodezhnaya (research centre) Antarctica 102 G10
Molokai (island) Hawaii, U.S.A. 44 C7
Moluccas (island group) Indonesia 75 P9
Mombasa Kenya 95 M4
Monaco 31 J5, 54 C10, **61**, 107
Mondego (river) Portugal 58 G5
Mongolia 31 N4, 74 D9, **86–87**, 113
Monrovia Liberia 92 E9
Montana (state) U.S.A. **45**
Montenegro (republic) Yugoslavia 68 D9
Monterrey Mexico 46 F6
Montevideo Uruguay 53 J10
Montgomery Alabama, U.S.A. 41 L6
Montpellier France 61 K9
Montpelier Vermont, U.S.A. 39 K4
Montréal Québec, Canada 37 J9
Montserrat (island) Caribbean Sea 47 O7, 119
Moorea (island) French Polynesia 101 P11
Moorhead Minnesota, U.S.A. 42 H3
Moosonee Ontario, Canada 36 F6
Morava (river) Czech Republic 68 F8, 69 F9
Morioka Japan 88 I6
Morocco 31 J5, 90 B7, **92**, 114
Moroni Comoros 95 N5
Moscow Russia 76 C7
Moselle (river) western Europe 61 M4, 65 B11
Mostar Bosnia and Herzegovina 68 D8
Mosul Iraq 31 I2
mountains 14, 16, 19
Mount Isa Queensland, Australia 99 K5
Mozambique 31 K7, 90 D10, **95**, 117
Mozambique Channel Madagascar/Mozambique 91 O8, 95 N7
Mulhacén (mountain) Spain 59 K8
Mull (island) Scotland, U.K. 56 E7
Munich Germany 65 F13
Münster Germany 64 C9
Mur (river) Austria 65 I14
Murcia Spain 59 M7
Mureș (river) Romania 68 G6
Murmansk Russia 76 E5, 103 O9
Murray (river) New South Wales/South Australia, Australia 29 O8, 97 K10, 99 L9
Murrumbidgee (river) New South Wales, Australia 97 K10
Musala, Mt. Bulgaria 69 G10
Muscat Oman 81 N7
Mwanza Tanzania 95 L3
Myanmar 31 N6, 74 C10, **84**, 112
Mykonos (island) Greece 69 I13

N

N'Djamena Chad 93 J8
Nagasaki Japan 89 B13
Nagoya Japan 89 G11
Nagpur India 83 F10
Naha Japan 88 B8
Nain Newfoundland, Canada 37 M4
Nairobi Kenya 95 M3
Namangan Kyrgyzstan 79 L10
Namib Desert south-western Africa 29 K8, 91 M8, 94 G8
Namibia 31 K8, 90 C11, **94**, 117
Nampula Malawi 95 M6
Nanchang China 87 N8
Nancy France 61 M3
Nanjing China 87 N7
Nan Mountains China 75 N6
Nanning China 87 L10
Nantes France 60 G5
Napier New Zealand 100 H5
Naples Italy 67 G12
Narvik Norway 72 F6
Nar'yan-Mar Russia 103 P8
Nashville Tennessee, U.S.A. 41 L4
Nassau The Bahamas 47 K6
Nasser, Lake (reservoir) Sudan 91 O4, 93 M6
natural resources **20–21**
Nauru 29 P7, 31 P7, 96 D8, 97 M7, 118
Naxos (island) Greece 69 I14
Ndola Zambia 95 J6
Nebraska (state) U.S.A. **42**
Negro (river) Argentina 53 F12
Negro (river) Brazil/Uruguay 49 M3, 51 J4
Negros (island) Philippines 85 L6
Nelson New Zealand 100 F6
Nelson (river) Manitoba, Canada 35 M9
Neman (river) Belarus/Lithuania 71 J5
Nepal 31 M5, 74 C10, **82**, 112
Netherlands, The 31 J4, 54 C9 **62–63**, 107
Netherlands Antilles 47 N9, 119
Nevada (state) U.S.A. **44**
New Britain (island) Papua New Guinea 97 K7, 98 C9

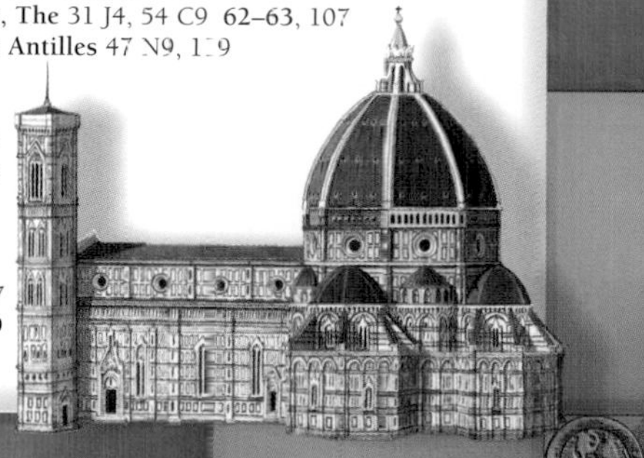

New Brunswick (province) Canada **37**
New Caledonia (island) Melanesia 29 P8, 31 P8, 96 D9, 97 M9, 101 J6, 119
Newcastle England, U.K. 57 H9
Newcastle New South Wales, Australia 99 N8
New Delhi India 82 E8
Newfoundland (island) Newfoundland, Canada 28 H4, 33 P5, 37 P8
Newfoundland (province) Canada **37**
New Georgia Islands Solomon Islands 101 J2
New Guinea (island) Indonesia/Papua New Guinea 29 O7, 75 Q8, 85 P9, 97 J7
New Hampshire (state) U.S.A. **39**
New Hanover (island) Papua New Guinea 98 C8
New Ireland (island) Papua New Guinea 98 C8
New Jersey (state) U.S.A. **39**
New Mexico (state) U.S.A. **45**
New Orleans Louisiana, U.S.A. 41 K7
New Plymouth New Zealand 100 F5
New Siberian Islands Russia 29 O3, 77 K4, 103 N4
New South Wales (state) Australia 99 M8
New York City New York, U.S.A. 39 K7
New York (state) U.S.A. **38–39**
New Zealand 29 P9, 31 P9, 96 D11, 97 M10, **100**, 118
Niamey Niger 92 H8
Nicaragua 30 G6, 32 D11, **47**, 104
Nicaragua, Lake Nicaragua 33 O10
Nice France 61 N9
Nicobar Islands India 29 M6, 31 M6, 75 M8, 83 K14
Nicosia Cyprus 78 B7
Niger 31 K6, 90 C8, **92–93**, 114
Niger (river) western Africa 29 J6, 91 L4, 92 G7, 92 H9
Nigeria 31 J6, 90 C9, **92–93**, 116
Niigata Japan 88 H8
Niihau (island) Hawaii, U.S.A. 44 A7
Nijmegen Netherlands 62 I9
Nile (river) northern Africa 29 K6, 91 N3, 93 M5, 93 N7
Ninety East Ridge Indian Ocean 29 M7
Nipigon Ontario, Canada 36 F6
Nipigon, Lake Ontario, Canada 33 N5, 36 F6
Niš Yugoslavia 68 F9
Niue (island) Polynesia 29 Q8, 31 Q7, 96 E9, 119
Nizhniy Novgorod Russia 76 D7
Nome Alaska (U.S.A) 34 D5
non-renewable resources 20
Nord Fjord Norway 73 B10
Nord-Ostsee Canal Germany 64 E6
Nordvik (research centre) Russia 77 J5, 103 O5
Norfolk Virginia, U.S.A. 39 I10
Norfolk Island Pacific Ocean 29 P8, 31 P8, 96 D10, 97 M10, 119
Norrköping Sweden 73 E13
North America (continent) 28, **32–47**, 104–105
North American Basin Atlantic Ocean 28 H5
North Cape Norway 72 G4, 103 N8
North Carolina (state) U.S.A. **41**
North Dakota (state) U.S.A. **42**
Northern Ireland U.K. **57**
Northern Mariana Islands Micronesia 31 O6, 96 C7, 119
Northern Sporades (island group) Greece 69 G12
Northern Territory Australia 99 J4
North Island New Zealand 29 P9, 97 N10, 100 F3
North Korea 31 O5, 74 D9, **87**, 113
North Platte Nebraska, U.S.A. 42 F7
North Pole 33 N1, 55 M2, 75 M1, 103 M6
North Sea western Europe 29 J4, 55 L5, 56 I8, 63 B10, 64 C6, 73 A14
North Uist (island) Hebrides, Scotland, U.K. 56 D6
North-west Pacific Basin northern Pacific Ocean 29 P5
North-west Territories (province) Canada **35**
Norway 31 J4, 54 C8, **72–73**, 109
Norwegian Sea Atlantic Ocean 29 J2, 55 M4, 72 C8, 103 M9
Norwich England, U.K. 57 K12
Nottingham England, U.K. 57 H12
Nouakchott Mauritania 92 E7
Nouméa New Caledonia 101 K8
Nova Scotia (province) Canada **37**
Novaya Zemlya (island group) Russia 29 L3, 76 G5, 103 O7
Novi Sud Yugoslavia 68 E7
Novosibirsk Russia 76 H9
Nubian Desert Sudan 29 K6, 91 O4, 93 N7
Nuku'alofa Tonga 101 J10
Nukus Uzbekistan 79 I8
Nullarbor Plain Western Australia, Australia 98 H7
Nuremburg 65 F12
Nuuk Greenland 103 J8
Nyasa, Lake Malawi 91 O7, 95 L6

O

Oahu (island) Hawaii, U.S.A. 44 B7
Oakland California, U.S.A. 44 F7
Oban Scotland, U.K. 56 E8
Ob' (river) Russia 29 M4, 76 F7, 76 G8
Oceania Pacific Ocean 29 P7, **96–101**
oceans 16, 18, 21, 24
Odense Denmark 73 C15
Oder (river) Germany 64 I8, 70 G6
Odessa Ukraine 71 L10
Ogden Utah, U.S.A. 45 J5
Ohio (river) U.S.A. 33 O7, 38 F8, 43 M9, 43 P7
Ohio (state) U.S.A. **43**
Ohonua Tonga 101 J10
oil 20
oil spills 27
Ojos del Salado, Cerro (mountain) Chile 49 M6, 52 E8
Okavango (river) southern Africa 91 M8, 94 H6
Okavango Delta Angola 91 N8
Okayama Japan 89 E11
Okeechobee Lake Florida, U.S.A. 41 O9
Okhotsk Russia 77 M6
Okhotsk, Sea of Japan/Russia 29 O4, 75 P3, 77 O7, 88 I1
Oki Islands Japan 89 D10
Okinawa Islands Japan 88 A7
Oklahoma (state) U.S.A. **40**
Oklahoma City Oklahoma, U.S.A. 40 H4
Öland (island) Sweden 73 F14
Oldenburg Germany 64 D7
Olympia Washington, U.S.A. 44 F2
Olympus, Mt. Greece 69 G11
Omaha Nebraska, U.S.A. 42 I7
Oman 31 L6, 74 B10, **81**, 111
Oman, Gulf of Arabia/Iran 75 K6, 81 N6
Omsk Russia 76 G9
Onega, Lake Russia 55 N5, 76 D6
Ontario (province) Canada **36**
Ontario, Lake Canada/U.S.A. 33 O6, 36 H10, 38 H4
Oradea Romania 68 F5
Oran Algeria 92 H4
Orange (river) southern Africa 29 K8, 91 N9, 94 H9
Örebro Sweden 73 E12
Oregon (state) U.S.A. **44**
Orinoco (river) Venezuela 28 H6, 49 M3, 51 I2
Orizaba (mountain) Mexico 33 M9, 46 F8
Orkney Islands Scotland, U.K. 56 G4
Orlando Florida, U.S.A. 41 O8
Ōsaka Japan 89 F11
Osh Kyrgyzstan 79 L10
Osijek Croatia 68 D7
Oskemen Kazakstan 79 N7
Oslo Norway 73 C12
Ostend Belgium 63 C11
Osterdal (river) Sweden 73 E11
Ōsumi Islands Japan 89 C15
Otaru Japan 88 H3
Otranto, Strait of Albania/Italy 67 K13
Ottawa Canada 37 I9
Ouagadougou Burkina Faso 92 G8
Oulu Finland 72 H8
Oulujärvi (lake) Finland 72 I9
Oviedo Spain 59 I1
Oxford England, U.K. 57 H13
Ozark Plateau Arkansas/Missouri, U.S.A. 41 I4, 43 K10
ozone layer 27

P

Pacific Ocean 28, 29, 30, 31, 34, 46, 49, 50, 52–53, 52–53, 75, 85, 87, 89, 97, 99, 100, 102
Padang Indonesia 84 G8
Padua Italy 66 G6
Pago-Pago American Samoa 101 P3
Pakistan 31 M5, 74 C10, **82**, 112
Palau 29 O6, 31 O6, 96 B8, 118
Palawan (island) Philippines 85 K5
Palembang 84 H9
Palermo Sicily, Italy 67 F15
Palma Majorca, Spain 59 P5
Palmer (research centre) Antarctica 102 F4
Palmer Land Antarctica 102 F5
Palmerston North New Zealand 100 G6
Pampas Argentina 28 H8, 49 M7, 53 G10
Pamplona Spain 59 L2
Panaji India 83 D12
Panama 30 G6, 32 D11, **47**, 104
Panama City Panama 47 K11
Panama, Gulf of Panama 49 L3
Panay (island) Philippines 85 L5
Paopao French Polynesia 101 P11
Papeete French Polynesia 101 P11
Papua New Guinea 31 O7, 96 C8, **98**, 118
Paraguay 30 F8, 48 C9, **52**, 106
Paraguay (river) South America 49 N6, 52 H8
Paramaribo Suriname 51 K2
Paraná (river) South America 28 H8, 49 N6, 50 L8, 52 G9
Paris France 61 J3
Parma Italy 66 E7
Páros (island) Greece 69 H14
Parry Islands North-west Territories, Canada 35 K3
Patagonia Argentina 28 H9, 49 M8, 53 F14
Patos, Lagoa dos (lake) Brazil 49 N7, 51 L11
Patras Greece 69 F13
Pavlodar Kazakstan 79 N6
Peace (river) British Columbia, Canada 35 I9
Pecos (river) New Mexico/Texas, U.S.A. 40 E6
Pécs Hungary 70 G10
Peloponnese (region) Greece 69 F13
Penang (island) Malaysia 84 G7
Pennines (mountain range) England, U.K. 57 G10
Pennsylvania (state) U.S.A. **38–39**
Pentecost (island) Vanuatu 101 K5
Peoria Illinois, U.S.A. 43 L7
Perm' Russia 76 E8
Perpignan France 61 J10
Persian Gulf Arabia/Iran 75 J5, 81 K5
Perth Western Australia, Australia 99 F8
Peru 30 G7, 48 C8, **50**, 106
Peru-Chile Trench Pacific Ocean 28 G7
Perugia Italy 66 F9
Pescara 67 H10
Peshawar Pakistan 82 D6
Petropavl Kazakstan 79 L5
Petropavlovsk-Kamchatskiy Russia 77 P6
Pevek Russia 103 N3
Philadelphia Pennsylvania, U.S.A. 39 J8
Philippine Basin Pacific Ocean 29 O6
Philippines 29 O6, 31 N6, 74 D10, 75 P7, **85**, 113
Philippine Sea Philippines 29 O6
Philippine Trench Pacific Ocean 29 O6
Phnom Penh Cambodia 84 H5
Phoenix Arizona, U.S.A. 45 J9
Phoenix Islands Kiribati 97 O7
Phuket Thailand 84 F6
Pico (island) Azores 58 B8
Pierre South Dakota, U.S.A. 42 G5
Pilcomayo (river) Bolivia/Paraguay 52 G7
Pinta (island) Galápagos Islands, Ecuador 50 C8
Piraeus Greece 69 G13
Pisa Italy 66 E8
Pitcairn Islands Polynesia 30 F8, 96 G10, 97 Q9, 119
Pittsburgh Pennsylvania, U.S.A. 38 G7
plants 18–19, 20
Plata, Río de la (river) Argentina/Uruguay 49 N7, 53 H10
plates, lithospheric 14–15
Platte (river) Nebraska, U.S.A. 42 F7
Plenty, Bay of New Zealand 100 H3
Ploiești Romania 68 I7
Plovdiv Bulgaria 69 H10
Plymouth England, U.K. 57 F15
Plzeň Czech Republic 70 E7
Po (river) Italy 66 F6
Podgorica Yugoslavia 69 E9
Pointe-Noire Congo 94 G4
Poland 31 K4, 54 D9, **70**, 109
polar regions 16, 19
pollution 20, 26–27
Polynesia Pacific Ocean 28 E7, 97 O10
Polynesia, French *see* French Polynesia
Pontianak Indonesia 84 I8
Poopó, Lake Bolivia 49 M6
Popocatépetl (volcano) Mexico 33 M9
population 22–23
Pori Finland 73 G11
Port Augusta South Australia, Australia 99 K8
Port-au-Prince Haiti 47 M7
Port Elizabeth 95 J11
Port-Gentil Gabon 94 F3
Port Hedland Western Australia, Australia 98 F5
Portland Maine, U.S.A. 39 M4
Portland Oregon, U.S.A. 44 F3
Port Louis Mauritius 95 Q8
Port Moresby Papua New Guinea 98 B10
Porto Portugal 58 G4
Pôrto Alegre Brazil 51 L11
Port-of-Spain Trinidad and Tobago 47 P9
Porto Novo Benin 92 H9
Port Said Egypt 93 M5
Port Sudan Sudan 93 O7
Portugal 31 J5, 54 B11, **58**, 107
Port Vila Vanuatu 101 J6
Pouembout New Caledonia 101 J7
Powell, Lake Utah, U.S.A. 45 K7
power (energy) 20–21
Poyang, Lake China 87 N8
Poznań Poland 70 G6
Prague Czech Republic 70 F7
Pretoria South Africa 95 J9
Prince Edward Island (province) Canada **37**
Prince Edward Islands South Africa 29 K9, 31 L9
Prince George British Columbia, Canada 34 H9
Prince of Wales Island North-west Territories, Canada 35 L4
Prince Rupert British Columbia, Canada 34 G9
Príncipe *see* São Tomé and Príncipe
Príncipe (island) São Tomé and Príncipe 91 L6, 94 E2
Pripyat' (river) eastern Europe 71 J6
Prītina Yugoslavia 69 F9
projections 9
Providence Rhode Island, U.S.A. 39 L6
Provo Utah, U.S.A. 45 J6
Prudhoe Bay Alaska, U.S.A. 103 L4
Prut (river) eastern Europe 68 J5, 71 K9
Prydz Bay Antarctica 102 F11
Pueblo Colorado, U.S.A. 45 M7
Puerto Ayora Santa Cruz, Galápagos Islands, Ecuador 50 C10
Puerto Baquerizo Moreno San Cristóbal, Galápagos Islands, Ecuador 50 D10
Puerto Deseado Argentina 53 G15
Puerto Montt Chile 53 E13
Puerto Rico (island) Caribbean Sea 30 H6, 32 F10, 47 N7, 119
Pula Croatia 68 A7
Puncak Jaya (mountain) Indonesia 85 P9
Punta Arenas Argentina 53 F16
Purus (river) Brazil/Peru 49 M4, 50 I5
Pusan South Korea 87 P5
Putumayo (river) Colombia 50 H4
P'yŏngyang North Korea 87 O4
Pyrenees (mountain range) western Europe 55 L7, 59 M2, 60 H10

Q

Qandahār Afghanistan 82 B7
Qaraghandy Kazakstan 79 M7
Qatar 31 L5, 74 B10, **81**, 111
Qinghai, Lake China 87 J6
Qiqihar Mongolia 87 N2
Qostanay Kazakstan 79 K5
Québec Québec, Canada 37 K9
Québec (province) Canada **37**
Queen Charlotte Islands British Columbia, Canada 33 K4, 34 G9
Queen Elizabeth Islands North-west Territories, Canada 28 F2, 33 M2, 35 K2, 103 K6
Queen Maud Land Antarctica 102 F9
Queensland (state) Australia 99 L5
Queenstown New Zealand 100 D9
Quimper France 60 F4
Quito Ecuador 50 F4

R

Rabat Morocco 92 G4
Raiatea (island) French Polynesia 101 N10
rainforests 18
Rainier, Mt. Washington, U.S.A. 44 F2
Raleigh North Carolina, U.S.A. 41 O4
Rangoon (Myanmar) 84 F4
Rapid City South Dakota, U.S.A. 42 E5
Ras Dashen (volcano) Ethiopia 91 O5, 93 O8
Rasht Iran 81 K2
Ravenna Italy 66 G7
Reading England, U.K. 57 I14
Rebun (island) Japan 88 H2
Recife Brazil 51 P5
Red (river) China/Vietnam 84 H3
Red Sea Arabia/Egypt 29 K6, 75 J6, 80 G7, 91 O4, 93 N6
Red (river) U.S.A. 40 G5, 42 H2
Reggio di Calabria Italy 67 H15
Regina Saskatchewan, Canada 35 K11
Reims France 61 K3
Reindeer Lake Saskatchewan, Canada 35 K9
Rejika Sovenia 68 A7
renewable resources 20
Rennell (island) Solomon Islands 101 K3
Rennes France 60 G4
Reno Nevada, U.S.A. 44 G6
Réservoir de la Grande Deux (lake) Québec, Canada 37 I5
Reshiri (island) Japan 88 H2
Resolute North-west Territories, Canada 103 K6
resources, natural **20–21**, 26
Réunion (island) Indian Ocean 29 L8, 31 L8, 90 E11, 91 P8, 95 P8, 119
Reykjavík Iceland 72 B5
Rhine (river) western Europe 55 M6, 62 I9, 65 C10, 65 C13
Rhode Island (state) U.S.A. **39**
Rhodes (island) Greece 69 J15
Rhodope Mountains Bulgaria/Greece 69 G10
Rhône (river) France/Switzerland 61 L7, 61 L8
Richmond Virginia, U.S.A. 38 I10
ridges 14
Riga Latvia 71 I3
Riga, Gulf of Estonia/Latvia 70 I2
Rimini Italy 66 G8
Rio de Janeiro Brazil 51 N9
Río Gallegos Argentina 53 F16
Rio Grande (river) Mexico/U.S.A. 33 M8, 40 F8, 45 L9, 46 F6
Riyadh Saudi Arabia 81 J7
Roanoke Virginia, U.S.A. 38 G10
Rochester Minnesota, U.S.A. 42 J5
Rockhampton Queensland, Australia 99 N5
Rock Island Illinois, U.S.A. 43 K7
Rock Springs Wyoming, U.S.A. 45 K5
Rocky Mountains North America 28 F4, 33 L4, 34 H9, 45 K4
Romania 31 K4, 54 D10, **68**, 108
Rome Italy 67 F10
Ronne Ice Shelf Antarctica 102 F6
Rosa, Monte (mountain) Italy/Switzerland 55 M7, 66 D5
Rosario Argentina 53 H10
Ross Ice Shelf Antarctica 102 D7
Ross Sea Pacific Ocean, Antarctica 29 P12, 102 C7
Rostock Germany 64 G6
Rostov-na-Donu Russia 76 B9
Roswell New Mexico, U.S.A. 45 M9
rotation of the Earth 12

Rotorua New Zealand 100 H4
Rotterdam Netherlands 62 F9
Rouen France 61 I3
Ruapehu (volcano) New Zealand 100 G5
Rub' Al-Khali Desert Saudi Arabia 81 K9
Ruhr Valley Germany 65 C9
Russia 31 N3, 74 8C, 76–77, 110
Russkaya (research centre) Antarctica 102 C6
Ruvuma (river) Mozambique/Tanzania 95 L5
Rwanda 31 K7, 90 D9, **95**, 116
Ryuku Islands eastern Asia 75 O6, 88 B5

S

Sabah Malaysia 85 K7
Sacramento California, U.S.A. 44 F7
Sacramento (river) California, U.S.A. 44 F6
Sado (island) Japan 88 G8
Saginaw Michigan, U.S.A. 43 N5
Saguenay (river) Québec, Canada 37 K8
Sahara Desert northern Africa 29 J6, 91 K4, 92 H6
Sahara, Western *see* Western Sahara
Sahel West Africa 29 J6, 91 L5, 92 G7
Saimaa, Lake Finland 73 I10
St. Croix (river) Minnesota/Wisconsin, U.S.A. 43 J4
St. Elias, Mt. Alaska, U.S.A. 33 K3, 34 F7
St-Étienne France 61 L7
St. George's Channel Ireland/U.K. 57 D13
St. Helena (island) Atlantic Ocean 29 J7, 31 J7, 90 B10, 91 K8, 119
Saint-Jean, Lac (lake) Québec, Canada 37 J8
Saint John New Brunswick, Canada 37 L9
St. John's Newfoundland, Canada 37 P9
St. Joseph Missouri, U.S.A. 43 J8
St. Kitts–Nevis 30 H6, 32 G10, **47**, 105
St. Lawrence (river) Québec, Canada 33 O6, 37 J9
St. Lawrence, Gulf of Canada 37 M8
St. Louis Missouri, U.S.A. 43 L8
St. Lucia 30 H6, 32 G11, **47**, 105
St-Nazaire France 60 G5
St. Paul Island Indian Ocean 29 M9, 31 M8
St. Paul Minnesota, U.S.A. 43 J4
St. Petersburg Russia 76 C6
St-Pierre and Miquelon (island group) Canada 28 H4, 30 H4, 37 O9, 119
St. Vincent and the Grenadines 30 H6, 32 G11, **47**, 105
St. Vincent, Cape Portugal 58 G8
Sakami, Lake Québec, Canada 37 I6
Sakhalin (island) Russia 75 P4, 77 O8
Salado, Rio (river) Argentina 52 G8
Sala'ilua Western Samoa 101 M2
Salālah Yemen 81 M9
Salamanca Spain 59 I4
Salem Oregon, U.S.A. 44 F3
Salerno Italy 67 H12
Salina Kansas, U.S.A. 42 H9
Salt Lake City Utah, U.S.A. 45 J6
Salvador Brazil 51 O7
Salzach (river) Austria/Germany 65 H14
Samara Russia 76 D8
Samar (island) Philippines 85 M5
Samarqand Uzbekistan 79 J10
Sambre (river) Belgium/France 63 F13
Samoa, American *see* American Samoa
Samoa Islands southern Pacific Ocean 29 Q7, 97 O8, 101 O1
Samoa, Western *see* Western Samoa
Sámos (island) Greece 69 J13
Samothrace (island) Greece 69 I11
Sanaa Yemen 81 I10
San Antonio Texasa, U.S.A. 40 G8
San Cristóbal (island) Galápagos Islands, Ecuador 50 D10
San Cristóbal (island) Solomon Islands 101 K3
San Diego California, U.S.A. 44 H10
Sandwich Islands, South *see* South Sandwich Islands
San Francisco California, U.S.A. 44 E7
San Jorge Gulf Argentina 49 M8
San José Costa Rica 47 J10
San Juan Argentina 53 E10
San Juan Puerto Rico 47 N7
San Marino 31 K4, 54 D10, **66**, 108
San Marino San Marino 66 G8
San Matías Gulf Argentina 49 M8
San Miguel de Tucumán Argentina 52 F8
San Salvador El Salvador 46 I10
San Salvador (island) Galápagos Islands, Ecuador 50 C9
Santa Barbara California, U.S.A. 44 G9
Santa Cruz Bolivia 52 G5
Santa Cruz (island) Galápagos Islands, Ecuador 50 C9
Santa Cruz de Tenerife Tenerife, Canary Islands 58 C10
Santa Cruz Islands southern Pacific Ocean 101 L3
Santa Fe New Mexico, U.S.A. 45 L8
Santa Isabel (island) Solomon Islands 101 J2
Santa Maria (island) Azores 58 C8
Santa María (island) Galápagos Islands, Ecuador 50 C10
Santander Spain 59 K1
Santiago Chile 53 E10
Santiago Spain 58 G2
Santo Domingo Dominican Republic 47 M7
São Francisco (river) Brazil 28 I7, 49 O5, 51 N7
São Jorge (island) Azores 58 B8
São Luís Brazil 51 N4
São Miguel (island) Azores 58 C8
Saône (river) France 61 L5, 61 L6
São Paulo Brazil 51 M9
São Tomé São Tomé and Príncipe 94 E2
São Tomé (island) São Tomé and Príncipe 91 L5, 94 E2
São Tomé and Príncipe 31 J7, 90 C9, **94**, 116
Sapporo Japan 88 H3
Saragossa Spain 59 M3
Sarajevo Bosnia and Herzegovina 68 D8
Saratov Russia 76 C8
Sarawak Malaysia 85 J7
Sardinia (island) Italy 55 M7, 67 B11
Sarh Chad 93 K9
Saskatchewan (province) Canada **35**
Saskatchewan (river) Saskatchewan, Canada 35 K10
Saskatoon Saskatchewan, Canada 35 K10
Sassari Sardinia, Italy 67 B11
Saudi Arabia 31 L6, 74 B10, **80–81**, 111
Sault Ste. Marie Michigan, U.S.A. 43 N3
Sault Ste. Marie Ontario, Canada 36 G8
Savai'i (island) Western Samoa 101 N2
Savannah Georgia, U.S.A. 41 N5
Savannah (river) Georgia, U.S.A. 41 N5
savannahs 18
Sayan Mountains Russia 77 I10
Scandinavia 29 K3, 55 M5, 72–73
Scilly, Isles of England, U.K. 57 E16
Scotia Sea Atlantic Ocean 102 H5
Scotland U.K. **56**
Scott (research centre) Antarctica 102 C8
Scott-Amundsen (research centre) Antarctica 102 E8
sea routes 24
seasons 13
Seattle Washington, U.S.A. 44 F2
Ségou Mali 92 F8
Segovia Spain 59 K4
Seine (river) France 55 L6, 61 K4
Selvas Brazil 28 H7, 49 L4
Semey Kazakstan 79 N7
semi-desert regions 17, 18
Sendai Japan 88 I7
Senegal 31 J6, 90 B8, **92**, 115
Senegal (river) western Africa 91 J4, 92 E7
Seoul South Korea 87 P5
Sepik (river) Papua New Guinea 97 K7
Serbia (republic) Yugoslavia 68 E8
Serra do Mar (mountain range) Brazil 49 O6
Setúbal Portugal 58 G7
Sevastapol' Ukraine 71 N11
Severnaya Zemlya (island group) Russia 29 N2, 76 H4, 103 O6
Severn (river) England, U.K. 57 G12
Severn (river) Ontario, Canada 36 F4
Seville Spain 59 I8
Seychelles 29 L7, 31 L7, 90 E10, 91 P7, **95**, 117
Shanghai China 87 O7
Shannon (river) Ireland 57 C12
Sheffield England, U.K. 57 H11
Shenyang China 87 O4
Shetland Islands Scotland, U.K. 56 G2
Shikoku (island) Japan 75 P5, 89 E12
Shinano (river) Japan 88 H8
Shizuoka Japan 89 H11
Shkodër Albania 69 E10
Shīrāz Iran 81 L5
Shymkent Kazakstan 79 K9
Siberia Russia 29 N4, 75 M4
Sibiu Romania 68 H6
Sicily (island) Italy 55 M7, 67 F15
Siena Italy 66 F8
Sierra Leone 31 J6, 90 B9, **92**, 115
Sierra Madre Occidental (mountain range) Mexico 33 L8, 46 D5
Sierra Madre Oriental (mountain range) Mexico 33 L8
Sierra Morena (mountain range) Spain 59 I8
Sierra Nevada (mountain range) California, U.S.A. 44 F6
Simpson Desert Central Australia 29 O8, 99 J6
Singapore 31 N7, 74 D11, **84**, 113
Singapore Singapore 84 H8
Sioux City Iowa, U.S.A. 42 H6
Sioux Falls South Dakota, U.S.A. 42 H5
Siret (river) Romania/Ukraine 68 I6
Sjaelland (island) Denmark 73 D15
Skagerrak (channel) Denmark/Norway 73 B13
Skellefte (river) Sweden 72 F8
Skopje Macedonia 69 F10
Skye (island) Scotland, U.K. 56 D6
Skyros (island) Greece 69 H12
Slave (river) Alberta, Canada 34 J8
Sligo Ireland 57 C10
Slovakia 31 K4, 54 D10, **70**, 109
Slovenia 31 K4, 54 D10, **68**, 108
small-scale maps 8
Smallwood Reservoir (lake) Newfoundland, Canada 37 J5
Snake (river) Idaho/Wyoming, U.S.A. 44 H4
Snowdon, Mt. Wales, U.K. 57 F12
Society Islands French Polynesia 28 E8, 97 Q9 101 N9
Socotra (island) Yemen 81 M11, 91 Q5
Sofia Bulgaria 69 G9
Sogne Fjord Norway 73 A11
solar power 20, 21
Solar System 12
Solomon Islands 29 P7, 31 P7, 96 D8, 97 L7, **101**, 118
Solomon Sea Papua New Guinea/Solomon Islands 98 C10
Somalia 31 L6, 90 D9, **93**, 115
Somerset Island North-west Territories, Canada 35 L4
South Africa 31 K8, 90 C11, **94–95**, 117
South America (continent) 28, **48–53**, **48–53**, 106
Southampton England, U.K. 57 H14
Southampton Island North-west Territories, Canada 35 N6
South Australia (state) Australia 99 J7
South Carolina (state) U.S.A. **41**
South China Sea south-eastern Asia 29 N6, 75 O7, 85 J6, 37 M10
South Dakota (state) U.S.A. **42**
South-east Indian Ridge Indian Ocean 29 M8
South-east Pacific Basin Pacific Ocean 28 G9
Southern Alps (mountain range) New Zealand 100 D8
South Georgia (island group) Atlantic Ocean 28 I9, 30 I9, 48 D11, 49 O9, 119
South Indian Basin Indian Ocean 29 N11
South Island New Zealand 29 P9, 97 N11, 100 F7
South Korea 31 O5, 74 D9, **87**, 113
South Orkney Islands Atlantic Ocean, Antarctica 102 F4
South Pole 102 E7
South Sandwich Islands Atlantic Ocean 29 I9, 31 I9, 119
South Shetland Islands Atlantic Ocean 102 F4
South Uist (island) Scotland, U.K. 56 D6
South-west Indian Ridge Indian Ocean 29 K9
South-west Pacific Basin Pacific Ocean 28 E8
Spain 31 J5, 54 B11, **58–59**, 107
species 15
Spitsbergen (island) Norway 29 K2, 103 M8
Split Croatia 68 B8
Spokane Washington, U.S.A. 44 H2
Sporades, Northern (island group) Greece 69 G12
Springfield Illinois, U.S.A. 43 L8
Springfield Missouri, U.S.A. 43 J10
Sri Lanka 29 M6, 31 M6, 74 C11, 75 L8, **83**, 112
Srinagar India 82 E6
Stanley Falkland Islands 53 H16
Stanovoy Mountains Russia 77 M8
Stavanger Norway 73 A12
Stewart Island New Zealand 97 M11, 100 C10
Stockholm Sweden 73 F12
Stornoway Scotland, U.K. 56 D5
Stranraer Scotland, U.K. 57 E9
Strasbourg France 61 N3
Stromboli (island) Italy 67 H14
Struma (river) Bulgaria/Greece 69 G10
Stuttgart Germany 65 D12
subtropical regions 17, 18
Sucre Bolivia 52 F6
Sudan 31 K6, 90 D9, **93**, 114
Sudbury Ontario, Canada 36 G8
Sudeten Mountains Czech Republic/Poland 70 F7
Suez Egypt 93 M5
Suez Canal Egypt 93 M5
Sulawesi (island) Indonesia 75 O9, 85 L9
Sulu Sea Malaysia/Philippines 85 K6
Sumatra (island) Indonesia 29 N7, 75 N9, 84 G8
Sumbawa (island) Indonesia 85 K10
Sun 12, 13, 16, 20, 21
Sunda Islands Indonesia 29 N7, 75 N9, 75 O9
Sundsvall Sweden 73 F10
Superior Wisconsin, U.S.A. 43 J3
Superior, Lake Canada/U.S.A. 33 N6, 36 F7, 43 L2
Surabaya Indonesia 85 J10
Suriname 30 H6, 48 D7, **51**, 106
Şūr Oman 81 O7
Suva Fiji 101 N7
Svalbard (island group) Arctic Ocean 28 K2, 29 K2, 31 K2, 103 N7, 119
Swansea Wales, U.K. 57 F13
Swaziland 31 K8, 90 D11, **95**, 117
Sweden 31 K3, 54 D8, **72–73**, 109
Switzerland 31 J4, 54 C10, **65**, 107
Sydney New South Wales, Australia 99 N8
Syracuse Sicily, Italy 67 G16
Syr Dar'ya (river) Central Asia 79 K8
Syria 31 L5, 74 B9, **80**, 110
Syrian Desert south-western Asia 75 J4, 80 H3
Szczecin Poland 70 F5

T

Ta'izz Yemen 81 I11
Tabrīz Iran 81 J2
Tacoma Washington, U.S.A. 44 F2
Tagus (river) Portugal/Spain 58 G6, 59 J5
Tahaa (island) French Polynesia 101 N9
Tahiti (island) French Polynesia 101 P11
Taipei Taiwan 87 O9
Taiwan 29 N6, 31 N5, 74 D10, **87**, 113
Taiwan Strait China/Taiwan 87 O9
Taiyuan China 87 M5
Tajikistan 31 M5, 74 C9, **79**, 110
Taklimakan Desert China 75 L5, 86 F4
Tallahassee Florida, U.S.A. 41 M7
Tallinn Estonia 71 J1
Tamanrasset Algeria 92 I6
Tampa Florida, U.S.A. 41 N8
Tampere Finland 73 H11
Tampico Mexico 46 F7
Tanganyika, Lake Central Africa 91 N7, 95 K4
Tangier Morocco 92 G3
Tangshan China 87 N5
Tanimbar (island group) Indonesia 85 N10
Tanna (island) Vanuatu 101 K7
Tanzania 31 K7, 90 D10, **95**, 116
Tapajós (river) Brazil 49 N4, 51 K5
Taranaki (mountain) New Zealand 100 F5
Taranto Italy 67 J13
Taranto, Gulf of Italy 67 J13
Taravao French Polynesia 101 P11
Tashkent Uzbekistan 79 K10
Tasmania (state) Australia 29 O9, 97 L10, 99 M11
Tasman, Mt. New Zealand 97 M11
Tasman Sea Australia/New Zealand 29 P9, 97 M10, 100 D7
Tau (island) Manua Islands 101 Q3
Taupo, Lake New Zealand 100 G4
Taveuni (island) Fiji 101 O6
Tay (river) Scotland, U.K. 56 G7
Tbilisi Georgia 78 F7
Tegucigalpa Honduras 46 I9
Tehran Iran 81 L2
Tel Aviv-Jaffa Israel 80 F4
temperate regions 16, 19
Tenerife (island) Canary Islands 58 B10
Tennessee (river) southern U.S.A. 41 K5
Tennessee (state) U.S.A. **41**
Terceira (island) Azores 58 B8
Terschelling (island) Netherlands 62 G4
Tetiaroa Atoll (island) French Polynesia 101 P10
Texas (state) U.S.A. **41**
Texel (island) Netherlands 62 F5
Thailand 31 N6, 74 D10, **84**, 112
Thailand, Gulf of Thailand 75 N8, 84 G6
Thames (river) England, U.K. 57 J14
Thar Desert India/Pakistan 75 K6, 82 D8
Thásos (island) Greece 69 H11
Thessaloníki Greece 69 G11
Thimphu Bhutan 82 I8
Thíra (island) Greece 69 I14
Thule Greenland 103 L7
Thunder Bay Ontario, Canada 36 E6
Thurso Scotland, U.K. 56 G5
Tianjin China 87 N5
Tian Shan China/Kyrgyzstan 29 M5, 75 L5, 79 N10, 86 F3
Tiber (river) Italy 67 F9
Tibesti Mountains Chad/Libya 91 M4, 93 K6
Tibet, Plateau of China 29 M5, 75 L6, 86 G6
Tierra del Fuego (island) Argentina/Chile 49 M9, 53 F17
Tigris (river) south-western Asia 29 L5, 78 D8, 81 J4
Tijuana Mexico 46 B4
Tilburg Netherlands 63 H10
Timaru New Zealand 100 E8
Timbuktu Mali 92 G7
time zones 25
Timişoara Romania 68 F6
Timor (island) Indonesia 85 M10
Timor Sea Australia/Indonesia 85 M11, 98 G2
Tindouf Algeria 92 F5
Tinos (island) Greece 69 I13
Tipperary Ireland 57 C12
Tiranë Albania 69 E10
Titicaca (lake) Bolivia/Peru 49 L5, 52 E5
Toamasina Madagascar 95 O7
Tobago *see* Trinidad and Tobago
Tocantins (river) Brazil 49 O5, 51 M6
Togo 31 J6, 90 B9, **92**, 115
Tokara Islands Japan 89 B16
Tokelau (island) Polynesia 29 Q7, 31 Q7, 96 E9, 97 O8, 119
Tokushima Japan 89 E12
Tokyo Japan 89 I10
Toledo Ohio, U.S.A. 43 O6
Toledo Spain 59 J5
Tombouctou Mali 92 G7
Tonga 29 Q8, 96 E9, 97 O9, **101**, 118
Tongatapu (island) Tonga 101 J10
Tongatapu Group (island group) Tonga 101 J9
Tonga Trench south-western Pacific Ocean 29 Q8
Toowoomba Queensland, Australia 99 O7
Topeka Kansas, U.S.A. 43 I8
Toronto Ontario, Canada 36 H9
Torrens, Lake South Australia, Australia 99 K7
Torreón Mexico 46 E6
Torres Strait Australia/Papua New Guinea 97 K8, 99 L1
Toubkal, Mt. Morocco 91 K3, 92 G4
Toulouse France 61 I9
Tours France 60 I5
Townsville Queensland, Australia 99 M4
trade 24–25
Transantarctic Mountains Antarctica 102 C8
transport 24, 26

Transylvanian Alps (mountain range) Romania 68 G7
Trent (river) England, U.K. 57 I11
Trenton New Jersey, U.S.A. 39 J7
Trieste Italy 66 H6
Trinidad Bolivia 52 F4
Trinidad and Tobago 30 H6, 32 E11, 47, 51, 105
Tripoli Libya 93 J4
Tripolis Greece 69 F13
Tristan da Cunha 119
Tristan da Cunha (island) Atlantic Ocean 29 J8, 31 J8
Trivandrum India 83 E15
Tromsø Norway 72 F5
Trondheim Norway 73 C10
tropical regions 16, 17, 18
Troyes France 61 K4
Trujillo Peru 50 F6
Tsugaru Strait Japan 88 H5
Tsushima (island) Japan 89 A12
Tsushima Strait Japan 89 A13
Tuamotu Archipelago (island group) French Polynesia 28 E7, 97 Q8
Tucson Arizona, U.S.A. 45 J10
Tulsa Oklahoma, U.S.A. 40 H4
tundra 19
Tunisia 31 K5, 90 C7, 93, 114
Tunis Tunisia 93 J3
Tupai Atoll (island) French Polynesia 101 M9
Turin Italy 66 C6
Turkana, Lake Ethiopia/Kenya 95 L2
Turkey 31 K5, 74 B9, 78, 110
Turkish Federated State of Cyprus Mediterranean Sea 78 B7, 119
Turkmenistan 31 L5, 74 B9, 78–79, 110
Turks and Caicos Islands 47 M6, 119
Turku Finland 73 H11
Tutuila (island) American Samoa 101 O3
Tuvalu 29 P7, 31 P7, 96 E8, 97 N8, 118
Tweed (river) Scotland, U.K. 56 G8
Twin Falls Idaho, U.S.A. 44 I5
Tyne (river) England, U.K. 57 H9
Tyrrhenian Sea southern Europe 67 E12

U

Ubangi (river) Central African Republic/Congo 29 K7, 91 M6, 94 H2
Uele (river) Democratic Republic of the Congo 29 K6, 91 N6, 95 J2
Ufa Russia 76 E8
Uganda 31 K7, 90 D9, 95, 116
U.K. see United Kingdom
Ukraine 31 K4, 54 E10, 71, 109
Ulaanbaatar Mongolia 87 K3
Ulan-Ude Russia 77 K10
Ume (river) Sweden 72 F9
Umeå Sweden 73 G9
Ungava Bay Canada 37 K2
Ungava Pensinsula Québec, Canada 37 J2
United Arab Emirates 31 L5, 74 B10, 81, 111
United Kingdom 31 J4, 54 B9, 55 L6, 56–57, 107
United States of America 30 F5, 32 D10, 38–45, 104
universe 12
Upernavik Greenland 103 K7
Upolu (island) Western Samoa 101 N2

Uppsala Sweden 73 F12
Ural Mountains Russia 29 L4, 55 O4, 75 K4, 76 F7
Uruguay 30 F8, 48 D10, 53, 106
Uruguay (river) South America 28 H8, 49 N7, 51 K10, 53 I10
Ürümqi China 86 H3
U.S.A. see United States of America
Ushuaia Argentina 53 G17
Ustica (island) Italy 67 F14
Utah (state) U.S.A. 45
Utrecht Netherlands 62 G8
Utsunomiya Japan 88 I9
Uvs, Lake Mongolia 87 I2
Uzbekistan 31 L5, 74 B9, 79, 110

V

Vaal (river) South Africa 95 I9
Vaasa Finland 73 G10
Vaduz Liechtenstein 65 D14
Valdés Peninsula Argentina 49 M8, 53 G13
Valencia Spain 59 M6
Valladolid Spain 59 J3
Valletta Malta 67 F17
Valparaíso Chile 53 D10
Vancouver British Columbia, Canada 34 H11
Vancouver Island British Columbia, Canada 33 K5, 34 G10
Vänern, Lake Sweden 55 M5
Van, Lake Turkey 78 E8
Vanua Levu (island) Fiji 101 O6
Vanuatu 29 P7, 31 P7, 96 D9, 97 M9, 101, 118
Varanasi India 82 G9
Vardar (river) Greece/Macedonia 69 F10
Varna Bulgaria 68 J9
Vatican City 31 K5, 54 C10, 67, 108
Vatnajökull Iceland 72 B6
Vättern, Lake Sweden 73 E13
Venezuela 30 H6, 48 C7, 50–51, 106
Venice Italy 66 G6
Venice, Gulf of Italy 66 G7
Veracruz Mexico 46 G8
Verkhoyansk Russia 77 L6
Verkhoyanski Mountains Russia 75 N3, 77 K5
Vermont (state) U.S.A. 39
Verona Italy 66 F6
Vesuvius, Mt. (volcano) Italy 67 G12
Victoria Seychelles 95 Q4
Victoria (state) Australia 99 L9
Victoria British Columbia, Canada 34 H11
Victoria Island North-west Territories, Canada 28 F2, 33 M3, 35 K5, 103 K5
Victoria, Lake eastern Africa 29 K7, 91 O6, 95 K3
Victoria, Mt. Papua New Guinea 97 K8
Vienna Austria 65 J13
Vientiane Laos 84 G4
Vietnam 31 N6, 74 D10, 84, 112
Vigo Spain 58 G2
Vilnius Lithuania 71 J4
Vinson Massif (mountain) Antarctica 102 E6
Virginia (state) U.S.A. 38–39
Virginia, West (state) U.S.A. see West Virginia
Virgin Islands Caribbean Sea 30 H6, 32 F10, 47 O7, 119
Vistula (river) Poland 70 H7
Viti Levu (island) Fiji 101 N7
Vitsyebsk Belarus 71 L4

Vladivostok Russia 77 N10
Vlieland (island) Netherlands 62 G5
Vlorë Albania 69 E11
volcanoes 14–15
Volga (river) Russia 29 L4, 55 O5, 76 C9
Volgograd Russia 76 C9
Volos Greece 69 G12
Volta, Lake (reservoir) Ghana 91 L5, 92 G9
Vostok (research centre) Antarctica 102 D9
Vyatka Russia 76 D7

W

Waal (river) Netherlands 62 G9
Wabash (river) Illinois/Indiana, U.S.A. 43 M7
Waddenzee Netherlands 62 G5
Waikato (river) New Zealand 100 G3
Waitaki (river) New Zealand 100 D9
Wakatipu, Lake New Zealand 100 D9
Wakayama Japan 89 F12
Wake Island Micronesia 29 P6, 31 P6, 96 D7, 119
Wakkanai Japan 88 H2
Wales U.K. 57
Wallis and Futuna Islands Polynesia 31 P7, 96 E9, 119
Walvis Bay Namibia 94 G8
Walvis Ridge Atlantic Ocean 29 J8
Wanganui New Zealand 100 G5
Wanganui (river) New Zealand 100 G5
Warsaw Poland 70 H6
Washington District of Columbia, U.S.A. 38 I8
Washington (state) U.S.A. 44
water 20, 21, 27
Waterford Ireland 57 D13
weather 16–17
Weddell Sea Antarctica 28 I11, 102 G6
Wellington New Zealand 100 G6
Weser (river) Germany 64 E9
West Bank south-western Asia 80 G4, 119
Western Australia (state) Australia 98 G7
Western Sahara northern Africa 31 J5, 90 B8, 92 E5, 119
Western Samoa 31 Q7, 96 E9, 101, 118
Western Siberian Plain Russia 29 M3
West Frisian Islands Netherlands 62 G5
West Indies (island group) Atlantic Ocean 28 G6
West Siberian Plain Russia 75 L3, 76 H7
West Virginia (state) U.S.A. 38
Whangarei New Zealand 100 G2
Wharton Basin Indian Ocean 29 N8
Whitehorse Yukon Territory, Canada 34 G7
White Nile (river) eastern Africa 91 O5, 93 N8
Whitney, Mt. California, U.S.A. 33 K7, 44 G8
Whyalla South Australia, Australia 99 K8
Wichita Kansas, U.S.A. 42 H9
Wiesbaden Germany 65 D11
Wight, Isle of England, U.K. 57 H15
Wilhelm, Mt. Papua New Guinea 97 K8, 98 B9
Wilkes Land Antarctica 102 D10
Williston Lake British Columbia, Canada 34 H9
Wilmington North Carolina, U.S.A. 41 P4
wind 16, 20, 21
Windhoek Namibia 94 H8
Windsor Ontario, Canada 36 G10
Windward Islands French Polynesia 101 O10
Winnemucca Nevada, U.S.A. 44 G5

Winnipeg Manitoba, Canada 35 M11
Winnipeg, Lake Manitoba, Canada 28 G4, 33 M5, 35 L11
Wisconsin (state) U.S.A. 43
Wollongong New South Wales, Australia 99 N9
Woods, Lake of the Canada/U.S.A. 42 I2
Wrangel Island Russia 103 M3
Wrocław Poland 70 G7
Wuhan China 87 M7
Wye (river) Wales, U.K. 57 G13
Wyoming (state) U.S.A. 45

X

Xiagazê China 86 G7
Xi'an China 87 L6
Xingu (river) Brazil 49 N4, 51 L5

Y

Yablanovyy Mountains Russia 77 K9
Yakutsk Russia 77 L7
Yamoussoukro Côte d'Ivoire 92 F9
Yangon (Myanmar) 84 F4
Yangtze (river) China 29 N5, 75 N6, 87 I7, 87 L8
Yaoundé Cameroon 93 J10
Yaroslavl' Russia 76 C7
Yekaterinburg Russia 76 E8
Yellow (river) China 29 N5, 75 N5, 87 L6
Yellowknife North-west Territories, Canada 35 J7
Yellow Sea China 75 O5, 87 O6
Yellowstone (river) Montana/Wyoming, U.S.A. 45 K2
Yemen 31 L6, 74 B10, 81, 111
Yenisey (river) Russia 29 M3, 29 M4, 75 M3, 76 H6, 76 H8
Yerevan Armenia 78 E7
Yogyakarta Indonesia 84 I10
Yokohama Japan 89 I10
York England, U.K. 57 H11
Yucután Peninsula Mexico 46 H8
Yugoslavia 31 K5, 54 D10, 68–69, 108
Yukon (river) Canada/U.S.A. 28 E2, 33 K3, 34 F5
Yukon Territory (province) Canada 34
Yumen China 87 J5

Z

Zagreb Croatia 68 C6
Zagros Mountains Iran 29 L5, 75 J5, 81 K3
Zaire see Democratic Republic of the Congo
Zaire (river) Central Africa 91 M6, 94 H2, 94 H3
Zákinthos (island) Greece 69 E13
Zambezi (river) southern Africa 29 K7, 91 O8, 95 I6, 95 L7
Zambia 31 K7, 90 C10, 95, 117
Zanzibar (island) Tanzania 91 O7, 95 M4
Zaysan, Lake Kazakstan 79 O8
Zhenzhou China 87 M6
Zibo China 87 N5
Zimbabwe 31 K7, 90 D10, 95, 117
Zinder Niger 93 I8
Zürich Switzerland 65 D14

Acknowledgments

Weldon Owen would like to thank the following people for their assistance in the production of this book:
Helen Bateman, Anthony Burton, Alastair Campbell, Jo Collard, Melanie Corfield, Simon Corfield, Sharon Dalgleish, Libby Frederico, Kathy Gammon, Kathy Gerrard, Janine Googan, Greg Hassall, Lynn Humphries, Chris Jackson, Megan Johnston, Ralph Kelly, Jennifer Le Gras, Rosemary McDonald, Kylie Mulquin, Nicholas Rowland, Rachel Smith, Julie Stanton, Dawn Titmus, Greg Tobin, Wendy van Buuren, Michael Wyatt.

Cartographic sources: U.S. Central Intelligence Agency; International Boundaries Research Unit, Durham University, United Kingdom; U.S. Geographer General

Photographic credits: 14 bottom left, David Weintraub/The Photo Library – Sydney; 14 bottom centre, Stephen Wilkes/The Image Bank; 14 bottom right, Mats Wibe Lund/Icelandic Photo; 15 centre far right, David Hardy/SPL/The Photo Library – Sydney; 15 bottom left, Francois Gohier/Ardea London; 15 bottom centre, B. McDairmant/Ardea London; 15 bottom right, International Photo Library; 16 top far right, Robert Harding Picture Library; 16 bottom, David W. Hamilton/The Image Bank; 17 top left, Jeffrey C. Drewitz/The Photo Library – Sydney; 17 top centre left, Sobel/Klonsky/The Image Bank; 17 top centre, Horizon International; 17 top centre right, Staffan Widstrand/Bruce Coleman Limited; 17 top right, Christer Fredriksson/Bruce Coleman Limited; 19 top centre, Alain Compost/Bruce Coleman Limited; 27 top, Horizon International; 27 centre, Shone/Gamma/Picturemedia; 27 bottom, Witt/Sipa Press/The Photo Library – Sydney.

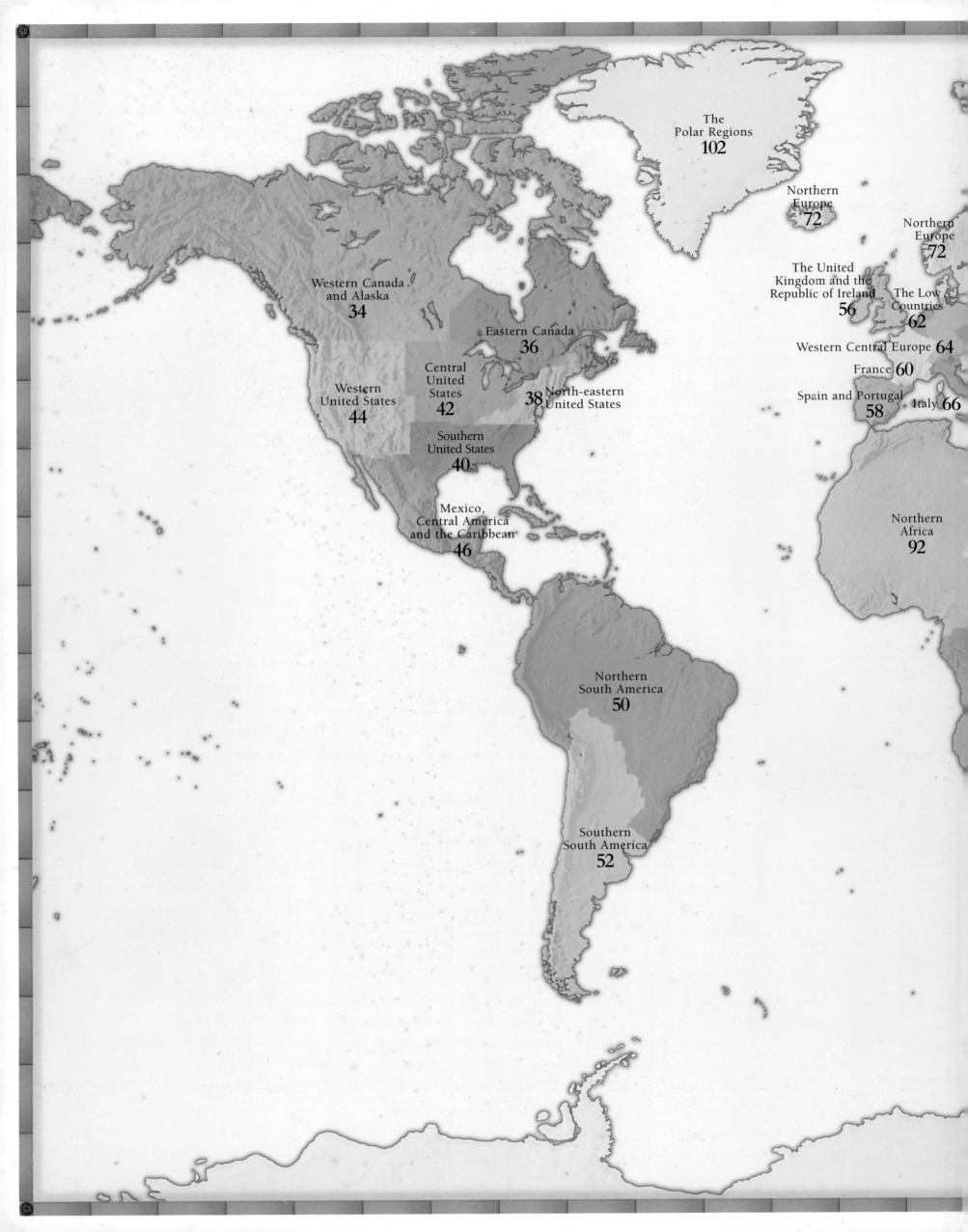

The Polar Regions
102

Northern
Europe
72

Northern
Europe
72

The United
Kingdom and the
Republic of Ireland
56

The Low
Countries
62

Western Central Europe 64

France 60

Spain and Portugal
58

Italy 66

Western Canada
and Alaska
34

Eastern Canada
36

Central
United
States
42

North-eastern
United States
38

Western
United States
44

Southern
United States
40

Mexico,
Central America
and the Caribbean
46

Northern
Africa
92

Northern
South America
50

Southern
South America
52